Learning and Teaching on the World Wide Web

This is a volume in the Academic Press
EDUCATIONAL PSYCHOLOGY SERIES

Critical comprehensive reviews of research knowledge, theories, principles, and practices

Under the editorship of Gary D. Phye

Learning and Teaching on the World Wide Web

EDITED BY

Christopher R. Wolfe

ACADEMIC PRESS

San Diego   San Francisco   New York   Boston   London   Sydney   Tokyo

Front cover image @ 2000 PhotoDisc, Inc.

The sponsoring editor for this book was Nikki Levy, the editorial coordinator was Barbara Makinster, and the book production manager was Monique Larson. The cover was designed by Suzanne Rogers. Composition was done by Inde-Dutch Systems, India, and the book was printed and bound by IPC Communications Services, St. Joseph, MI.

This book is printed on acid-free paper.

Academic Press
A Harcourt Science and Technology Company
525 B Street, Suite 1900, San Diego, California 92101-4495, USA
http://www.academicpress.com

Academic Press
Harcourt Place, 32, Jamestown Road, London NW1 7BY, UK
http://www.academicpress.com

Library of Congress Catalog Card Numbe: 00-00-110179
International Standard Book Number: 0-12-761891-0

PRINTED IN THE UNITED STATES OF AMERICA
01 02 03 04 05 06 IPC 9 8 7 6 5 4 3 2 1

Contents

1. LEARNING AND TEACHING ON THE WORLD WIDE WEB

Christopher R. *Wolfe*

2. THE PSYCHOLOGY OF HUMAN–COMPUTER MISMATCHES

Valerie F. Reyna, Charles J. Brainerd, Judith Effken, Richard Bootzin, and Farrell J. Lloyd

3. INDIVIDUAL CHARACTERISTICS AND WEB-BASED COURSES

Margaret D. Anderson

4. TEACHING ADVANCED LITERACY SKILLS FOR THE WORLD WIDE WEB

M. Anne Britt and Gareth L. Gabrys

5. CREATING INFORMAL LEARNING ENVIRONMENTS ON THE WORLD WIDE WEB

Christopher R. Wolfe

6. COOPERATIVE LEARNING AND COMPUTER-SUPPORTED INTENTIONAL LEARNING EXPERIENCES

Lawrence W. Sherman

7. FROM REAL TO VIRTUAL COMMUNITIES: COGNITION, KNOWLEDGE, AND INTERACTION IN THE WORLD WIDE WEB

Giuseppe Riva

8. HOW CAN THE WEB SUPPORT THE LEARNING OF PSYCHOLOGY?

Nick Hammond and Annie Trapp

9. GENDER IDENTITIES ON THE WORLD WIDE WEB

Christine H. Jazwinski

10. CAUGHT IN THE WEB: RESEARCH AND CRITICISM OF INTERNET ABUSE WITH APPLICATION TO COLLEGE STUDENTS

Janet Morahan-Martin

I I. DOING EDUCATIONAL RESEARCH
ON THE INTERNET

Adam N. Joinson and Tom Buchanan

12. THE MENTAL WEB: PEDAGOGICAL AND COGNITIVE IMPLICATIONS OF THE NET

Jennifer Wiley and Jonathan W. Schooler

Contributors

Numbers in parentheses indicate the pages on which the authors' contributions begin.

Margaret Anderson (45), Psychology Department, State University New York, Cortland, New York 13045

Richard Bootzin (23), Department of Psychology, University of Arizona, Tucson, Arizona 85724–5031

Charles Brainerd (23), College of Education, University of Arizona, Tucson, Arizona 85724–5031

M. Anne Britt (73), Psychology Department, Northern Illinois University, DeKalb, Illinois 60115

Tom Buchanan (221), Department of Psychology, School of Social and Behavioral Sciences, University of Westminster, London W1R 8AL, United Kingdom

Judith Effken (23), College of Nursing, University of Arizona, Tucson, Arizona 85724–5031

Gareth L. Gabrys (73), Naperville, Illinois 60563

Nick Hammond (153), Learning and Teaching Support Network, Department of Psychology, University of York, York YO1 5DD, United Kingdom

Christine H. Jazwinski (171), Department of Psychology, St. Cloud State University, St. Cloud, Minnesota 56301

Adam Joinson (221), Institute of Educational Technology, The Open University, Milton Keynes MK7 6AA, United Kingdom

Farrell J. Lloyd (23), Department of Medicine, University of Arizona, Tucson, Arizona 85724

Janet Morahan-Martin (191), Department of Social Sciences, Bryant College, Smithfield, Rhode Island 02917–1284

Valerie Reyna (23), Informatics and Decision-Making Lab, Department of Surgery and Medicine, University of Arizona, Tucson, Arizona 85724–5031

Giuseppe Riva (131), Applied Technology for Neuropsychology Lab, Istituto Auxologico Italiano, 28044 Verbania, Italy

Jonathan W. Schooler (243), Learning Research and Development Center, University of Pittsburgh, Pittsburgh, Pennsylvania 15260

Lawrence W. Sherman (113), Department of Educational Psychology, Miami University, Oxford, Ohio 45056

Annie Trapp (153), Learning and Teaching Support Network, Department of Psychology, University of York, York YO1 5DD, United Kingdom

Jennifer Wiley (243), Department of Psychology, University of Illinois, Chicago, Illinois 60607

Christopher R. Wolfe (1, 91), Western College Program, Miami University, Oxford, Ohio 45056

About the Authors

Dr. Margaret Anderson (Chapter 3) completed her doctorate in educational technology at Concordia University in Montreal, Canada, and is now a member of the Psychology Department at SUNY Cortland. She is past president of the Society for Computers in Psychology. Dr. Anderson developed and teaches a Web-based asynchronous distance graduate course in educational psychology. She has published 45 articles that deal with individual learning styles and the integration of computers into the curriculum. Her current research focuses on the assessment of individual learning styles and on the developmental and cultural components of those styles as they relate to academic performance. Correspondence regarding Chapter 3 should be sent to:

Margaret Anderson, Ph.D.
Psychology Department
SUNY
Cortland, NY 13045
e-mail:andersmd@snycorva.cortland.edu

Dr. Richard Bootzin (Chapter 2) is a professor of psychology and of psychiatry at the University of Arizona and holds a doctorate from Purdue University. Dr. Bootzin's primary research areas are cognitive processing during sleep and understanding the treatment of insomnia. He directs the Sleep Research Laboratory in the University of Arizona Psychology Department and the Insomnia Clinic of the University of Arizona Sleep Disorders Center. Dr. Bootzin is president of the Academy of Psychological Clinical Sciences and a fellow of both the American Psychological Association and the American Psychological Society. He has written or co-authored over 200 books, articles, and chapters.

Dr. Charles Brainerd (Chapter 2) has a doctorate in experimental psychology from Michigan State University and is a professor of educational psychology at the University of Arizona. He has published over 150 research articles and books in areas such as learning and decision making, mathematical modeling, assessment, and cognitive development. He is an APS Founding Fellow and an APA Fellow of the Division of General Psychology, the Division of Developmental Psychology, and the Division of Educational Psychology. His current research focuses on assessing learning outcomes in technology-infused classrooms.

Dr. M. Anne Britt (Chapter 4) received her doctoral degree in cognitive psychology from the University of Pittsburgh and is currently an assistant professor of psychology at Northern Illinois University. Her research is on advanced literacy skills in history learning. She has published articles in the *Journal of Memory and Language, Journal of Educational Psychology, and Cognition and Instruction*, as well as many book chapters. She is the designer of the *Sourcer's Apprentice* software, a historical reasoning tutor that has been developed over 5 years and used in 10 high school classrooms in two states. Correspondence regarding Chapter 4 should be sent to:

Ann Britt, Ph.D.
Northern Illinois University
Psychology Department
DeKalb, IL 60115
e-mail:britt@niu.edu

Dr. Tom Buchanan (Chapter 11) is a senior lecturer in psychology at the University of Westminster in London. His research interests encompass a number of areas in social and personality psychology (e.g., media violence and aggressiveness), and he has recently been interested and active in the use of the Internet for psychology teaching (e.g., Web-mediated formative assessment) and research (particularly the administration of personality tests over the Internet).

Dr. Judith Effken (Chapter 2) is currently an assistant professor at the University of Arizona College of Nursing, where she teaches health care informatics. She holds a M.S. in nursing management and a Ph.D. in experimental psychology with a focus on cognition and instruction from the University of Connecticut.

Gareth Gabrys (Chapter 4) received a master's degree in cognitive psychology from the University of Pittsburgh. He is currently a software engineer at MessageBlaster.com, where he designs and develops Web interfaces. He has also created user interfaces for graphical and speech-recognition applications and has contributed to articles published in the *Journal of Memory and Language and Human Factors*.

Dr. Nick Hammond (Chapter 8) is a reader in psychology at the University of York and director of the Learning and Teaching Support Network, Psychology. He completed a psychology degree at Birmingham University and a Ph.D. in attention and performance at Birkbeck College, London His interests in cognition and computing and in educational technology stem from a 6-year appointment at the MRC Applied Psychology

Unit at Cambridge. His research interests are in skilled performance, human–computer interaction, and learning technology. He is chair of the Central Executive Committee of the Association for Learning Technology and is the UK national representative of the European Academic Software Award Programme. Correspondence regarding Chapter 8 should be sent to:

Nick Hammond, Ph.D.
Learning and Teaching Support Network
Department of Psychology
University of York
York YO1 5DD, United Kingdom
e-mail: N.Hammond@psych.york.ac.uk

Dr. *Christine Jazwinski* (Chapter 9) has a Ph.D. in social psychology from Purdue University. She is currently employed as a professor of psychology at St. Cloud State University in Minnesota. Jazwinski has been actively involved in studying the WWW and exploring its educational potential since she first learned about Mosaic and considered it the best invention since sliced bread. Jazwinski's scholarly interests include the social psychology of the WWW, educational applications of the Web for teaching psychology, laboratory applications of the WWW for data collection, psychobiography, and the psychology of altruism and rescue during the Holocaust. Correspondence regarding Chapter 9 should be sent to:

Chris Jazwinski, Ph.D.
Department of Psychology
St. Cloud State University
St. Cloud, MN 56301
e-mail: jaz@STCLOUDSTATE.EDU

Dr. *Adam Joinson* (Chapter 11) is a lecturer in educational technology at the Institute of Educational Technology at the Open University in the United Kingdom. In the past he has lectured in social psychology and has worked as a freelance technology journalist. His research interests include self-disclosure and intimacy online, conducting research using the WWW, and the development of online learning communities. Correspondence regarding Chapter 11 should be sent to:

Adam N. Joinson, Ph.D.
Student Research Centre
Institute of Educational Technology
The Open University
Walton Hall
Milton Keynes MK7 6AA, United Kingdom
e-mail: A.N.Joinson@open.ac.uk

Farrel J. Lloyd (Chapter 2) is a practicing general internal medicine physician with postgraduate training in public health and medical informatics. He earned his M.D. from the University of Utah School of Medicine and his M.P.H. from the University of Arizona Graduate Program in Public Health. He is on the faculty of the medical school at the University of Arizona and directs the clinical arm of the Arizona Health Science Center's initiatives in medical informatics and outcomes assessment. Dr. Lloyd was awarded the Dean's Physician Scientist Career Development Award in 1999. He is also an elected fellow of the American College of Physicians/American Society of Internal Medicine.

Dr. Janet Morahan-Martin (Chapter 10) is a professor of psychology at Bryant College in Smithfield, Rhode Island. Her Internet-related research has focused on pathological Internet use and gender differences in Internet behaviors and attitudes. She has published and presented papers on psychological aspects of Internet use and organized and chaired symposia for the American Psychological Association on both pathological Internet use and gender and the Internet. She is on the editorial board of *CyberPsychology & Behavior*, a founding member of the International Society of On-line Mental Health, a member of the Society for Computers in Psychology, and on the first executive committee for the Internet Advisory Board of the Society for the Teaching of Psychology. Correspondence regarding Chapter 10 should be sent to:

Janet Morahan-Martin, Ph.D.
Department of Social Sciences
Bryant College
1150 Douglas Pike
Smithfield, RI 02917–1284
e-mail:jmorahan@bryant.edu

Dr. Valerie F. Reyna (Chapter 2) holds a doctorate in psychology from Rockefeller University. She has published over 80 articles and books on such topics as reasoning and decision making and false memories. She has received numerous awards and distinctions, including election to fellowship status in the AAAS and the APA. Professor Reyna holds joint appointments in the Department of Surgery and Medicine and the Arizona Research Laboratories at the University of Arizona. She is the director of the Informatics and Decision-Making Laboratory and director of the Division of Learning, Technology, and Assessment. Correspondence regarding Chapter 2 should be sent to:

Valerie F. Reyna, Ph.D.
Informatics and Decision-Making Lab
Department of Surgery and Medicine

P.O. Box 245031
University of Arizona
Tucson, AZ 85724–5031
e-mail: vreyna@U.Ariziona.EDU

Giuseppe Riva (Chapter 7) is professor of communication psychology and general psychology at the Catholic University of Milan, Italy, and senior researcher at the Applied Technology for Neuro-Psychology Laboratory (ATN-P Lab) Istituto Auxologico Italino, Milan, Italy. He has published many papers on computer-mediated communication and the role of virtual reality in medicine and training. Dr. Riva is associate editor of *CyberPsychology & Behavior and content editor of International Journal of Virtual Reality.* Correspondence regarding Chapter 7 should be sent to:

Giuseppe Riva, Ph.D.
Applied Technology for Neuro-Psychology Lab
Istituto Auxologico Italiano
P.O. Box 1
28044 Verbania, Italty
e-mail:auxo.psylab@auxologico.it

Dr. Jonathan Schooler (Chapter 12) is an associate professor of psychology and a research scientist at the Learning Research and Development Center at the University of Pittsburgh. He received his B.A. from Hamilton College and his M.S. and Ph.D. from the University of Washington. One of his long-standing research interests is understanding the mechanisms that lead to memory distortions in naturalistic settings, including examining the impact of postevent suggestion on event memories and assessing the disruptive consequences of verbalizing nonverbal memories. Other interests include consciousness, creativity, problem solving, decision making, the relationship between language and thought, and learning in science museums. He has been an author of more than 50 publications and coauthored the book *Scientific Approaches of Consciouseness.* He serves on the editorial boards of *Memory and Cognition* and *Consciousness and Cognition* and is an associate editor of *Cognitive Technology.*

Dr. *Lawrence Sherman* (Chapter 6) obtained his Ph.D. from Wayne State University (1971) and has taught educational psychology classes at Miami University since that time. He is currently the president of the Ohio Association for the Study of Cooperation in Education (OASCE) and is also on the Executive Board of the International Association for the Study of Cooperation in Education (IASCE), where he serves as the treasurer. He is the Webmaster of both the OASCE and the IASCE. He is also a past president of the International Society of Humor Studies. For further information see his Web page at http://www.muohio.edu/~shermalw. Correspondence regarding Chapter 6 should be sent to:

Lawrence Sherman, Ph.D.
Department of Educational Psychology
Miami University
Oxford, OH 45056
e-mail:Shermalw@muohio.edu

Annie Trapp (Chapter 8) has a PGCE and an M.Sc. in organizational psychology. She lectures part-time in the Department of Psychology at the University of York and has published on institutional drivers and inhibitors to the take-up of communication and information technologies, as well as on other topics related to educational technology. She manages the Learning and Teaching Support Network, Psychology, and works part-time on a project related to communication and information technologies in small-group teaching.

Dr. *Jennifer Wiley* (Chapter 12) is an assistant professor of psychology at the University of Illinois, Chicago. She received her Ph.D. in psychology from the University of Pittsburgh and completed a postdoctoral fellowship at the University of Massachusetts, Amherst. Dr. Wiley's research is generally concerned with contexts that promote successful text comprehension and problem solving, including studies on learning from Web pages. She has specifically investigated what design features and tasks help students to understand what they read online. Other areas of research include the effects of domain knowledge on the processing of ambiguous text and the contexts that allow experts to solve creative problems effectively. Correspondence regarding Chapter 12 should be sent to:

Jennifer Wiley
Department of Psychology
Univerisity of Illinois
1007 W. Harrison Street
Chicago, Il 60607
e-mail: jwiley@uic.edu

Dr. *Christopher* R. *Wolfe* (editor, Chapters 1 and 5) earned a doctorate in cognitive psychology from the University of Pittsburgh and is an associate professor of interdisciplinary studies at Miami University. He serves as the director of quantitative reasoning and instructional computing for the School of Interdisciplinary Studies and is an affiliate of Miami's departments of psychology and educational psychology. He is secretary/treasurer of the Society for Computers in Psychology (SCiP), an executive officer of Miami's Center for Human Development Learning and Teaching, and an associate of the Division of Learning, Technology, and Assessment at the University of Arizona. His research interests include learning technologies and cognition and instruction. His work places particular emphasis on higher-order cognitive processes and the relationship between learning, reasoning, and representation of knowledge. He has published articles in many leading journals, including the *Journal of Behavioral Decision Making, Behavioral Research Methods, Instruments, and Computers, Computers & Education: An International Journal, Journal of Educational Technology Systems, Journal on Excellence in College Teaching,* and *Teaching of Psychology.* Since 1996 he has been the founding editor of the Dragonfly Web Pages, an award-winning Web site for science and children. Correspondence should be sent to:

Christopher Wolfe, Ph.D.
Western College Program
Miami University
Oxford, OH 45056
e-mail:WolfeCR@muohio.edu

Preface

This book comes at a time when interest in the Web and "learning technologies" is keen. Bold claims are being made about the technology revolutionary in education, with little in the way of empirical or theoretical guidance on how to use the Web effectively in teaching. Today, 40% of college courses list Web resources in the syllabus, and more than a quarter of college courses have their own Web pages. It has been estimated that by the year 2002, 2.2 million college students will be enrolled in distance-learning courses, up from 710,000 in 1998 (Riva, Chapter 7). Already the vast majority of college students on U.S. campuses are "wired" (or wireless!), with 50% having Internet access from their dorm rooms (Morahan-Martin, Chapter 10). Yet too often the rush to technology is led by hyperbola and the fear of being left behind, rather than by a principled and evidence-based consideration of what works best for students. A goal of this book is to place the development of Web-based learning resources on solid psychological foundations. Thus, the positions advanced in this book are theoretically grounded and empirically supported.

This book draws on a broad range of psychological theory and research to create an "intradisciplinary" perspective on Web-based learning and teaching. This book will be indispensable to both psychologists and educational researchers interested in learning, as well as to practitioners of educational technology. Although the book is by no means a "how to" manual, teachers and trainers who use the Web in their teaching (or are thinking about it) will find it an especially useful compilation of relevant theory and research. Imperative for the researcher, this book is nevertheless accessible to students and educated laypersons.

Learning and Teaching on the World Wide Web addresses the application of psychological theory and research to the development and assessment of learning resources on the Web. The book explores Web-based learning and demands on the learner, the psychology of the learner, psychologically powerful dimensions of the Web, and online research. This work is greatly enhanced by a broad understanding of the social and psychological context of Web-based learning. For example, learning styles, the interaction between individual characteristics and technologies, and issues of anonymity and identity in cyberspace are some of the important dimensions of the learning context considered here. This book is built on solid foundations. The work is informed by early luminaries such as Johann Von Neumann, William Estes, James Gibson, Kurt Llewin, Lev Vygotsky, and Seymour Papert, as well as by the most reliable recent research. Recent research is applied to learning and teaching on the Web from several fields, including the study of individual differences in personality and cognitive style; basic cognitive research on perception, memory, and higher-order thinking; social–psychological research on virtual communities and online interaction; and clinical research on pathological Internet use. Recent technological advances such as shared hypermedia are also considered.

The organization of this book is from the individual learner to learning communities and the broader contexts in which learning and teaching take place. The authors of this volume are among the most influential psychologists in their respective fields. More than "early adopters," they are recognized experts from around the world. Five leading European psychologists and 14 experts from the United States contributed to this volume. Christopher Wolfe, editor and author of Chapters 1 and 5, is the director of quantitative reasoning and instructional computing in the School of Interdisciplinary Studies at Miami University. The first chapter, "Learning and Teaching on the World Wide Web," provides a conceptual introduction and overview. Chapter 2, "The Psychology of Human–Computer Mismatches," was coauthored by Valerie Reyna, Charles Brainerd, Judith Effken, Charles Bootzin, and Farrell Lloyd, the director and members of the executive board of the Division of Learning, Technology, and Assessment at the University of Arizona. Together they have published over 400 books, articles, and chapters. The past president of the Society for Computers in Psychology, Margaret Anderson wrote Chapter 3, "Individual Characteristics and Web-Based Courses." Anderson has published 45 articles that deal with individual learning styles and integrating computers into the curriculum. Anne Britt and Gareth Gabrys are the authors of Chapter 4, "Teaching Advanced Literacy Skills for the World Wide Web." They have published extensively in journals, including *Journal of Memory and Language, Journal of Educational Psychology, Cognition and Instruction, and Human Factors.* The editor is the secretary/treasurer for the Society for Computers in Psychology and also wrote the fifth chapter, on "Creating Informal Learning Environments on the World Wide Web." Lawrence Sherman is the author of Chapter 6, "Cooperative Learning and Computer-Supported Intentional Learning Experiences." He serves on the executive board of the International Association for the Study of Cooperation in Education and is the president of the Ohio Association for the Study of Cooperation in Education. Giuseppe Riva, a professor of communication psychology and general psychology at the Catholic University of Milan, Italy, wrote Chapter 7, "From Real to Virtual Communities: Cognition, Knowledge, and Interaction in the World Wide Web." The director and manager of the United Kingdom's Learning and Teaching Support Network, Psychology, Nick Hammond and Annie Trapp, coauthored Chapter 8, "How Can the Web Support the Learning of Psychology?" Christine Jazwinski wrote Chapter 9, "Gender Identities on the World Wide Web." She is a professor of psychology at St. Cloud State University in Minnesota and has been actively involved in studying the Web and its educational potential for several years. Janet Morahan-Martin is the author of Chapter 10, "Caught in the Web: Research and Criticism of Internet Abuse with Application to College Students." She is a professor of psychology at Bryant College in Smithfield, Rhode Island, and has conducted research and chaired symposia for the American Psychological Association on both pathological Internet use and gender and the Internet. Adam Joinson, a lecturer in educational technology at the Institute of Educational Technology at the Open University in the United Kingdom, and Tom Buchanan, a senior lecturer in psychology at the University of Westminster in London, coauthored Chapter 11, "Doing Educational Research on the Internet." The final chapter, "The Mental Web: Pedagogical and Cognitive Implications of the Net," was written by Jennifer Wiley and Jonathan Schooler. Wiley's research is concerned with contexts that promote successful text comprehension and problem solving, including studies on learning from Web pages. Jonathan Schooler has been the author of more than 50 publications and coauthored a book titled *Scientific Approaches to Consciousness*. He serves on the editorial boards of *Memory and Cognition* and *Consciousness and Cognition* and is an associate editor of *Cognitive Technology*.

When I first began recruiting the authors of this work, I wrote in my first e-mail message that I envisioned a book that takes a long view, one that will still be relevant years after publication. A person reading this book years from now will undoubtedly have better and faster computers and networks, and perhaps technologies that I had not imagined. I trust he or she will also benefit from advances in the science of learning and the scholarship of teaching. It is my hope that this volume will still be of service. I hope that in some small way this volume will help you, the reader, set the paradigm for learning and teaching on the World Wide Web.

Christopher R. *Wolfe*

Acknowledgments

I am indebted to the students of the Western College Program at Miami University for much of what I have learned about learning and teaching on the Web. In our interdisciplinary Technology courses and work on the Dragonfly Web Pages, we have learned from experience together. I trust they have learned as much from my mistakes as I have. Project Dragonfly (Chapter 5) is a cooperative effort, and I am grateful to my colleagues Jamie Bercaw, Hays Cummins, Carolyn Haynes, Chris Myers, and Lynne Myers for years of productive collaboration.

I also acknowledge the Society for Computers in Psychology (SCiP) for playing many roles in the creation of this book. SCiP serves as both an "incubator" for young researchers and an opportunity for exchanges among senior scientists working with technology. I first met several of the authors of this volume at SCiP meetings. I also thank my hosts at the Division of Learning, Technology, and Assessment at the University of Arizona and the Learning and Teaching Support Network Psychology (formerly the Centre for Technological Innovation in Psychology) at the University of York in the United Kingdom. They provided invaluable assistance with early work on this project when I was a visiting scholar. Finally, I thank my wife, Shari, for commenting on a draft of the Introduction, and especially for keeping it all in perspective. I dedicate this book to Michael and Patrick: the future belongs to you.

CHAPTER

1

Learning and Teaching on the World Wide Web

CHRISTOPHER R. WOLFE

Miami University

I. FROM 3 RS TO 3 WS?

This book is more about learning and teaching than technology. Teaching on the Web is an art that can — and should — be informed by empirical research and sound psychological principles. First, teaching on the Web *is* teaching. Some of the qualities that make a gifted teacher effective in face-to-face contexts also apply on the Web, even as the Web requires new teaching skills. Second, teaching on the Web is an art. Whether on-line learning resources are created by individuals or multidisciplinary teams, they require artistry and creativity. The tools for creating Web-based learning experiences are becoming more powerful and easier to use, and the technology is advancing at an astonishing rate. Finally, in order to be effective, teaching on the Web must be informed by research and theory. It is in the domains of psychological research, theory, and their application that this volume makes its contribution.

   Although the authors of this work are all appreciative of the potential of the Web, we are far from "cheerleaders." There has been too much booster-ism and not enough empirical research about what works on the Web, and what does not. Technology cheerleaders have made extreme claims, such as the notion that technology will soon replace universities. For example, in 1997 Lewis Perelman argued that "education is in a 'metastable' situation and will come to a 'systems break' within years, or even months," and that "even virtual universities are irrelevant" (Eamon, 1999, p. 200). This is accompanied by the claim that "the teaching function of the university will be completely replaced by 'knowledge industries,' which will deliver needed 'just in time' knowledge to workers who will have no formal university training" (Eamon, 1999, p. 197).

The Web provides "fingertip access" to worlds of information, and some technology cheerleaders behave as if access to information was the primary issue in education. Clearly, mere access to information is not enough. In fact, ordinary people have access to an astonishing array of free, reliable information. For example, the Cleveland Public Library in Cleveland, Ohio (in consortium with other public libraries in northeastern Ohio), has combined holdings of over 2.6 million titles and over 10 million items total (CLEVNET, 2000a). Among these holdings are thousands of scientific journals — among them 116 psychology periodicals — including *Acta Psychologica*, the *British Journal of Psychology*, the *Journal of Consulting and Clinical Psychology*, and *Psychological Review* (CLEVNET, 2000b). If access to information were the major obstacle to higher education, then Cleveland would be peopled by scholars and scientists. It is time to take the "hype" out of hypermedia.

The range of research relevant to learning and teaching on the Web is unusually broad. Obviously, there has been important work on Web-based learning itself, and clearly, recent advances in the psychology of learning should inform our thinking and practice. Yet, upon reflection, it soon becomes apparent that other areas of psychology cannot be ignored. The Web is a cognitive technology. Cognitive research on topics ranging from basic perception and memory to reasoning, integration, and other kinds of higher-order thinking is of great relevance. The Web is increasingly a social medium. Recent advances, such as shared hypermedia (SHY), allow people to "chat" while Web browsing. People using software such as Firetalk, Gooey, and Instant Rendezvous can communicate with others who are simultaneously browsing the same Web pages. This makes any page on the Web potentially the occasion for "virtual communities" of common interest. This SHY technology, explored by Riva in chapter 7, promises to make Web browsing even more of a social experience. Thus, research on computer-mediated communication (CMC), virtual communities, and computer-supported cooperative learning are part of a comprehensive understanding of the Web as a tool for learning and teaching. The Web is also a highly personal technology. Basic issues of personal identity play out on the Web, including gender issues, and the interaction of personality and technology. The Web offers unique opportunities and pitfalls associated with individual differences in areas such as cognitive style, tolerance of ambiguity, and locus of control.

Recent research, along with firmly established lines of inquiry, suggest four fundamental themes that are explored in this book. First, contrary to the rhetoric of the cheerleaders, and despite its overall promise, the *Web places greater demands on students* than traditional modes of instruction. These include cognitive demands on text processing stemming from the nonlinear nature of the Web, mismatches between learners and technologies arising from the heterogeneity of information on the Web, demands for greater cognitive flexibility, and more demanding environments for social interaction. Second, our understanding of the psychology of the learner suggests that Web-based learning is likely to be most successful when researchers and practitioners employ a broad "intradisciplinary" framework. This kind of framework is advocated by Reyna, Brainerd, Effken, Bootzin, and Lloyd in chapter 2, and Anderson in chapter 3. Such a framework takes into account basic cognitive processes (such as memory and perception), individual differences among learners, the learner's sensitivity to context, and acknowledges that people are social animals and learning is a social act. To a limited extent, an awareness of these dimensions represents current best teaching practices in psychology departments in the United Kingdom, as evidenced by Hammond and Trapp's exploration in chapter 8. Third, recent research on the psychological dimensions of the Web suggest a number of factors that are likely to influence learning and teaching. These include the power of the Internet as a tool for exploring and shaping personal identity, the recognition of the Web as a social technology, and the power of the (perceived) anonymity of on-line interactions. Finally, there is an urgent need for valid and reliable research on the Web, including research on basic psychological processes, and applied educational research. Our understanding of the learning and teaching on the Web will only be advanced through sound on-line research.

II. WEB-BASED LEARNING AND DEMANDS ON THE LEARNER

A. Demands on the Reader

The Web places greater demands on the learner than traditional learning environments. At the level of text processing, the Web places high demands on the reader's ability to make connections between new and existing knowledge. In chapter 4, Britt and Gabrys report research suggesting that the Web is a more difficult reading environment, for several reasons. First, as a nonlinear "hypertextual" environment, the Web strips out text devices that typically build coherence in linear texts such as textbooks. Second, learning experiences on the Web are generally created from "building blocks" of several shorter texts (for example, the Dragonfly Web Pages described by Wolfe in chapter 5). From the standpoint of the reader, this increases the number of documents that must be integrated, placing increased cognitive demands on the reader. Third, even superficial explorations of the Web reveal inconsistencies among sources that must be reconciled by the reader. This, too, is more taxing than reading traditional texts.

B. Demands of Heterogeneous Information

Heterogeneity of information is a mixed blessing. On the one hand, learning from diverse sources of information offers the potential for a richer, more subtle and nuanced understanding of the world. On the other hand, heterogeneity leads to greater complexity, and places additional burdens on the learner. In chapter 2, Reyna et al. argue persuasively that increased heterogeneity of information is an intrinsic property of learning technologies such as the Web. The heterogeneity of information available through the Web creates dilemmas for teachers and learners at micro and macro levels of analysis. These dilemmas, or "mismatches," as Reyna et al. dub them, include tensions between learning materials and memory systems, individual differences and on-line teaching techniques, mode of presentation and perception, and socialization and on-line experience. Heterogeneous representations of information on the Web often overlap substantially at the level of gist memory, with little or no overlap in their verbatim details. It is now well established that gist and verbatim memories are used quite differently in many learning and reasoning tasks (Reyna & Brainerd, 1995; Reyna et al., chapter 2). All students working with heterogeneous information must confront contradictions among sources and address issues of quality. These are among the advanced literacy skills discussed by Britt and Gabrys in chapter 4.

C. Demands for Cognitive Flexibility

Rapid technological changes, and a nonlinear rhetorical structure, make the Web less predictable than traditional learning environments. Some individuals are more comfortable learning in unpredictable environments than others, a trait Reyna et al. describe as "cognitive flexibility" in chapter 2. The Web requires more cognitive flexibility of learners than other settings, and these demands interact with several personality traits. Research reviewed by Anderson in chapter 3 suggests that students with a certain set of personality traits are most likely to benefit from Web-based learning experiences. These traits include high tolerance of ambiguity, low anxiety, field independence, and internal locus of control. Unfortunately, this same research implies that learning from the Web may be more difficult for people who do not share these traits.

D. Social Demands

Communication on the Internet is radically different from other forms of communication, a point made by Morahan-Martin in chapter 10, and echoed elsewhere. Some of the social cues we rely upon in face-to-face communication are missing in on-line communication. The Internet also has the paradoxical effect of decreasing social interaction for some users, and increasing social interaction for others. As Reyna et al. note, for susceptible individuals, the Web may lead to isolation and withdrawal from peer and family relationships, to the detriment of learning and general well-being. This may also lead some users to pathological Internet use, an issue explored extensively by Morahan-Martin in chapter 10.

Social interactions involve not only the communicators, but also contexts. However, contexts are created, not given, and are subject to continual change. Social actors not only respond to their technological environments, but those very responses change the technological context. As Riva notes in chapter 7, communication involves interpreting situations in which actors are involved. Actors clarify meanings, in part, by relating them to a shared context. Yet, these acts require greater metacognitive skills, and many students lack the metacognitive ability to monitor and control their learning in Web-based instructional settings.

The point of the preceding discussion is not that the Web is unsuited to learning. The Web has enormous potential as a tool for learning and teaching. However, the Web is unlikely to live up to its potential until researchers and practitioners recognize that the Web places additional demands on learners. Social demands, demands for high levels of cognitive flexibility, demands of heterogeneous information, and greater demands on the reader are part of the fabric of the Web. We should not be daunted by these issues, but we ignore them at our peril.

III. THE PSYCHOLOGY OF THE LEARNER AND WEB-BASED LEARNING

Recent advances in the psychology of learning suggest four areas of special relevance to learning and teaching on the Web. The first of these is the study of individual differences. The Web holds the promise of "tailoring" educational experiences to individuals. Relevant dimensions include differences in learning styles and differences in personality. Second is the view of learning as a social act, including work on Web-based cooperative learning, and the creation and maintenance of "virtual learning communities." Third is a consideration of basic cognitive process including perception, memory, and metacognition. These considerations should inform the creation of instructional displays and the way information is structured. Finally, a large body of evidence suggests that learners are highly sensitive to the context of learning. The context includes not only the technology and other learners, but also the goal structure and several characteristics of instructional materials.

A. Individual Differences

1. Learning Styles

There are reliable individual differences among students in their ability to benefit from learning technologies such as the Web. According to dual coding theory (Paivo, 1991), people differ in their preference for visual or verbal modes of presentation corresponding to preferred forms of mental representation. Although the evidence is not conclusive, Reyna et al. in chapter 2, and Anderson in chapter 3, suggest that there are reasons to believe that students who prefer a visual style of learning might benefit most from multimedia presentations. Conversely, students who prefer verbal styles may actually be hindered by multimedia. Another dimension of potential relevance is serialist versus holist styles of information processing. Reyna et al. review literature, suggesting that the serialist–holist dimension is a good predictor of learning in complex environments. Those teaching with the Web may wish to ensure that they are providing appropriate environments for learners with different preferences. These preferences may interact with presentation format and knowledge domain. Thus, in some instances, tailoring the educational experience to accommodate these preferences may be warranted.

2. Personality

The Web requires greater cognitive flexibility of learners than other settings, and these demands interact with several personality traits. First, the Web requires a heightened tolerance of ambiguity. As Anderson notes in chapter 3, ambiguity tolerance is an individual's ability to accommodate uncertain situations and ideas. Individuals with low tolerance for ambiguity may require more frequent feedback than is typically provided in Web-based learning contexts. Another personality dimension of relevance is field dependence/independence. Field-dependent people are characterized as oriented toward the global, social, and interpersonal. Field-independent individuals are characterized as analytic, self-referent, and impersonal. As Anderson notes, the data seem to suggest that field-independent students learn more from hypermedia, such as the Web, than field-dependent students. Locus of control refers to the degree to which individuals attribute their success and failure as resulting from either internal or external causes. Anderson reports evidence that students with internal locus of control are better able to structure their navigation, suggesting that they may be better able to take advantage of Web-based learning environments.

The literature on on-line research demonstrates that personality traits can be validly assessed using on-line measures, as Joinson and Buchanan indicate in chapter 11. These on-line measures could form the basis of educational research, testing hypotheses about learning and personality. Such measures could also form the basis of branching decisions, providing different learners with different versions of an educational experience depending on their personality characteristics.

B. Learning as a Social Act

There is something special about the sensibility of a good college seminar. Participating in a small seminar in the first year of college has been linked to higher retention rates, better academic performance, and more positive uses of student services (Fidler & Hunter, 1989). On-line interactions have been used successfully to strengthen community, enrich intellectual exchanges among students, and create rich "feedback webs" among faculty, students, and others, (Wolfe, Crider, Mayer, McBride, Sherman, & Vogel, 1998). Hammond and Trapp (chapter 8) found that psychology departments often use the Web to support dialogical processes, including preparing students for face-to-face communication, providing a forum for on-line discussions, and sharing electronic resources that will become the focus of subsequent discussions.

Communication is a reciprocal process. Educators and researchers increasingly reject the "parcel-post" model of communication (i.e., delivery of information) in favor of models of "inter-subjectivity" where communicators share their understandings of the world and engage one another's constructions of reality. Drawing upon the "classic" theory and research of Kurt Lewin, Jerome Bruner, Jean Piaget, and Lev Vygotsky, as well as post-modern thinking, practitioners such as Sherman (chapter 6) are beginning to build computer-supported intentional learning experiences on the Web. Cooperative learning starts with the premise that learning is a social act, and emphasizes the co-construction of meaningful narratives in the learning process.

The process of co-construction is at the heart of the "dialogic approach" to learning, which views cognition as an extension of conversation. Higher-order thinking is seen as the result of internalizing social interactions. Riva (chapter 7) uses the term "brainframe" to describe the matrices of cognitive functions that determine how we see the world and interact with it. He describes "interbrainframes" as the brainframes resulting from the networking of minds: the simultaneous interconnecting of many frames that are active in communication. Interbrainframes form the basis of virtual learning communities. Learners in Web-based learning environments must navigate paths through nodes and links created by others. It is in the interplay of navigator and Web-based hypermedia, of self and others, and of interlocutors and context that learning takes place. This is what Riva calls "the space between minds" where knowledge is generated and competencies are developed.

C. Basic Cognitive Processes

1. Perception

There is often a mismatch between human perceptual capabilities and the way learning materials are presented to students. People are dynamic visual information processors. We are highly efficient movement detectors, and sensitive to subtle changes in the visual field. Traditional media, such as textbooks, are capable of presenting only static visual displays, whereas the Web is well suited for presenting dynamic displays. In chapter 2, Reyna et al. report research suggesting interactions among instructional display format, instructional objectives, and characteristics of the learner that should be considered in designing dynamic displays.

Building on work in ecological psychology, Reyna et al. suggest that perception is guided by patterns of information in the environment, rather than sensory elements. J.J. Gibson's theory of affordances suggests that organisms use these patterns of information to direct actions based on perceived opportunities afforded by the environment. Affordances are constrained by the goals, knowledge, and skills of the perceiver, as well as inherent characteristics of the perceptual environment. Obviously, on the Web, designers have a good deal to say about the perceptual environment. Ecological psychology suggests that relationships should lawfully map onto relevant facets of the environment to take advantage of the nature of the perceptual system. Reyna et al. provide evidence that people are able to handle intricacies efficiently when complex relationships clearly map onto the perceptual environment. However, the creators of Web sites must deliberately design such lawful relationships into their visual displays. For example, in a unit for nursing students, Effken and her colleagues (chapter 2) varied the size and shape of a rectangle to demonstrate how oxygenation is a function of breaths per minute and units of air per breath. Similarly, on the Dragonfly Web Pages, Wolfe (chapter 5) created an interactive exercise where children "designed" a human-powered aircraft after reading a brief expository passage. Participants' decisions about the characteristics of the aircraft, such as weight and wingspan, were systematically tied to pictorial feedback about the aircraft and text describing its success or failure.

2. Memory

Recent research on human learning and memory suggests that when information is encoded, multiple memory traces are formed along a continuum from precise verbatim traces to fuzzy gist representations (Reyna & Brainerd, 1995; Reyna et al., chapter 2; Wolfe, chapter 5). Although verbatim memory traces are more precise, they also deteriorate more rapidly than fuzzy traces. Moreover, gist memories are generally the basis for creative transfer. As Wolfe notes, young children initially reason with verbatim representations, and, as they develop, begin gaining the ability to reason with increasingly fuzzy representations. Paradoxically, as Reyna et al. argue, these findings suggest that reasoning becomes more accurate as memories become less precise.

Wolfe reports that a goal of the Dragonfly Web Pages is to facilitate the encoding of useful and meaningful gist memories by creating tasks with "the right mix" of novel and familiar elements. The goal is to help children develop and refine intuitions (gist) by putting learners in the position of having to reason about situations where their existing knowledge is inadequate to the task at hand. Because gist representations are usually the basis for creative transfer, which is after all the ultimate goal of education, it is important to avoid teaching and testing at the level of verbatim information to the neglect of appropriate gist.

3. Metacognition

Metacognition is a person's knowledge about his or her own mental processes, and the ability to monitor and regulate those processes accordingly. In chapter 3, Anderson reviews the literature and concludes that metacognition is the best single predictor of academic performance, surpassing intelligence and other relevant variables. Generally, learning from the Web requires higher levels of metacognitive ability than other forms of instruction. Thus, those who teach Web-based courses are wise to consider the metacognitive demands made by their courses. Fortunately, the evidence seems to suggest that metacognitive abilities are somewhat malleable. Although metacognition is largely a function of cognitive development and domain knowledge, the right kinds of Web-based learning experiences may improve self-monitoring and other metacognitive processes. Indeed, as Wiley and Schooler suggest in chapter 12, developing proficiency in Web browsing, and the judicious application of "mental web" metaphors, may enhance metacognition.

D. Sensitivity to the Learning Context

It is well established that learners are highly attuned to the contexts in which learning takes place. These contexts include other learners (considered above), characteristics of the technology, and demand characteristics of the learning experience. Of particular importance to learning and teaching on the Web are characteristics of the Web as a medium and the goal structure of the learning experience.

1. Characteristics of the Web

The Web is an ephemeral medium. As Wolfe notes in chapter 5, we use phrases such as "browsing" and "surfing" to characterize our interactions with the Web, rather than, say, "studying" or "examining." The Web favors graphics over words, and pithy text over exhaustive treatises. Although it is technologically simple to put book length texts (or longer) on the Web, such documents violate our assumptions. Indeed, even with shorter documents, the tendency is for students to "print and run" (Joinson & Buchanan, chapter 11), eliminating the expressive power of networked hypermedia. Wolfe argues for creating brief, high-quality interactive experiences on the Web, rather than trying to be exhaustive. However, as Britt and Gabrys demonstrate in chapter 4, this increases the number of documents that must be integrated, placing greater cognitive demands on students.

Harnessing the expressive power of the Web requires one to work with, rather than against, the rhetorical structure of the medium. As previously noted, the Web is well suited to dynamic displays and systematic visual (and auditory) analogues of complex relationships. More broadly, the Web is a medium for concretizing abstractions. Wolfe argues for "reifying" abstract concepts. This entails manifesting them in a form where people can explore them in a more natural way, thus capitalizing on mechanisms of everyday learning.

2. Goal Structure

Intentional learning places the learner's goals at the center of learning. As Wolfe notes in chapter 5, the strategic nature of learning requires students to be goal directed. The goal structure of a learning experience is how goals are manifest in the behavioral setting, generally by a system of external rewards. Thus, the goal structure is one of the most important aspects of the learning context. In chapter 6, Sherman distinguishes among three kinds of goal structures: cooperative goal structures, competitive goal structures, and individual goal structures.

Cooperative goal structures are those in which two or more learners are rewarded for helping one another on learning tasks. As Sherman suggests, the jigsaw technique, reciprocal peer learning, and group-investigation models have been demonstrated to be effective. Cooperative goal structures have been included in "computer-supported cooperative learning" environments on the Web.

Competitive goal structures pit learners against one another. Here a student can only achieve his or her goals at the expense of others, a condition Sherman describes as "mutually exclusive goal attainment" (MEGA). Examples of competitive goal structures are games with winners and losers, and some traditional classrooms where students are graded on a bell curve. MEGA conditions create negative interdependencies among students, and are probably inappropriate for many learning situations. However, as Wolfe notes, play is a potent force in learning. Competitive learning games may have a place on the Web.

An individual goal structure is one in which learners are rewarded for their behavior independently from the rewards bestowed on others. For example, learners work independently on the Sourcer's Apprentice (chapter 4) and the Dragonfly Web Pages (chapter 5), and are given feedback based solely on the behavior of the individual learner. Individual goal structures work best with criterion-referenced evaluation systems, rather than norm-based systems. Too often in traditional classrooms, the teacher's rhetoric of independent evaluation is mismatched with a competitive goal structure, either through norm-referenced grading or through informal social comparisons of who is the better student. Individual goal structures work particularly well in informal learning environments of the kind described by Wolfe in chapter 5. However, those who would like to foster cooperative learning are bound to be disappointed if the learning context is guided by individual goal structures.

IV. PSYCHOLOGICAL DIMENSIONS OF THE WEB AND WEB-BASED LEARNING

The Web is a psychologically rich environment. It often transforms the lives of people who use it. To illustrate, a recent issue of the American Psychological Association's (APA) *Monitor on Psychology* was devoted to "how the Internet is changing psychology as we know it" (APA, 2000), including clinical practice, empirical research, education, and psychological phenomena such as on-line interaction and the impact of the technology on the self. Because the Web is such a psychologically potent medium, those who study and use the Web as a learning environment must broadly consider the intersection of psychology and the Web. Four areas are of particular importance: the impact of the Web on personal identity, the social psychology of on-line interactions, the psychological power of anonymity, and the potential for Internet abuse. For educational researchers, these psychological dimensions suggest new hypotheses and new variables to study. For those teaching with the Web, these areas suggest unrecognized promises and pitfalls. Those who capitalize on these powerful psychological dimensions of the Web have the potential to create transformative educational experiences that change students' lives. However, this body of research also suggests that teachers of Web-based courses may, unwittingly, be "playing with fire," or at least powerful psychological forces.

A. Identity and the Internet

The Internet has been called "the ultimate identity tool" (Murray, 2000). Sherry Turkle suggests that "the Internet is *the* identity technology — much of what people do online is self exploration and presentation, from searching and e-mailing, to chatting or creating a home page" (quoted in Murray, 2000, p. 17). There are historical reasons to believe that our basic notions about "the self" have undergone radical transformations since the Protestant reformation (Baumeister, 1987). There has been a progression from relatively simple, stable self-concepts to increasingly problematic, fragmented, and contradictory "postmodern" identities.

In chapter 9, Jazwinski raises the question of whether a key aspect of identity, our concept of gender, will undergo fundamental historic changes as the result of on-line experimentation. On many interactive Internet sites, people may assume gender identities of male, female, and neuter, and one popular site gives users 11 gender options to choose from. As Jazwinski notes, the social construction of gender is obvious on-line. She uses the phrase "doing gender" to describe how gender identities are constructed through social interactions. Doing gender on-line occurs on several levels. It can be the deliberate choosing of a gender when prompted. Those choices include gender switching, gender masking, or choosing the gender corresponding to biological sex. However, gender can be constructed less self-consciously when everyday habits are carried over into virtual environments, or when men and women use technology differently. Some have argued that the Internet places men and women on "even footing." However, there is evidence that gender stereotypes are even more pronounced on-line. The intricacies of these positions are explored in detail in chapter 9.

One way in which the Web influences a person's sense of identity is in the creation of home pages where people must decide how to present themselves. The very act of creating a home page is an exploration of identity. There is evidence that the creators of home pages overestimate how positively others will view their pages (Sherman et al., 1999; in press). However, the data suggest that the Web is neither a grossly impoverished social environment, nor a superior environment for impression management relative to face-to-face communication.

Another way the Web influences the self is through on-line interactions, such as those in SHY environments, and more established synchronous communication forums, such as chat rooms. People play with identities on the Internet, cycling through many possible selves and experimenting radically with self-presentation. As Jazwinski warns in chapter 9, the ease of changing identities on the Internet may lead to shallow and rigid on-line personae. This can lead to structurally weak virtual communities with ineffective conflict resolution strategies. These issues of identity and self-presentation can quickly spill over into educational contexts.

B. The Power of Anonymity

Perceived anonymity is a ubiquitous characteristic of the Internet, and a psychologically potent social condition. Whether surfing the Web or interacting in chat rooms, users generally think of themselves as anonymous. In chapter 9, Jazwinski notes that, in reality, most users are far less hidden than they think they are, with systems administrators having access to Internet Protocol (IP) addresses and other personal data. Nonetheless, users generally think of their "true" identities as being hidden. Moreover, as Joinson and Buchanan describe in chapter 11, simply not being seen by others, visual anonymity, has many of the same psychological effects as "pure" anonymity, even if users must provide their real names.

Among the consequences of perceived anonymity is the potential for heightened group affiliation and "hyperpersonal" interaction. Under conditions of perceived or visual anonymity, people will share more intimate details of their lives, and express thoughts and feelings that they would not express as readily in other contexts. Joinson and Buchanan argue that the use of computer-mediated communication in education encourages the development of highly affiliated groups when students are visually anonymous and share a social identity. Conversely, when students must reveal their identities, on-line class discussions are often stilted. If students are required to participate, discussion can become forced and skewed to due dates. If not required, students often avoid on-line discussions altogether. Students may also be less willing to access remedial materials on the Web if they believe they are being watched. For these reasons, Joinson and Buchanan suggest that if one wants students to make full use of Web-based courses, one should allow them to do so anonymously.

Of course, there is a catch. Students may be more willing to engage in hostile behaviors or divulge bigoted opinions under conditions of anonymity. For example, Sherman and Dietz-Uhler (2000) describe an experience in a psychology class combining face-to-face seminar meetings with anonymous on-line discussions. Students read materials on adolescent development suggesting that adolescence is a time when many people come to terms with their sexual orientation. Face-to-face discussions were matter of fact, however, anonymous on-line discussions included surprising levels of "gay bashing." When Dietz-Uhler confronted the students about this in seminar, students admitted that anonymity made them feel free to express "politically incorrect" sentiments. The moral of the story is not that anonymity is good or bad. Rather, it is that conditions of perceived anonymity bring a psychological depth to the learning environment that may be harnessed or harmful, depending on how they are handled.

C. User Perceptions and Social Stereotypes

Given the issues outlined above, it is not surprising that the way people perceive one another on-line raises important problems for educators. Jazwinski (chapter 9) suggests that when individuating information about the self and others is absent, people will rely more heavily on social categories that are known and salient. This suggests that people will interact with others on-line as if they were highly representative of those categories. For example, if someone thinks they know another's gender or ethnicity (say, by interpreting a nickname), they may respond on the basis of social stereotypes associated with those categories. Unfortunately, rather than freeing us from stereotypes, the Internet may lead people to rely more heavily on gender and ethnic stereotypes than face-to-face settings.

In chapter 7, Riva suggests that in constructing false identities on-line, people make significant use of social stereotypes in an attempt to have the identity recognized and accepted. This may force others to resort to highly stereotypical attitudes and behaviors so they can share a basic understanding of the social situation. These findings suggest caution in using the Internet to experience "what it is like" to have another gender or ethnicity. For example, a white male trying to experience what it's like to be an African-American woman may instead find his own racial and gender stereotypes exaggerated in his behavior, and find others over reliant on those social categories in their responses to him. Thus, his experiences may reflect an exaggerated and distorted version of his own stereotypes, with little resemblance to the life of real African-American women.

D. The Potential for Internet Abuse

Magazines, newspapers, and television have featured many lurid and sensationalistic stories about Internet abuse. Thus, it is reasonable to ask whether it is a real phenomenon or a creation of the media. Following a thorough review of the literature in chapter 10, Morahan-Martin concludes that a small minority of Internet users do indeed develop problematic behaviors related to their Internet use. Unfortunately, however, there is not universal agreement upon the etiology or basic definition of Internet abuse. For example, duration of disturbed Internet use has not been considered in any of the studies Morahan-Martin reviewed. Still, it is reasonable to assume that those who employ on-line discussions in their Web-based teaching may find themselves occasionally dealing with unexpected psychological issues.

Morahan-Martin finds that many of the psychologically powerful aspects of the Internet discussed above are associated with pathological Internet use. Her review of the literature (including her own research) suggests that people who are dependent on the Internet are much more likely than others to socially experiment on-line. Internet abusers seem to be about twice as likely as others to create false identities and to gender-swap on-line. They are more likely to report that they find on-line anonymity liberating, and are much more likely to report that the Internet makes it easier for them to communicate. Other factors associated with Internet abuse are a desire for excitement, particularly in the form of on-line gambling and "cybersex," the desire to escape negative emotions, and the desire to achieve a sense of power and mastery unavailable in the real world.

Morahan-Martin finds that college students are the group most prone to Internet abuse. The Internet provides avenues for dealing with issues of isolation, identity, intimacy, and sexuality that are particularly relevant to the college years. At this time, there is no evidence that Web-based courses are directly linked with pathological uses of the Internet. More research needs to be conducted on any relationship between educational practice and Internet abuse. However, the issues of anonymity, identity, and on-line interaction appear to be strongly associated with Internet abuse. This further attests to the psychological force of these aspects of the Internet, and suggests that educators should be cognizant of Internet abuse.

V. ON-LINE RESEARCH ON WEB-BASED LEARNING

The Web raises key research questions about learning and teaching — for both basic and applied researchers. The Web is still in its infancy, and there is a desperate need for good basic research about learning and teaching on the Web, and rigorous assessment of Web-based courses. As Anderson argues in chapter 3, it is time to turn away from simple comparisons of Web-based courses to those employing other formats. We need to study learning in all its complexity. In chapter 2, Reyna et al. contend that long-term changes in learning and memory should be the most important objective of research on learning technologies. They note that the quality of learning includes the organization of the learner's knowledge and learning strategies. Anderson echoes these insights in her discussion of the importance and malleability of metacognition. Modifying attitudes, beliefs, critical thinking skills, and procedural knowledge is also among the most important objectives of many educational experiences. Yet too often assessment is limited to declarative knowledge measured by the ability to recognize text.

The Web offers exciting new tools for the psychological researcher (Batinic, Reips, & Bosnjak, in press; Birnbaum, 2000). These tools for on-line research are powerful and increasingly easy to use. There are several high-quality Web sites where researchers can run their experiments and visitors can participate in psychological research. These include the Web's Experimental Psychology Lab (http://www.psych.unizh.ch/genpsy/Ulf/Lab/WebExpPsyLab.html) maintained by Reips at the University of Zurich, and Psychology Experiments on the Internet (http://www.olemiss.edu/psychexps/) maintained by McGraw, Tew, and Williams at the University of Mississippi. However, Web-based research raises fundamental methodological and ethical issues. These include whether on-line methods are always justified, which on-line methods to use, and how best to interpret the results of on-line research.

The most important question about on-line research is whether it provides valid and reliable results. Joinson and Buchanan (chapter 11) have conducted a review of psychological studies comparing on-line and off-line methods, including survey questionnaires, personality instruments, and controlled experiments. Their findings are generally encouraging. Both research settings produced similar patterns of results. The most common finding is that participants' responses stem from the same psychological processes in both Web-based and off-line studies. Web-based research offers large heterogeneous samples, including the potential for cross-cultural comparisons of participants from around the world. Joinson and Buchanan also suggest that Web-based research reduces demand characteristics of experiments and decreases experimenter bias.

However, the news is not all good. In chapter 10, Morahan-Martin reports large differences in the incidence of Internet abuse when measured in on-line and off-line studies. Of all the off-line studies she reviewed, the *highest* incidence of Internet abuse was 13% of Internet users, whereas in the on-line studies reviewed, the *lowest* rate of Internet abuse was 46% of participants. In one on-line study, 80% of the participants met the researcher's criteria for Internet abuse. These differences can be attributed to the highly skewed self-selected sample that participated in the on-line studies.

Issues of self-selection, technological sophistication, and demographic differences between Internet users and the general population may affect the results of on-line investigations. Although the gap is narrowing, denizens of the Internet are still disproportionately white and male. Sometimes there are interactions between demographics and research setting. Morahan-Martin found that males were two to five times as likely as females to abuse the Internet in off-line studies, but on-line studies that reported gender either found no difference or reported that females were more likely to be Internet abusers. Joinson and Buchanan suggest that individual differences in computer anxiety may interact with the research medium to affect research results. This indicates that researchers must be particularly clever and careful in how they recruit participants and interpret their results. Perhaps differences in research setting will be greatest when parameters of the general population are being estimated, and Web-based research will be the most reliable when participants are randomly assigned to experimental conditions.

The Web also raises ethical issues for researchers. First, it is less clear what constitutes informed consent on the Web. Asking potential participants to read a statement before clicking an "informed consent button" does not guarantee that they will read and understand the statement. Moreover, we can easily track the Web browsing patterns of people visiting a Web site, including which sites they visited immediately before and after they accessed the site. This can be accomplished without the visitor's knowledge or consent by using a "cookie," or examining the IP addresses in the server's log file. These practices are common on commercial Web sites, but may not be compatible with existing ethical standards.

Finally, it is less clear on the Internet what constitutes "public behavior," and whether on-line researchers need to take additional precautions to protect the confidentiality of research participants. To illustrate these points, a graduate student in our psychology department took a direct quote from an academic journal made by a participant in a chat room. Typing the exact quote into a search engine, he soon found an archived version of the conversation. In less than five minutes he was able to produce the nickname and e-mail address of the participant quoted in the journal article. Reporting about behavior taking place in public settings on-line may leave a data trail that could be used to violate a participant's privacy. Even concealing individuating information may not be adequate to protect the confidentiality of participants when exact quotes — or even low-frequency key words — might be used to track down their identities.

In chapter 9 Jazwinski laments that there are not widely accepted methods for collecting valid data on the Internet (however, see Batinic et al., in press; Birnbaum, 2000), and that much of the research on computer-mediated communication uses ethnographic methods. Reyna et al. argue that randomized control trials are required to evaluate educational interventions, and indeed are the only ethical avenue for introducing major educational changes. Web-based research requires us to revisit fundamental research issues. For example, in chapter 5, Wolfe discusses informal learning experiences on the Web that generally draw visitors on the basis of intrinsic motivation rather than as a course requirement. Self-selection is thus a key characteristic of visitors to informal learning sites. Therefore, one set of research questions concern how people are drawn to a Web site and characteristics of the visiting population. Another set of issues concern what, if anything, people learn as a result of their visit. The first set of questions may be best addressed by survey methods, and the second by experimental methods.

Consistent with a broad intradisciplinary framework is the use of converging on-line research methods. Examining phenomena from a variety of perspectives — using a set of methodological lenses to achieve a comprehensive understanding — is the hallmark of converging methodologies. This offers the best hope for fully comprehending learning on the Web in all its subtlety. Ultimately, the research question should dictate which on-line method is used for a particular part of a research campaign.

Controlled experiments are the only way to tease apart causal relationships among teaching methods and learning outcomes. Moreover, the personal, professional, and financial investments that are made in Web-based teaching provide powerful incentives for exaggerating the effectiveness of Web-based courses. Controlled experiments offer a proven antidote to these tendencies, and can reliably be performed on-line. As Wiley and

Schooler note in chapter 12, verification, problem solving, and sorting tasks (as well as experiments employing discourse analysis) can be used to measure deep conceptual learning. For a comprehensive list of experiments on the Web, see the American Psychological Society Psychological Research on the Net site (http://psych.hanover.edu/APS/exponnet.html) maintained by John Krantz.

Other procedures, including surveys, participant feedback, and third party evaluations, employ both quantitative and qualitative methods. On-line surveys are useful for reaching a large number of participants and exploring the impact of demographic variables such as ethnicity, gender, and socioeconomic status. Feedback from students and unbiased third parties provides useful information that the researcher may not have considered.

Qualitative methods, including on-line interviews and ethnographies, permit the researcher to ask questions about the nature of virtual learning communities. There have been several well-known ethnographic studies on the Internet (e.g., Baym, 1996; Turkle, 1995). Unfortunately, few educational researchers are well trained in face-to-face ethnographic methods, let alone Internet-based ethnographies. In anthropology, ethnographers often spend years engaged in research, not just a week or two as has happened in some educational studies. Many anthropologists employ the logic of disconfirmation. They recognize the influence of their culturally bound prejudices, and actively look for evidence *against* their own interpretations (Emerson, Fretz, & Shaw, 1995; Bernard, 1995). Devices such as triangulation, and attempts to corroborate information from informants are also used to guard against misinterpretation.

The use of co-constructive methods, sometimes called cooperative inquiry, participatory action research, and co-inquiry, might also be beneficial in understanding the learner's experience. The basic premise of co-inquiry is that the "researcher" and "participant" are both sentient beings capable of making sense of their experience together (Reason, 1994; Reason & Bradbury, in press). This approach may be particularly enriching when used with more mature nontraditional students engaged in informal, "life long" learning.

A converging methodology research campaign conducted on-line might proceed by repeating a cycle of deep methods, broad methods, and controlled experiments. Qualitative methods such as interviews, ethnography, and co-inquiry may give the researcher a rich understanding of the learner's experience. Broad methods such as surveys, participant feedback, and input from outside parties may expand the understanding gained from qualitative research and provide a more inclusive view. The results of these methods, along with theory and other research findings, may in turn be used to form more sophisticated hypotheses to be tested by controlled experiments. These experiments can be used to disentangle causal relationships among specific aspects of Web-based teaching and specific learning outcomes. Since experimental research generally raises as many questions as it answers, a return to qualitative methods may be the next step, thus completing the cycle. Although it may not always be necessary to conduct such a full-blown research campaign, this approach is the most likely to address learning in all of its complexity. That this full range of methods could be employed on-line is a testament to the rich potential of the Internet for research.

VI. STRUCTURE AND ORGANIZATION

The general organization of this book is from the individual learner to learning communities and the broader contexts in which learning and teaching take place. Chapters 2 and 3 each provide a comprehensive framework for considering learning and teaching on the Web. In chapter 2, Reyna et al. examine four dilemmas for learners created by Web-based learning: the learning and memory mismatch, the individual differences mismatch, the perception–presentation mismatch, and the socialization mismatch. The theme of individual differences and Web-based courses is explored more fully by Anderson in chapter 3. Anderson develops an interactive model of learner characteristics and Web-based courses by considering characteristics of the individual and key aspects of Web-based course design.

Chapters 4 and 5 consider learning environments that teach higher-order thinking skills. In chapter 4 Britt and Gabrys examine the advanced literacy skills required for learning on the Web. These skills include integration, sourcing, and corroboration. Advanced literacy skills have been taught with the Sourcer's Apprentice, a Web-based application that has been demonstrated to be effective with high school students. In chapter 5, Wolfe explores informal learning environments on the Web. Drawing from his experience with the Dragonfly Web Pages, Wolfe describes the principles and strategies used to create interactive decision-making experiences on the Web.

Chapters 6, 7, and 8 examine the social dimensions of Web-based learning. Sherman discusses cooperative learning and intentional learning experiences on the Internet in chapter 6. Drawing from the classic research of Kurt Lewin, as well as postmodern theory, he shows how the goal structure of a learning experience affects the nature and degree of cooperation. In chapter 7, Riva considers the nature of virtual learning communities. He explores the interplay of cognition, conversation, and community in creating shared contextual understanding. He argues that an understanding of the inherent integration of cognition, knowledge, and social interaction is necessary for creating Web-based social learning environments. Hammond and Trapp, in chapter 8, present a taxonomy of the ways psychology departments in the United Kingdom use the Web to support learning. They find that departments use the Web for teaching primary content materials (reception), to facilitate exploration (construction and integration), to support communication (dialogue), and to support communities of learners and manage the "nuts and bolts" of the learning experience (communities of practice).

Psychologically powerful dimensions of the Web are considered in chapters 9 and 10, along with their ramifications for students and teachers. In chapter 9, Jazwinski explores the creation of gender identities on the Web. Characteristics of virtual social interaction and issues such as virtual gender, gender bending, gender concealment, and unequal power and access are important strands in the psychological fabric of the Web. Morahan-Martin considers the potential of the Internet for abuse in chapter 10, with special consideration of college students. Understanding the psychologically compelling dimensions of the Internet may suggest new hypotheses for educational researchers, and unrecognized pitfalls for those who teach with the Web.

Joinson and Buchanan examine educational research on the Internet in chapter 11. Issues associated with on-line research include assessment of Web-based courses, ethical issues, participant characteristics, and validity. The relationship between behavior on the Internet and education, including the design of educational materials, receives special consideration. Finally, in chapter 12, Wiley and Schooler provide a conclusion to the book. They discuss differences between learning from the Web and both classroom learning and learning from textbooks. They also consider the ramifications of the Web as a metaphor for the mind and directions for future research.

VII. CONCLUSIONS

Too many working on the Web seem to have forgotten the most basic maxim of the information age: garbage in, garbage out. Today "content" has become ghettoized, separated from the glitzy cutting edge of technology, and relegated a minor subspecialty. Many of us who have been working on the Web for years are impressed by its explosive expansion, but are also discouraged by the banality and crass commercialism of the Web today. For example, as Morahan-Martin notes, the most sought after search term on most search engines is "sex" (with "MP3" topping one list in January 2000). It is not that I am alarmed by the evils of pornography so much as disappointed by the distance between where we are today and the Web's potential as an instrument of human development.

It is time for us to pay more attention to what we are putting on the Web, and why. For most of my lifetime, the hardware has been ahead of the software, and the software has been ahead of theory. By this I mean, first, that software engineers have not fully utilized the capacities of computers, and second, that "know-how" and craftsmanship exceed erudition and artistry. In the case of on-line learning, there has been a paucity of good ideas. Educational thinking has lagged behind the potential of networked information technology. Theory and research have been the real "bottlenecks" in the creation of effective learning technologies.

Perhaps the cheerleaders are correct that this is the last generation that will experience a college education. Conversely, maybe something very much like a traditional liberal arts education will provide the best basis for life long learning on the Web. In any case, we must get beyond boosterism and down to the serious work of studying learning in all its complexity and creating rich learning environments on the Web. Teaching on the Web is an art. Only by applying hard work, rigorous research, and imagination to that art will we create a world-class World Wide Web.

References

APA (2000). *Monitor on Psychology*, 31 (4), whole issue.

Batinic, B., Reips, U.-D., & Bosnjak, M. (Eds.). (In press). *Online social sciences*. Seattle: Hogrefe & Huber.

Baumeister, R. F. (1987). How the self became a problem: A psychological review of historical research. *Journal of Personality and Social Psychology*, 52, 163–176.

Baym, N. K. (1996). The emergence of community in computer-mediated communication. In R. Shields (Ed.), *Cultures of Internet: Virtual spaces, real histories, living bodies* (pp. 138–163). London: Sage.

Bernard, H. R. (1995). *Research methods in anthropology: Qualitative and quantitative approaches* (2nd ed.). Thousand Oaks, CA: Sage Publications

Birnbaum, M. H. (Ed.). (2000). *Psychology experiments on the Internet*. San Diego, CA: Academic Press.

CLEVNET (2000a, May 18). *The CLEVNET library consortium* [on-line]. Available; http://www.cpl.org/Locations.asp

CLEVNET (2000b, MAY 18). *The library catalog of the Cleveland Public Library and the CLEVNET libraries* [ON-LINE]. Available: http://js-catalog.cpl.org:60100/newcat.html

Eamon, D. B. (1999). Distance education: Has technology become a threat to the academy? *Behavioral Research, Measurement, Instruments, & Computers*, 31, 197–207.

Emerson, R. M., Fretz, R. I., & Shaw, L. L. (1995). *Writing ethnographic fieldnotes*. Chicago: University of Chicago Press.

Fidler, P. P., & Hunter, M. S. (1989). How seminars enhance student success. In M. L. Upcraft and J. N. Hunter (Eds.), *The freshman year experience: Helping students survive and succeed in college*. San Francisco: Jossey-Bass.

Murray, B. (2000). A mirror on the self. *Monitor on Psychology*, 31, 16–19.

Paivio, A. (1991). Dual coding theory: Retrospect and current status. *Canadian Journal of Psychology*, 45, 255–287.

Reason, P. (Ed.). (1994). *Participation in human inquiry*. London: Sage Publications.

Reason, P., & Bradbury, H. (Eds.). (In press). *Handbook of action research: Participative inquiry in practice*. London: Sage Publications.

Reyna, V. F., & Brainerd, C. J. (1995). Fuzzy-trace theory: An interim synthesis. *Learning and Individual Differences*, 7, 1–75.

Sherman, R. C., End, C., Kraan, E., Cole, A., Campbell, J., Klausner, J., & Birchmeier, Z. (in press). *Meta-perception in cyberspace*, Cyber Psychology & Behaviour.

Sherman, R. C., End, C., Kraan, E., Cole, A., Martin, J., & Klausner, J. (1999, June). *The nature of impressions formed from World Wide Web home pages.* Presentation to the American Psychological Society, Denver, CO. Available: http://miavx1.muohio.edu/~shermarc/aps99.htm

Sherman, R. C., & Dietz-Uhler, B. (2000, April). *Active and collaborative learning: Technological applications.* Psychology Department Colloquium Presentation, Miami University, Oxford, Ohio.

Turkle, S. (1995). *Life on the screen: Identity in the age of the Internet.* New York: Simon and Schuster.

Wolfe, C. R., Crider, L., Mayer, L., McBride, M., Sherman, R., & Vogel, R. (1998). Toward a Miami University model for Internet-intensive higher education. *Journal on Excellence in College Teaching, 9,* 29–51.

The Psychology of
Human–Computer Mismatches

VALERIE F. REYNA,* CHARLES J. BRAINERD,† JUDITH EFFKEN,‡
RICHARD BOOTZIN,§ AND FARRELL J. LLOYD¶

*Departments of Surgery and Medicine, †Division of Learning, Technology, and
Assessment, ‡College of Nursing, §Department of Psychology, and ¶Department of Medicine,
University of Arizona

I. HUMAN–COMPUTER MISMATCHES: A
FRAMEWORK FOR ASSESSMENT

Technology-infused instructional environments (e.g., electronic interactive-learning systems and real-time video conferencing) have evolved at a much more rapid pace than the scientific study of how and what people learn in those environments (Alavi, 1994; Mayer, 1997; Ross, 1994). Consequently, new instructional technologies are proliferating in classrooms, but little is known about their effects on learning. For example, computer-based graphics, including animation, photographs, and video, have reached high levels of refinement. However, these advances have not been matched by advances in research on how such graphics influence the learning of course material (Reiber, 1990). Because the effects of technology on instructional outcomes are poorly understood, decisions as to when to implement them, how to implement them, and how to design improved technologies often proceed in an empirical vacuum.

Decisions about the cost-effectiveness of investments in instructional technology should obviously hinge on outcome assessment. In this chapter, we propose a framework for the assessment of learning outcomes

Learning and Teaching on the World Wide Web

associated with technology. We discuss the kind of expertise that is required for such assessment, the nature of current instructional technologies, and potential mismatches between technologies and human learning. These mismatches occur with respect to four classes of characteristics of human learners: natural learning and memory processes, perception, individual differences in learning styles and other cognitive factors, and individual differences in social and personality factors. The human–machine mismatches in each of these domains, we ultimately argue, determine the instructional outcomes produced by learning technologies.

Current educational uses of technology suggest five conclusions that should inform a research agenda. First, although many technological options are available to instructors, four options predominate in university courses: Web-based instruction, video-delivered distance learning, electronic interactive-learning environments, and simulated environments (including virtual reality). Second, technology-infused instruction poses some fundamental dilemmas for learners—dilemmas that are rooted in mismatches between the capabilities of humans and those of machines. These dilemmas are of four general sorts: mismatches between properties of technology and (1) natural human learning and memory processes, (2) perception, (3) individual differences in cognitive characteristics of learners, and (4) individual differences in social and personality characteristics of learners. Specific studies should therefore be undertaken to determine how human-machine mismatches in each of these domains influence the instructional outcomes of learning technologies. Third, each category of dilemmas is more prominent with some technologies than with others. For instance, mismatches that involve natural learning and memory processes are especially likely with Web-based instruction, whereas mismatches that involve social and emotional factors are especially likely with electronic interactive learning. To encompass all of the categories of dilemmas, it is therefore necessary to investigate all of these technological options. Fourth, to achieve generality of findings, technological options must be studied in multiple disciplines and in heterogeneous populations of students. The test beds for research should therefore be diverse with respect to disciplinary content, student populations, and geographical regions. Fifth, to achieve standardization of findings, new tools will have to be developed to categorize and analyze instructional choices. For instance, software systems must be designed to support and analyze the processes of goal selection, learning activity selection, technology selection, lesson planning, and evaluation of learning outcomes in courses with varied disciplinary content and instructional objectives. Also, software systems will be required that are capable of logging and tracking students' interactions with diverse course material.

Dilemmas within each category of human–machine mismatch should be investigated, and initial studies are likely to be category specific (i.e., designed to identify factors that are important within each mismatch category). As research proceeds, findings within each category should be summarized in appropriate mathematical models, especially structural equation models. Initially, important mismatches within the spheres of learning and memory processes, cognitive individual differences, and social-personality individual differences should be identified and captured in mathematical models. Then, research on interactions among factors in different spheres becomes possible. Therefore, subsequent studies should span categories of mismatches. As results from these later, cross-category investigations become available, they should also be represented in appropriate mathematical models. The ultimate goal is an integrated theoretical model that specifies how factors in each domain interact with each other and how, taken together, they determine the instructional outcomes of particular technologies.

II. RESEARCH AGENDA

The research agenda we advocate employs a comprehensive framework consisting of four principles:

1. Research on learning technologies must address multiple levels of analysis, from the individual to the institutional (e.g., Dutta, 1997).

2. Learning technologies show, as an intrinsic property, that they increase the amount and heterogeneity of information available (but not necessarily accessible) to learners (e.g., Mayer, 1997).

3. The amount and heterogeneity of information available through learning technologies creates dilemmas at each level of analysis (e.g., Friedman, 1994).

4. In addition to traditional learning outcomes, the scientific study of the effects of learning technologies must include basic learning and memory processes, cognitive individual differences factors, and social-personality factors (e.g., Alavi, 1994).

The rationale for these principles is straightforward. Empirical research indicates that learning technologies have different effects on different individuals (e.g., Mayer, Steinhoof, Bower, & Mars, 1995), on different aspects of learning (e.g., Lloyd & Reyna, in press-a; Reyna & Brainerd, 1995), on groups, as opposed to individuals (e.g., Kipnis, 1997), and on learning in different disciplines (e.g., Reiber, 1990). Unless these differences are taken into account, many beneficial effects of technology-infused instruction may go undetected (Mayer, 1997). Such differences are predicted by modern cognitive learning theories, and these theories have sometimes been used in the design of learning technologies, especially in the design of user interfaces (e.g., Jones & Farquhar, 1995). However, there is little systematic research on these predictions. For instance, although certain theories expect that computer-based graphics (animation, photographs, and live video) will have paradoxical effects on learners' retention of course content (e.g., Brainerd & Reyna, 1993, 1995), experimental findings on how and what people learn from these graphics are limited (Reiber, 1990).

It is now widely conceded that the quality of learning includes processes such as the organization of learners' knowledge bases and their strategies for learning and retaining course material (e.g., Kizlik, 1996; Reimann & Schult, 1996; Scardamalia, 1994; Zhou & Whang, 1996). Although university courses must impart skills and knowledge, changes in learning and memory processes that encourage creative transfer, in addition to sheer retention, are also fundamental goals. Hence, a standard instructional issue is that learners are often able to retain course content in considerable detail and yet not be able to use it creatively to solve new problems or make decisions in new contexts (e.g., Mayer, 1997; Reyna, Lloyd, & Brainerd, in press; Reyna & Brainerd, 1993, 1995). From this perspective, long-term changes in learning and memory processes may be the most important objective of research on learning technologies because these changes enable learners to engage in sophisticated problem solving, to make informed decisions in real-world contexts, and to understand how to learn in new situations (Njoo & de Jong, 1993; Puntambekar, 1995).

Finally, although individual projects will have varied aims, they should ideally support a series of concrete objectives derived from the four principles. The first objective is to distinguish different effects of learning technologies for individuals, for learners generally, for groups, and for disciplines. The second objective is to determine the impact of the amount and heterogeneity of information available through technology on learning processes and outcomes. The third objective is to advance knowledge of the mechanisms responsible for improvements in learning processes and outcomes through technology. The final objective is to develop new technologies and refine existing ones to produce desired effects on learning processes and outcomes.

III. DILEMMAS IN THE APPLICATION OF LEARNING TECHNOLOGIES

The substantive focus of our proposed research agenda consists of some key dilemmas in the use of learning technologies. Johann Von Neumann (1958), writing at the dawn of the computer age, foresaw a mismatch between the capabilities of human and machine intelligence. Subsequent research has confirmed Von Neumann's conjecture and articulated it in two ways. First, insofar as human versus machine intelligence is concerned, the nature of the mismatch is better understood than it was in Von Neumann's time. The mismatch is rooted in differences between the natural learning and memory processes of humans and the corresponding processes of computers. Computers are specialized for storing vast quantities of information in precise verbatim form, exhaustively retrieving it, and processing it via step-by-step computations. Human learners are specialized for extracting and storing the core gist of information, retrieving it in selective and strategic ways, and processing it intuitively (e.g., Estes, 1980). In addition, three other classes of human–machine mismatch have been identified that modulate the effects of learning technologies: mismatches arising from individual differences in cognitive, perceptual, and social-personality factors. We sketch the four classes of mismatches separately.

A. Dilemma 1: The Learning and Memory Mismatch

Because learning technologies capitalize on the strengths of computers, it is foreseeable that they will mesh well with some natural learning processes but not others. For instance, a hallmark of courses that rely on the World Wide Web is that learners are provided with access to multiple representations of course content in multiple media (text, still pictures, voice, video). Although these multiple representations overlap at the level of core gist, they are extremely heterogeneous in their verbatim details. Although the potential benefits of multiple representations of course material have been widely acknowledged (e.g., Schnotz, 1993; Schnotz & Kulhavy, 1994), research on verbatim and gist memory suggests that this aspect of Web-based instruction will enhance students' retention of core gists, but may interfere with their retention of exact verbatim features of material (Brainerd & Reyna, 1993; Reyna & Kiernan, 1994). This, in turn, has implications for the traditional outcome measures of retention and creative transfer. Because gist memories are the usual basis for creative transfer (e.g., Reyna, 1996b; Reyna & Brainerd, 1993), such multiple representations may increase performance on transfer measures while decreasing it on measures of sheer retention. Some evidence of this pattern can be found in recent studies of multimedia learning (e.g., Mayer & Anderson, 1991, 1992).

Because the effects of learning technologies are modulated by interactions with natural learning and memory processes, those interactions should be the focus of research on technology-infused courses in multiple disciplines (for example, arts and humanities, physical and biological sciences, education, engineering, geosciences, mathematics, medicine, and the social sciences). Instructors in these disciplines can distinguish important core gists and verbatim facts from their courses. (For example, the exact form of the ideal gas law, which must be remembered for accurate calculation, is $PV = nRT$, whereas the gist is that pressure increases directly with temperature and inversely with volume; the exact biochemical structure of DNA is made up of adenine forming hydrogen bonds with thymine and guanine forming hydrogen bonds with cytosine, whereas the gist is that the four nucleic acids bond in two types of pairs.) Research should concentrate on measuring how the two forms of learning interact with specific features of the learning technologies.

Because natural learning and memory processes are enduring properties of the human nervous system, it is possible to identify processes that, on the basis of extant research, are most likely to interact with features of learning technologies, and then to refine technologies to accommodate verified interactions. Prior research provides two classes of generalizations, one about the memory representations that learners store, and the other about how those representations are processed during reasoning. Both can be used to generate hypotheses about the effects of learning technologies.

Recent research suggests a set of key predictive generalizations about memory representations. Learners store dissociated verbatim memories (e.g., exact values of variables in equations, exact appearances of graphs and figures in textbooks, and exact factors included in particular laboratory demonstrations) and gist memories (concepts, patterns, elaborations, inferences) in parallel as they process course material (Brainerd & Reyna, 1993). Because verbatim and gist memories are stored in parallel, conceptual understanding of material can be present even though learners have not fully processed its verbatim form, and precise verbatim memories of material can be present without conceptual understanding (Reyna & Brainerd, 1995; Reyna et al., in press). When verbatim and gist memories of material have been stored, the former deteriorate more rapidly over time (Gernsbacher, 1985; Murphy & Shapiro, 1994). Certain methods of presentation, which can be manipulated with learning technologies, favor verbatim memories over gist memories, while others favor gist memories over verbatim memories (Brainerd & Gordon, 1994; Brainerd, Reyna, & Kneer, 1995). Similarly, some types of materials themselves favor verbatim memories over gist memories, while other types favor gist memories over verbatim memories (Reyna & Kiernan, 1994, 1995). Moreover, once verbatim and gist memories of material are formed, certain testing procedures selectively preserve verbatim memories while others selectively preserve gist memories (Brainerd, Reyna, Howe, & Kingma, 1990; Reyna & Titcomb, 1997). Finally, when verbatim and gist memories of material are both available in memory, learners access them via quite different retrieval cues (Brainerd & Reyna, 1995; Reyna, 1995).

Key predictive generalizations about memory–reasoning relations are suggested by recent research. The forms of reasoning demanded in university courses, from scientific inference to aesthetic judgments about art, are strongly biased to operate on the simplest available gist memories (Reyna & Brainerd, 1992). Gist even plays a key role in mathematical reasoning (Reyna & Brainerd, 1993). The gist bias of reasoning is determined by multiple factors, the most critical of which is that gist memories are more resistant to forgetting than verbatim memories, and are more readily accessible via nonspecific retrieval cues in reasoning tasks (Reyna & Brainerd, 1991a). Although the gist bias of reasoning normally promotes accuracy, it sometimes creates powerful reasoning illusions that make certain material, such as conditional probability concepts in statistics, or equilibrium principles in thermodynamics, very difficult to learn (Brainerd & Reyna, 1990). Although reasoning is biased to operate on the simplest available gist, certain features of learning technologies can prod reasoning to operate on more complex gist memories or on verbatim memories (Reyna & Brainerd, 1991b). As learning of course material progresses, there is a shift in reasoning toward increased formation of new gist memories and decreased reliance on new verbatim memories (Reyna & Brainerd, 1994), creating a paradoxical situation in which learners' reasoning becomes more accurate as their memories become less precise (Reyna & Ellis, 1994). Because forgetting rates are higher for verbatim memories than for gist memories, after long delays (e.g., when learners take a later course in a sequence), there is a shift toward even greater reliance on gist memories (Brainerd et al., 1990).

Each of these features of natural learning processes is expected to interact with features of learning technologies. For example, learners who remember primarily gist-level information may be stymied in navigating through large amounts of verbatim information if searches can only be based on full, or even partial, verbatim matches. Lloyd & Reyna (in press-b) provide several examples of such verbatim interference in the use of search engines to navigate the Web. Prototype on-line assessment tools have been developed that track students' progress through electronic course materials, including Web sites. A student's progress through materials can then be evaluated in terms of its disparity from the paths taken by more advanced users (i.e., experts) and its disparity from earlier paths taken by that student. Conversely, if learning technologies make verbatim information far more accessible to students, they may rely on it unduly, lowering performance on measures of creative transfer and problem solving (cf. Brainerd & Reyna, 1993; Reyna & Kiernan, 1995). An important aim of research should be to identify features of learning technologies that support different aspects of learning and memory (e.g., gist versus verbatim), and that have different effects on learning outcomes (e.g., retention versus creative transfer).

B. Dilemma 2: The Individual-Differences Mismatch

A consistent finding reported by faculty who have redesigned their courses around learning technologies is that there are surprising individual differences in students' tendencies to benefit from the technologies (e.g., Oshima & Scardamalia, 1996; see Anderson, chapter 3, this volume, for a detailed discussion of individual characteristics and Web-based courses). This is an instance of the general phenomenon of aptitude-by-treatment interactions:

stable individual differences in cognitive factors that modulate learners' ability to benefit from particular innovations. These include differences in learning styles, attitudes, and prior exposure to both relevant knowledge and to technology. Thus, the second dilemma is that learners may not benefit equally from particular varieties of learning technologies.

Indeed, incompatibilities between individuals' cognitive styles and learning technologies may produce lower levels of learning relative to traditional instructional approaches. In order to develop learning technologies that are able to produce specific instructional outcomes, the individual-differences factors that have strong effects on learners' ability to benefit from the features of those technologies must be identified. Because learning technologies are merely tools that can efficiently deliver a variety of content, however, these technologies provide unprecedented opportunities to incorporate information about individual differences in learning into instructional delivery. Although some data on the question of individual differences in the effects of learning technologies are available (e.g., Ayerson, 1995), findings are limited, and the major factors that must be accommodated in the design of such technologies remain open questions. However, by tapping the broader research literature on individual differences, both common-sense hypotheses and theoretical hypotheses can be generated to guide initial research on this dilemma.

An obvious common-sense hypothesis is that with computer-based technologies, factors such as learners' computer skills, the availability of computers for learners' use, and learners' access to the Internet, the Web, e-mail, and related resources will be predictors of learning outcomes. Research is already underway on this hypothesis. An instrument that measures these factors, as well as learners' attitudes toward computer-based learning environments, has been constructed. The instrument is continuing to be revised to incorporate relevant research, especially research demonstrating effects of attitudes, as well as student goals and perceptions, on learning outcomes (e.g., Cooney & Swanson, 1990). This instrument has been administered to several hundred students in diverse courses at the University of Arizona, and at other universities via the Web.

Existing theories of aptitude-by-treatment interactions point to additional individual-differences factors that are likely to modulate the effects of most instructional treatments. With technology-infused instruction, the following three are promising candidates for modulating factors: prior knowledge of course content (e.g., Mayer & Gallini, 1990; Reyna, 1996a), verbal versus spatial learning style (e.g., Collins & Tellier, 1994), and cognitive flexibility (e.g., Vosniadou, De Corte, Glaser, & Mandl, 1996). The first of these three factors, prior knowledge, can be measured in multiple ways, including assessing the number of prior courses in the area (and level of prior achievement), distinguishing majors versus nonmajors, and using the sorts of knowledge pretests that are common in university courses (e.g., a bank of normed pretests is available in mathematics at the University of Arizona). Statistical data reduction methods can be used to extract independent predictors of learning outcomes from these multiple measures. As for the other two factors, standardized instruments are available in the literature that measure them with high reliability and validity.

Prior knowledge should predict learners' ability to benefit from technologies that emphasize conceptual understanding of material and learning outcomes that involve creative transfer. This prediction is based on the finding that prior knowledge increases students' ability to derive meaningful representations of learned material. The second dimension, verbal versus visual learning style, should predict students' ability to benefit from technologies that add rich visual support to traditional text material. The third factor, cognitive flexibility, should predict learners' ability to benefit from just about any technology that departs from familiar classroom or laboratory learning environments — especially technologies that involve radical departures from traditional instructional approaches (e.g., electronic interactive-learning systems, and virtual reality demonstrations). Some evidence that is consistent with the first two predictions is available from studies of multimedia environments (e.g., Mayer, 1997), and some evidence that is consistent with the third prediction is available from studies of hypertext environments (e.g., Jacobson & Spiro, 1995).

Global relations among technological interventions, individual differences, memory contents, and learning outcomes can be captured in structural equation models. However, underlying detailed process models should also be developed using Markov models for recursive learning processes (e.g., acquisition) and multinomial models for nonrecursive processes (e.g., memory retrieval). The structures of such models can be briefly characterized as follows (cf. Brainerd & Reyna, 1995; Brainerd et al., 1990). The effects of technology-infused instruction on learning outcomes are indirect. They are modulated by two classes of factors, one that is proximal to learning outcomes and the other that it is more distal to learning outcomes. The proximal class of factors is the nature of the memory representations, verbatim and gist, that are acquired on the basis of technology-infused instruction. The distal class of factors consists of stable individual differences variables of two sorts, cognitive and social-personality. These individual differences factors will also affect the content of memory representations, so model-based representations of research findings should be interactive at the level of proximal versus distal controlling factors.

C. Dilemma 3: The Perception–Presentation Mismatch

Learning technologies offer new ways to present information to students. For example, instructors can integrate video clips into traditional expository text to create simulations, or mirror the complexity of an intensive care unit or airline control room (e.g., Reinhardt, 1995). However, despite the allure of new technology, there is often a mismatch between human perceptual skills and the way information is typically presented to students.

1. Basic Processes in Perception

Current applications in learning technologies can benefit from an understanding of basic processes in perception. For example, humans are excellent "movement detectors." A bird in the underbrush can be hard to detect—until the bird moves. Similarly, a perceptually dense display can be better navigated with motion cues. People also easily detect breaks in symmetry, such as pictures hanging crooked on a wall or musical dissonance that goes unresolved. Our abilities to detect asymmetries are not so surprising given that much of the information we depend on to survive involves detecting asymmetries. For example, breaks in the usual symmetry of the highway can suddenly arouse drivers from daydreaming into a heightened state of awareness, although they may not be able to determine immediately what it was that was different.

Another human perceptual capability was identified by James J. Gibson (1966, 1986), the founder of ecological psychology. Traditional perceptual theories assumed that our perceptions of the world (for example, a chair or an old friend) were built up by combining a myriad of discrete, atomic sensory impressions. Gibson argued instead that the visual information in the environment that supports our ability to get around is the unique patterning of light and textures. These patterns tell us what opportunities for action the world affords us. Gibson argued that the "affordances" defined by these patterns could be detected by animals that have become attuned to the relevant patterns through evolution or learning. Further investigations in ecological psychology suggest that whether or not an individual detects a particular affordance can be constrained by his or her current goal, his or her prior knowledge and skill (as well as physical development), and the way information is presented. In short, as Kosslyn (1994) notes, the mind is not a camera. We do not view everything at one level of sharpness or acuity. What we focus on, or observe, depends on the task at hand and the salience of the available information for accomplishing that task.

2. What Does Perceptual Psychology Tell Us About Instructional Technology?

Research on computer display design has focused considerable attention on how to build computer displays that capitalize on human perceptual strengths. One design strategy is to build diagrams that mimic, or model, the physical design of real-world systems. This is very common for engineering displays or for modeling physiology. Another strategy uses abstract objects to show the relationships between specific variables. For example, the size and shape of a rectangle might be used to show how oxygenation is a function of how much air one takes in with each breath and how many breaths one takes per minute. Research shows that subjects can detect problems more quickly with displays like these, but only if the complex variables or relationships shown map clearly onto the relevant environmental facts. The difference between the designer of the computer display and nature is that the designer has to engineer the lawful relationships into the display. In nature, such relationships are given in the invariance of experience.

Further work has shown that there is a hierarchy of relationships that compose the structure of an affordance. For example, one can define the affordance structure of heart disease at various levels (e.g., cellular, tissue, organ, and system). Each of these levels places some constraints on the others. The way the heart is connected to the arteries and veins constrains the values that vascular pressures can take in any of these areas. Similarly, oxygen needs at the tissue level place constraints on organ and system functioning. Depending on the nature of the observer's task, different levels of information become critical. To support performance optimally, it is necessary to make available the particular level of information that is key to the task.

D. Dilemma 4: The Socialization Mismatch

Preliminary evidence suggests that technology can be expected to have contradictory effects on the socialization of different individuals (e.g., Digman, 1990). Technology has enormous potential to connect people — as in distance learning, the Web, and software that supports group communication (in this volume see Sherman, chapter 6, for a discussion of technologically-mediated cooperative learning, and Riva, chapter 7, for a thorough discussion of virtual communities). Although the efficiency and relative anonymity of those connections should facilitate social interaction (e.g., factors such as race, gender, and disability are less obvious), technology can also have the paradoxical effect of increasing social isolation when it usurps normal activities or replaces face-to-face interaction. Such cases, often involving college students, have been documented increasingly in the psychological literature. Research should distinguish these contradictory effects of technology on social interaction with a view toward identifying factors that foster appropriate socialization.

Specifically, exposure to technology can be expected to increase or decrease the amount and quality of students' social interactions, depending on the individual. Based on prior research, such effects should interact with personality characteristics (e.g., Bernard, Hutchison, Lavin, & Pennington, 1996; Mooradian & Nezlek, 1996). The amount and quality of social interactions have been found to act as buffers against stress and to promote both emotional and physical health (Cohen & Willis, 1985; Monroe, Bromet, Connell, & Steiner, 1986). The use of technologies may increase some social interactions and decrease others. For example, communication technology could be used by susceptible individuals to support a pattern of increasing social exclusivity and withdrawal from peer and familial relationships by substituting virtual social interactions (in this volume see Morahan-Martin, chapter 10, for a review of the literature on Internet abuse). Thus, students who are highly introverted might increase technologically mediated social interaction, but limit face-to-face interaction. Given our present state of knowledge, however, it is not possible to predict whether the use of technologies will increase or decrease the types of social interactions that have been found to be beneficial for emotional and physical health. Traditional self-report and other-report measures (e.g., peer judgments) of social interaction and measures of stress have yet to be studied.

Social and personality factors (e.g., sociability and openness to new experience; Martin & Rubin, 1995) also play an important role in the group interactions that are increasingly part of the educational process. The assumption has long been that interaction improves both learning and performance accuracy (the latter accounting for the adoption of group interaction in the modern workplace). Until recently, however, research has not uniformly supported this assumption (for a review, see Gigone & Hastie, 1997). For example, in the research literature on group assessment, judgment tasks in which groups consistently outperform individuals are rare. In the classroom, effects of social facilitation can be offset by social inhibition and so-called "loafing," in which some individuals enjoy the product of others' labors without contributing their fair share.

The contradictory effects of group interaction on performance can be teased apart with focused measures. Using such measures, group interaction has been found to enhance performance, especially when tasks are informationally complex, such as when information is incomplete and multiple perspectives and sources of information must be combined (Gigone & Hastie, 1997). Technology provides multiple means of representing, storing, and communicating complex information to facilitate group interaction, and therefore might be expected to improve group performance. Judgment and decision-making tasks are examples of such informationally rich tasks, and we should expect beneficial effects of technology on group versus individual performance on classroom tasks of this sort. For example, group versus individual performance using technology can be compared in disciplines in which judgments of risk and probability are a hallmark of decision making (e.g., mechanical engineering, environmental biology, and geosciences). Student-based and instructor-based measures of team skills (e.g., ratings of students' ability to work well in groups) can then be elicited and related to learning outcomes.

Finally, a major issue in the evaluation of learning technologies is disentangling their effects on social processes from their effects on learning processes. Although technology may produce exciting new ways of learning, it is also possible that most of its impact is due to social factors, such as motivating students to spend more time with the subject matter than they otherwise would have. Thus, motivation, expectancy, and other nonspecific effects are especially important factors to consider with novel interventions (Bootzin, 1985; Grencavage, Bootzin, & Shoham, 1993). By measuring such factors as amount of exposure to course materials (e.g., students' time on Web sites, and ratings of frequency of use of technologies), it is possible to separate social effects of technologies, such as generalized increases in motivation, from unique and specific effects on learning.

IV. TEACHING HEMODYNAMICS: AN EMPIRICAL EXAMPLE

Effken (1993; Effken, Kim, & Shaw, 1997) developed an instructional program to teach nursing students the underlying principles of hemodynamics and the effects of drugs on hemodynamics. This program serves as an empirical example of an instructional program created in cognizance of human–computer mismatches. Of particular interest are dilemmas caused by differences between human perception and display techniques, and mismatches of cognitive style, especially verbal versus visual learning. In research on this instructional program, three different displays were designed to present the same fundamental information in different ways: the strip chart display, the integrated balloon display, and the moving square display. The strip chart display presents information as discrete bar graphs. The student must then integrate the information to arrive at a diagnosis. The other two displays present higher-order variables (i.e., relationships). The integrated balloon display shows how the physical connectivity of the cardiovascular system constrains the values that pressure and blood flow can take at each point in the system. The etiological potentials (moving square) display shows how pressure and flow are constrained by the underlying factors of resistance, heart strength, and fluid volume. We have found that each enhancement of the display results in more accurate and faster problem solution by students. Students learn to solve simulated clinical problems very quickly with the moving square display, primarily because it uses symmetry effectively. Any break in symmetry indicates a problem. Furthermore, the display shows clearly what the course of corrective action should be. Each drug maps directly onto one element of the display. Students find it more difficult to learn to use the other two displays because the relationship between the drugs they use and the clinical problems is a one-to-many relationship.

However, the balloon display has been shown to be the best learning tool for teaching *principles* of hemodynamics. There are two reasons for this finding. First, the balloon display contains more of the semantic context of the clinical situation. The connected balloons resemble a cardiovascular system diagram often shown in physiology texts. Second, the balloon display requires that students actively explore the display to discover the relationships between pressure and flow, and the drugs they must use to control them. A number of other findings from the general display design literature are relevant to instructional display design. Learning is often tailored to a particular environment. That is, the learning activity is situated in a particular domain and focused on specific learning goals. Students need guidance in what to treat as important, and need experience in dealing with novel situations. This suggests that simply making information visual will not be enough. Extra clues or constraints need to be provided to limit the student's search and help them find the important information.

A. Visual Display and Learning

For learning to transfer to other problems, invariants (relationships) must also be shown to be appropriate for the new tasks (Lintern, 1991). Procedures or techniques that accentuate the invariant relationships to be learned will enhance the student's ability to differentiate the relevant information. For example, providing explanatory illustrations can help students understand the key relationships they are trying to learn (Mayer & Gallini, 1990). Illustrations by themselves are much less effective. The Dragonfly Web Pages (see Wolfe, chapter 5 this volume) provide a good example of how techniques can be used to help students find the crucial information. In a recent edition on flight, students were asked to invent a plane that would meet particular design goals, but were constrained in choosing their design parameters from a limited set of possible wing lengths and weights. A picture that mapped easily onto the relevant relationships (weight and wing length) showed the results of their choices. Picture, text, and task goal complemented each other.

For a visual display to support learning, visual objects shown in the display should be compatible with the properties they represent (Kosslyn, 1994). For example, when an object in a display represents "more" of a substance, it should be shown as relatively larger, longer, or higher than the object with which it is compared. Size is relatively easy to map accurately (although errors still can be made), but other relationships and concepts are not as easily mapped onto a display's geometry. Indeed, this is one of the real challenges for designers of learning environments. A related issue is whether the mapping presented should be based on the learner's naïve model, which makes the relationship more intuitive for the student, or whether it should be based on the laws or principles (e.g., mathematical, physical, or ethical) that support it, which may be quite counterintuitive for the student. Because education is the goal, one might assume that the latter would be the case, but this may not be so. It may be necessary to begin with the naive worldview, particularly for initial navigation, and then progress to the more scientifically based view. Instructional technology has the potential to be helpful to a broad range of students. However, ultimately it needs to support the weakest student without frustrating the strongest (cf. Rasmussen, Pejtersen, & Goodstein, 1994).

B. Constraints on Perception

Research on learning and perception shows that students learn best when instructors build on their prior knowledge (Ausbel's 1982 scaffolding, for example; see also Reyna, 1996a). We cannot expect students to understand visual displays that do not build on their prior knowledge. The designers of the Macintosh Operating System were quick to recognize this. Their design for the desktop capitalizes on what people normally see on and around their desks and offices: files, wastebaskets, clipboards, scissors, etc. As Rasmussen and colleagues (1994) note, "An artifact [or an instructional system] that is well designed should, through the appropriate use of invariant features make obvious what it is for and how it should be used (p. 116)." Unfortunately, display designers have been less quick to exploit the strengths (e.g., symmetry detection and change detection) and compensate for the limitations of perception (e.g., visual acuity and tiny icons).

Identified constraints on perception include prior experience and perceptual or related cognitive skills. Research by Vicente and his colleagues (Vicente & Rasmussen, 1990, 1992) suggests that cognitive style is a variable that affects perceptual learning. The particular dimensions of cognitive style that have been imputed by various researchers to have a role are deep versus surface processing (Biggs, 1987), serial versus holistic processing (Pask & Scott, 1972), and verbal versus visual processing (Richardson, 1977). Vicente and colleagues have found that the serialist–holist dimension is the best predictor of students' learning in a complex control task. Our preliminary data reveal some differences in students' performance with the hemodynamic instructional displays along the verbalizer–visualizer dimension. Specifically, students' scores on the visual scale correlated significantly with their speed and accuracy in solving hemodynamic problems using the balloon display.

Following Christoffersen's use of "control recipes" to assess understanding (Christoffersen, Hunter, & Vicente, 1996), Effken and colleagues asked students to list the steps they used to correct the last problem encountered so that someone else could solve the problem easily. They then asked students for their opinions about the display. Participants were asked to list the "best" and "worst" things about the display, and then were asked, "What, if anything, did you learn about hemodynamics and the drugs used to treat problems with blood pressure and flow by participating in this experiment?" Finally the students were asked to list three words that best described their response to the computer display.

Of the seven students who worked with the balloon display, six addressed pressures and flow explicitly (e.g., "Adjust volume to bring pressures within safe range," "When the veins are bigger than the artery, then …," and "If the ventricle decreased [sic] pumping …"). The seventh wrote the recipe solely in terms of the drugs used (e.g., decrease fluid). In contrast, none of the students using the moving square display addressed pressures or flow in their descriptions; most simply described how to use the drugs to adjust the square's position on the cross. For example, one student wrote, "Try to position the 'heart' at the center of the cross, either by manipulating the heart drugs or the resistance drugs." Another student stated that she or he "first looked to see where the square was in terms of being high or low in either resistance or heart strength." This supports our hypothesis that, with the moving square display, much of the semantics of the clinical situation is lost.

These results are consistent with what three student users told us they did not like about the moving square display: "It was confusing at first and also when you learn how to manipulate the little box, you aren't using your knowledge of hemodynamics. . . , you use the mouse and arrows"; "a little confusing to get used to — guess I had trouble with the abstract idea of the box because it is hard to see how the drugs are affecting the heart"; and "it was a little difficult to connect this to what drugs/actual events were occurring with a patient." Their lists of the three words that best described their experience support these comments. For the moving square group, two of the first words written were "confused" and "stressed."

Students' descriptions of what they learned also suggest that there are major differences in the instructional support provided by the two displays. If this self-report is reliable, then the moving square user groups' learning stayed largely at the drug (or etiological) level. There is little connection verbalized between the etiological (drug) factors and the pressures and flow. The connections they made were largely between the drugs they gave and the etiological factors (resistance, heart strength, and volume) shown as the three dimensions in the display. It may be that the salience of the 1:1 mapping between drugs and etiological factors for control makes mastering the more difficult relationship of the drugs to pressure and flow redundant. The learning of the student users of the balloon display, on the other hand, seems to be directed at how the drugs affect pressure and flow ("the system"), which is the purpose of that display. It seems that the strengths of the moving square display, that is, its support for detecting and treating hemodynamic problems quickly, are not as well suited to its use as a learning tool.

C. Instructional Display Formats

Based on the convergence of several measures (self-report of learning, what they liked and disliked about the displays, and control recipes), it seems safe to conclude that working with each display induces in students a different conceptualization of hemodynamics and problem treatment. That difference in understanding seems to be due to two design aspects: the level of analysis at which the problem is described (which relationships, or constraints, are made visible or emphasized) and the way the semantics of the problem are mapped onto the display geometry. The integrated balloon display makes clear how pressures at several points relate to each other and to cardiac output and resistance, but does not make clear how the drug components (which are directed at the underlying etiological factors of resistance, contractility, and fluid volume) relate to the pressures and flows. Students have to discover that complex and highly nonlinear relationship for themselves. The responses from the balloon display group suggest that they were engaged in a discovery process. The moving square display, on the other hand, embeds the pressures and flows in the etiological space to make that relationship clear. At the same time, it makes the use of a simple, linear solution to solve problems possible. Students learn that if they use the corresponding drugs to correct the visible deviations in heart strength, resistance, and volume, the pressures and flows will take care of themselves. This solution essentially changes the nature of the problem and allows the student to ignore the harder question of how the drugs relate to pressures and flow. Indeed such displays make it possible to solve the presented problems without even considering the variations in pressures and flow.

Research has shown that for instructional tasks requiring both individual values and integrated knowledge, mixed formats (e.g., analog bar graphs and text displays) are better; but for a task requiring only integrated knowledge, the integrated format is better (e.g., Boles & Wickens, 1983; Carswell & Wickens, 1987). Therefore, depending on the task goal, it may be useful to complement the more holistic displays (balloon and moving square) with the traditional strip chart display, which presents data more discretely. This combination of formats might enable our students to have the best of all worlds: discrete data elements presented sequentially plus those same elements and their critical relationships presented holistically. Students might be better able to see how a particular treatment affects the system, not only at the more global, or holistic, level, but also at the more elemental component level.

Effken looked at only one measure of cognitive style — verbal versus visual learner. Selection of the verbalizer–visualizer instrument was based on its content, as well as on its brevity and simplicity. Instruments that purport to measure other cognitive style dimensions are available. One of the more promising for complex problem-solving tasks is Pask and Scott's

(1972) Spy Ring History Test, which measures the holist–serialist distinction. Using this instrument, Howie (1996) has reported significant positive correlations between a holist learning style and normal trial completion time, fault detection time, fault diagnosis accuracy, and fault compensation time in a process control learning task. Further research using multiple instruments that measure various dimensions of cognitive style would be helpful to distinguish which dimensions are relevant.

V. SUMMARY AND CONCLUSIONS

Although learning technologies have evolved more rapidly than the scientific study of how and what people learn from such technologies, prior research offers a solid foundation for predictions. In this chapter, we have reviewed relevant research and proposed a framework for the assessment of learning outcomes associated with technology. We discuss the kind of expertise that is required for such assessment, the nature of current instructional technologies, and potential mismatches between current technologies and human learning. The extent to which designers overcome these human–machine mismatches ultimately determines the instructional outcomes produced by learning technologies.

Given the magnitude of investment and the rate of obsolescence, outcomes assessment is increasingly demanded in order to justify investments in educational interventions, primarily because actual learning outcomes often violate intuitive assumptions. Prior to full implementation, a multidisciplinary team should assess the expected effects of major technological innovations, and such effects should also be monitored after implementation. Experts are required with knowledge of current applications of learning technologies, human–computer interaction, human learning and memory processes, individual differences in learning styles and other cognitive-perceptual factors, and individual differences in social and personality factors. Related areas that are also important include design of learning technologies, educational assessment, aptitude-by-treatment interactions, and mathematical modeling.

Because such teams are multidisciplinary, it is necessary to integrate theories and methods across many disciplines. However, recommendations that are valid and generalizable are most likely when assessment is based on evidence, not only from the project at hand, but also from the research literature. Randomized control trials are not only required for proper evaluation of interventions, they are the only ethical avenue for introducing major educational changes that affect students. Because intuitions or plausibility are not reliable guides to effectiveness, educational innovations can be harmful to students, despite good intentions. Furthermore, contrary to popular belief, randomized control trials are not necessarily more expensive than observational or correlational studies, and their payoff in knowledge about the effectiveness of interventions is always superior to other designs. Expenses can be minimized by forming research partnerships with faculty at other universities who are using specific technologies and with corporations in the learning technology industry. Many of the issues at stake in instructional technology are also relevant to other cognitive applications in business and industry, such as using technology to train employees or to enhance judgment and decision making on the job. The aim of such collaboration should be a comprehensive research agenda that will generate data to address the instructional outcomes problem and to stimulate the creation of improved technologies.

Our analysis suggests a research agenda based on four findings of basic and applied research. First, technology-infused instruction poses some fundamental dilemmas for learners that are rooted in mismatches between the capabilities of humans and those of machines. These dilemmas are of four kinds: mismatches between properties of technology and (1) natural human learning and memory processes, (2) individual differences in cognitive characteristics of learners, (3) ecological properties of human perception, and (4) individual differences in social and personality characteristics of learners. Second, each category of dilemmas is more prominent with some technologies than with others. For instance, mismatches that involve natural learning and memory processes are especially likely with Web-based instruction. Mismatches that involve social and emotional factors are especially likely with electronic interactive learning. Third, to achieve generality of findings, technological options must be studied in multiple disciplines and in heterogeneous populations of students. Finally, new tools will have to be developed to categorize and analyze instructional choices. As research proceeds, findings within each category should be summarized in appropriate mathematical models, such as structural equation models. The ultimate goal is an integrated theoretical model that specifies how factors in each domain interact with each other and how, taken together, they determine the instructional outcomes of particular technologies.

Acknowledgments

Preparation of this paper was supported in part by grants from the National Science Foundation (SBR9730143), U.S. Department of Commerce (04–60–98039) National Institutes of Health (P50HL61212) and the Academic Medicine and Managed Care Forum (SPS Log 38347).

References

Alavi, M. (1994). Computer-mediated collaborative learning: An empirical evaluation. MIS Quarterly, 18, 159–174.
Ausbel, D. P. (1982). Schemata, advance organizers, and anchoring ideas: A reply to Anderson, Spiro, & Anderson. Journal of Structural Learning 7 (1), 63–73.

Ayerson, D. J. (1995). Individual differences, computers, and instruction. *Computers in Human Behavior*, 11, 371–390.

Bernard, L. C., Hutchinson, S., Lavin, A., & Pennington, P. (1996). Ego-strength, hardiness, self-esteem, self-efficacy, optimism, and maladjustment: Health-related personality constructs and the "Big Five" model of personality. *Assessment*, 3, 115–131.

Biggs, J. B. (1987). *Student approaches to learning.* Hawthorn, Australia: Australian Council for Educational Research.

Boles, D., & Wickens, C. D. (1983). *A comparison of homogeneous and heterogeneous display formats in information integration and nonintegration tasks* (Tech. Rep. EPL–8306/ONR–83806). Champaign, IL: University of Illinois Engineering Psychology Laboratory, Department of Psychology.

Bootzin, R. R. (1985). The role of expectancy in behavior change. In L. White, G. E. Schwartz, & B. Tursky (Eds.), *Placebo: Theory, research, and mechanisms.* New York: Guilford Press.

Brainerd, C. J., & Gordon, L. L. (1994). Development of verbatim and gist memory for numbers. *Developmental Psychology*, 30, 163–177.

Brainerd, C. J., & Reyna, V. F. (1990). Inclusion illusions: Fuzzy-trace theory and perceptual salience effects in cognitive development. *Developmental Review*, 10, 365–403.

Brainerd, C. J., & Reyna, V. F. (1993). Memory independence and memory interference in cognitive development. *Psychological Review*, 100, 42–67.

Brainerd, C. J., & Reyna, V. F. (1995). Autosuggestibility in memory development. *Cognitive Psychology*, 28, 65–101.

Brainerd, C. J., Reyna, V. F., Howe, M. L., & Kingma, J. (1990). The development of forgetting and reminiscence. *Monographs of the Society for Research in Child Development*, 53, (3–4, Serial No. 222).

Brainerd, C. J., Reyna, V. F., & Kneer, R. (1995). False-recognition reversal: When similarity is distinctive. *Journal of Memory and Language*, 34, 157–185.

Carswell, C. M., & Wickens, C. D. (1987). Information and the object display. *Ergonomics*, 30, 511–527.

Christoffersen, K., Hunter, C. N., & Vicente, K. J. (1996). A longitudinal study of the effects of ecological interface design on skill acquisition. *Human Factors*, 38, 523–541.

Cohen, S., & Willis, T. A. (1985). Stress, social support, and the buffering hypothesis. *Psychological Bulletin*, 98, 310–357.

Collins, R., & Tellier, A. (1994). Differences in conceptual flexibility with age as measured by a modified version of the Visual Verbal test. *Canadian Journal on Aging*, 13, 368–377.

Cooney, J. B., & Swanson, H. L. (1990). Individual differences in memory for mathematical story problems: Memory span and problem perception. *Journal of Educational Psychology*, 82, 570–577.

Digman, J. M. (1990). Personality structure: Emergence of the five-factor model. *Annual Review of Psychology*, 41, 417–440.

Dutta, S. (1997). Strategies for implementing knowledge-base systems. *IEEE Transactions on Engineering Management*, 44, 79–90.

Effken, J. A. (1993). *Coordination of hemodynamic monitoring and treatment performance.* Unpublished dissertation, University of Connecticut.

Effken, J. A., Kim, N-G., & Shaw, R. E. (1997). Making the constraints visible: Testing the ecological approach to interface design. *Ergonomics*, 40 (1), 1–27.

Estes, W. K. (1980). Is human memory obsolete? *American Scientist*, 68, 62–69.

Friedman, E. A. (1994). A management perspective on effective technology integration: Top ten questions for school administrators. THE *Journal*, 22, 89–90.

Gernsbacher, M. A. (1985). Surface information loss in comprehension. *Cognitive Psychology*, 17, 324–363.

Gibson, J. J. (1966). *The senses considered as perceptual systems.* Boston: Houghton Mifflin.

Gibson, J. J. (1986). *The ecological approach to visual perception.* Hillsdale, NJ: Lawrence Erlbaum Associates. (First published in 1979)

Gigone, D., & Hastie, R. (1997). Proper analysis of the accuracy of group judgments. *Psychological Bulletin*, 121, 149–167.

Grencavage, L., Bootzin, R. R., & Shoham, S. V. (1993). Specific and nonspecific effects in psychological treatments. In C. G. Costello (Ed.), *Basic issues in psychopathology.* New York: Guilford Press.

Howie, D. E. (1996). *Shaping expertise through ecological interface design: Strategies, metacognition, and individual differences* (CEL 96–01). Toronto: University of Toronto, Cognitive Engineering Laboratory.

Jacobson, J., & Spiro, R. J. (1995). Hypertext learning environments, cognitive flexibility, and the transfer of complex knowledge: An empirical investigation. *Journal of Educational Computing Research*, 12, 301–333.

Jones, M. G., & Farquhar, J. D. (1995). Using metacognitive theories to design user interfaces for computer-based learning. *Educational Technology*, 35, 12–22.

Kipnis, D. (1997). Ghosts, taxonomies, and social psychology. *American Psychologist*, 52, 205–211.

Kizlik, R. (1996). Connective transactions — technology and thinking skills for the 21st century. *International Journal of Instructional Media*, 23, 115–122.

Kosslyn, S. M. (1994). *Elements of graph design*. New York: Freeman.

Lintern, G. (1991). An informational perspective on skill transfer in human-machine systems. *Human Factors*, 33 (3), 251–266.

Lloyd, F., & Reyna, V. F. (In press-a). Clinical decision-making and information management in the era of managed care. In R. C. Becker, I. Ockene and J. S. Alpert (Eds.), *New cardiology: Textbook of cardiovascular management for clinical practice*. New York: Arnold Publishing.

Lloyd, F. J., & Reyna, V. F. (in press-b). A Web exercise in evidence-based medicine using cognitive theory *Journal of General Internal Medicine*.

Martin, M. M., & Rubin, R. B. (1995). A new measure of cognitive flexibility. *Psychological Reports*, 76, 623–626.

Mayer, R. E. (1997). Multimedia learning: Are we asking the right questions? *Educational Psychologist*, 32, 1–19.

Mayer, R. E., & Anderson, R. B. (1991). Animations need narrations: An experimental test of a dual-coding hypothesis. *Journal of Educational Psychology*, 83, 484–490.

Mayer, R. E., & Anderson, R. B. (1992). The instructive animation: Helping students build connections between words and pictures in multimedia learning. *Journal of Educational Psychology*, 84, 444–452.

Mayer, R. E., & Gallini, J. K. (1990). When is an illustration worth a thousand words? *Journal of Educational Psychology*, 82, 715–726.

Mayer, R. E., Steinhoof, K., Bower, G., & Mars, R. L. (1995). A generative theory of textbook design. *Educational Technology Research and Development*, 43, 31–44.

Monroe, S. M., Bromet, E. J., Connell, M. M., & Steiner, S. C. (1986). Social support, life events and depressive symptoms: A one-year prospective study. *Journal of Consulting and Clinical Psychology*, 54, 424–431.

Mooradian, T. A., & Nezlek, J. B. (1996). Comparing the NEO-FFI and Saucier's minimarkers as measures of the Big Five. *Personality and Individual Differences*, 21, 213–215.

Murphy, G. L., & Shapiro, A. M. (1994). Forgetting of verbatim information in discourse. *Memory & Cognition*, 22, 85–94.

Njoo, M., & de Jong, T. (1993). Exploratory learning with a computer simulation for control theory. *Journal of Research in Science Teaching*, 30, 821–844.

Oshima, J., & Scardamalia, M. (1996). Collaborative learning processes associated with high and low conceptual progress. *Instructional Science*, 24, 125–155.

Pask, G., & Scott, B. C. (1972). Learning styles and individual competence. *International Journal of Man-Machine Studies*, 4, 217–253.

Puntambekar, S. (1995). Helping students learn "how to learn" from texts: Towards an ITS for developing metacognition. *Instructional Science*, 23, 163–182.

Rasmussen, J., Pejtersen, A. M., & Goodstein, L. P. (1994). Cognitive systems engineering. New York: Wiley.

Reiber, L. P. (1990). Animation in computer-based instruction. *Educational Technology Research and Development*, 38, 77–86.

Reimann, P., & Schult, T. J. (1996). Turning examples into cases: Acquiring knowledge structures for analogical problem solving. *Educational Psychologist*, 31, 123–122.

Reinhardt, A. (1995, March). New ways to learn. *Byte*, 50–71.

Reyna, V. F. (1995). Interference effects in memory and reasoning: A fuzzy-trace theory analysis. In F. N. Dempster and C. J. Brainerd (Eds.), *Interference and inhibition in cognition* (pp. 29–59). San Diego, CA: Academic Press.

Reyna, V. F. (1996a). Conceptions of memory development, with implications for reasoning and decision-making. *Annals of Child Development*, 12, 87–118.

Reyna, V. F. (1996b). Meaning, memory, and the interpretation of metaphors. In J. Mio & A. Katz (Eds.), *Metaphor: Implications and applications* (pp. 39–57). Hillsdale, NJ: Erlbaum.

Reyna, V. F., & Brainerd, C. J. (1991a). Fuzzy-trace theory and the acquisition of scientific and mathematical concepts. *Learning and Individual Differences*, 3, 27–60.

Reyna, V. F., & Brainerd, C. J. (1991b). Fuzzy-trace theory and framing effects in choice: Gist extraction, truncation, and conversion. *Journal of Behavioral Decision Making*, 4, 249–262.

Reyna, V. F., & Brainerd, C. J. (1992). A fuzzy-trace theory of reasoning and remembering: Patterns, paradoxes, and parallelism. In A. Healy, S. Kosslyn, & R. Shiffrin (Eds.), *From learning processes to cognitive processes: Essays in honor of William K. Estes*. Hillsdale, NJ: Erlbaum.

Reyna, V. F., & Brainerd, C. J. (1993). Fuzzy memory and mathematics in the classroom. In R. Logie & G. Davies (Eds.), *Everyday memory*. Amsterdam: North-Holland.

Reyna, V. F. & Brainerd, C. J. (1994). The origins of probability judgment: A review of data and theories. In G. Wright and P. Ayton (Eds), *Subjective Probability* (pp. 239-272). New York: Wiley.

Reyna, V. F., & Brainerd, C. J. (1995). Fuzzy-trace theory: An interim synthesis. *Learning and Individual Differences*, 7, 1–75.

Reyna, V. F., & Ellis, S. C. (1994). Fuzzy-trace theory and framing effects in children's risky decision making. *Psychological Science*, 5, 275–279.

Reyna, V. F., & Kiernan, B. (1994). The development of gist versus verbatim memory in sentence recognition: Effects of lexical familiarity, semantic content, encoding instructions, and retention interval. *Developmental Psychology*, 30, 178–191.

Reyna, V. F., & Kiernan, B. (1995). Children's memory and interpretation of psychological metaphors. *Metaphor and Symbolic Activity*, 10, 309–331.

Reyna, V. F., Lloyd, F. J., & Brainerd, C. J. (In press). Memory, development, and rationality: An integrative theory of judgment and decision-making. In S. Schneider and J. Shanteau (Eds.), *Emerging perspectives on decision research*. Cambridge: Cambridge University Press.

Reyna, V. F., & Titcomb, A. (1997). Constraints on the suggestibility of eyewitness testimony: A fuzzy-trace theory analysis. In D. G. Payne & F. G. Conrad (Eds.), *Intersections in basic and applied memory research* (pp. 157–174). Hillsdale, NJ: Erlbaum.

Richardson, A. (1977). Verbalizer-visualizer: A cognitive style dimension. *Journal of Mental Imagery*, 1, 109–126.

Ross, S. M. (1994). Delivery trucks or groceries? More food for thought on whether media (will, may, can't) influence learning: Introduction to the special issue. *Educational Technology Research and Development*, 42, 5–6.

Scardamalia, M. (1994). Computer support for knowledge-base building communities. *Journal of the Learning Sciences*, 3, 265–283.

Schnotz, W. (1993). On the relation between dual coding and mental models in graphics comprehension. *Learning and Instruction*, 3, 247–249.

Schnotz, W., & Kulhavy, R. (Eds.). (1994). *Comprehension of graphics*. London: Pergamon.

Vicente, K. J., & Rasmussen, J. (1990). The ecology of human-machine systems II: Mediating direct perception in complex work domains, *Ecological Psychology*, 2, 207–250.

Vicente, K. J., and Rasmussen, J. (1992). Ecological interface design: Theoretical foundations. *IEEE Transactions on Systems, Man, and Cybernetics*, SMC–22, 589–606.

Von Neumann, J. (1958). *The computer and the brain*. New Haven, CT: Yale University Press.

Vosniadou, S., De Corte, E., Glaser, R., & Mandl, H. (Eds.). (1996). International perspectives on the design of technology-supported learning environments. Mahwah, NJ: LEA.

Zhou, G., & Whang, J. (1996). Curriculum knowledge representation and manipulation in knowledge-base tutoring systems. *IEEE Transactions on Knowledge & Data Engineering*, 8, 679–689.

CHAPTER

3

Individual Characteristics and Web-Based Courses

MARGARET D. ANDERSON

State University of New York at Cortland

Educators have a rich history of exploring the different ways of presenting material to students. Psychologists have an equally long record of inquiry into the learning process. When we combine the results from these two areas we have a very potent mix — one able to bewilder the best-intentioned practitioner, and at the same time provide fertile ground for the researcher. Educational psychologists have consistently worked to integrate the information gleaned from these two disciplines. Perhaps the best example of this merger is in the area of aptitude–treatment interaction.

The research on aptitude–treatment interaction (ATI) focuses on performance and how it is influenced by the individual characteristics of the student when the presentation format differs. The basic assumption is that for some instructional strategies, the treatments, are more or less effective for particular individuals depending upon their specific abilities and aptitudes (Cronbach & Snow, 1977). ATI suggests that optimal learning occurs when the instruction is exactly matched to the aptitudes of the learner. However, the major impediments to arriving at conclusive results in this line of research have been in defining and measuring aptitude and outcome. Thus, while most educators and laypeople intuitively believe that individual differences and teaching methods make a difference in performance, the empirical evidence on this issue has been inconclusive.

When researchers initially began studying the impact of various instructional treatments on students' performance they focused on classroom presentation techniques. At that time, educators were trying to determine the comparable benefits of such techniques as expository teaching, discovery learning, and collaborative activities. While the results of comparative studies were at best inconclusive, they suggested that each technique produced superior results under some conditions. This naturally raises the question of what were those conditions? How can we predict which treatment would be most effective in any given situation?

One way to begin to understand the seemingly conflicting empirical results was to look at another element in the equation, namely, the student. Once this line of inquiry was embraced, it opened a Pandora's box for researchers. If there were some salient differences between students that determined which treatment would be most effective, what were those critical elements? Thus, hundreds of studies were conducted exploring a veritable plethora of individual characteristics and how they influenced academic performance.

Despite the massive amount of research generated by the quest to identify the impact of the aptitude–treatment interaction, the formula continued to be elusive. As Snow (1989) concluded, "many ATI combinations are complex and difficult to demonstrate clearly, and no particular ATI effect is sufficiently understood to be the basis for instructional practice" (p. 51). A major factor contributing to the inconclusive results was the idiosyncratic nature of the studies. There was never a consensus as to which aptitudes, treatments, or outcomes should be systematically explored. Coupled with the inconsistent variables used in the studies was the fact that they were measured using a wide array of assessment instruments and methods. As each researcher fixed upon an interaction he or she wished to explore, the investigative process began over again, in seeming disregard for the studies that had preceded it in the domain. As Dillon and Gabbard (1998) have lamented, with each new stage of technological development the lessons learned from user studies of previous technologies tend to be ignored. This unconnected process of research seems to typify what Meehl (1978) was referring to when he said that researchers in the soft sciences seem to forget the basic guidelines that have been proven to work in the older sciences. Replication and a cumulative set of results are requisites for any endeavor to generate a body of knowledge. We need to build on the results of prior studies if we are to advance our understanding of the complex interaction between aptitude and treatment. If we do not make a concerted effort to systemically and systematically explore all the variables related to a particular theory of learning and performance, it is likely that these theories, like many others, "will come and go, more as a function of baffled boredom than anything else" (Meehl, 1978, p. 807).

It is within the historical perspective of research on aptitude–treatment interaction that I propose exploring the impact individual differences have on student performance in Web-based courses. In this case, the relevant medium is the World Wide Web (Web). It remains for us to determine which specific aptitudes and treatments might be predictive of success in courses using this medium. Due to the breadth of research in this area, it is not practical to provide a comprehensive review of all the potentially related areas; neither is it feasible to review all publications within any one domain. Rather, I have selected seminal papers within representative areas to allow for the creation of a hypothetical model of the interaction of the individual learner characteristics and participation in Web-based courses.

I. PRESENTATION MEDIUM

The medium of education has undergone a slow but steady evolution from the initial interactive dialogues to verbal expository presentation of material and then text-based formats, culminating in the digital representations of information. Each of these media has been able to support a wide variety of instructional approaches. Each, in turn, has been the subject of extensive research attempting to demonstrate its superiority over other delivery media. To date, most of the comparative studies between instructional media — face-to-face teaching; paper, television, video, or computer-based formats; and various distance delivery media — have found no significant differences in student learning (Anderson, 1999; Dillon & Gabbard, 1998; Maki, Maki, Patterson, & Whittaker, 1999; McIsacc & Gunawardena, 1996; Romero, Berger, Healy, & Aberson, 1999; Schulman & Sims, 1999). Applying this base of research findings to the study of the impact the World Wide Web has on education, it would seem appropriate to turn away from simple comparisons of Web-based courses to those employing any other format. We should instead focus on unraveling the other salient elements that are predictive of student success in Web-based courses. Kozma (1991) proposed that technology may impact learners more in some situations than it does in others because of the interaction between the task, the learners, and the technology. He believes that this view is compatible with Snow's (1989) evolving aptitude–treatment interaction theory. The questions that now need to be asked are not which medium works best, but rather, how best to incorporate media attributes into the design of effective instruction (McIsacc & Gunawardena, 1996). To take this line of inquiry one step further, we should ask not only what the impact of the individual elements of the design are on the outcome, but also what impact the components ultimately have on shaping the learners involved in the situation.

II. CHARACTERISTICS OF THE INDIVIDUAL

There is an ever-growing body of literature tracking the impact of individual variables on students' academic performance. Unfortunately, while there is a great deal of breadth to the research in this area, there is not a lot of depth. Researchers have used a wide range of differing criterion and outcome variables. The predictive variables of interest range from personality dimensions to cognitive and learning styles, motivation, and the impact of prior knowledge and affect. One of the major obstacles to fitting these variables into a comprehensive framework is the lack of consensus over the relevant terminology to employ when discussing the approach students use (e.g., Biggs, 1993; Curry, 1983; Messick, 1994; Riding & Cheema, 1991; Schmeck, 1988). Until such a resolution is arrived at, it behooves us to examine the wealth of diverse studies available to us, and attempt to extract information from them that is relevant to predicting students' performance in Web-based courses.

A. Personality Dimensions

Personality dimensions constitute individual differences at the most global level. Of these dimensions the ones that have received the most research attention related to academic performance include field dependence/independence, locus of control, and an active/passive orientation. In addition, such general personal attributes as ambiguity tolerance, general anxiety, and self-efficacy have also been studied in relation to students' academic performance.

I. Ambiguity Tolerance

Since the concept of ambiguity tolerance was first articulated by Frenkel-Brunswik (1948), this personality variable has received consistent attention from various branches of psychology. While this attribute was originally studied by clinical, cognitive, personality and social psychologists, it is currently being researched primarily by organizational psychologists (Furnham & Ribchester, 1995). In examining the construct it appears that it could prove to be a possible predictive variable of performance in distance education courses.

Ambiguity tolerance refers to an individual's willingness to accommodate or adapt to ambiguous situations or ideas. Ambiguous situations develop from novel circumstances that have no familiar cues, complex situations with many cues to be considered, contradictory situations where different elements or cues suggest different structures, or unstructured situations containing cues that cannot be interpreted. Tolerant individuals accept or invite new situations in which the rules or procedures are not known. They also like complex problem situations where the answers are uncertain. These individuals perform well when faced with a learning situation containing a great deal of novelty, complexity, contradiction, or lack of structure (MacDonald, 1970). These are precisely the environmental characteristics that are often evident in a Web–based learning environment.

While a summary of the research to date (Jonassen & Grabowski, 1993) suggests that individuals who are able to tolerate ambiguity are likely to perform well in situations that require complex problem-solving and divergent learning approaches, much more research will be necessary to conclusively relate this personality characteristic to performance in Web-based courses. Of particular importance to Web-based course designers is the Furnham and Ribchester (1995) review of the research relating ambiguity tolerance to the need for feedback during educational pursuits. They conclude that individuals with a low ambiguity tolerance rely on feedback and seek it out whenever possible.

2. Anxiety

Anxiety has received a great deal of attention in the psychological literature. It can be characterized as either a "trait," indicating that it is a semipermanent general personality predisposition, or a "state," representing a transient emotional mood or condition. There is usually a curvilinear relationship between anxiety and performance, indicated by a decrement in performance if anxiety levels are extremely high or low. An early study (O'Neil, Spielberger, & Hansen, 1969) indicated that college students with high state anxiety make more errors using computer-based instruction on the more difficult materials and fewer errors on the easier materials than low state anxiety students. After reviewing the literature on anxiety and academic performance Jonassen and Grabowski (1993) proposed that low-anxiety students are more likely to benefit from instruction that encourages self-regulation tasks, provides changes in routine, and is visually based. On the other hand, the highly anxious students prefer situations that provide a structured routine and include externally imposed goals. These individualistic requirements for externally imposed structure are also salient characteristics for course designers.

3. Field Dependence/Independence

A personality dimension that has received considerable attention is the construct of field dependence and field independence. Not only are there major differences in attributes between individuals with these contrasting traits, but these differences are also evidenced in the students' approaches to learning. The field-independent person is characterized as analytic, self-referent, and impersonal in orientation, whereas the field-dependent person is characterized as global, socially sensitive, and interpersonal in orientation (Witkin & Goodenough, 1981). Field-dependent students are influenced by their physical and social backgrounds, and are less able to rely on their own judgments, organize their own learning activities, and maintain their own direction. In contrast, field-independent students have clear ideas of their own standards and values, and are logical, organized, abstract, and analytical when approaching intellectual activities (Luk Suet Ching, 1998). Field-independent students typically demonstrate high levels of self-directed learning.

The influence of this personality trait on academic performance was articulated early in the ATI research by McLeod and Adams (1979) who found that field-dependent students performed better with maximum guidance and that field-independent students performed better using discovery instructional methods, like distance education, that provide minimum guidance. Similarly, Messick (1976, 1994) indicates that field-independent individuals are likely to learn more effectively under conditions of intrinsic motivation such as self-study, which are less influenced by social reinforcement. They also appear to be more efficient in the selection and implementation of executive strategies that coordinate information processes. In a review of the research dealing with the relationship between field dependence/independence and academic performance, Jonassen and Grabowski (1993) concluded that field independence was the strongest predictor of divergent tasks in a course, including media skills; field-independent individuals were better at transferring rules to new contexts as well as generating rules to solve novel problems; and field independence is important in analyzing and categorizing visual stimuli.

Numerous studies have investigated the interaction of field dependence/independence with the use of multimedia. Jonassen and Wang (1993) report that field independent processors generally prefer to impose their own structure rather than have the structure imposed externally. They conclude from their research that field-independent learners are better hypertext processors, especially as the form of the hypermedia becomes more inferential and less overtly structured. Burton, Moore, and Holmes' (1995) research revealed that field-dependent learners prefer a slower pace, test fewer hypotheses, generate fewer combinations, recall fewer cues, and are more passive in a multimedia environment. Weller, Repman, Lan, and Rooze (1995) succinctly summarize the results when they claim that field-independent students learn more effectively from hypermedia-based instruction than field-dependent students.

4. Active/Passive Learners

Researchers have hypothesized that the activity/passivity of learners might be directly related to their academic performance, especially when the instruction involves the use of hypermedia. A review of the relevant literature by Dillon and Gabbard (1998) reports limited support for this hypothesis, revealing a slight tendency for active learners to outperform all others in a hypermedia environment. Passive learners seem to depend on prompts and explicit cues to accomplish their tasks. MacGregor (1999) reconfirmed the connection between active learners and superior performance.

5. Locus of Control

Another personality dimension that has been actively studied in relation to student's academic performance is locus of control. This dimension, which has its roots in Rotter's (1966) social learning theory, refers to the individual's belief regarding the causes of his or her experiences, and those factors to which an individual attributes his or her successes and failures. Representative of the results in this field is Wilhite's (1990) finding that an internal locus of control appears to be a reliable predictor of superior academic performance. Biggs (1985) demonstrated that there is a relationship between locus of control and the learning style a student adopts, specifically that a student with an internal locus of control is more likely to demonstrate a deep approach to learning. This finding is consistent with Watkins' (1984) results, indicating that if students perceive that they have control over their own learning, they are more likely to use information processing approaches in which they focus on the content as a whole, try to see connections between the parts, and actively think about the structure of the information. Perceived lack of control is most likely to lead to the view of learning as a memory task. This interaction of locus of control and learning style is typical of the empirical findings in this domain. It rapidly becomes evident that there is not a simple, direct relationship between any one personality trait and performance in an academic setting. The relationship is probably mediated by a number of other important individual and environmental factors.

In a review of the literature relating locus of control to academic performance, Jonassen and Grabowski (1993) report that internality predicts better academic performance: internals avail themselves of information more than externals because they believe that they can act on their own behalf; internals have better study habits; internals perform better under a contract-for-grade plan, whereas externals perform better under teacher control; when given control of instruction on videocassette, internals make greater use of the controls than externals because internals will search harder for information; and internality positively affects achievement, time on instruction, attitude toward content, and task interaction frequency in a computer-based instruction lesson. Recent research by MacGregor (1999) also indicates that students with an internal locus of control are better able to structure their navigation and take advantage of hypertext learning environments.

6. Self-Efficacy

The concept of self-efficacy, or one's belief in one's ability to successfully perform a given behavior, has been most fully developed by Bandura (1997). There is accumulating evidence for the importance of this construct on academic performance. Multon, Brown and Lent (1991) emphasize the potentially pivotal role of self-efficacy in students' academic performance when they indicate that it has proven to be more robust than any other variable in explaining and predicting academic performance among college students.

In addition, Zimmerman, Bandura and Martinez-Pons (1992) demonstrated that students' beliefs in their ability to self-regulate their learning affected their perceived self-efficacy for academic achievement, which in turn influenced their personal academic goal setting, and ultimately their academic performance. Furthermore, Zimmerman (1990) reports that self-efficacy is the ultimate source of students' motivation.

B. Learning Style

There is probably no term in the psychological vocabulary that is more shrouded in ambiguity than "learning style." This term can alternately be used to designate a cognitive depth of processing (for example deep/surface or holist/serialist), a preference for instructional modality (such as verbal, visual, or haptic), or a variety of social factors (individual versus group study). Within each designation there is further confusion caused by a lack of consensus over the appropriate assessment instrument and inconsistent application of performance measures. However, despite the multifaceted confounds resulting from these discrepancies, it appears possible to identify some useful patterns relating learning style to performance.

1. Depth of Cognitive Processing

The majority of the research dealing with learning style has focused on the student's depth of cognitive processing, specifically describing a deep–surface dimension. This dimension was first articulated by Ausubel (1963), who investigated what he termed "meaningful" versus "rote" approaches to learning. Since that time numerous researchers (Biggs, 1978; Entwistle, 1981; Marton & Saljo, 1976; Pask, 1976; Riding & Douglas, 1993; Schmeck, 1988; Svensson, 1977) have adopted this conceptual framework, if not the exact terminology. In general, the distinction between the approaches indicates that the deep approach is typified by an interest in the academic task, an enjoyment in carrying it out, and a concentration on theorizing about the task at hand and its relationship to previous knowledge. On the other hand, a student who adopts a surface approach sees the task as a demand to be met, relies on memorization of the factual components, and concentrates on discrete components of the task unrelated to other tasks.

Over the past 30 years researchers using this deep–surface dimension of the student's approach to learning have attempted to ascertain how it relates to academic performance. Again, there is no consistent definition of performance. Some researchers (Beckwith, 1991; Busato, Prins, Elshout, & Hamaker, 1998; Trigwell & Prosser, 1991; Watkins, 1983) have used performance in university courses as the outcome measure, while others (Biggs, 1979; Christensen, Massey, & Isaacs, 1991; Marton & Saljo, 1976; Ramsden & Entwistle, 1981; Riding & Douglas, 1993; Schmeck & Phillips, 1982) have used specific cognitive tasks as performance measures.

Regardless of the outcome measure used, the research results have been inconclusive at best. Some papers have reported positive relationships between approach to learning and performance (Biggs, 1979; Biggs & Rihn, 1984; Kirby & Biggs, 1981; Saljo, 1981; Schmeck & Phillips, 1982). Other studies have failed to find any relationship between the approach used and the outcome measure (Beckwith, 1991; Busato et al., 1998; Christensen et al., 1991; Trigwell & Prosser, 1991; Watkins, 1983).

The uncertainty of the superiority of adopting either a deep or a surface approach is still evident when the medium of presentation is hypertext. In a series of studies, Beishuizen, Stoutjesdijk, and van Putten (1994) demonstrated that deep processors were able to consistently produce more effective study behaviors when they were working in a hypertext environment.

With the inconclusive nature of the results in this domain, perhaps our goal should be to create learners who are able to adopt either deep or surface approaches and strategies depending on the demands of the task characteristics. Pask (1988) describes versatile learners as students who are proficient at learning from most or all modes of instruction. They can employ both holist (deep) and serialist (surface) learning strategies; they succeed in achieving a full understanding that is composed of both descriptions and procedures.

2. Instructional Modality

Much of the current research in this area goes back to Paivio's (1971, 1991) dual coding theory, which addresses a person's preferred method of processing information. This theory proposes that information is either coded in a network composed of language-based information (the verbal subsystem) or coded in a network composed of nonverbal information (the imagery subsystem). This theory suggests that although everyone codes information in both subsystems to some extent, individuals differ in their preferred representational style. While the two subsystems are assumed to be structurally and functionally distinct, cue summation predicts that learning is increased as the number of available cues or stimuli is increased, both within and across channels. Kozma's (1991) review of the research related to simultaneous presentation of visual and audio material confirmed the hypothesis that combined use of audio and visual information results in more recall than visual-only or audio-only presentations.

In reviewing the literature related to these dimensions, Jonassen and Grabowski (1993) propose that students who demonstrate a visual prefer- ence should excel at tasks that require imaginal (generating mental images) instructional sequences, deductive (general-to-detailed) sequencing, and verbal advanced organizers. They are able to take full advantage of imagery- intensive materials including pictures, graphs and charts, and are proficient at video games. Verbal learners succeed with material that is presented in lectures, tapes, and nonillustrated texts. Becker and Dwyer (1998) directly addressed these differences when they studied the preferences of visual and verbal learners for using a groupware product in a Web-based course. They reported that students who preferred a visual style of learning felt that the groupware enhanced their group project, while students who favored a more verbal style found significantly less enhancement from the use of groupware and did not feel that it helped their on-line project.

The findings on the relationship between various instructional media and dual coding theory are far from conclusive. It appears that much depends on the exact nature of the material being presented and the type of media employed. Butler and Mautz (1996) found that multimedia does not effect all students in a similar manner. Students who preferred a graphical learning setting benefited most from multimedia presentations, however; students who prefer verbal presentations may actually be hindered by multimedia.

C. Executive Cognitive Processes

The relationship between learning style and performance is not simple and direct. Recent research findings point to the prominent role of executive cognitive processes in the individual learner's management of the strategies and tactics he or she employs. Among these higher-order processes are metacognition and self-regulated learning.

1. Metacognition

While the concept of metacognition, or "knowing about knowing," is not new, empirical studies into the effects of this attribute on performance have dramatically increased over the past 10 years. Flavell (1976) was one of the first researchers to study metacognition, which he defines as "one's knowl- edge concerning one's own cognitive processes and products and the active monitoring and consequential regulation of those processes in relation to the cognitive objects or data on which they bear" (p. 232). Subsequently, he distinguished between three types of metacognitive knowledge: knowl- edge about the self, knowledge about various cognitive tasks, and strategy knowledge (Flavell, 1987).

Research findings concerning the relationship of metacognition to acade-mic performance in general seem to be very consistent. Biggs (1988) indi-cates that increasing degrees of metacognition lead to deeper performance outcomes. Everson and Tobias (1998) clearly demonstrate the positive rela-tionship between high metacognitive abilities and course grades, and Kurtz and Weinert (1989) demonstrated that metacognition was a better predictor of performance than either effort attributions or scores on traditional intelli-gence tests. Anderson (1995) goes so far as to assert that metacognition is the single best predictor of students' academic performance.

Bernt and Bugbee (1993) review the research relating metacognition specifically to performance in distance education courses and conclude that distance learners often fail to monitor their progress and comprehension of course material. This lack of metacognition results in less than optimal use of time and produces poor results.

Applying the elements of metacognition, Mitchell (1993) proposes a cybernetic model of the learner whose central component is the learner as an active agent or control system attempting to attain goals in specific situ-ations, and being aware of one or more metastrategies for goal attainment. This model of the learner is consistent with the notion that the effective learner is highly motivated and needs to engage in a number of steps either consciously or unconsciously to reach the desired goal.

2. Self-Regulated Learning

An executive cognitive process that is now receiving a great deal of research attention is self-regulated learning (SRL), which combines metacog-nition with motivational and perceptual components. Various theorists have included other individual aspects such as student perceptions of themselves, of others, and of the learning environment; attention; orga-nization; goal setting; and self-evaluation (Boekaerts, 1997; Schunk, 1995; Zimmerman, 1990). Winne (1996) indicates that SRL includes both deliberate and nondeliberate forms of cognitive engagement.

Self-regulated learners are characterized as those students who rely on internal resources to govern their own learning process. They seem to be aware of what they know and feel about the domain of study, including which general cognitive and motivational strategies are effective to attain the learning goals, how easy or difficult it is to gain mastery in that domain, and whether they have the capacity and the motivation to invest the neces-sary resources. Thus, these are learners who are aware when they know a fact, or possess a skill, and when they do not. They proactively seek out information and are metacognitively, motivationally, and behaviorally active participants in their own learning. They display high self-efficacy, self-attribution, and intrinsic task interest. They are able to self-instruct during acquisition and self-reinforce during performance enactment. This self-monitoring depends on continuing feedback of learning effectiveness. Numerous empirical studies (e.g., Bouffard, Boisvert, Vezeau, & Larouche, 1995; Butler & Winne, 1995; Cantwell & Moore, 1996) have demonstrated a clear relationship between students' ability to self-regulate their learning and academic performance.

The importance of SRL is only just beginning to be understood. However, at this point it is fair to say that this characteristic seems to be a critical element in understanding what sets superior performers apart from the average. As our educational demands increasingly become entwined with the recovery and creation of new information, individuals will find it essential to be able to initiate, direct, and maintain their own performance.

3. Motivation

Self-regulated learning has been described as containing abilities both to direct and monitor metacognitive and cognitive activities and to sustain the motivation necessary to achieve goals. Wolters (1998) has convincingly demonstrated that self-regulated learners actively monitor and regulate their willingness to provide effort and persistence for academic tasks. He further reports that these students consciously adapt or modify the motivational strategy they use to fit situational demands.

One critical aspect of motivation, and especially of self-regulated motivation, is the ability of the student to establish goals and to monitor progress toward those goals. Schunk (1995) articulates the importance of goal setting, and describes methods teachers can implement to assist students in becoming more proficient at this facet of self-regulation.

Another facet of motivation is linked to effort or the allocation of resources. Efficient self-regulators are able to assess how much effort is needed to accomplish a particular task, and then determine if they are willing to expend that effort to accomplish their goals. This effort may take the form of the appropriate use of a learning strategy to support their goals, even if it is not their preferred strategy, or it may involve a temporal measure of persistence. In either case there is a growing body of literature that asserts that motivational beliefs are associated with whether students exert effort and the type of effort they expend. This effort is directly related to success and failure in school (Boekaerts, 1997).

D. Learner Profile

Extrapolating from the research reviewed above it is possible to build a predictive model of the learner characteristics that should be most suited to, and benefit most from participation in, a Web-based course. In general, the successful student would be able to tolerate ambiguity and be relatively free of anxiety. This individual would be field independent, adopt an active approach, and have an internal locus of control. The successful student will be a versatile learner, able to effectively employ deep or surface learning approaches as necessary. Regardless of the favored learning style, he or she will exhibit a high degree of metacognitive awareness and a strong ability to self-regulate his or her own learning.

The characteristics described above will significantly affect several different outcome measures. Students matching the described profile should produce academically superior performance outcomes when compared to students who do not demonstrate those characteristics. This superior performance should be evidenced by better educational products and higher scores on graded activities. In addition, students with the facilitative profile should report greater satisfaction with the course, its content, and their own performance.

Those students who most closely resemble the profile described above will be those most likely to thrive in a Web-based course. However, the larger issue is not just the appropriate placement of students, but whether or not it is possible to cultivate (or instill) those facilitative attributes in other students by virtue of their participation in an appropriately structured course.

III. MALLEABILITY OF INDIVIDUAL CHARACTERISTICS

Questions concerning the extent to which individual characteristics can be modified have resulted in mixed responses. Historically, such individual characteristics as field dependence/independence, locus of control, and activity/passivity have been considered personality traits, and as such, relatively permanent attributes. However, there have been empirical demonstrations that even these characteristics may be responsive to some forms of intervention. Approaches to learning are also considered relatively permanent attributes but again, may show some modifications in certain situations. There is also some evidence that self-regulated learning and metacognition are amenable to training programs and that the learning strategies that individuals use are quite responsive to training.

A. Personality Characteristics

The claim that curriculum and teaching approaches can influence individual characteristics was supported by Luk Suet Ching (1998) when she demonstrated that nursing students became more field independent during their participation in a distance education undergraduate program. She hypothesized that this shift in approach was a response to the self-directed nature of the particular educational program.

Warner (1981) reported that students in individualized, computer-based learning became more internal because they could relate success to their own efforts, whereas non-computer-based students became more dependent on the teacher. Similarly Dertinger (1984) discovered that students in a mastery learning situation became more internal as a result of the method.

However, despite some indications that these characteristics may be responsive to interventions, questions still remain regarding the extent to which it is possible to modify them. The most effective mechanism for realizing the changes, and the relative permanence of the changes, is unclear.

B. Approach to Learning

The results are also mixed concerning the extent to which an individual's preferred approach to learning can be modified by training. It has been proposed that the individual's basic preference toward adopting a deep or surface style of learning may be a relatively permanent trait; however, it is likely that it undergoes some modification as the individual matures, with young children displaying more of a surface orientation than adults. In addition, these approaches are also sensitive to some forms of direct instruction (Biggs, 1988). On the other hand, the use of learning strategies appears to be readily modifiable through appropriate instructional interventions (Schmeck, Ribich, & Ramaniah, 1977; Weinstein & Underwood, 1985).

In addition to changes brought about through explicitly instructional situations, changes may also be realized as a result of engaging in tasks that implicitly require students to adopt certain strategies. Anderson (1996) reports on the results of involving students in creating Web-based learning modules — an activity which forced them to become familiar with the nonlinear mechanisms of hypertext. As a result of this instructional format, students showed a significant increase in their use of deep learning strategies as compared to their use prior to engaging in the activity.

C. Executive Cognitive Processes

The research findings dealing with the impact of experience or training on metacognition and especially on self-regulated learning are more encouraging as there is a body of literature that demonstrates that both of these characteristics are somewhat malleable. The extent to which the enhancement of metacognitive skills and knowledge is a natural part of development is still an unanswered question. There appears to be a developmental component to this attribute (Brown & Palinscar, 1989), however, it may be based more on experience with the specific domain rather than a simple function of natural development. Zimmermann (1990) indicates that young children are ineffective self-regulated learners. A developmental progression may also be evidenced by adult learners when they endeavor to regulate their learning in a domain which is novel to them.

Winne (1996) describes self-regulated learning as a "developable" aptitude — one that changes incrementally with experience and instruction. He proceeds to develop the theory that self-regulated learning may occur in the form of conscious deliberation, or can be carried out automatically. This level of self-regulatory automaticity is only possible once the student has become proficient at a task, and no longer needs conscious effort for self-direction. Given this progression, the more extensive one's domain knowledge, the more control is embedded within the domain knowledge, and the less of one's resources need to be devoted to search for, use, and metacognitively monitor appropriate strategies. Therefore, a novice in a domain cannot be expected to display the same sorts of self-regulation that an expert would employ.

There are several comprehensive models for improving self-regulation in students. After completing a review of the literature documenting changes in students' ability to self-regulate, Boekaerts (1997) concludes that when students are not able to regulate their own learning, teachers can compensate for suboptimal self-regulatory skills. However, there is a fine line between a beneficial level of external regulation and so much external regulation that the student has little opportunity — or need — to develop his or her own regulatory abilities. Therefore, the external regulation needs to be presented in such a way as to provide a scaffolding structure for the student — one which can be gradually removed as the student's own self-regulation develops. Hofer, Yu, and Pintrich (1998) provide a detailed description of the effective components and design of a program to enhance self-regulated learning. Finally, Romero et al. (1999) describe the need to include mechanisms and feedback to improve students self-regulation in a Web-based tutorial lesson.

Despite the optimism about the potential for enhancing self-regulation, several authors caution that trying to teach students to self-regulate their academic learning is more complex than initially envisioned (Pressley, 1995; Zimmerman, 1990). The development of self-regulated learning is a long-term endeavor requiring modeling and explanation of mature thought embedded in an extensive practice of doing interesting and authentic tasks with appropriate scaffolding. It is also unclear to what extent newly learned self-regulatory strategies will transfer because of the motivational component required.

IV. CHARACTERISTICS OF EXPERIENCE

A. Knowledge (Declarative and Procedural)

There is a vast literature documenting the differences in the thought processes of novices and experts in any given domain. Butler and Winne

(1995) argue that the ability to fuse knowledge and information processing without teacher or text scaffolding is what sets experts apart from novices. In the early stages of skill development, students cannot "time-share" among various self-regulatory skills and the learning process itself. If SRL is a result of experience with both procedural and declarative knowledge, less experienced students simply have not had the time or requisite experiences to develop their skills in this area and as such are not able to self-regulate their learning.

There is a wide range of knowledge that is required for students to move from novice to expert and be able to self-regulate their learning in any domain. Butler and Winne (1995) and Boekaerts (1997) both elaborate on the need for domain knowledge, knowledge of cognitive and metacognitive strategies, knowledge of conditions underlying effective strategy use, knowledge about allocation of cognitive resources, and knowledge of motivational strategies in the development of proficient self-regulating learners.

The difference between novices and experts is readily evident in the manner in which they navigate through hypertext environments. MacGregor (1999) demonstrated that students who had greater domain knowledge evidenced more purposeful navigation and allocated time more variably to different information nodes when they were studying using hypertext environments. In addition, novices who possess less domain knowledge do not benefit from menu choices as much as competents or experts (Draper, 1999). These changes in the effective use of hypermedia may be the result of the development of more elaborate mental representations of the structure of the domain knowledge. Experts in a domain are distinguished from novices, in part, by the nature of their mental models and how they use them to represent and manipulate knowledge. The processing capabilities of the computer can help novices build and refine mental models so that they are more like those of experts (Kozma, 1991).

Jonassen and Wang (1993) demonstrate that one of the significant effects of the computerized presentation of hypertext material is the mapping of the cognitive structure of an expert onto the information to be presented. If students are directed explicitly to attend to this structure, the novice is able to acquire the structural knowledge of the expert. However, simply guiding the students though the structure does not necessarily modify their own cognitive representation of the information. Dillon and Gabbard (1998) support the contention that hypermedia can model knowledge structures of experts in a manner that makes their assimilation by learners more likely. The argument appears to be that hypermedia may support production of more effective pedagogical resources if it is designed in such a way as to model knowledge structures explicitly. In this way, hypermedia's support of structural mapping would ideally lend itself to helping novices acquire an expert's representation of a subject domain.

Using the media to support the acquisition of complex mental representations indicates how electronic technology can be developed to simulate teacher–student encounters and serve as a technological partner in an environment resembling Vygotsky's (1978) zone of proximal development. This student–technology interaction also has implications for bringing about the changes evidenced while interacting "with" computers and those that remain resident in the student as a result "of" the interaction with technology (Salomon, Perkins, & Globerson, 1991).

B. Attitude

There is clear empirical support for the connection between attitude and performance. Munger and Loyd (1989) report that students with more positive attitudes toward computers performed better than students with more negative attitudes. In addition, Kozma (1991) suggests that the perceptions students have about the medium used to present instruction along with the purpose of learning the material influence the amount of effort they put into processing the message.

Bernt and Bugbee (1993) reviewed the literature specifically to relate attitude to performance in distance courses and concluded that "while ability is a more critical factor in achievement among younger students, attitudinal, motivational and personality factors may contribute more to differences in achievement among older students" (p. 100). More recently, Papa, Perugini, and Spedaletti (1998) also studied the role of attitude in affecting the use of technologically advanced systems and concluded that positive perceptions and a positive attitude toward tele-education may lead to positive influences on performance. If the person thinks he or she is able to master the distance learning system, his or her performance improves. However, if he or she thinks it is not possible to do so, his or her performance deteriorates.

In general, the factor that appears to be the single best predictor of attitudes toward computers appears to be previous experience. Given the importance of a positive attitude on performance, it is encouraging to note that most students' attitudes improve with exposure to the use of enhanced media (Anderson & Hornby, 1996). Butler and Mautz (1996) demonstrated that even though multimedia does not uniformly lead to higher recall, positive attitudes resulted from the presentations regardless of the students' preferred presentation style.

V. SALIENT ELEMENTS OF WEB-BASED COURSE DESIGN

There is adequate information to allow us to construct a predictive model of the successful student in a Web-based course, and we can also draw on the literature to suggest which of the relevant traits might be malleable. The question remains as to which design elements of a Web-based course are most likely to positively impact learner characteristics. In recent years, numerous studies have been conducted into several critical elements of course design. Much of this literature is very relevant to the design of Web-based courses as it investigates the relationship of course design with an individual student's performance. By exploiting the interactivity and individualization possible in Web-based courses, we are perfectly situated to take advantage of this body of research and construct Web-based courses that not only cater to certain individual characteristics, but also help to develop those characteristics beyond their native state.

While it is certainly true that not all Web-based courses follow the same format, there are, nonetheless, certain common core characteristics. Most Web-based courses are asynchronous, and students are frequently expected to carry out a great deal of the learning on their own, often at a geographic distance from the educational institution. The expectation that students can and should be independent underlies much of the distance education literature. Participation in a distance education course requires greater personal motivation and interest than in the more traditional forms of education. In general, these courses provide limited interpersonal interaction, require large amounts of reading and writing, and do not involve expository lectures. Students need to become proficient in the use of advanced technologies in novel environments with limited external support (Anderson, 1997–1998; Baynton, 1992; Keegan, 1996; Misra, 1993).

One of the course design elements that varies the most and has received a great deal of attention is the amount of control the program offers the student, in terms of both navigational freedom and pacing of course-related activities. A second salient design element is the amount and nature of feedback provided to the student. A final area of concern centers on the nature of the individual tasks within the overall course structure and the requisite level of prior knowledge.

A. Control

One of the frequently cited advantages of asynchronous distance courses is that it gives students control of their learning. However, this opportunity for students to influence, direct, and determine decisions related to the educational process is not seen as a universally beneficial aspect of instruction. Baynton (1992) provides a comprehensive description of the critical elements of control and relates them to development of distance education courses. According to her model, the ability to effectively control the learning process results from an interaction of the student's independence, competence, and support (both human/emotional and resource/content). Earlier, Snow (1989) indicated that the effective use of control takes into account students' abilities (high or low) and involves treatments that differ in the structure and completeness of instruction. He claimed that structured treatments, specifically those with high levels of external control and well-defined sequences, help students with low ability, but hinder those with high abilities. In their review of the impact of learner control on the use of hypermedia, Dillon and Gabbard (1998) find support for the claim that, in general, the ability to control pace and delivery of information appears insufficient to affect learning outcomes significantly for all but high-ability learners.

These findings reinforce the description of the characteristics of the student most likely to benefit from a Web-based course presented earlier in this chapter. The student who possess those characteristics is likely to be able to take full advantage of the opportunity afforded by an asynchronous distance course to control the learning environment. However, for students who do not have the native ability to benefit from this freedom, appropriate external controls can be designed into the system itself. Hapeshi and Jones (1992) provide some guidelines on the importance of determining the degree of flexibility to allow the student when navigating through a hyper-text environment. A critical element in the transition from text to hypertext is the removal of a forced linear presentation of material. However, in many cases guidelines still need to be provided to ensure that students success-fully navigate through the space. Beishuizen et al. 1994) demonstrate that students who combine self-regulation with deep processing benefit from limited external structure, while students who demonstrate surface process-ing and less self-regulation require additional structure in a hypertext learn-ing situation. Ideally the external control would be available on demand, and would be able to be phased out as the student developed the ability to self-regulate learning.

B. Feedback

Butler and Winne (1995) acknowledge that "self-regulated learning is a pivot upon which students' achievement turns" (p. 245). They proceed to detail the central role that the effective use of feedback plays in students' ability to select and evaluate their choice of learning approaches. They claim that feedback is an inherent catalyst for all self-regulated activities. While learn-ers are more effective when they attend to externally provided feedback, this feedback is not usually available during learning activities, but is given after a task has been completed. Availability of feedback while engaged in the task is critical to the development of self-monitoring skills. Feedback which is usually available to students at the completion of a task is consid-ered to be "outcome feedback" and only describes whether or not the results are correct. Butler and Winne (1995) contend that this type of feedback carries no information about the task other than its state of achievement, and hence provides minimal external guidance for a learner to learn how to self-regulate.

In addition to the temporal availability of feedback, the nature of the feedback and its interpretation are dependent on a number of individual variables. Chinn and Brewer (1993) describe the mediating effects of the learners' beliefs and knowledge. Essentially, if students' knowledge is incorrect and entrenched, they are likely to be erratic in applying productive learning strategies. As domain-specific knowledge increases, students' use of cognitive strategies that support self-regulated learning is enhanced.

Self-regulating learners are able to effectively generate internal feedback while engaged in an activity, and use that feedback to monitor their progress toward their goals. However, if students are not already self-regulating, they will not spontaneously monitor their performance, and will need to have mechanisms for generating external feedback built into their instructional modules. These external feedback protocols should stimulate students to develop the ability to self-monitor and become sensitive to intrinsic feedback, thus reducing their dependence on external support.

Bernt and Bugbee (1993) demonstrated that feedback in the form of practice tests while engaged in coursework has a beneficial impact on subsequent course performance. This supports the inclusion of formative evaluations in order to modify students' approaches to learning, a critical element in a distance situation where the student is working independently to master a set body of knowledge. It is especially true for the student who is not proficient at self-monitoring. Butler and Winne (1995) conclude that learning improves when feedback informs students about their monitoring of learning needs and guides them in how to achieve learning objectives.

C. Task Characteristics

Each Web-based course consists of a number of learning and performance activities. It is critical that the course developer conduct a thorough task analysis for each individual task within the course. Such a task analysis needs to clearly articulate the goals of the activity and identify the learning strategies most suitable for achieving those goals. In order to accomplish this the course designers need to be experts in the field, or have access to such expertise. Once the most efficient means of completing each task has been identified, the course developer needs to build the supporting "scaffolding" for using those strategies into the program. By delineating the most effective approach to learning, and including that structure in the course, the designer can capitalize on the interactive individualization available through Web courses. This provides the opportunity to model the appropriate approach and thus help the novice accomplish the task. But the structure should be flexible enough to allow the expert to bypass the externally imposed structure and complete the task according to his or her preferred heuristic.

Coincident with this task analysis is the development of the actual course materials. Regardless of the nature of the specific activity, the importance of the quality of the material cannot be overemphasized. One of the basic conclusions of studies comparing varying media and instructional treatments is that any course is only as good as the materials used to support it — with poor materials even good students cannot succeed (e.g., Draper, 1999; Parlangeli, Marchigiani, & Bagnara, 1999).

VI. INTERACTIVE MODEL OF LEARNER CHARACTERISTICS AND WEB-BASED COURSES

We are now in a position to create an interactive model of the learner and the effects of participation in Web-based courses on academic performance. We can predict which learner characteristics are most likely to facilitate performance in a Web-based course. We can also indicate the importance of certain preexisting experiential elements. In addition, certain design characteristics of Web-based courses can be critical to individual performance. Throughout the model, the crucial element becomes understanding the recursive interaction between the student, the course, and the outcome measures.

Figure 3.1 represents the interaction of the individual, the course design and the outcomes of a Web-based course. The learner characteristics indicated earlier in the chapter as being predictive of success form the core of the salient individual differences. Coupled with these core traits are aspects of the individual that result from prior experience. These include attitude and previous knowledge. The individual's attitude upon entering the Web-based course is based on previous experience, as well as the predisposing effects of the core characteristics. Both the declarative and procedural knowledge the individual possesses at the outset of the course result from experiences in the individual's past.

All three aspects of the individual — core characteristics, attitude, and prior knowledge — directly impact the student's participation in a Web based-course. This is where the design elements of the course itself become critical. The program should be able to provide adequate scaffolding to guide students through the activities. For students who do not intuitively self-monitor and assess their own progress and satisfaction, explicit prompts should be made by the program. As the student progresses the prompts regarding appropriate approaches should recede and more control should reside in the student. This explicit and implicit feedback while the student is engaged in the tasks of the course will serve to modify all three aspects of the individual, thus affecting his or her subsequent performance in the course.

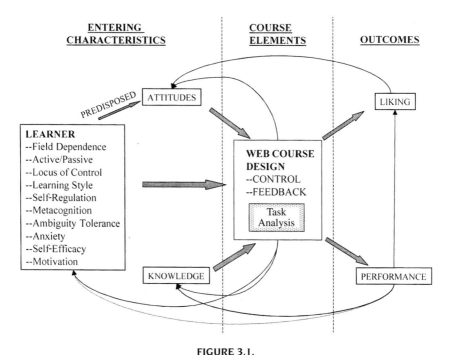

FIGURE 3.1.
Interactive model of learner characteristics and Web-based courses.

Upon completion of the course two outcome measures (student performance and satisfaction with the course) can be assessed directly. Each of these terminal outcome measures is a direct result of participation in the course. In addition, final performance will influence the ultimate level of satisfaction. These terminal measures also provide feedback to be incorporated into the student's experiential base. However, the terminal outcome measures do not provide any constructive feedback to the student while he or she is engaged in the course. As such, they need to be supplemented with interim feedback while the student is engaged in the course. As students with certain individual characteristics may not intuitively take advantage of the available feedback, the feedback needs to be made explicit.

Thus, in the complete model, as the student engages in the Web-based learning activities, he or she receives both implicit and explicit feedback concerning level of performance and liking of the course while engaged in the activities. This feedback influences the basic characteristics and approaches to the remainder of the course tasks. At the conclusion of the course, performance outcome measures play a role in determining satisfaction with the overall experience, and in modifying the basic learner characteristics. They will also provide feedback as to what changes would be most beneficial to future learning attempts and the likelihood of engaging in subsequent Web-based learning.

VII. CONCLUSIONS

The issue facing distance educators is not just the impact of the medium or the individual characteristics of the successful learner. The issue is how to determine the significance of the interaction between the two. This is part of a larger question of which design elements need to be considered in constructing Web-based courses. I suggest that we need to revisit the basic curriculum design issues. We need to determine exactly what it is we are trying to teach and to whom. Then we need to design the best materials to do that job. No matter what the medium is, poorly designed materials will never produce top quality learning. We need to develop materials that teach not only the declarative knowledge, but also the procedural knowledge of our disciplines. We need to provide students with facts, as well as the abilities to think critically about those facts, to learn how to gather new information, and to become life-long self-directed learners.

We can adequately construct a profile of the student most likely to thrive in a Web-based environment. However, we should not restrict participation in Web-based courses to those students. Rather, it becomes our responsibility to ensure that all students can benefit — academically and personally — from engaging in Web-based learning opportunities. We should be able to take advantage of knowledge from a wide range of disciplines to exploit this new medium and create a learning environment that is truly adaptive to each individual and is able to foster those abilities most likely to guarantee academic success. Our major research issue needs to be what impact the design of our Web-based courses can have on the development of the cognitive abilities of our students.

As the Web removes geographic boundaries for education, the cultural and individual differences of students that instructors will need to contend with will become even more complex. It will become increasingly more difficult to ensure the appropriate treatment of each student. Developing instructional materials for a homogeneous audience is a relatively simple task; as the audience becomes more heterogeneous the materials need to include sufficiently structured guidance which the student may elect to follow or avoid according to his or her preference and idiosyncratic navigational system. Therefore, it will become even more critical that course designers fully understand the cognitive demands of the tasks in their curriculum. They must be aware of the approach or aptitude that is most effective for the treatment they have designed. Finally, they must be able to incorporate the appropriate scaffolding to enable each student to implement that strategy which will ensure his or her successful completion of individual tasks and ultimately, of an entire course.

References

Anderson, M. D. (1995). *Relating college students' learning approach to their quality of learning outcome.* Unpublished dissertation, Concordia University.

Anderson, M. D. (1996). *Effecting changes in cognition through the use of* HTML. Paper presented at the 26th Annual Meeting of the Society for Computers in Psychology, Chicago.

Anderson, M. D. (1997–1998). Critical elements of an Internet based asynchronous distance education course. *Journal of Educational Technology Systems, 26,* 383–388.

Anderson, M. D. (1999). Does the medium affect the message? *Supporting instructional technology: What really counts?* Proceedings of the Eighth Annual SUNY FACT Conference on Instructional Technologies, pp. 6–8. State University of New York.

Anderson, M. D. & Hornby, P. A. (1996). Computer attitudes and the use of computers in psychology courses. *Behavior Research Methods, Instruments, & Computers, 28,* 341–346.

Ausubel, D. P. (1963). *The psychology of meaningful verbal learning.* New York: Grune & Stratton.

Bandura, A. (1997). *Self-efficacy: The exercise of control.* New York: Freeman.

Baynton, M. (1992). Dimensions of "control" in distance education: A factor analysis. *The American Journal of Distance Education, 6.* 17–31.

Becker, D., & Dwyer, M. (1998). The impact of student verbal/visual learning style preferences on implementing groupware in the classroom. *Journal of Asynchronous Learning Networks, 2.*

Beckwith, J. B. (1991). Approaches to learning, their context and relationship to assessment performance. *Higher Education, 22,* 17–30.

Beishuizen, J., Stoutjesdijk, E., & van Putten, K. (1994). Studying textbooks: Effects of learning styles, study task, and instruction. *Learning and Instruction, 4,* 151–174.

Bernt, F. M., & Bugbee, A. C., Jr. (1993). Study practices and attitudes related to academic success in a distance learning programme. *Distance Education, 14,* 97–113.

Biggs, J. (1978). Individual and group differences in study processes. *British Journal of Educational Psychology, 48,* 266–279.

Biggs, J. (1979). Individual differences in study process and the quality of learning outcomes. *Higher Education, 18,* 384–394.

Biggs, J. (1985). The role of meta-learning in study processes. *British Journal of Educational Psychology, 55,* 185–212.

Biggs, J. (1988). The role of metacognition in enhancing learning. *Australian Journal of Education, 32,* 127–138.

Biggs, J. (1993). What do inventories of students' learning processes really measure? A theoretical review and clarification. *British Journal of Educational Psychology, 63,* 3–19.

Biggs, J. B., & Rhin, B. A. (1984). The effects of intervention on deep and surface approaches to learning. In J. R. Kirby (Ed.), *Cognitive strategies and educational performance.* New York: Academic Press.

Boekaerts, M. (1997). Self-regulated learning: A new concept embraced by researchers, policy makers, educators, teachers, and students. *Learning and Instruction, 7,* 161–186.

Bouffard, T., Boisvert, J., Vezeau, C., & Larouche, C. (1995). The impact of goal orientation on self-regulation and performance among college students. *British Journal of Educational Psychology, 65,* 317–329.

Brown, A. L., & Palinscar, A. S. (1989). Guided, cooperative learning and individual knowledge acquisition. In L. B. Resnick (Ed.), *Knowing, learning and instruction: Essays in honor of Robert Glaser* (pp. 393–451). Hillsdale, NJ: Erlbaum.

Burton, J. K., Moore, D. M. & Holmes, G. A. (1995). Hypermedia concepts and research: An overview. *Computers in Human Behavior, 11,* 345–369.

Busato, V. V., Prins, F. J., Elshout, J. J., & Hamaker, C. (1998). Learning styles: a cross-sectional and longitudinal study in higher education. *British Journal of Educational Psychology*, 68, 427–441.

Butler, D. L., & Winne, P. H. (1995). Feedback and self-regulated learning: A theoretical synthesis. *Review of Educational Research*, 65, 245–281.

Butler, J. B., & Mautz, R. D., Jr. (1996). Multimedia presentations and learning: A laboratory experiment. *Issues in Accounting Education*, 11, 259–280.

Cantwell, R. H., & Moore, P. J. (1996). The development of measures of individual differences in self-regulatory control and their relationship to academic performance. *Contemporary Educational Psychology*, 21, 500–517.

Chinn, C. A., & Brewer, W. F. (1993). The role of anomalous data in knowledge acquisition: A theoretical framework and implications for science instruction. *Review of Educational Research*, 63, 1–49.

Christensen, C. A., Massey, D. R., & Isaacs, P. J. (1991). Cognitive strategies and study habits: An analysis of the measurement of tertiary students' learning. *British Journal of Educational Psychology*, 61, 290–299.

Cronbach, L. J., & Snow, R. E. (1977). *Aptitudes and instructional methods: A handbook for research on interactions*. New York: Irvington Publishers.

Curry, L. (1983). *An organization of learning styles theory and constructs*. Paper presented at the 67th Annual Meeting of the American Educational Research Association. Montreal, Quebec.

Dertinger, T. D. (1984). An experimental study of the effects of mastery learning on the locus of control of sixth-grade science students. *Dissertation Abstracts International*, 13, 107.

Dillon, A., & Gabbard, R. (1998). Hypermedia as an educational technology: A review of the quantitative research literature on learner comprehension, control, and style. *Review of Educational Research*, 68, 322–349.

Draper, S. W. (1999). *Learning styles* [Notes on-line]. Available: http://medusa.psy.gla.ac.uk/~steve/lstyles.htm

Entwistle, N. (1981). *Styles of learning and teaching*. Chichester: Wiley.

Everson, H. T. & Tobias, S. (1998). The ability to estimate knowledge and performance in college. *Instructional Science*, 26, 65–79.

Flavelle, J. H. (1976). Metacognitive aspects of problem solving. In L. B. Resnick (Ed.), *The nature of intelligence* (pp. 231–236). Hillsdale, NJ: Erlbaum.

Flavelle, J. H. (1987). Speculation abut the nature and development of metacognition. In F. E. Weinert & R. H. Kluwe (Eds.), *Metacognition, motivation and understanding* (pp. 21–29). Hillsdale, NJ: Erlbaum.

Frenkel-Brunswik, E. (1948). Intolerance of ambiguity as an emotional perceptual personality variable. *Journal of Personality*, 18, 108–143.

Furnham, A., & Ribchester, T. (1995). Tolerance of ambiguity: A review of the concept, its measurement and applications. *Current Psychology: Development, Learning, Personality, Social*, 14, 179–199.

Hapeshi, K., & Jones, D. (1992). Interactive multimedia for instruction: A cognitive analysis of the role of audition and vision. *International Journal of Human-Computer Interaction*, 4, 79–99.

Hofer, B. K., Yu, S. L., & Pintrich, P. R. (1998). Teaching college students to be self-regulated learners. In D. H. Schunk & B. J. Zimmerman (Eds.), *Self-regulated learning: From teaching to self-reflective practice* (pp. 57–85). New York: Guilford Publications.

Jonassen, D. H. & Grabowski, B. L. (1993). *Handbook of individual differences, learning, and instruction*. Hillside, NJ: Erlbaum.

Jonassen, D. H. & Wang, S. (1993). Acquiring structural knowledge from semantically structured hypertext. *Journal of Computer-Based Instruction*, 20, 1–8.

Keegan, D. (1996). *Foundations of distance education*. North Yorkshire: Biddles.

Kirby, J. R., & Biggs, J. B. (1981). *Learning styles, information processing abilities, and academic achievement* [Final report]. Australian Research Grants Committee, Belconnen ACT.

Kozma, R. B. (1991). Learning with media. *Review of Educational Research*, 61, 179–211.

Kurtz, B. E., & Weinert, F. E. (1989). Metamemory, metaperformance, and causal attributions in gifted and average children. *Journal of Experimental Child Psychology*, 48, 45–61.

Luk Suet Ching, W. (1998). The influence of a distance-learning environment on student's field dependence/independence. *Journal of Experimental Education*, 66, 149–160

MacDonald, A. P. (1970). Revised scale for ambiguity tolerance: Reliability and validity. *Psychological Reports*, 26, 791–798.

MacGregor, S. K. (1999). Hypermedia navigation profiles: Cognitive characteristics and information processing strategies. *Journal of Educational Computing Research*, 20, 189–206.

Maki, R. H., Maki, W. S., Patterson, M., & Whittaker, P. D. (1999). *Evaluation of a Web-based introductory psychology course.* Paper presented at the annual meeting of the Society for Computers in Psychology, Los Angeles, CA.

Marton, F., & Saljo, R. (1976). On qualitative differences in learning: I. Outcome and process. *British Journal of Educational Psychology*, 46, 4–11.

McIsaac, M. S., & Gunawardena, C. N. (1996). Distance education. In D. H. Jonassen (Ed.), *Handbook of research for educational communications and technology: A project of the Association for Educational Communications and Technology* (pp. 403–437). New York: Simon & Schuster Macmillan.

McLeod, D. B., & Adams, V. M. (1979). The interaction of field independence with discovery learning in mathematics. *The Journal of Experimental Education*, 48, 32–35.

Meehl, P. E. (1978). Theoretical risks and tabular asterisks: Sir Karl, Sir Ronald, and the slow progress of soft psychology. *Journal of Consulting and Clinical Psychology*, 46, 806–834.

Messick, S. (1976). Personal styles and educational options. In S. Messick (Ed.), *Individuality in learning: Implications of cognitive styles and creativity for human development.* (pp. 310–327). San Francisco: Jossey-Bass.

Messick, S. (1994). The matter of style: Manifestations of personality in cognition, learning, and teaching. *Educational Psychologist*, 29, 121–136.

Misra, G. (1993). Development of learning skills in the context of distance education. *Indian Journal of Psychometry & Education*, 24, 1–6.

Mitchell, P. D. (1993). Are theories of learning essential or misleading for educational technology? In N. Estes & M. Thomas (Eds.), *Rethinking the roles of technology in education* (Vol. 2, pp. 1086–1088). Austin, TX: College of Education, University of Texas at Austin.

Multon, K. D., Brown, S. D., & Lent, R. W. (1991). Relation of self-efficacy beliefs to academic outcomes: A meta-analytic investigation. *Journal of Counseling Psychology*, 38, 30–38.

Munger, G. F., & Loyd, B. H. (1989). Gender and attitudes toward computers and calculators: Their relationship to math performance. *Journal of Educational & Computing Research*, 5, 167–177.

O'Neil, H. F., Spielberger, C. D., & Hansen, D. N. (1969). The effects of state-anxiety and task difficulty on computer-assisted learning. *Journal of Educational Psychology*, 60, 343–350.

Paivio, A. (1971). *Imagery and verbal processes.* New York: Holt, Rinehart & Winston.

Paivio, A. (1991). Dual coding theory: Retrospect and current status. *Canadian Journal of Psychology*, 45, 255–287.

Papa, F., Perugini, M., & Spedaletti, S. (1998). Psychological factors in virtual classroom situations: A pilot study for a model of learning through technological devices. *Behavior and Informational Technology*, 17, 187–94.

Parlangeli, O., Marchigiani, E., & Bagnara, S. (1999). Multimedia systems in distance education: Effects of usability on learning. *Interacting with Computers*, 12, 37–49.

Pask, G. (1976). Styles and strategies of learning. *British Journal of Educational Psychology*, 46, 128–148.

Pask, G. (1988). Learning strategies, teaching strategies, and conceptual or learning style. In R. R. Schmeck (Ed.), *Learning strategies and learning styles* (pp. 83–100). New York: Plenum.

Pressley, M. (1995). More about the development of self-regulation: Complex, long-term, and thoroughly social. *Educational Psychologist*, 30, 207–212.

Ramsden, P., & Entwistle, N. (1981). Effects of academic department on students' approaches to studying. *British Journal of Educational Psychology*, 57, 368–383.

Riding, R. & Cheema, I. (1991). Cognitive styles — An overview and integration. *Educational Psychology*, 11, 193–215.

Riding, R., & Douglas, G. (1993). The effect of cognitive style and mode of presentation on learning performance. *British Journal of Educational Psychology*, 63, 297–307.

Romero, V. L., Berger, D. E., Healy, M. R., & Aberson, C. L. (1999). *Using cognitive learning theory to design effective on-line statistics tutorials.* Paper presented at the annual meeting of the Society for Computers in Psychology, Los Angeles, CA.

Rotter, J. B. (1966). Generalized expectancies for internal versus external control of reinforcement. *Psychological Monographs*, 80, 1–28.

Saljo, R. (1981). Learning approach and outcome: some empirical observations. *Instructional Science*, 10, 47–65.

Salomon, G., Perkins, D. N., & Globerson, T. (1991). Partners in cognition: Extending human intelligence with intelligent technologies. *Educational Researcher*, 20, 2–9.

Schmeck, R. R. (1988). *Learning strategies and learning styles.* New York: Plenum Press.

Schmeck, R. R., & Phillips, J. (1982). Levels of processing as a dimension of differences between individuals. *Human Learning*, 1, 95–103.

Schmeck, R. R., Ribich, F. D., & Ramanaiah, N. (1977). Development of a self-report inventory for assessing individual differences in learning processes. *Applied Psychological Measurement*, 1, 413–431.

Schulman, A. H., & Sims, R. L. (1999, June). Learning in an online format versus an in-class format: An experimental study. *THE Journal*, 26, 54–56.

Schunk, D. H. (1995). Inherent details of self-regulated learning include self perceptions. *Educational Psychologist*, 30, 213–216.

Snow, R. (1989). Aptitude-treatment interaction as a framework for research on individual differences in learning. In P. Ackerman, R. Sternberg, & R. Glaser (Eds.), *Learning and individual differences* (pp. 13–60). New York: Freeman.

Svensson, L. (1977). On qualitative differences: III. Study skill and learning. *British Journal of Educational Psychology*, 47, 233–243.

Trigwell, K., & Prosser, M. (1991). Relating approaches to study and quality of learning outcomes at the course level. *British Journal of Educational Psychology*, 61, 265–275.

Vygotsky, L. S. (1978). Mind in society. Cambridge, MA: Harvard University Press.

Warner, T. D. (1981). The effects of computer-based education on sixth-grade students' self-concept, locus of control, and mathematics achievement. *Dissertation Abstracts International*, 42, 1040.

Watkins, D. (1983). Assessing tertiary study processes. *Human Learning*, 2, 29–37.

Watkins, D. (1984). Students' perceptions of factors influencing tertiary learning. *Higher Education Research and Development*, 3, 33–50.

Weinstein, C. E., & Underwood, V. L. (1985). Learning strategies: The how of learning. In J. W. Segal, S. F. Chipman, & R. Glaser (Eds.), *Thinking and learning skills: Vol. 1. Relating instruction to research* (pp. 241–258). New York: Erlbaum.

Weller, H. G., Repman, J., Lan, W., & Rooze, G. (1995). Improving the effectiveness of learning through hypermedia-based instruction: The importance of learner characteristics. *Computers in Human Behavior*, 11, 451–465.

Wilhite, S. C. (1990). Self-efficacy, locus of control, self-assessment of memory ability, and study activities as predictors of college course achievement. *Journal of Educational Psychology*, 82, 696–700.

Winne, P. H. (1996). A metacognitive view of individual differences in self-regulated learning. *Learning and Individual Differences*, 8, 327–353.

Witkin, H. A., & Goodenough, D. R. (1981). *Cognitive styles: Essence and origins — Field dependence and field independence.* New York: International University Press.

Wolters, C. A. (1998). Self-regulated learning and college student's regulation of motivation. *Journal of Educational Psychology*, 90, 224–235.

Zimmerman, B. J. (1990). Self-regulated learning and academic achievement: An overview. *Educational Psychologist*, 25, 3–17.

Zimmerman, B. J., Bandura, A., & Martinez-Pons, M. (1992). Self-motivation for academic attainment: The role of self-efficacy beliefs and personal goal setting. *American Educational Research Journal*, 29, 663–676.

CHAPTER 4

Teaching Advanced Literacy Skills for the World Wide Web

M. ANNE BRITT

Northern Illinois University

GARETH L. GABRYS

MessageBlaster.com

A major goal of the U.S. government has been to connect America's public schools to the Internet. As of the fall of 1998, 89% were connected and the rest were expected to be connected by the beginning of 2000 (NCES, 1999). The expectation of many politicians, and educational thinkers, is that connecting schools to the Internet will cure our national educational ills. Some think that learning will be promoted by opening up the classrooms to more, and potentially better, educational opportunities than are currently present. Students can learn from lesson plans developed by other teachers; they can exchange e-mail with scientists doing the research described in their textbooks; and they can read original documents rather than excerpts in textbooks. Unfortunately, there is also a downside to opening up a world of quick, cheap information to students: Without specific training, many students are unprepared to differentiate sound information from unsound materials. Students can use the World Wide Web (Web) to visit the Holocaust museum to learn about WWII atrocities; but they can also visit neo-Nazi sites that "prove" that the Holocaust never occurred. They can confuse advertising and fiction with historical information, or they may simply become overwhelmed by the daunting task of locating and organizing the vast quantities of information that they can retrieve with a single click.

Learning and Teaching on the World Wide Web
73

The skills that students need in order to utilize the potential of the Internet are quite similar to those we have found essential for high school students learning to use primary documents in history classes (Britt, Rouet, & Perfetti, 1994; Rouet, Britt, Mason, & Perfetti, 1997; Wineburg, 1991). In this chapter we describe these skills and examine how they apply to the situation of students learning from the Web. We also describe the Sourcer's Apprentice, a Java application we created to provide tutoring and practice opportunities for learning these skills.

I. LITERACY SKILLS FOR INTERNET USERS

Before the Internet, publishers and the high cost of publishing acted as a kind of gatekeeper of document quality. Though far from infallible, this mechanism at least restricted publication to those with either enough funds to publish themselves or enough drive, credibility, and talent to convince a publisher that he or she could attract an audience to some work. The Internet has eliminated this barrier by reducing the cost of disseminating information to virtually nothing. While this has made possible the widespread availability of virtual libraries and tremendous repositories of government information, it has also made it possible for anyone with a computer and $20 per month (or less) to access the Internet and create a Web site that publishes almost anything.

We have observed an analogous situation in history education where textbooks once acted as the gatekeepers of historical "truths." As standards have changed, students are now increasingly expected to use the textbook as one source among many — with a greater reliance on primary and secondary sources (National Center for History in the Schools, 1996). This places students in the position of having to deal with integrating information from multiple accounts of a story by different authors who have different motives for telling the story and who do not necessarily agree in their accounts.

Likewise, we believe that students need explicit instruction in skills that would enable them to evaluate and filter the myriad kinds of information they will encounter on the Web. The skills we have identified, though derived from research on history learning, are not specifically the purview of any one domain but are used by all disciplines to some extent. One might think of them as advanced literacy skills: abilities that expert readers typically acquire on their own that enable them to read and comprehend complex texts. The three skills that we consider most important for students are *sourcing*, *corroborating*, and *integrating*. Two additional skills we think are very important, but do not discuss in this chapter, are argumentation and the use of search strategies. We discuss each of the three skills in detail below.

A. Integration

The World Wide Web is, by definition, organized nonlinearly, and users almost inevitably read multiple pages on the same topic written by different authors. One problem this causes for students is the need to take information garnered from one page and integrate it with what one has learned from other pages. Students must become skilled in making connections across pages, reading occasions, and authors. For example, a student learning about the events leading up to the Gulf of Tonkin Resolution (which effectively started America's official involvement in the Vietnam War) can access firsthand accounts, commentaries, newspaper articles, photographs, official U.S. documents including the Gulf of Tonkin Resolution itself, and speeches by U.S. officials. When reading each selected document, a student will want to assimilate all relevant information. In this case, they gather information about the main participants and their motives as well as the major events and their sequence in time. The student must gradually build up a coherent understanding of the "story" and continually add to, or modify, this story based on information gained from each new page they visit. This is what we mean by integration, though it should be noted that we do not restrict the skill of integration to learning about a situation or story. We think of it in the most general way as adding to or modifying any complex argument, procedure, situation, or concept.

Integration involves making connections between prior and new knowledge. Nonlinear reading (i.e., following links on hypertext pages) places high demands on the reader's ability to build links between new and prior knowledge in several ways. First, nonlinear texts tend to strip out text devices that create coherence because the author cannot make assumptions about what the reader may have already read. Integration requires that one activate one's existing representation in order to modify it based on new information. Authors of a single text carefully add text devices that invoke this representation before giving new information. This tends to reduce the reader's need to expend mental effort to spontaneously notice the association. When one reads multiple documents, these text devices are lacking. Readers must actively work to find associations between the new information and the prior representation in order to maintain coherence. Research by Britt, Goldman, and Perfetti (1999) suggests that high school students do poorly at integrating information when they must spontaneously notice associations between accounts given in multiple documents. They gave high school students either two texts describing the same historical events or the same information in a single integrated text. Furthermore, students given two texts were either instructed to read simply for comprehension or explicitly instructed to integrate the information in both documents. After reading, students were asked to write an essay describing the events and answer several detailed questions. The results

showed that students who read two texts with only comprehension instructions made more errors, recalled less information, and provided less integrated answers to questions than either students who read a single
document or those who read two documents with integration instructions.
This indicates that high school students are certainly capable of integrating
multiple documents, but may be unlikely to do so spontaneously. This
conclusion is consistent with another study by Perfetti, Britt, and Georgi
(1995) which found little evidence of spontaneous integration on the part
of six college students who read several documents on a single topic over a
14-week period.

A second difficulty created by nonlinear reading is that it increases the
number of documents that require integration. Nonlinear presentation
tends to favor short documents, meaning that more documents must be
read to gain the same amount of information as in a more traditional linear
document. A student doing a research paper from library sources may select
three or four books. A student doing a research paper from Web documents
may select 10 or 12 pages by different authors, considerably increasing the
number of documents to integrate.

A third difficulty of using nonlinear texts is that readers of multiple documents, and especially readers of Web documents, must deal with inconsistencies. Authors can and will disagree about the situations they describe
and readers need to be able to represent inconsistent and conflicting information. This can be very confusing to students. In a recent study, Britt et al.
(1999) found that 27% of high school students who were given two texts to
read on the same topic found the experience confusing or difficult. To quote
one student, "I thought it was confusing reading the two different stories
about the same thing. And because of that I forgot some parts of the
stories." Another student wrote, "The fact that there was 2 different versions
made it harder. I wasn't sure which one to believe so I combined both."
Finally, another said, "It is a little confusing how 2 essays on the same topic
can differ so much." Other recent findings show that even college students
have difficulty modifying their model of the situation formed from a previously read text on the same topic (Johnson & Seifert, 1996, 1999; Millis &
Erdman, 1998; van Oostendorp & Bonebakker, 1999).

A final difficulty with nonlinear reading is that readers are expected to
guide their own learning process. Authors of linear texts tend to order their
presentations very carefully, giving background information, for instance,
before delving into complicated arguments. When students guide their own
reading, there is nothing to stop them from jumping right into a complicated
argument without understanding much about its context — leading to a
potentially impoverished representation of the situation. In many ways,
hypertext is better suited to users with some amount of domain knowledge
who are primarily searching for information than to novices learning about
the domain for the first time.

Although we point out all of these integration difficulties with nonlinear reading, we are certainly not arguing that students should return to learning from single textbooks. We merely note that many students are likely to experience integration difficulties when they read nonlinear texts, and they need explicit instruction on making interdocument connections. Other things being equal, students who have difficulties, and who do not receive such instruction from parents and teachers, may find learning from the Web a difficult, confusing experience, and may fail to build the kind of integrated knowledge representations that we would hope they would.

B. Sourcing

Sourcing is the skill of noticing and evaluating the source of a document one is reading, usually for the purpose of assessing the credibility of the information contained in the document. We differentiate between the source's credibility and the document's trustworthiness. It is quite possible for credible authors to write untrustworthy works and for noncredible authors to pen tomes of objective fact. Source evaluation is a heuristic that we use to assess document trustworthiness when we have no other means of verifying the veracity of the document. Mentally, sourcing involves constructing a more or less elaborated model of the author, based on available source information, and then evaluating the content of the document with respect to this model. Source information can include the author's name, credentials, and motives as well as information about the type of document and when it was written. There are three general components to skilled sourcing *identification*, *evaluation*, and *use*. A student using the Web for research, for example, may find a relevant page by using a search engine, or by following a path of links. In order to fully evaluate the information contained on the page, the student must identify the page's source and evaluate it as part of determining how trustworthy and reliable the information on the page might be. Finally, if the student intends to use the page as a reference or cite it in a research paper, he or she will need to keep a record of the source that is sufficient to return to the page at a later time.

With Web documents, perhaps the most difficult of these three components of sourcing is identifying the source. Printed documents tend to carry very standard information about the author and the type of document (e.g., a copyright page and an "About the author" description in an appendix or on a dust jacket). Identifying the source of a Web document differs in many ways from identifying the source of printed documents. In some cases, obtaining author information can be easier and richer for Web documents than for printed documents. On some pages, authors specify source information at the bottom of the page. This information usually includes the author's name, affiliation, and contact information (usually an e-mail address), and the date the page was created and/or last updated. On other pages, the author's name and other information may appear with the title (similar to a newspaper byline). Furthermore, when it is available, the quality of author information for Web documents can be better than that of printed documents. Some authors provide a link to their homepage where one can find out more about their credentials, background, perspective, and other documents they have written. Additionally, students are not necessarily limited to the author's autobiographical information. They can consult third party sources such as Contemporary Authors or other sites that carry biographical information on many current authors.

Unfortunately, many Web documents do not provide such rich source information. Frequently, author information is provided only on the first page of a multi page document. If someone locates one of the linked pages through a search engine, he or she may have a difficult time finding the title page and author information (depending on the quality of the navigation tools on the page or the obviousness of the page naming scheme). All too often, Web pages have no explicit source information at all. In these situations, a user can discover some clues about the legitimacy of a source by parsing the Uniform Resource Locator (URL) address, or visiting the homepage of the site. Evaluating a URL requires some understanding of standard patterns, such as that in the United States .com, .gov, .org, and .edu signify that a company, the government, a nonprofit organization, or an educational institution are the domains of the page, respectively. In the case of .com and .org sites one can also use familiar company names and brand names (e.g., "nytimes.com" or "microsoft.com") as indicators of authorship and credibility. In the case where a student finds a page by following a link, he or she might obtain information from the referring source. Unfortunately, Web pages tend to provide links in lieu of bibliographic information. Thus, the reader is left to infer something about the quality of the page's source by the quality and possible motives of the referring site (e.g., is this a link carried for a fee, or is it represented as a reliable source by the referrer?).

Another difficulty with obtaining source information on the Web is that many cues regarding document type are lost. Printed documents vary considerably and fairly consistently with document type. Paperback novels, for instance, look very different from bound legal proceedings. On the Web, these cues are lost or obscured. Pulp fiction and legal proceedings both appear as uniform text in a browser. Furthermore, one has a tendency to classify documents according to the application with which one views them (e.g., HTML viewed through a browser compared to a PDF file viewed through a plug-in) rather than the type of document.

Once a student identifies the source of a page (or obtains as much source information as possible), he or she is in a position to evaluate the source. In many ways, evaluating a Web document's source is the same as evaluating the source of a printed document. To evaluate a source, one must use everything one knows about the author and document to make a determination of the source's trustworthiness. Source evaluation depends on such features as the author's credentials, potential for bias, vantage point, and skill. It also depends on features of the document such as who published it, when it was written, and the type of document it is. One feature that is extremely important is the author's motive or purpose for writing the document. Authors may write to entertain, to persuade, to inform, and, frequently, to persuade in the guise of informing. Detecting an author's hidden bias is often difficult because texts are rarely completely biased and one-sided, but rather they subtly hide their bias and adopt an air of objectivity. Often source features that prove reliable in the print world are much less reliable in the Web world. For instance, reliance on brand names such as "the New York Times" for source evaluation may be less reliable in the on-line world where "time-to-story" is no longer once per day but once per hour, or less.

After evaluating a source, students need to keep track of the source information in order to later use it as a reference or as part of a research paper. Source information has several uses. First, supporting one's argument with a credible citation of an external source strengthens its support. Second, students make decisions about what sources to include in a paper and they can use their knowledge of sources to make sure to select the best or most important source to use (e.g., most relevant, most direct knowledge of events, or least bias). Third, in devising a plan for searching for information on a topic, students can use source information to help decide what type of documents to look for. For example, scholars can provide explanations and thoughtful analysis whereas primary sources provide crucial details. However, one general difficulty with keeping track of information found exclusively on the Internet is that links change and often become dead ends.

While the skill of sourcing is necessary, it is not generally in the repertoire of the average high school student. Wineburg (1991) found that experts, but not high school Advanced Placement students, sourced the texts they were given in a multiple-document learning situation. Our previous studies have shown that college students make restricted use of this skill and high school students are even less able or inclined to use it (Rouet et al., 1997; Britt et al., 1994). For instance, Rouet et al. (1997) found that college students asked to justify the trustworthiness and usefulness of a set of documents did mention many features of the author (e.g., author's credentials, motivations or participation in the events) and features of the document type (e.g., when it was written). In contrast, Britt et al. (1994) found that regular high school students rarely used the source of the document to justify their ranking when given the same task.

Further evidence that high school students are not skilled sourcers comes from an analysis of pretest data for a recent study (Britt & Aglinskas, in preparation). Students were given six short excerpts describing and analyzing the U.S. involvement in the Panamanian revolution. The set of documents included four excerpts that directly described a meeting between

U.S. President Theodore Roosevelt and a Panamanian revolutionary that occurred prior to the revolution. Three of these excerpts were from participants in that meeting (two letters from Roosevelt and the memoirs of the revolutionary); the fourth excerpt was from a novel. Students read the documents with sources at the bottom of the excerpt and were able to take notes that they could later use when answering questions. One of the questions asked students to list three facts that could be used to support or oppose US involvement in the revolution. We found that approximately 25% of the students listed an event that was only mentioned in the novel despite the fact that the novel was clearly indicated to be a work of fiction. These students clearly disregarded the fictional nature of the source when selecting an answer for the question.

Although college students do attend to sources more often then high school students, they are not experts in evaluating this information. Perfetti, Britt, Rouet, Georgi, and Mason (1994) found that while college students tend to notice author information, they are not always influenced by it. Thus, we find that college students, as well as high school students, need to improve their ability to identify, evaluate, and use source information. This skill is especially important as reliance on the Internet for research material increases.

C. Corroboration

Another way to assess the credibility of information in a document is to look for corroboration by other sources. Corroboration is the general skill of checking facts or interpretations from a particular document against other independent sources. It is commonly used by historians (Wineburg, 1991), print journalists, and academics, and is a necessary skill for anyone using the Internet for research. For example, while doing research for this chapter, the first author came across a story in a *Boston Globe Online* article about a UCLA survey of U.S. college freshmen that found that 83% of freshman used the Web for research and homework in the fall of 1999 (Sax, Astin, Korn, & Mahoney, 1999). In order to use this information in a paper or talk, the accuracy of the information first needed to be verified. This was done by locating the original source, in this case the home page for the Higher Education Research Institute at UCLA. This allowed not only verification of the study's findings but also provided elaborative details that enabled a fuller analysis of the information. While six months later the exact link used to verify the *Globe* information was "dead," it was still possible to write to the Institute and receive a copy of the report. This example illustrates both the need for corroboration and one of the major problems with corroborating information on the Internet: dead links or "link rot."

Corroboration is an important skill for students to have for several reasons. First, corroboration enables students to verify the accuracy of information before relying on it too heavily. Students can check new information against other independent documents or find the most direct source. Second, corroboration enables students to identify agreed upon facts, events, and interpretations and to weigh them appropriately. Third, because no single document can offer a complete picture of the situation or argument supplied, the act of corroboration enables students to locate unique information not mentioned in the original source. Finally, through corroboration, students can identify information sources that omit important generally agreed upon facts, interpretations, or alternatives, and this may serve as a red flag to identify whether an author may be intentionally deceptive or misleading.

The process of corroboration generally involves searching for comparison documents, comparing them, and appropriately using corroborating evidence. Searching for comparison documents generally involves using what one knows about the availability of bibliographic information. This includes using sources mentioned in the current document, collected bibliographies on the topic area, citation indexes, and databases (e.g., PsychInfo). The Web tends to replace these standard sources with archival sites (e.g., ftp://rtfm.mit.edu), links, and search engines. Of these, the search engine is the most ubiquitous and useful, but also one that requires skill to use. Nonspecific queries are likely to return millions of links to irrelevant Web pages. Selecting appropriate key words and constructing a Boolean query requires some knowledge of the domain, some metaknowledge about searching a large database of pages that contain many overlapping words, and a little understanding of Boolean logic. College students vary greatly in how they represent and carry out a Web search task. For example, in a recent upper division college course, the first author asked students to use the Web to find a page that could be helpful in writing chapters they were working on all term. An analysis of the pages shows that one-third of the students used the Web in a manner consistent with the course (e.g., using PsychInfo to locate a relevant article), while most located information that would not typically be usable in a term paper. Almost 25% located class notes from a professor's web site and 41% located summary information or articles from .com and .org sites. Many students reported frustration with the time taken to find relevant information.

After locating appropriate comparison documents, the student can then begin the comparison process. This process involves directly comparing the information from the various sources to identify which important statements are agreed upon, which are uniquely mentioned, and which are discrepant. A student may wish to differentially weight the credibility of statements that are uniquely mentioned or discrepant. Finally, once other sources have been located and the content compared, the student is in a situation where he or she can begin to use this information. The student will generally want to report a complete summary of the full story, including much of the agreed upon information. In addition, he or she will also want to include some of the more interesting less agreed upon unique information. When using this information, the student has a responsibility to the reader to provide support for this controversial information, noting it as uncorroborated and citing alternative sources if it is actually discrepant. Finally, the actual material used should be from the most primary source of information available. There is no reason to rely on another author's description or quotation of what is written in a particular document if that source is actually available.

As we found with sourcing, corroboration is typical of expert reading but not of high school readers (Wineburg, 1991). Not only is there a lack of spontaneous corroboration in high school students, there is also a problem that younger readers are not skilled navigators of hypertext, and do not have strategies for systematically searching through links (Rouet & Levonen, 1996). Having an adequate representation of the interconnections between supporting and conflicting sources is central to being able to use corroboration.

D. Summary

The three skills we have described, integrating, sourcing, and corroboration, are all characteristics of expert readers. We generally expect students to acquire these skills by the time they are in college, but they are generally not explicitly taught these skills in school. The research on multiple-document reading has shown that high school, and even college, students do not always have or use these skills. Thus, by introducing the Internet into grade school and high school classrooms, we are making new demands on students. Optimistically, the Internet might foster the development of these skills at an earlier age simply due to exposure to multiple documents. This will undoubtedly be the case for some students. More realistically, we need to develop methods for explicitly training these skills if we want students to become educated consumers of the vast quantities of information that are now available to them.

II. TEACHING ADVANCED LITERACY SKILLS

Our interest in training advanced literacy skills led us to create the Sourcer's Apprentice (SA), a Java application that tutors and provides practice opportunities for students to engage in sourcing and corroboration. Students use SA to read a small number of excerpts from multiple documents, identify various source components, answer source and content questions, and write short essays. These activities are all centered on content modules that currently involve historical controversies (e.g., to what extent was Andrew Carnegie responsible for the violent breaking of the Homestead steel strike).

The design of SA was driven by six principles from cognitive and educational theories: (1) learn by solving problems with richly integrated sets of documents, (2) support construction of expert representations such as document and argument models, (3) create an interface by decomposing the task into necessary elements, (4) support transfer by using a real world environment and providing several problems of very different types, (5) provide students with explicit and interactive instruction on the relevant skills, and (6) motivate student engagement through challenges and immediate feedback. A detailed description of these principles is given in Britt, Perfetti, van Dyke, and Gabrys (in press). We used these principles to guide the design of the skills tutorial, the content modules, and the practice environment. In the next section we briefly describe each of these three components of SA.

A. Skills Tutorial

Students using SA for the first time begin with an interactive skills tutorial. We are currently writing tutorials and designing the environment for the other literacy skills (e.g., integration, argumentation, and information search). SA provides a short interactive tutorial on sourcing and corroboration. The tutorial instructs students about a set of critical elements (see Figure 4.1), such as features of the author (i.e., Who, who wrote it; Position, what their position is; and How Know, how authors happen to know the information they are writing about), features of the document (i.e., When, when it was written; and Type, what type of document it is), and features of the content (i.e., Main Point, statement summarizing document's relevance to the controversy; Documents Mentioned, any external documents sited in the excerpt; and Comments, anything mentioned by the document of which the student may wish to take note). The tutorial then devotes an entire page of instruction to each of these components where students are briefly instructed on *identifying*, *using*, and *evaluating* each component. The How Know feature, for example, first instructs students on identifying the How Know information from the texts provided. Then they are given information on using the How Know information later such as when writing a paper. Finally they are taught how to evaluate information based on the How Know feature (e.g., judging the trustworthiness of the content). As with all the tutorial screens, just enough information is provided for each segment to get the student started. After reading a single tutorial page for a component of the target skill, students are asked two questions. The first question always addresses identification of the feature and the second question addresses something about either its use or its evaluation. For the tutorial, students read approximately eight pages of text and answer two questions following each page of instruction.

B. Content Modules

A content module is a set of documents and a set of questions about an historical controversy. The term "controversy" is used here to describe an event about which historians offer conflicting interpretations. For example, the controversy for our Homestead Steel Strike module is, "to what extent was Carnegie responsible for breaking the Union at Homestead?" The main task of students using SA is to read the set of documents, fill in on-screen note cards with source and content information, and then answer targeted questions and write a short essay about the controversy. The main screen is shown in Figure 4.1. Students are given the controversy statement at the top of the screen and a bookshelf representing excerpts from seven actual documents that are hierarchically structured with respect to generality. The most general document is an overview, usually a textbook excerpt. Next are works by two historians that provide analysis and interpretation of the controversy from opposing viewpoints. Finally, the most specific documents are four primary documents, such as letters and treaties, that provide data about very specific points made by each of the historians. Each document is generally 100 to 500 words in length. The order in which the books are presented

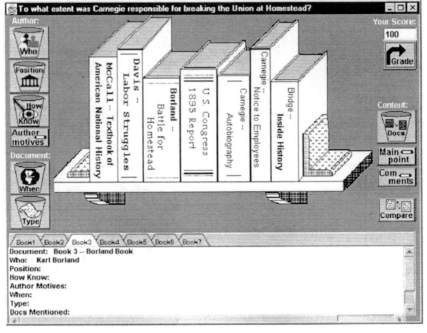

FIGURE 4.1
Structured note card from the Sourcer's Apprentice.

on the screen was selected based on previous studies showing that students do better in a complex reading situation when the document set is structured (Britt, Rouet, & Perfetti, 1996) and that domain novices often lack the knowledge to guide decision making through a document set (Foltz, 1996; Rouet, Favart, Britt, & Perfetti, 1998). This order we used is most general to most specific, from left to right. Students click on each book to open it and read information about the author, document type, and content. While they read each document they collect some information in on-screen note cards so they can later write an essay on this controversy using only their notes.

C. Practice Environment

The way that students practice sourcing and corroborating is by filling in the structured note cards shown at the bottom of Figure 4.1. Students read the excerpts from the books on the bookshelf by clicking on the book and bringing up a multitabbed window (see Figure 4.2). Students can change pages by clicking on the tabs at the bottom of the book to reveal four scrollable pages: a table of contents, an author page, a document page, and a content page. In Figure 4.2, the book is open to the author page which provides detailed

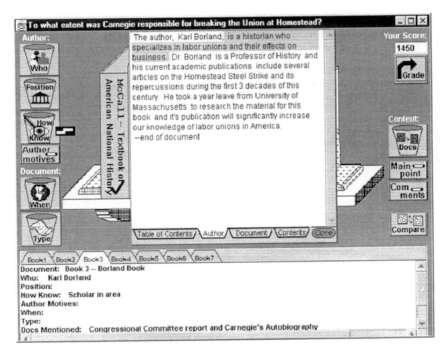

FIGURE 4.2
Author page from the Sourcer's Apprentice.

source information about the author's credentials and motives. The document page explains the type of document it is, who publishes it, and when it was written. Much of this information is of the type provided on the copyright page of actual books or in the reference book *Contemporary Authors* that is available electronically in many libraries. The actual excerpt can be found on the content page. Each time a book is opened a checkmark appears at the bottom of the book; a red checkmark indicates the most recently opened book and a blue checkmark indicates that the book was previously opened. This procedure for helping students keep track of their progress has proven useful in earlier studies (Britt et al., 1996; Rouet, 1990).

We do not presently have between-document hypertext links because previous research failed to show beneficial effects of such links (Britt et al., 1996; Rouet, 1990). In fact, Britt et al. (1996) found that rather than using document-to-document evidence links, students preferred to make selections from a table of contents instead. To support corroboration, we encourage students to make document-to-document comparisons by opening two documents on the screen simultaneously. By clicking the "Compare" button on the main screen, the student can display a second document next to the already opened document. For example, with the bookshelf shown in Figure 4.1, a reader might bring up Davis's book on the left and Carnegie's *Autobiography* on the right. This would be an interesting comparison for a student to make because Davis's book explicitly mentions Carnegie's *Autobiography*. This feature enables students to make a direct comparison between Davis's summary of Carnegie's excerpt and Carnegie's actual excerpt. In addition to checking interpretations of cited material, this feature also enables the student to compare arguments on opposing sides of a controversy.

While reading the documents, students fill in structured note cards that focus their attention on the source properties described earlier. Each note card has slots for the author's name (Who), title (Position), how the author knows this information (How Know), why it was written (Author Motives), date written (When), type of document (Type), and which other documents are explicitly mentioned in the current excerpt (Docs Mentioned). There is a separate note card for each document. To insert text into a note card, a student selects a phrase from the author, document, or content page of a document and drags it to the appropriate "bucket" icon on the left side of the screen. For example, for the document depicted in Figure 4.2, the phrase "is a historian who specializes in labor unions and their effects on business" is the correct answer to how the author knows the information in the excerpt. Clicking anywhere on this phrase causes it to be highlighted and dragging it to the "How Know" bucket causes the tutor to evaluate it. If this answer is correct, SA awards points (upper right-hand corner) and an abstracted and abbreviated form of the information is inserted into the note card (e.g., "Scholar in area"). If the answer is incorrect, SA pops up a dialog box indicating the error and offers a hint toward the right answer. These hints are graduated — starting vague (e.g., an historian would probably have an opinion on that point) and becoming more specific (e.g., Carnegie mentions that information in the last paragraph of his autobiography) until after a few incorrect attempts it literally tells the student which phrase to select. This is done to ensure that every student can complete the task even if they do not initially know what they are doing. The score awarded for an answer decreases with the number of hints received.

If, at any time, the student needs a reminder about the type of information that should be inserted into a line on the note card, he or she can click on the corresponding bucket. The text from the tutorial screens then appears in a pop-up window. For example, when a student clicks the "Why" bucket they see a screen that displays the tutor information on author motives in a slightly more elaborated form. By using the bucket help, students can obtain direct instruction on any of the note card features, but these screens only appear when a student asks for it. Students also use these screens to insert text directly into the note cards for three of the features (Author Motives, Main Point, and Comments). We decided that these features were too awkward to answer by dragging a phrase from the document, so students construct their own answer and are later graded on these by the teacher. Our intention is eventually to have all note cards be filled in this way after students have had repeated exposure to the environment, and training for that skill. At this point, they should no longer need immediate feedback.

After students finish reading the books, they write a short essay on the controversy. The bookshelf is replaced by a large window into which the students type their essay. The note cards the students filled in are always available to help them during the writing process. The books, on the other hand, are not available (unless the teacher wants them to be).

After writing the essay, a small question window appears at the bottom of the screen and students receive several questions about the documents they read. These questions are intended to verify that the information presented by the documents was understood. An example of a question to test students' sourcing ability is, "Which document was written earliest?" To answer each question, students must drag a phrase from one of the books into an "answer" bucket. If correct, the student receives 300 points. If incorrect, the student receives fewer points and gets the next in a series of graduated hints. These skill questions are interspersed with content questions to make sure that students are not ignoring the content while learning the target skill.

D. Effectiveness of the Sourcer's Apprentice

We have tested SA's effectiveness in two studies with high school students using a pretest–post-test methodology with treatment and control groups (Britt & Aglinskas, in preparation). Both the pretest and the post-test involved students reading a booklet containing six related documents, one document per page, with source information at the bottom (i.e., similar to an SA module). While reading, students took notes that they could use later when answering questions, including several targeted at attention to sourcing, such as which document was written earliest or which document was the least trustworthy. Different historical topics were used for the pretest, post-test, and treatment module.

In the first study, two 11th grade history classes were given the sourcing tutorial followed by a module over two to three consecutive class periods. One class used the Homestead Steel Strike module and the other used the Vietnam War module. Two matching classes were given no treatment. On the day after, the treatment students used the Sourcer's Apprentice, all students were given the post-test in their regular classroom, and no mention was made to the treatment students that this had anything to do with the prior activities in the computer room. On the post-test, we found that students given SA tutorial and practice mentioned more source features in their notes and answered more source questions correctly (relative to their pretest baseline) than did control subjects receiving no treatment. The pretest scores of the two groups did not differ.

Our second study was similar except for the control condition. In this experiment, both the experimental and the control groups were exposed to the same documents, however, we manipulated the organization of the materials. The treatment class was given the Homestead module through the Sourcer's Apprentice's environment. The control class was given the same documents in a textbook format in which each source was provided (e.g., either an indented quotation or as a footnote) but immediately interpreted to tell a single coherent story. As in the first experiment, we found that using the Sourcer's Apprentice resulted in significantly better sourcing performance on the transfer task compared to the pretest baseline.

These studies indicate that students' sourcing skills can be greatly improved through a simple training procedure. We expect similar results could be obtained for the other skills we described. Our intention with writing the Sourcer's Apprentice in Java was to make it available over the Web to any teacher who wished to use it in his or her classroom. We have put it on the Web, but we still need to do further development to improve the program before any widespread use can be considered. Interested readers are invited to try out the program at http://www.pitt.edu/~sourcers, while the link is still alive.

III. CONCLUSIONS

We have argued in this chapter that despite hopes for the Internet to be an educational panacea, it will actually create new learning demands on students. The situation faced by students using the Web for research is similar to that faced by history students learning to use primary and secondary sources: they must construct integrated representations from multiple documents of varying quality. Dealing with this situation requires the ability to integrate information from different documents, identify and evaluate the credibility of those documents based on source information, and corroborate the information extracted from those documents with other credible documents. Considerable research shows that high school students — and many college students — do not have, or do not readily use, these skills when reading. Thus, we conclude that efforts must be made to explicitly train these skills in order to enable students to make sense of the vast quantities of information the Internet makes available to them.

Finally, we described the Sourcer's Apprentice, an application to provide tutorial and practice opportunities in sourcing. This application, though relatively simple, has proven quite effective at increasing students' attention to source information. In the future, we expect to expand this program to include other advanced literacy skills — thus helping to prepare students for learning in the 21st century.

References

Britt, M. A., & Aglinskas, C. T. (In preparation). *Using the Sourcer's Apprentice to enhance high school students' sourcing in history.*

Britt, M. A., Goldman, S. R., & Perfetti, C. A. (1999, August). *Content integration in learning from multiple texts.* Paper presented at the Meeting of the Society for Text and Discourse, Vancouver, BC, Canada.

Britt, M. A., Perfetti, C. A., van Dyke, J., & Gabrys, G. L. (In press). The Sourcer's Apprentice: A tool for document-supported history instruction. In P. Stearns (Eds.), *Knowing, teaching and learning history: National and international perspectives.* New York: New York University Press.

Britt, M. A., Rouet, J.-F., & Perfetti, C. A. (1994, April). *Evaluation of source information in learning with history documents.* Paper presented at the Annual Meeting of the American Educational Research Association, New Orleans, LA.

Britt, M. A., Rouet, J.-F., & Perfetti, C. A. (1996). Using hypertext to study and reason about historical evidence. In J.-F. Rouet, J. J. Levonen, A. P. Dillon, & R. J. Spiro (Eds.), *Hypertext and cognition* (pp. 43–72). Mahwah, NJ: Erlbaum.

Foltz, P. (1996). Comprehension, coherence, and strategies in hypertext and linear texts. In J.-F. Rouet, J. J. Levonen, A. P. Dillon, & R. J. Spiro (Eds.), *Hypertext and cognition* (pp. 109–136). Mahwah, NJ: Erlbaum.

Johnson, C., & Seifert, C. M. (1996). Sources of the continued influence effect: When misinformation in memory affects later inferences. *Journal of Experimental Psychology: Learning, Memory, and Cognition, 20,* 1420–1436.

Johnson, C., & Seifert, C. M. (1999). Modifying mental representations: Comprehending corrections. In H. van Oostendorp, & S. R. Goldman (Eds.), *The construction of mental representations during reading.* Mahwah, NJ: Erlbaum.

Millis, K. K., & Erdman, B. J. (1998). Comprehending news articles: Updating the news. *Poetics, 25,* 343–361.

National Center for History in the Schools (1996). *National standards for United States history: Exploring the American experience.* Los Angeles: University of California, Los Angeles.

NCES (U. S. Department of Education, National Center for Educational Statistics). (1999, June 24). *Issue brief: Internet access in public schools and classrooms: 1994–98.* [on-line]. Available: http://nces.ed.gov/pubsearch/pubsinfo.asp?pubid=1999017

Perfetti, C. A., Britt, M. A., & Georgi, M. C. (1995). *Text-based learning and reasoning: Studies in history.* Hillsdale, NJ: Erlbaum.

Perfetti, C. A., Britt, M. A., Rouet, J.-F., Georgi, M. C., & Mason, R A. (1994). How students use texts to learn and reason about historical uncertainty. In M. Carretero & J. F. Voss (Eds.), *Cognitive and instructional processes in history and the social sciences* (pp. 257–283). Hillsdale, NJ: Erlbaum.

Rouet, J.-F (1990). Interactive text processing by inexperienced (hyper-) readers. In A. Rizk, N. Streitz, & J. Andre (Eds.), *Hypertexts: Concepts, systems, and applications* (pp. 250–260). Cambridge: Cambridge University Press.

Rouet, J.-F., Britt, M. A., Mason, R. A., & Perfetti, C. A. (1997). Using multiple sources of evidence to reason about history. *Journal of Educational Psychology, 88,* 478–493.

Rouet, J.-F., Favart, M., Britt, M. A., & Perfetti, C. A. (1998). Studying and using multiple documents in history: Effects of discipline expertise. *Cognition and Instruction, 15* (1), 85–106.

Rouet, J.-F., & Levonen, J. J. (1996). Studying and learning with hypertext: Empirical studies and their implications. In J.-F. Rouet, J. J. Levonen, A. P. Dillon, & R. J. Spiro (Eds.), *Hypertext and cognition* (pp. 9–24). Mahwah, NJ: Erlbaum.

Sax, L. J., Astin, A. W., Korn, W. S., & Mahoney, K. M. (1999, June 24). *The American freshman: National norms for fall 1999* [on-line]. Cooperative Institutional Research Program from the Higher Education Research Institute, UCLA. Available: http://www.gseis.ucla.edu/heri/cirp.htm

Van Oostendorp, H., & Bonebakker, C. (1999). Difficulties in updating mental representations during reading news reports. In H. van Oostendorp & S. R. Goldman (Eds.), *The construction of mental representations during reading.* Mahwah, NJ: Erlbaum.

Wineburg, S. S. (1991). Historical problem solving: A study of the cognitive processes used in the evaluation of documentary and pictorial evidence. *Journal of Educational Psychology, 83,* 73–87

CHAPTER

5

Creating Informal Learning Environments on the World Wide Web

CHRISTOPHER R. WOLFE

Miami University

In an early essay, Seymour Papert (1984) presents what seems to be a paradox about children and learning. He notes that without formal instruction, children in every culture learn a great deal in a very short period of time. Speaking and comprehending language, using everyday objects, and even manipulating parents are but a few of the skills that are mastered in the first years of life. Yet when children get to school the pace of learning seems to slow. Years of formal schooling lead to small changes at best, especially in the areas of science and mathematics. Does this imply that schools retard learning? Obviously not. Clearly, the difference lies in the nature of the material to be learned. Many skills are learned through direct experience, and these are generally "picked up" outside of school through experiential learning (Kolb, 1984). Other knowledge domains (e.g., science) entail a much higher degree of abstraction, and concrete experience is often insufficient to acquire abstract concepts. Thus, children do not seem to learn as well in school because it is harder to learn abstractions through "natural" methods such as play.

It was Papert's insight that if one could "reify abstractions," to manifest them in a form where children could explore them in a natural way, more of the experiential learning that stems from "everyday" activities could take place in abstract knowledge domains such as mathematics. The World Wide

Web (Web) is a cognitive technology that makes it possible to concretize scientific abstractions. Children have a natural curiosity that is expressed in exploring and manipulating the tangible world. Yet formal education rarely builds upon this curiosity. Perhaps Albert Einstein was correct in saying, "it is in fact nothing short of a miracle that modern methods of instruction have not entirely strangled the holy curiosity of inquiry. ... It is a very grave mistake to think that the enjoyment of seeing and searching can be promoted by means of coercion and a sense of duty" (quoted in Henniger, 1987, p. 169).

The Web is particularly well suited to promoting scientific reasoning and "the enjoyment of seeing and searching" favored by Einstein. A good deal of recent literature suggests that children are capable of learning scientific reasoning in schools through inquiry-based education (Herrenkohl & Guerra, 1998; White & Frederiksen, 1998; Zuckerman, Chudinova, & Khavkin, 1998). However, developing proficiency in scientific reasoning is difficult, and innovative informal education holds the promise of having a profound effect on children. This chapter describes principles and strategies that support the creation of informal learning environments on the Web. This discussion is informed by over five years of experience developing the Dragonfly Web Pages, an informal science education environment on the Web.

I. INFORMAL EDUCATION

Formal education refers to traditional approaches to teaching and learning in academic settings such as schools. The phrase "informal learning" is used more loosely. Informal education often refers to voluntary educational activities outside of traditional contexts such as the educational programming of museums, zoos, and educational television. An example of this approach is seen in a position statement of the National Science Teachers Association (NSTA):

> Informal science education generally refers to programs and experiences developed outside the classroom by institutions and organizations that include: Children's and natural history museums, science-technology centers, planetaria, zoos and aquaria, botanical gardens and arboreta, parks, nature centers and environmental education centers, and scientific research laboratories; Media, involving print, film, broadcast, and electronic forms; Community-based organizations and projects, including youth organizations and community outreach services. (NSTA, 1998, paragraph 1).

Other uses of the phrase "informal education" emphasize the pedagogical approach to learning, rather than the institutional setting. For example, according to the National Science Foundation's (NSF) Informal Science Education Program, informal education is characterized by learning that is voluntary and self-directed, life-long, and motivated mainly by intrinsic interests, curiosity, exploration, manipulation, fantasy, task completion, and social interaction. Informal learning can be linear or non-linear and often is self-paced and visual- or object-oriented. It provides an experiential base and motivation for further activity and learning. (NSF, 2000, paragraph 1).

Obviously, these components of the learning experience are not restricted to setting, and can occur either inside or outside the classroom.

Advocates of informal learning who focus on pedagogy often view the informal–formal dichotomy as an oversimplification. For example, taking an anthropological perspective, Strauss (1984) argues that this dichotomy is ethnocentric. He offers an alternative taxonomic framework that includes incidental learning, intentional learning with ill-defined procedures, and intentional learning with well-defined procedures, with different acquisition strategies. For present purposes it is useful to recognize that informal education is conceptualized in various ways, including by the settings in which it occurs, the practices of instruction, and particular cognitive learning processes. In the case of the Dragonfly Web Pages, some children visit the pages from classrooms and home schooling environments, and many more visit of their own volition. Thus, all of these considerations should influence the development of informal learning environments on the Web. Most important, perhaps, is the rich potential of the Web as a medium of informal education, however conceived. Emerging Web technologies may lead to a renaissance in informal education because the Web holds the promise of promoting self-directed life-long learning, expanding learning beyond the classroom, and supporting alternative social organizations for learning and teaching.

II. THE NATURE OF THE WEB

The Web is a medium that encourages brief encounters. We use phrases such as "browsing" and "surfing" to describe our experience with the Web rather than "studying" and "contemplation." These phrases highlight the ephemeral nature of these interactions. Thus, as a medium, the Web is not well suited to lengthy presentations of text, although book-length manuscripts can easily be made into Web pages. Rather, the Web is well suited to drawing children into brief, voluntary, interactive learning experiences. However, theoretical approaches to designing such informal learning experiences on the Web have not yet been articulated.

Unlike traditional media, interactive technologies afford opportunities for new forms of interaction and communication. Recent research on interactive satellite-based training suggests that high levels of interaction and participant empowerment are key ingredients of successful technology-based education (Wolfe, Wang, & Bergen, 1999). Children today appear more receptive than their elders to taking charge of their own learning in digital domains (Tapscott, 1998) and interaction and empowerment are likely to be central to creating successful educational Web pages.

The Web is, first and foremost, an interactive medium. However, "interactivity" refers to a number of characteristics, and it is necessary to distinguish among them. One sense in which the Web is interactive is that it facilitates communication among a community of people (Jonassen, 1995; Riva, chapter 7 this volume). E-mail links, feedback forms, integrated databases, and threaded discussions are all ways in which the Web facilitates interaction among people. For example, the Dragonfly Web Pages make extensive use of feedback forms, and the site provides access to e-mail discussion lists. The Web is a medium that connects people in many-to-one any many-to-many communities (Harasim, 1989). Some Web sites contain "mutable spaces" where visitors change the content experienced by themselves and others. Virtual white boards and threaded discussion lists are two examples of mutable spaces. In these cases, visitors actually change the pages in ways that are visible to subsequent visitors, as when a visitor draws a picture of a cat on a white board. Other visitors may then add whiskers or erase the drawing entirely.

Simulation is the third approach to interactivity, and a major thrust of the Dragonfly Web Pages. Some simulations, such as flight simulators, seek to mimic an environment in great detail. Others, such as the popular computer games SimEarth and SimCity, and the Dragonfly Web Pages, abstract key variables and present the user with a set of critical decisions. In this approach, users make a number of decisions and receive images, sound, and text that are tailored to their responses. In these simulations, users navigate nonlinear "texts," and different users may have different experiences depending on their behavior. Simulations of this kind promote some of the same critical thinking skills as hypertext (Wolfe, 1995a) and share some of the rhetorical structure of hypermedia (Landow, 1991).

Computer-based learning technologies have frequently been used in ways that alter the traditional roles of student and teacher by shifting the focus from instructor-centered to student-centered activities (Locatis & Weisberg, 1997; Menges, 1994; Wolfe, Crider, et al., 1998). Applying a student-centered approach to informal education represents a logical extension of these efforts. Within the last several years there has been much speculation that the Internet will transform teaching and learning, and replace traditional schools altogether (see Eamon, 1999, for a thoughtful discussion of extreme claims about the Internet and higher education). These discussions have generally focused upon the Web as a medium of distance learning. In considering distance learning, the chief psychological issues are "which theories, strategies, and approaches promote learning at a distance."

Technologies used to promote learning at a distance have historically been based on "positivistic" instructional design theory (Dick, 1996; Dick &

Carey, 1996), or no theory at all. "There is no question that the major principles of instructional design have been derived from Skinnerian psychology and Gagne's conditions of learning" (Dick, 1991, p. 41). However, recently cognitive psychologists have come to the forefront in the research and development of distance learning experiences (e.g. Anderson, 1997–1998). I find behaviorist instructional design principles particularly inappropriate for promoting informal education on the Web. Computers are cognitive tools (Lajoie & Derry, 1993), and cognitive technologies such as the Web can be used to create rich learning environments. Rather than asking which theories promote learning at a distance, this analysis suggests the question, "which theories, strategies, and approaches best aid the development of Web resources that lead children to voluntarily engage in higher-order thinking, develop and refine their mental representations of complex subject matter, and increase intrinsic motivation to explore and learn?" Fostering scientific reasoning, and increasing motivation, and the ability to engage in inquiry are the goals of the Dragonfly Web Pages.

III. THE DRAGONFLY WEB PAGES

The Dragonfly Web Pages are located at http://www.muohio.edu/dragonfly/ and have been on the Web since March 25, 1996. As of this writing, the Dragonfly Web Pages have received over 400,000 visits to the main Dragonfly home page, with the hit rate increasing over time (Wolfe, Myers, & Cummins, in press). The Dragonfly Web Pages consist of nearly 400 interlinked pages. Today about 800 people visit the main home page of the Dragonfly Web Pages each day, or over 23,000 per month, compared with 420 total visitors in the month of April 1996. A number of independent organizations have honored the Dragonfly Web Pages with unsolicited awards. The British Broadcasting Corporation *Education Web Guide* states that they are "particularly impressed by the quality and educational content." The pages were awarded the Digital Dozen for "outstanding math and science Internet sites" from the Eisenhower National Clearinghouse for Science and Mathematics. *Web This Week* awarded the Dragonfly Web Pages four stars based on detailed reviews. They were also "Hot Site of the Day" in USA *Today*.

The Dragonfly Web Pages are organized around themes such as trees, space, time, navigation, and skeletons. There is a new edition for each theme, and generally, each edition has several features or departments represented by several interlinking Web pages. The departments of each edition of the Dragonfly Web Pages are (1) brief illustrated expository text; (2) an interactive experience where children apply what they learn; (3) a side bar designed to be of interest to children; (4) links to related resources; and (5) off-line investigations. Each edition has most of these departments, but relatively few have all. Editions vary greatly in their popularity, as measured

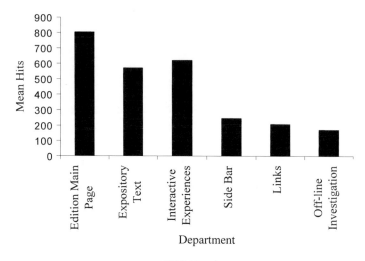

FIGURE 5.1

Mean hits per department across 16 editions in January 2000.

by the number of visitors per month. For example, in the month of January 2000, the main page of the Ice and Snow edition had 2606 visitors and the main page of Earth Sounds had 469 visitors. There are many reasons for these differences. New editions are featured on the top of the Dragonfly home page, and thus get more attention. Conversely, older editions are better represented in search engines. Finally, of course, some themes are more popular with children than others.

Departments also vary greatly in popularity from edition to edition. Figure 5.1 (from Wolfe et al., in press) depicts mean hits per department over 16 editions in the month of January 2000. Because the Water edition, and especially the off-line inquiry, "create your own water cycle," received so many visitors (8325), it was excluded from this figure. It can be seen that, generally, the interactive experiences were the most popular. Interactive Experiences received a mean of 622 visitors in January 2000. However, the great range in popularity from edition to edition makes generalization unwarranted (for a more detailed analysis of the hit rate data and patterns of visitation to the Dragonfly Web Pages, see Wolfe et al., in press). Below, each department is considered in greater detail.

A. Expository Text

Articles by adult scientists such as Jane Goodall, and children's reports of their own investigations, teach visitors scientific principles related to each theme. Because the Web is a graphic medium, these pages are illustrated and relatively brief. By modeling processes of inquiry, they also teach scientific reasoning skills such as formulating testable hypotheses. For example, in the Flight edition of the Dragonfly Web Pages (http://www.muohio.edu/dragonfly/flight/), the expository text explains the influences of thrust, drag, lift, and gravity on an airplane. This is combined with a piece about Paul MacCready, who won the first Kremer Prize for building a human-powered airplane that could fly around a mile-long, figure-eight course. Thus, students learn scientific principles in the context of investigations, such as MacCready's exploration of human-powered flight.

B. Interactive Experiences

The interactive experiences on the Dragonfly Web Pages are brief interactive decision making games. They are "bite-sized" experiences, generally taking less than 10 minutes to complete, and interactive in the sense of other simulations, as previously discussed. These experiences are game-like in that the visitor is placed in a fanciful hypothetical situation and given a goal. To achieve these goals, the visitor must make decisions about how to apply what they are learning. For example, on the Ice and Snow pages (http://www.muohio.edu/dragonfly/snow/) visitors read about characteristics of snow, and then they are invited to "make a flake." Visitors are encouraged to "create your own 'virtual' snowflakes for different weather conditions" by describing the air temperature, flake size, and the shape of the snowflake in three climates within the United States. Visitors read a brief statement and get to see a picture of their type of snowflake (for example, hexagonal stellar crystals or a "stud" snowflake composed of two snowflakes attached through their centers by an ice crystal). They learn that hexagonal stellar crystal flakes can be found anywhere it snows, hexagon plate flakes form high in the clouds, and stud snowflakes form only in very cold conditions. Other interactive decision-making games invite visitors to go on a virtual dinosaur dig, design an experiment to see if chimps can make tools, guide an expedition to Mars searching for evidence of life, and design a tree to grow in the understory of a temperate forest. Each of these games distills key points from expository text to create choice points in the simulation. Generally, visitors are put in a powerful position, sometimes even "playing god" as when designing a tree or a snowflake.

It is well established that context has demonstrable effects on learning and instruction (Tessmer & Richey, 1997). These games provide meaningful contexts for applying what is being learned. By striving to achieve goals in meaningful contexts, visitors think through the relationships among key variables such as the shape of a tree and its ability to compete for sunlight in the understory of a forest. In addition to setting goals and creating meaningful contexts, the Dragonfly Web Pages make interactive decision-making games of optimal difficulty for a wide range of children. Games that are too difficult lead to frustration, guessing, and quitting. A game that is too easy is not a game at all.

An index to the difficulty of these interactive decision-making games is the pattern of hits across various options. Each decision can be thought of as a pathway, and the terminal points of those pathways are unique Web pages containing specific feedback tailored to a constellation of responses. For example, on "Spider Paradise Island," visitors must decide whether or not there is a colony of seabirds on the island, whether the island is large or small, and whether the ocean currents around the island are swift or still. Visitors then get to see a picture of their island and read about its suitability for spiders.

The three binary decisions lead to eight possible outcomes. According to research by Gary Polis presented on the Dragonfly Web Pages, the optimal choice is a small island with nesting birds, in swift currents. Visitors who choose this option are told, "Your spiders share their island with a colony of seabirds. Dr. Polis found eight times more spiders on islands with bird colonies. Your island is small and, thus, has a lot of shoreline per square meter of island. Finally, the currents off your island are swift, bringing plenty of food from the sea. You have described a paradise for spiders."

From June 1997 through January 2000, 3949 visitors completed this interactive decision-making game. The page corresponding to the best answers was visited 1021 times, or by about 26% of those completing the game. The next most popular set of responses corresponded to a small island with nesting birds in still currents, with 535 hits (14%), and the least popular set of decisions described the island as large, free of seabirds, and surrounded by swift currents, with 325 hits (8%). All told, of those completing the game, 2445 (62%) described the island as inhabited by seabirds; 2340 (59%) described the island as small; and 2225 (56%) described it as surrounded by swift currents. These data suggest a game of moderate difficulty. Although the optimal set of responses was much more popular than each of the others (26% versus 14% or less), 74% described the island with a less than ideal set of responses. However, the best choice on each of the three options was made by only slightly more than half of the visitors. This may suggest, for example, that the expository text describing the importance of swift currents could be improved. Of course, the ability to provide detailed, tailored feedback facilitates learning for everyone who plays. Other interactive decision making games yielded similar patterns (Wolfe et al., in press).

C. Side Bars

A side bar in a magazine or textbook refers to a brief piece often appearing in a highlighted column that is distinct from, yet tangentially related to, an article. On the Dragonfly Web Pages, many editions have side bars on materials that are related to the theme, and of interest to children. Popular side bars include bird-eating spiders, the cries of wolf puppies, and the most accurate clock in the world. The lesser black bird-eating spider (*Xementhis immensis*) is described and illustrated in the Webs of Life edition. In the Animal Communication edition, children can click on a picture of a wolf pup to hear vocalizations. Finally, on the Time pages, visitors can see a picture of an atomic clock, and learn about how it works. Side bars vary in popularity. The kinds of information found in these side bars are relatively common among children's magazines and Web sites. Moreover, it can be seen that this department is not as popular as the interactive experiences that are the heart of the Dragonfly Web Pages (see Figure 5.1). Side bars are a means of "spicing up" the pages; however, they are not a substitute for the more substantive experiences.

D. Links to Related Resources

As stated previously, building curiosity and increasing motivation are among the goals of the Dragonfly Web Pages. As visitors become interested in a topic, it is important to channel their heightened curiosity toward further investigations. Links to related resources, and assistance with off-line investigations (below), are ways of capitalizing on increased motivation. The strategy is to "strike while the iron is hot." Providing links to related Web sites is one way to make related resources immediately available to children. The Dragonfly Hot Links page (http://www.muohio.edu/dragonfly/links.htmlx) provides annotated links to 118 Web sites on topics ranging from art and astronomy to writings by children. There have been 26,129 visitors to this page since April 1996, and in January 2000 it received 556 visitors. Each of these sites has been screened for children. Several editions of the Dragonfly Web Pages have their own focused hot links pages, for example, Map and Orienteering Hot Links in the Navigation edition, Space Links in the Space edition, and Spider Web Links in the Webs of Life edition. Of course, books are an excellent source of information (and a better medium than the Web for going in depth into some topics). The Dragonfly Web Pages provides annotated bibliographies for children, such as Further Reading About Ice and Snow. The Web puts a good deal of information at the visitor's fingertips. Strategically placed links to relevant information for children encourages additional learning.

E. Off-line Investigations

Perhaps the most important goal of Project Dragonfly is to encourage children to pursue their own investigations of the natural world. The Dragonfly Web Pages encourage "off-line" investigations (generally outdoors) by providing resources to help children engage in inquiries related to the theme of the edition. For example, in the Flight edition, the Great Airplane

Challenge encourages children to collect data about the flight of paper airplanes. A Pet Communication Survey in the Animal Communication edition invites children to ask questions about how their pets communicate. In the Houses edition, children learn how best to observe bats, and they can take part in a national survey on the observed behavior of bats. These pages differ dramatically in popularity. For example, in January 2000 the airplane challenge was visited 558 times, the pet communication survey was visited 214 times, and the bat behavior survey was visited only 34 times. Children's interests, seasonal variations, and differing popularity of the themes may account for some of these differences (Wolfe et al., in press).

The strategy for the off-line investigation department is to provide enough detail so that children will be able to conduct an investigation with little or no adult supervision, while at the same time providing opportunities to allow children to empirically address their own questions. The purpose of this department is to encourage and legitimate inquiry. Combining specific procedures with open-ended questions promotes investigation. Resources such as these help visitors to the Web site turn their interests into action.

F. Assessment and Evaluation

Informal education of any kind poses a number of problems of assessment and evaluation — particularly on the Web. The complexities of assessing informal learning environments are best addressed by employing converging research methodologies. Experimental comparisons, observational studies, visitor feedback, and detailed visitor activity data work together to create a composite portrait of the learner. Each method has its strengths and weaknesses, and those weaknesses can be overcome by considering the research problem from more than one perspective (see Wolfe et al., in press, for a more thorough discussion of the assessment of the Dragonfly Web Pages).

In chapter 2, Reyna and her colleagues argue that "randomized control trials are required for proper evaluation of interventions, and they are the only ethical avenue for introducing major educational changes that affect students." Although this is generally true of formal education, the voluntary nature of informal learning experiences makes experimental comparisons problematic, and standard practice inappropriate. Visitors to informal learning environments on the Web visit of their own volition. Thus, as contrasted with traditional educational research methods, comparisons to alternative teaching methods lose their meaning. The purpose of most empirical research is to reliably generalize from a sample to a population. When considering informal learning environments, the population of interest is visitors to the Web site rather then children everywhere. A random sample of this population would be taken from people who would choose to visit a Web site, or potential visitors, rather than the larger population as a whole. Both the popularity of a site and what visitors actually learn are of interest. A

Web site without any visitors would obviously be of little educational value, but so would a Web site that teaches what visitors already know. Thus, if a Web site were pitched at a level well beneath its actual visitors, it too would be of little educational value — even if those visitors knew more than a random sample of children who might benefit from the information.

Randomized experimental comparisons can be employed in informal learning environments by treating "all visitors" as the population of interest. In this approach, visitors arrive at the page of their own volition, without any additional prodding. Visitors are then invited to participate is a study where they agree to be randomly assigned to control or experimental conditions. However, they may be promised access to the information of interest, and other rewards, once the experiment has been completed. It is not known whether experimental comparisons such as this lead to unacceptably high dropout rates. This technique is similar to the use of a "wait list control" in assessing the impact of Dragonfly magazine on scientific reasoning in classrooms (see Wolfe, Halas, & Arthur, 1999). Unfortunately, there were insufficient resources to include an experimental investigation of the Dragonfly Web Pages. Readers are encouraged to see Joinson and Buchanan, chapter 11, (this volume) for a discussion of conducting educational research on the Web.

Methods of assessment for the Dragonfly Web Pages include patterns of hits across pages, feedback from visitors via e-mail and feedback forms, a small observational study of children interacting with The Dragonfly Web Pages, and unsolicited awards from independent organizations. The Web site has a feedback form and e-mail links that provide feedback from visitors (see Wolfe et al., in press, for a thorough discussion of the assessment of the Dragonfly Web Pages). Ninety-two percent (92%) of visitors made positive evaluations, and only 8% made negative evaluations (Wolfe et al., under review). The adjectives most frequently used to describe the Dragonfly Web Pages were "Great," "Good," "Like," and "Cool." Examples of positive feed-back include the following comments from parents, teachers, and children. From a parent, "This is a terrific site! I came here looking for some basic information to explain to my 9 year old about how trees grow, how they're shaped, and how the seeds are spread in the forest. This site is very educational, well written and entertaining." A teacher wrote, "It is a wonderful site. I will use this to make students active participants in science activities and experiments. Excellent!" Another teacher said, "I thoroughly enjoyed your site. I was delighted to find factual informational and 'virtual' experiences for my students. I will be teaching fourth grade for the first time this year. Needless to say, but I will anyway, I'll be showing this site to my kids." Not surprisingly, children wrote many of the comments. For example, one child wrote, "IT'S AWESOME!!!!!!!!!!!!!!!!!!!! I am the head of a club in school that I started to save trees. We learn about and plant and save trees. I will show this Web site to all the members. I think it is great because you're just not learning but you're having fun to!" Another child wrote, "I love this site! It is soooo much fun! I found it by accident and am glad that I did. I am doing a Web site summary for one of my classes and this site is my favorite so far." Negative comments tended to be brief. Examples of negative statements include, " it is very boring," "I hate it," "it is very bad," and "it was terribal" (sic). Judging from hit rate data, less that 1 in 1000 visitors made evaluative comments, and the sample is far from random (Wolfe et al., in press). Nonetheless, the overwhelming positive feedback suggests that many parents, teachers, and children enjoy the Web site, and believe it has educational merit.

IV. PRINCIPLES GUIDING THE DRAGONFLY WEB PAGES

The Dragonfly Web Pages are built upon the pedagogy of Project Dragonfly as well as a set of psychological principles adapted to informal science education on the Web. In developing these pages, the nature of the Web, the informal context, and children's interests have all been taken into account. From the perspective of children, the interactive decision-making games are a form of play. The literature on play provides insights useful to creating informal learning environments. Informal education is, almost by definition, learner centered. Thus, learner-centered educational principles have helped guide the creation of these pages. Finally, giving visitors a better "feel" for scientific phenomena is a major goal of these pages. Thus, research on gist formation informs the development of the Dragonfly Web Pages.

A. APA Learner-Centered Psychological Principles

The Dragonfly Web Pages are founded upon student-centered pedagogy (Wolfe, 1992), requiring visitors to take an active role in their own learning. It is well established that learning takes place when children are actively engaged (e.g., Brooks & Brooks, 1993) and have meaningful experiences (Resnick, 1989). The work of the Learner-Centered Principles Work Group of the American Psychological Association's Board of Educational Affairs has been particularly helpful in informing these efforts. The Work Group outlined 14 principles based on a thorough review of the literature. Five of these principles address cognitive and motivational factors influencing learning, and because of their utility, are discussed here in some detail.

The nature of the learning process is the theme of the first APA principle: "The learning of complex subject matter is most effective when it is an intentional process of constructing meaning from information and experience. ... Successful learners are active, goal-directed, self-regulating, and assume personal responsibility for contributing to their own learning" (Learner-

Centered Principles Work Group, 1997, paragraph 3). For the most part, children interacting with the Dragonfly Web Pages are there because they want to be, and actively construct meaning from experience. The pages endeavor to provide learning experiences that children find personally meaningful. This is accomplished by providing many choices for visitors, and many choice points in their interactive experience. Intentional learning is supported in environments where learners play a decision-making role and are challenged with tasks that require them to construct a mental representation from new and existing information to achieve meaningful goals.

The second APA principle considered here describes the role of goals in the learning process: "The successful learner, over time and with support and instructional guidance, can create meaningful, coherent representations of knowledge. The strategic nature of learning requires students to be goal directed" (paragraph 4). The interactive experiences at the heart of the Dragonfly Web Pages are goal directed. Children try to "design" a tree for a specific environment, "construct" a human-powered aircraft, or find hidden sea creatures. Successfully completing these virtual tasks requires developing a cognitive representation that integrates ideas from ecology, such as competition; concepts from physics, such as thrust and drag; and gestalt psychology principles of camouflage. These interactive experiences tap into the "strategic nature of learning" by confronting visitors with environments where they must apply what they are learning to achieve relevant goals.

The construction of knowledge is the topic of the third learner-centered principle discussed here: "The successful learner can link new information with existing knowledge in meaningful ways. Knowledge widens and deepens as students continue to build links between new information and experiences and their existing knowledge base" (paragraph 5). Materials on the Dragonfly Web Pages are integrated with children's previous knowledge, and children are explicitly encouraged to make links to existing knowledge. Materials on topics such as trees, water, and sports take what children know as the starting point for learning science. Links between new experiences and existing knowledge are further refined through constructivist inquiry exercises. For example, in the Webs of Life edition, visitors read about Gary Polis's explorations of scorpion populations on islands off the coast of Baja California. They are then encouraged to explore "backyard islands" — ecosystems that can be found in a park or lawn. Visitors learn that just as ocean currents transport food and energy to islands, detritus — dead leaves, insect shells, and other organic matter — is often a major source of energy in their backyard environments. By exploring how leaves that blow into a schoolyard from a nearby wood affect local plants and animals, children begin to construct integrated representations of scientific principles that incorporate newly learned materials, existing scientific knowledge, and lived experience.

The context of learning is the subject of the fourth APA principle considered here: "Learning is influenced by environmental factors, including culture, technology, and instructional practices. ... Technologies and instructional practices must be appropriate for learners' level of prior knowledge, cognitive abilities, and their learning and thinking strategies" (paragraph 8). The Dragonfly Web Pages provide meaningful contexts for learning and use technology in developmentally appropriately ways. Although the decisions visitors make may be sophisticated from a cognitive standpoint, navigation is accomplished through simple point-and-click procedures. A global medium such as the Web requires a good deal of cultural sensitivity. For example, I have received e-mail from children in every region of the United States, and from 19 other countries including Bahran, China, India, Israel, Malaysia, Mexico, Morocco, and Singapore. Even if published in only one language, issues of culture, as well as geography and climate, abound.

The last APA learner-centered principle addressed in this chapter concerns intrinsic motivation to learn:

> The learner's creativity, higher order thinking, and natural curiosity all contribute to motivation to learn. Intrinsic motivation is stimulated by tasks of optimal novelty and difficulty, relevant to personal interests, and providing for personal choice and control. ... Intrinsic motivation is facilitated on tasks that learners perceive as interesting and personally relevant and meaningful, appropriate in complexity and difficulty to the learners' abilities, and on which they believe they can succeed. Intrinsic motivation is also facilitated on tasks that are comparable to real-world situations and meet needs for choice and control. (Paragraph 10)

The Dragonfly Web Pages foster intrinsic motivation by providing choices and decision points that give visitors a sense of control. As previously noted, one interactive experience invites children to "make" a snowflake that would typically fall in an Ohio winter. The child must manipulate parameters such as temperature and shape. They then get to see a picture of their snowflake and learn about the environments where they are most typically found. The goal is to create problems of appropriate difficulty that are intrinsically interesting and relevant to children. Problems such as these are novel in the sense that they fall outside of a child's everyday experience, and yet rely on familiar and engaging materials. On-line interactive experiences such as this require some degree of intrinsic motivation to attract visitors in the first place. They in turn increase intrinsic motivation for subsequent exploration and discovery. In fostering curiosity and promoting intrinsic motivation, the Dragonfly Web Pages seek to increase the degree of effort children put into their own inquiries. Thus on-line activities legitimize and support the extended efforts required by off-line investigation.

B. Play and Learning

Trumbull (1990) describes scientists as "people who play with ideas in order to change the complex into the simple" (in Goldhaber, 1994, p. 26). Play is important in the development of a scientist (Wolfe, Cummins, & Myers,

1998), and the Dragonfly Web Pages are designed to be a place where children play to learn. From an educational perspective, some key characteristics of play are that it is internally motivated, motivating, self-directed, and characterized by some degree of divergent "as if" thinking (Spodek & Saracho, 1987). Science is a process of shared systematic inquiry. Exploratory representational play (ERP) in the late elementary school years (roughly 8 to 12 years old) is a pivotal experience in developing the ability to engage in shared systematic inquiry (Wolfe, Cummins, & Myers, 1998). The term "exploratory representational play" means play comprised of intrinsically motivated, self-directed explorations with a significant symbolic or representational dimension. Although important to developing scientific thinking, ERP is not the predominate mode of play for older children (see Bergen, 1988, p. 64, for a clear portrait of developmental trends in play).

In considering what is meant by ERP it is useful to distinguish it from related concepts. ERP is not identical to exploration. Children and adults often engage in explorations that are serious, extrinsically motivated, other directed, or otherwise not play. Recent research supports the notion that children are capable of scientific reasoning in schools through inquiry-based instruction (Herrenkohl & Guerra, 1998; White & Frederiksen, 1998; Zuckerman, et al., 1998). My assessment of Project Dragonfly further demonstrates that 8- to 12-year-old children are capable of engaging in shared systematic inquiry — science — in schools (see Wolfe, Halas, & Arthur, 1999, for a brief account of preliminary findings). However, shared systematic inquiry need not be "play" in any of the ways described above. ERP is also different from the exploratory play common among infants and toddlers. ERP is primarily goal directed and cognitive, rather than kinesthetic in nature. ERP is representational in the sense of mental representations that are personally meaningful to the individual, and may or may not manifest themselves concretely, (Wolfe, Cummins, & Myers, 1998).

The observation that play is important in the development of scientific reasoning seems to be supported by the literature. Henniger (1987) argued that learning science and mathematics through play promotes curiosity, motivation to learn, and divergent thinking. Pepler and Ross (1981) compared the effects of children's playing with convergent and divergent materials (form boards and puzzles) on subsequent convergent and divergent problem solving. They found that the divergent playgroup performed better on divergent tasks, and that the convergent playgroup employed more strategy-based moves in solving convergent problems. Tracy (1987) conducted a review of the literature on the relationship between spatial abilities, scientific achievement, toy playing habits, and gender roles. She found indirect evidence that socially stereotyped "boy toys" promote spatial abilities which are employed extensively in some kinds of scientific thinking. In subsequent research, Tracy (1990) found a positive correlation between spatial ability and science achievement scores. Although science can be serious business, the literature suggests that learning to do science can be facilitated by play.

The concept of ERP guides the creation of the interactive decision-making games. First, the game must be intrinsically motivating. The data from the hit counters suggest that the interactive experiences are, in aggregate, the most popular department of the Dragonfly Web Pages (see Figure 5.1). Second, to play the games, children must play with their mental representation. For example, to determine which shape of tree works best in the understory of an Ohio woods, the child must develop a mental representation of the forest and consider the dimensions of competition for light and the relative position of the sun throughout the day. Of course, a player could simply guess at responses, but the instructions and feedback promote playing with the mental representation. Part of what makes the games "playful" is that they ask the visitor to take on roles that are outside everyday experience. Perhaps this is why having visitors take a fanciful role such as the creator of a tree or a snowflake has proved popular and successful. For example, data from hit counters reveal that in January 2000, 3268 children completed "Make a Flake." Reciting facts about snow and playing with one's mental representation of how snowflakes are formed are two distinct mental activities. Below we will consider how ERP can serve to "educate intuitions."

C. "Intuition" and Mental Representation

A scientific understanding of the nature of "intuition" is informed by fuzzy-trace theory (Reyna & Brainerd, 1995), which describes the process of gist formation in a comprehensive framework. Fuzzy-trace theory has important ramifications for cognitive processes such as learning, reasoning, and memory, and enjoys strong empirical support (Brainerd & Reyna, 1990a,b; Reyna, 1991; Reyna & Brainerd, 1989, 1995; Wolfe, 1995b).

> The basic claim is that when information is encoded, global gist-like patterns, impressions, and essences are encoded along with verbatim information. The result is a multifaceted fuzzy-to-verbatim representation of information. Individual knowledge items are represented along a continuum such that vague, fuzzy-traces coexist with more precise verbatim representations. Moreover, people exhibit a strong preference to reason with the vaguest gist-like representations allowable for a given task (Wolfe, 1995b, p. 86).

Research on cognitive development suggests that young children initially reason with verbatim representations, and as they develop, gain an ability to reason with increasingly fuzzy representations (Reyna, 1991).

From a fuzzy-trace perspective, the interactions that takes place on the Dragonfly Web Pages facilitate the encoding of useful and meaningful gist by creating tasks with "the right mix" of familiar and novel components. For example, an exploration of conditions on different planets in our solar system invites children to play a "virtual baseball game" on planets that differ in gravity and prevailing wind speed. By adjusting the strength of the bat, children get an intuitive feel for the differences between the gravitational fields of Earth and Jupiter that exceeds a mere recitation of facts. The Dragonfly Web Pages help children develop and refine intuitions (gist) because it puts them into the position of attempting tasks where existing intuitions and verbatim representations are inadequate. Although science is a matter of precision, scientific insight and understanding require the development of subtle and nuanced intuitions.

V. STRATEGIES FOR CREATING INFORMAL LEARNING ENVIRONMENTS ON THE WEB

A major impetus for this chapter is to encourage others to develop informal learning environments on the Web. Toward that end, we will consider theories, strategies, and techniques that facilitate the creation of effective learning environments. These strategies are based on my experience with the Dragonfly Web Pages and my understanding of the research literature on cognition, instruction, development, and technology. The preceding discussion suggests a model of the learner in an informal environment. Ideally, the learner is curious, intrinsically motivated, and playful. Such learners are active, self-regulating, and goal directed. They form complex mental representations by successfully integrating previous knowledge and new experiences. These mental representations include memory traces that are vague, fuzzy, and gist-like intuitions, as well as more precise verbatim memories.

Only the most naive educator would expect all learners to spontaneously visit a Web site displaying all of the attributes outlined above. In addition to serving as descriptions of the ideal learner, fostering these learner characteristics should be a major goal of informal education. Below we will consider how to support informal learning and nurture characteristics of effective informal learners by creating meaningful contexts, making interactive experiences, and working with the rhetorical structure of the Web.

A. Create Meaningful Contexts

The phrase "learning environment" embodies a place metaphor, evoking a setting where learning takes place. An informal learning environment on the Web should create an atmosphere for learning rather then serve as an information delivery vehicle. To create a meaningful context is to share a metaphoric, fictionalized understanding with the visitor. For example, on the Dragonfly Web Pages, visitors "jump" into the Dragonfly Pond, "hunt" for hidden sea creatures, "design" an airplane, and "go on a virtual dinosaur dig." Each of these activities embodies an action taken within a fictitious context. From a technological standpoint these are equivalent to presenting a multiple choice test, or a point-and-click interface. Yet the context permits visitors to play at "hunting," "designing," "digging," and the like, which has a profound effect on their experience. Making an island paradise for spiders is fun and intrinsically motivating in ways that answering multiple choice questions about research is not.

One approach to creating meaningful and motivating contexts is to allow the user to "play god" and take a "god's eye view" of the world. Designing a tree is something outside of our everyday experience. For this very reason, visitors are eager to play god in the context of an interactive decision-making game. Of course, when visitors are given a context and asked to play a decision-making role, they usually want to generate their own course of action. Unfortunately, it is not possible to anticipate every course of action that a visitor may invent to achieve a given goal. This creates a dilemma for the designers of informal learning environments. It is pragmatically necessary to limit the visitors options, and yet limiting options may detract from the visitor's illusion of control.

In addressing the dilemma of control, the designer may be aided by a clever cover story — a narrative that plausibly limits the visitor's options. For example, someone playing the role of President of the United States may wish to create government policy. It would not be possible to anticipate every policy every visitor to a Web site might think of. A reasonable strategy for limiting options would be to create a "cover story" like the following, suggested by the game Hidden Agenda. Perhaps, the story might suggest, the President is a compromise candidate who is politically weak and presides over an uneasy coalition government. According to the cover story, he or she must choose among alternative policies suggested by a set of cabinet officers (or campaign contributors). The President must weigh how these options will be treated by various constituencies and choose how to best achieve his or her goals in a particular political context. Such a cover story explains the narrow range of options in a plausible way and permits detailed feedback about how others would respond to various policy options. Although players may still wish that they could generate options themselves, the integrity of the experience is maintained by the cover story. In short, creating meaningful contexts has a dramatic impact on the visitor's experience. Careful attention to context may serve the designer by steering the visitor toward an appropriate set of alternative actions, provide opportunities for useful and appropriate feedback, and hide technical and practical limitations.

B. Make the Experience Interactive

The Web is an interactive medium, and, as previously argued, interactivity takes a number of forms on the Web. If we want visitors to become active learners, we must find ways for them to do something with their knowledge.

Many advocate "learning by doing," and, especially when considering informal learning environments, it is reasonable to ask, "learn by doing what?" At the most general level, the answer is integrating previous knowledge and new experiences, and applying them to achieve meaningful goals.

This approach to active learning is embodied in interactive decision-making games. The quality of the interaction is largely a function of the quality of the visitor's decisions. Turning expository statements of declarative knowledge into a procedural course of action for the visitor is the key to making successful simulations of this kind. The trick is to create "choice points" where visitors must make substantial decisions, applying what they are learning to accomplish a meaningful goal. In creating interactive experiences on the Dragonfly Web Pages, for example, I often start with the expository writings of scientists and try to create choice points based on scientific principles or key research findings. The quality of the interaction is also largely a function of the quality of the feedback visitors receive. It is necessary to provide useful and supportive feedback when visitors are ready to receive it. "Right" and "wrong" are only slightly better than no feedback at all. Effective feedback demonstrates the consequences of the visitor's decisions. It encourages visitors to revise their mental representations, and invites them to play again — whether they gave the best answer or not. Part of the fun of interactive decision-making games is seeing what happens when you make the wrong choice. It should be part of the learning too.

C. Work with the Web (Not against It)

As previously argued, the Web is an ephemeral medium that encourages brief interactive encounters. The Web favors graphics over text, browsing over contemplation, and economy over depth. It is understandable that many of us lament the banality and superficiality of most Web sites for children. Yet if we are to use the Web to create successful informal learning environments, then we must work with, rather than against, the rhetorical structure of a medium that emphasizes attention-grabbing graphics and pithy, precise text.

The dilemma for educators is how to build on the strengths of the Web without being shallow. The solution is quality over quantity. We are better off creating brief, high-caliber experiences then expecting a Web site to be comprehensive and exhaustive. It is imperative to provide a substantive experience, however brief. Yet a successful informal learning environment does not need to accomplish everything. An excellent appetizer is better than a mediocre main course. Moreover, superficiality is combated by extensions to other experiences. Links to other Web sites, annotated bibliographies, suggestions for further inquiry, and even links to more elaborate experiences within the same Web site are proven devices for piquing visitor interest and encouraging further exploration.

Experience is the best teacher and the source of the most profound learning. However, in many domains, the abstract nature of the subject matter makes learning from experience difficult. The Web holds great promise as a learning technology, in large measure, because of its potential for making abstract notions tangible. Informal learning environments are places where visitors can explore, interact, play, and learn from experience. Technology is evolving at an astonishing rate, and the Web is changing daily. Yet the power of experience as the ultimate teacher is an enduring truth of the human condition.

References

Anderson, M. D. (1997–1998). Critical elements of an Internet based asynchronous distance education course. *Journal of Educational Technology Systems, 26,* 383–388.

Bergen, D. (1988). Stages of play development. In D. Bergen (Ed.), *Play as a medium for learning and development: A handbook of theory and practice* (pp. 49–66). Portsmith, NH: Heinmann.

Brainerd, C. J., & Reyna, V. F. (1990a). Gist is the grist: Fuzzy-trace theory and the new intuitionism. *Developmental Review, 10,* 3–47.

Brainerd, C. J., & Reyna, V. F. (1990b). Inclusion illusions: Fuzzy-trace theory and perceptual salience effects in cognitive development. *Developmental Review, 10,* 365–403.

Brooks, J. G., & Brooks, M. G. (1993). *In search of understanding: The case for constructivist classrooms.* Alexandria, VA: Association for Supervision and Curriculum Development.

Dick, W. (1991). An instructional designer's view of constructivism. *Educational Technology, 31,* 41–50.

Dick, W. (1996). The Dick and Carey model: Will it survive the decade? *Educational Technology Research & Development, 44,* 55–63.

Dick, W., & Carey, L. M. (1996). *The systematic design of instruction* (4th ed.). New York: Harper Collins.

Eamon, D. B. (1999). Distance education: Has technology become a threat to the academy? *Behavior Research Methods, Instruments, & Computers, 31,* 197–207.

Goldhaber, J. (1994). If we call it science, then can we let the children play? *Childhood Education, 71,* 24–27.

Harasim, L. (1989). On-line education: A new domain. In R. Mason & A. Kaye (Eds.), *Mindweave: Communication, computers, and distance education* (pp. 50–62). Oxford: Pergamon.

Henniger, M. L. (1987). Learning mathematics and science through play. *Childhood Education, 64,* 167–171.

Herrenkohl, L. R., & Guerra, M. R. (1998). Participant structures, scientific discourse, and student engagement in fourth grade. *Cognition and Instruction, 16,* 431–473.

Jonassen, D. H. (1995). Supporting communities of learners with technology: A vision for integrating technology with learning in schools. *Educational Technology, 34,* 34–37.

Kolb, D. A. (1984). *Experiential learning : Experience as the source of learning and development.* Englewood Cliffs, NJ: Prentice-Hall.

Lajoie, S. P., & Derry, S. J. (Eds.). (1993). *Computers as cognitive tools.* Hillsdale, NJ: Erlbaum.

Landow, G. P. (1991). The rhetoric of hypermedia: Some rules for authors. In P. Delany, & G. P. Landow (Eds.), *Hypermedia and literary studies* (pp. 81–103). Cambridge, MA: MIT Press.

Learner-Centered Principles Work Group of the American Psychological Association's Board of Educational Affairs (1997, November). *Learner-centered psychological principles* [16 paragraphs on-line]. Available (March 10, 2000): http://www.apa.org/ed/lcp2/lcp14.html

Locatis, C., & Weisberg, M. (1997). Distributed learning and the Internet. *Contemporary Education, 68,* 100–103.

Menges, R. J. (1994). Teaching in the age of electronic information. In W. J. McKeachie (Ed.), *Teaching tips: Strategies, research, and theory for college and university teachers* (9th ed., pp. 183–193). Lexington, MA: D.C. Heath.

National Science Foundation (2000, March 10). *Informal science education program* [13 paragraphs on-line]. Available: http://www.ehr.nsf.gov/ehr/esie/ISE.htm

National Science Teachers Association (1998, January). An NSTA *position statement: Informal science education* [3 paragraphs on-line].Available (March 10, 2000): http://www.nsta.org/handbook/informaleducation.asp

Papert, S. (1984). Computer as mudpie. In D. Peterson (Ed.), *Intelligent schoolhouse* (pp. 17–26). Reston, VA: Reston Publishing.

Pepler, D. J., & Ross, H. S. (1981). The effects of play on convergent and divergent problem solving. *Child Development, 52,* 1202–1210.

Resnick, L. B. (1989). *Knowing, learning, and instruction: Essays in honor of Robert Glaser.* Hillside, NJ: Erlbaum.

Reyna, V. F. (1991). Class inclusion, the conjunction fallacy, and other cognitive illusions. *Developmental Review, 11,* 317–336.

Reyna, V. F., & Brainerd, C. J. (1989). Output interference, generic resources, and cognitive development. *Journal of Experimental Child Psychology, 47,* 42–46.

Reyna, V. F., & Brainerd, C. J. (1995). Fuzzy-trace theory: An interim synthesis. *Learning and Individual Differences, 7,* 1–75.

Spodek, B., & Saracho, O. N. (1987). The challenge of educational play. In D. Bergen (Ed.), *Play as a medium for learning and development: A handbook of theory and practice* (pp. 9–26). Portsmith, NH: Heinmann.

Strauss, C. (1984). Beyond "formal" versus "informal" education: Uses of psychological theory in anthropological research. *Ethos, 12,* 195–222.

Tapscott, D. (1998). *Growing up digital.* New York: McGraw Hill.

Tessmer, M., & Richey, R. C. (1997). The role of context in learning and instructional design. *Educational Technology Research and Development, 45,* 85–115.

Tracy, D. M. (1987). Toys, spatial ability, and science and mathematics achievement: Are they related? *Sex Roles, 17,* 115–138.

Tracy, D. M. (1990). Toy-playing behavior, sex-role orientation, spatial ability, and science achievement. *Journal of Research in Science Teaching, 27,* 637–649.

Trumbull, D. (1990). Introduction. In E. Duckworth, J. Easley, D. Hawkins, & J. K. Smith (Eds.), *Science education: A minds-on approach for the elementary years* (pp. 1–20). Hillside, NJ: Erlbaum.

White, B. Y., & Frederiksen, J. R. (1998). Inquiry, modeling, and metacognition: Making science accessible to all students. *Cognition and Instruction, 16,* 3–118.

Wolfe, C. R. (1992). Using an authoring system to facilitate student-centered discovery oriented learning. *Computers & Education: An International Journal, 19,* 335–340.

Wolfe, C. R. (1995a). Homespun hypertext: Student-constructed hypertext as a tool for teaching critical thinking. *Teaching of Psychology, 22,* 29–33.

Wolfe, C. R. (1995b). Information seeking on Bayesian conditional probability problems: A Fuzzy-trace theory account. *Journal of Behavioral Decision Making, 8,* 85–108.

Wolfe, C. R., Crider, L., Mayer, L., McBride, M., Sherman, R., & Vogel, R. (1998). Toward a Miami University model for Internet-intensive higher education. *Journal on Excellence in College Teaching, 9,* 29–51.

Wolfe, C. R., Cummins, R. H., & Myers, C. A. (1998). Dabbling, discovery, and dragonflies: Scientific inquiry and exploratory representational play. In D. P. Fromberg & D. Bergen (Eds.), *Play From birth to twelve: Contexts, perspectives, and meanings.* New York, NY: Garland.

Wolfe, C. R., Halas, J. W., & Arthur, S. (1999). Scoring procedures manual for the scientific reasoning scenarios. *Technical report of the Center for Human Development, Learning, and Teaching. Miami University, Oxford, Ohio* [On-line] (pp. 1–19). Available (March 10, 2000): http://miavx1.muohio.edu/~chdltcwis/wolfchris_instrument.html

Wolfe, C. R., & Myers C. A. (1996). The Dragonfly's Web: Courseware for children created by college students on the World Wide Web. *Behavioral Research Measurement, Instruments, and Computers, 28*, 161–164.

Wolfe, C. R., Myers, C. A., & Cummins, R. H. (in press). The Dragonfly Web Pages: Informal science education on the World Wide Web. *Cognitive Technology.*

Wolfe, C. R., Wang, A., & Bergen, D. (1999). Assessing the winning teams program of interactive satellite-based training. *Behavior Research Methods, Instruments, & Computers, 31*, 275–280.

Zuckerman, G. A., Chudinova, E. V., & Khavkin, E. E. (1998). Inquiry as a pivotal element of knowledge acquisition within the Vygotskian paradigm: Building a science curriculum for the elementary school. *Cognition and Instruction, 16*, 201–233.

Cooperative Learning and Computer-Supported Intentional Learning Experiences

LAWRENCE W. SHERMAN

Department of Educational Psychology, Miami University

I. INTRODUCTION

In this chapter I describe how various uses of technology are associated with cognitive and social psychology as applied to peer learning in technologically enriched behavior settings. This explanation should provide historical and theoretical foundations for peer learning in the classroom as well as the workplace. I will attempt to show that the discipline of psychology, specifically social and cognitive psychology, has originated various cooperative learning strategies that are based upon a strong theoretical foundation. These applications have been designed to improve human relations, as well as more efficient knowledge acquisition and problem solving among communities of diverse learners. The role of new computer-supported technologies will be discussed as a medium through which collaboration among peer learning groups is facilitated. Recent concerns by the U. S. Secretary of Labor's "SCANS Report" (Lankard, 1995) will be used to demonstrate the significance of making classroom learning experience more authentically congruent with the needs of a highly diverse, interdependent, and technologically enriched workplace.

II. THE INFLUENCE OF KURT LEWIN: A BRIEF HISTORY

At the end of the last century, the American Psychological Association (APA) summarized the development and significance of various subdisciplines of the field of psychology (APA, 1999). Both social psychology and cognitive psychology were briefly described. Interestingly, several significant people and their theoretical contributions appeared in both of the subdisciplines of social and cognitive psychology, specifically, Jean Piaget, Lev Vygotsky, and Kurt Lewin. Thus, it is appropriate to look to these foundational theorists when considering cooperative learning and computer-supported intentional learning experiences.

The "contructivist" theories of Piaget and Vygotsky are widely acknowledged as significant foundations upon which to build peer learning experiences. For example, the role of elaboration, equilabration, metacognition, and scaffolding all stem from contructivist theory (see O'Donnell & King, 1999, for a more thorough discussion of these topics). The present discussion will focus on the influence of Kurt Lewin. I will also draw upon a postmodern cognitive perspective with regard to the role of plural realities, narrative, and writing (Sherman, 2000).

The cognitive field psychologist Kurt Lewin was an important founding father of social psychology who influenced the development of the group dynamics movement (APA, 1999, p. 21). Lewin's concern for the resolution of social conflict (Lewin, 1948) influenced many of his students. Several of them have continued that interest. The generations of Lewinian influence are detailed in Figure 6.1. One of his students, Morton Deutsch, has had a long and continuing interest in "applied" social psychology. Deutch's research interests have ranged from studying the productivity of work groups experiencing cooperative or competitive conditions to attempts at resolving the nuclear arms race. Interest in Deutsch's (1949) earlier research led several scholars to reexamine the influence of cooperation and competition on instruction. Other students of Lewin have also had a strong interest in concepts of group dynamics and their applications in educational settings (e.g., Leon Festinger in cognitive dissonance and social comparison theory; Ronald Lippitt in group atmospheres and leadership; and Jacob Kounin in psychological ecology of behavior settings, discipline and classroom management). Lewin's heritage continues on through a third generation of students of the students of Lewin (e.g., David Johnson, a student of Morton Deutsch; Eliot Aronson, a student of Leon Festinger; Richard Schmuck, a student of Ronald Lippitt; and myself, a student of Jacob Kounin). Schmuck (1995) has given us a detailed history of this progression, especially as it relates to the growth and development of an international organization, the International Association for the Study of Cooperation in Education (IASCE), whose primary focus is research

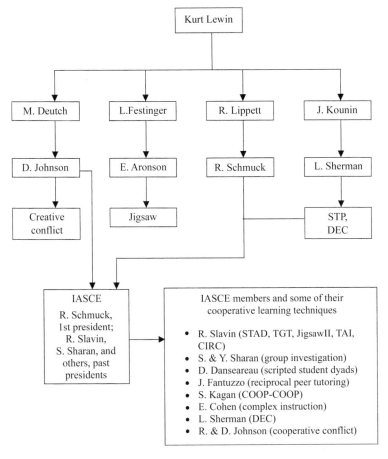

FIGURE 6.1.

Generations of Lewinian cooperative learning theorists and their techniques.

on and application of cooperative learning strategies in educational settings.

Strongly influenced by the *Equality of Educational Opportunity Report* (Coleman, 1966), the United States enacted many programs of voluntary as well as court-ordered desegregation of public schools. It should be noted that "desegregating" an environment such as a school system or individual classrooms, does not necessarily result in the integration of the diverse communities of individuals which have merely been put together in the same behavior setting. From an ecological perspective, the very structures of these behavior settings may either promote social acceptance or increase social distance (exacerbate social conflict and intergroup tensions) among the diverse individuals who occupy these settings (Hertz-Lazarowitz & Miller,

1992). Social psychologists have recognized this (Hewstone & Brown, 1986) and responded with theory-based pedagogical applications that have been attempts at facilitating integration and improved human relations in these newly created diverse learning communities. These applications were primarily based on Lewinian social-psychological theory and were concerned with promoting democracy and reducing conflict. A variety of cooperative learning strategies have been created. Some examples include Eliot Aronson's Jigsaw approach, and Johnson and Johnson's "creative conflict." These techniques were also found to be highly effective with regard to improving academic achievement. Throughout the 1970s and continuing into the present century, other cognitive and social psychologists began to create a great variety of cooperative learning strategies.

Lewinian-oriented cognitive psychologists subscribe to the theory that human behavior is a result of the interaction of persons with their environments. This has led to much speculation about "action theory." An action theory examines the actions needed to achieve a desired consequence (goal attainment) in a given situation. Johnson and Johnson (1991) have stated that "when you generate an action theory from your own experiences and then continually modify it to improve its effectiveness, you are learning experientially" (pp. 16–17; see Figure 6.2). Experiential learning affects the learner in three ways: (1) cognitive structures are altered, (2) attitudes are modified, and (3) behavioral skills are expanded. This is thought to be a cyclical process: (1) taking action by behaviorally trying out the strategies and procedures in one's action theory leads to; (2) experiencing the consequences of one's actions, receiving feedback on one's behaviors, and reflecting on and examining one's experiences leads to; (3) organizing present information and experiences into an action theory, which leads back to taking action and perpetuates the cycle.

FIGURE 6.2.
The experiential learning cycle (after Johnson & Johnson, 1987, p. 18).

TABLE 6.1
Twelve Lewinian Principles of experiential learning[a]

Principle 1. Effective experiential learning will affect the learner's cognitive structures (action theories), attitudes and values, perceptions, and behavioral patterns.

Principle 2. People will believe more in knowledge they have discovered themselves than in knowledge presented by others.

Principle 3. Learning is more effective when it is an active rather than a passive process.

Principle 4. Acceptance of new action theories, attitudes, and behavioral patterns cannot be brought about by a piecemeal approach — one's whole cognitive–affective–behavioral system has to change.

Principle 5. It takes more than information to change action theories, attitudes, and behavioral patterns.

Principle 6. It takes more than firsthand experience to generate valid knowledge. Besides experience, there needs to be a theoretical system that the experience tests out, and reflection on the meaning of the experience.

Principle 7. Behavior changes will be temporary unless the action theories and attitudes underlying them are changed.

Principle 8. Changes in perceptions of oneself and one's social environment are necessary before changes in action theories, attitudes, and behavior will take place.

Principle 9. The more supportive, accepting, and caring the social environment, the freer a person is to experiment with new behaviors, attitudes, and action theories.

Principle 10. In order for changes in behavior patterns, attitudes, and action theories to be permanent, both the person and the social environment have to change.

Principle 11. It is easier to change a person's action theories, attitudes, and behavioral patterns in a group context than in an individual context.

Principle 12. A person accepts a new system of action theories, attitudes, and behavioral patterns when he or she accepts membership in a new group.

[a]After Johnson & Johnson (1987, pp. 18–20)

Experiential learning, then, may facilitate the development of an action theory. The Johnsons (Johnson & Johnson, 1991) have presented 12 principles of experiential learning (see Table 6.1). The last 4 principles focus on the influence of environments on individuals, especially within the context of social groups "experiencing" cooperative learning. Membership in a group will free a person to experiment with new behaviors, attitudes, and action theories, especially if that group is supportive and accepting. One such group might be a classroom of individuals experiencing cooperative learning.

In summary, this brief history has been a modest attempt to link Lewinian-influenced "cognitive field theorists" and their contributions to the world of cooperative learning. Action theory and experiential learning are the primary foundations upon which cooperative pedagogy was created. In the next section I will discuss cooperative learning as presently being used in primary, secondary and postsecondary environments. I will describe cognitive and action theories in which cooperative learning strategies make use of computer web-based technology.

III. COOPERATIVE LEARNING

Because there is widespread confusion about both theory and terminology, some clarification regarding the term "cooperative learning" is in order. Johnson (1979) described three types of behavior settings which are called "goal structures." The three goal structures are *cooperative, competitive,* and *individualistic.* These goal structures are primarily based on the presence or absence of interdependence among classroom members. It is acknowledged that one form of cooperative learning has been labeled "collaborative learning" and has been used extensively in the teaching of writing at the postsecondary level of education. While elements of collaborative learning are present in many cooperative programs, some have felt it necessary to make a distinction between collaborative and cooperative learning (Bruffee, 1993). Others believe that the terms "cooperative" and "collaborative" complement each other (Brody, 1995). I will use the terms "cooperative" and "collaborative" interchangeably.

A. Cooperative Goal Structures

Cooperative goal structures are in operation when two or more individuals are in a situation where the task-related efforts of individuals help others to be rewarded. Group members behave in a positively interdependent fashion and are rewarded on the basis of the quality or quantity of a group product according to a fixed set of standards — those standards being mastery or criterion-referenced performance standards. Other attributes considered important in defining a cooperative goal structure are face-to-face interactions, heterogeneous groupings, individual accountability, group processing, and positive interdependence.

Face-to-face interactions imply reciprocal communications. It will be noted later that these communications could also be accomplished at a distance in either an asynchronous or a synchronous manner utilizing computer-supported technologies. The notion of "heterogeneous groupings" implies recognition of the "diversity" of individual group members, parameters of which may be gender, ethnic background, physical disabilities, achievement ability, and so on. Group processing also involves acts of communication in which members exchange views about what actually happens in cooperative group experiences. This, too, can take place at a distance utilizing computer-supported technology. It is believed that the term "collaborative learning" fits into this category of goal structure. Peer tutoring models such as Aronson's (Aronson et al., 1978) Jigsaw technique,

TABLE 6.2
Categorization of cooperative learning methods by incentive and task structures with an example of each

Task structure	Incentive structure		
	Group reward for individual learning	Group reward for group product	Individual reward
Group study (no specialization)	STAD and TGT (Slavin, 1995); Humphries et. al., (1982); Hamblin, et al., (1971); and Sherman (1986)	Learning together (Wheeler & Ryan, 1973)	Peterson & Janicki (1979); Webb & Kenderski (1984); Starr & Schuermann (1986)
Task (with individual specialization)	Jigsaw II (Slavin, 1995)	GI (Sharan, 1980) and STP (Sherman & Woy-Hazleton, 1988)	Jigsaw (Aronson et al., 1978) and DEC (Millis et al., 1993)

Fantuzzo's (Fantuzzo, Riggio, Connelly, & Dimeff, 1989) reciprocal peer learning, or Dansereau's (Dansereau, et al., 1986) scripted peer dyads would also be located here. The Johnsons' (Johnson & Johnson, 1994) and Sharans' (Sharan & Sharan, 1992) group-investigation models are considered cooperative goal structures as well. Sherman's (1990) dyadic essay confrontations (DECs) might also be considered an example of cooperative learning.

Slavin (1983) has further differentiated cooperative goal structures on the basis of two types of task structures (those with or without task specialization) and three types of incentive structures including group rewards for (1) individual learning or (2) group products, and (3) individual rewards (See Table 6.2).

B. Competitive Goal Structure

Individually competitive goal structures give students individual goals and reward them by means of a comparative or normative evaluation system. In an individually competitive structure a student can attain his or her goal only if the other participants cannot attain their's. One achieves one's goal at the expense of others. Kohn (1992) has described this as MEGA (mutually exclusive goal attainment). In a sense, there is some interdependence among students, though it is primarily negative interdependence. Under MEGA conditions, mutual assistance is generally counterproductive. Cheating and "dirty tricks" are some examples of negative interdependence. Some have described this as the "traditional" structure of learning in many college classrooms (Wolff, 1969). Grades which are assigned on a normal distribution would be an example of a competitive goal structure.

C. Individual Goal Structures

An individual goal structure is one in which students are given individual goals, and by using a criterion-referenced evaluation system, students are assigned individual rewards based on the quality or quantity of their personal performances or products and achievements. Whereas student interdependence is required in the cooperative structure, students behave quite independently of each other in an individualist goal structure. Being given individual credit for completing a series of rote drill exercises in a programmed instruction computer medium might be a good example. Another example might be receiving one's driving license after "passing a performance-based test": everyone who has reached the minimal standard of performance receives the license.

D. Goal Structures and Evaluation

Obviously there is a relationship between goal structures and evaluation methods. Evaluation has been described as either norm-referenced or criterion-referenced (Bloom, Hastings, & Madaus, 1971). Competitive goal structures logically demand a norm-referenced form of evaluation. Likewise, cooperative and individualistic goal structures usually demand a criterion-referenced system of evaluation. It might also be noted that many times "peer evaluations" are used in cooperative goal structures, whereas in competitive and individual goal structured activities some powerful authority (e.g., a teacher) is the primary evaluator and distributor of rewards.

Although earlier interest in cooperative pedagogy is acknowledged (e.g., Hains & McKeachie, 1967), Kohn (1992) presents some of the strongest arguments in favor of teaching through cooperation. Over the past 30 years social and educational psychologists have produced a considerable volume of research demonstrating the effectiveness of a great variety of small group cooperative structures, especially at the elementary and secondary education level — for example, the Johnsons (Johnson & Johnson, 1975, 1987), Eliot Aronson (Aronson, Blaney, Sikes, Stephan, & Snapp, 1975; Lucker, Rosenfeld, Sikes, & Aronson, 1976; Blaney et al., 1977; Aronson et al., 1978), Robert Slavin (1978ab, 1983, 1995), and the Sharans (Sharan, 1980, 1994; Sharan et al., 1985; Sharan & Sharan, 1992).

A modest amount of research has been accomplished in the postsecondary college or university environment where the mode of instruction remains, many believe, as individually competitive as Wolff's (1969) earlier descriptions. A few examples of cooperation in university settings might be Carroll's (1986) or Lamberights' (1988) studies using Aronson's jigsaw technique in undergraduate psychology classrooms. Wolfe (1995) reported on the collaborative construction of hypertext as a tool for teaching critical thinking. Sherman (1986; Sherman & Woy-Hazelton, 1988) and Gnagey

(1988) have described the use of Slavin's "student teams and achievement divisions" (STAD) technique as well as Sharan's group-investigation (GI) model in undergraduate and graduate educational psychology classes. Several other studies have analyzed the uses of cooperative learning in a variety of postsecondary educational settings (Dansereau, 1985; Dansereau et al., 1986; Fantuzzo et al., 1989; Millis, 1990; Millis, Sherman, & Cottell, 1993; Nolinske & Millis, 1999). Sharan (2000) provides a thorough review of recent research on cooperative learning in a variety of settings.

Most social psychology textbooks contain considerable discussions about conflict, sometimes instigated by individual or intergroup competition, and its resolution and/or reduction through the use of cooperative techniques. Social psychologists' interests in intergroup relations acknowledge the effectiveness of cooperative learning (e.g., see Messick & Mackie, 1989). Almost all introductory educational psychology textbooks (e.g., Dembo, 1994; Good & Brophy, 1990; Slavin, 2000; Woolfolk, 1999) now contain extended discussions of cooperative learning and its effectiveness with regard to improved racial relations, positive self-esteem, greater internal attributions of control, and higher academic achievement. The most current editions of many of these texts also provide web sites and CDs that support the delivery of course content utilizing cooperative learning strategies.

E. Postmodern Thought and Cooperative Learning

Sherman (2000) has defined and discussed various attributes of "postmodern" thinking in education. These attributes include: (1) challenging the idea of a single meaning of reality (objectivism); (2) accepting randomness, incoherence, indeterminacy, and paradox; (3) being skeptical about the positivist tradition in science and essentialist theories; and (4) assuming that meanings are historically situated and constructed and reconstructed through language. Wilber (1998) has suggested three additional core assumptions. First, reality is not in all ways pregiven (objectivism), but in some significant ways is a construction or interpretation (this view is often called *"constructivism,"* while the belief that reality is simply given, and not also partly constructed, is referred to as "the myth of the given". Second, meaning is context dependent — contexts are boundless (this is often called "contextualism"). Finally, cognition must therefore privilege no single perspective (this is called the "integral-aperspective" view; Wilber, 1998, p. 121).

Sherman (2000) has suggested that one implication of postmodern thinking concerns how teachers take into consideration the subjective nature of various disciplines. The act of communication is a reciprocal process (Schmuck & Schmuck, 1997) of discourse in which we engage each others' constructions of reality. Encountering each others constructions of reality might be considered an "interdependent" action which some would describe as a primary element of cooperative learning. Bruner (1990, 1996) discusses this as an act of "intersubjectivity" and emphasizes the important role of "narrative" in this process. Communicating through face-to-face dialogue, as well as through the acts of writing and reading, offers an opportunity to construct and determine a credible reality. This is thought to be similar in meaning to the notion of developing an "action theory" as described earlier in Figure 6.1 and Table 6.1. Constructivism from a Piagetian and Vygotskian perspective would also explain this learning process. It is believed, then, that computer-supported collaborative learning environments might facilitate this process of intersubjectivity.

IV. TECHNOLOGY

Historically, technological advancements in communication have influenced teaching and learning, for example, the migration from stone and clay tablets, parchment, papyrus scrolls, and the printing press in the past to typewriters, Xerox duplications, word processors, e-mail, listservs, and the World Wide Web in the present. In the postindustrial global economy of the present (see B. M. Friedman, 1999; T. L. Friedman, 1999) people encounter great diversity of thought from a variety of different people representing many different cultures or what some refer to as different "communities of practice" (Goldman, 1996; see Hammond & Trapp, chapter 8, this volume, for more on using the web to support communities of practice). Postmodern theory recognizes diversity in the form of plural constructions of realities that one is likely to encounter. Technologically sophisticated communication skills are a necessary component of this new global environment. In 1990 Elizabeth Dole, U.S. Secretary of Labor, presented what has been called the "SCANS Report" (The Secretary's Commission on Achieving Necessary Skills, 1991; Whetzel, 1992; Lankard, 1995), where she suggested five goals for public school education. The goals are presented in Table 6.3, and include the ability to use sophisticated technology to communicate and collaborate. Collaborative teaching and learning experiences that make use of various technologies would be congruent with the skills necessary to achieve an effective postindustrial global economy. Margaret Riel (1996) has contributed an excellent description of these processes within and among networked learning environments.

My own experience with adapting computer-based technology to enhance learning began in the 1970s. I began to use computer-mediated communication (CMC) facilitated by mainframe computer-generated reports in undergraduate educational psychology classes (Sherman, 1976, 1979). Throughout the 1980s and into the 1990s internet access and mainframe computers facilitated CMC using "listservs" and "newsgroups" (Sherman, 1995). During the spring of 1993 I was fortunate to be part of a collaborative

TABLE 6 3
Five Workplace Skills Identified in the SCANS Report[a]

1. Resources—identifying, organizing, planning, and allocating time, money, materials, and workers

2. Interpersonal skills—negotiating, exercising leadership, working with diversity, teaching others new skills, serving clients and customers, and participating as a team member

3. Information skills—using computers to process information and acquiring and evaluating, organizing and maintaining, and interpreting and communicating information

4. Systems skills—understanding systems, monitoring and correcting system performance, and improving and designing systems

5. Technology utilization skills—selecting technology, applying technology to a task, and maintaining and troubleshooting technology

[a]After Whetzel (1992).

effort that brought the world's first CMC message by a dignitary of state (U.S. President William Clinton) to a fifth grade classroom in Oxford, Ohio (Sherman, McMahon-Klosterman, Meyer, & Stephens, 1994). This event transpired asynchronously through the Internet medium of KIDCAFE, at that time an Internet "netnews group" founded by Odd de Presno and Dan Wheeler (KIDCAFE@vm1.nodak.edu, presently at http://www.kidlink.org). President Clinton's message was featured as a major accomplishment in networking for the year 1993 (Clement & Abrahams, 1994). Not discussed in Clement and Abrahams (1994) was the cooperative group activities that proceeded and eventually generated President Clinton's message. These fifth grade children were involved in a group-investigation inquiry project that focused on the President's inaugural speech, where they perceived his emphasis to be on determining how to reduce the national debt. The children's collaboratively determined solution to this problem involved having every child in the country donate their pennies. They communicated this solution asynchronously via the Internet from their classroom KIDLINK connection to a larger community of children throughout the United States as well as a much broader international community of children. Not only did this generate a response from President Clinton, as well as the vice-president's wife, Tipper Gore (via a telephone call to the classroom), but it also resulted in several hundred dollars in donations that were eventually sent to Washington, DC. It is believed that in this cooperative learning event we witnessed all three elements of the experiential learning cycle described earlier in Figure 6.2: (1) the children tried out an action theory strategy that (2) provided them with considerable feedback, which (3) altered their previous perceptions about the role of children in solving problems. Those of us who were involved with this project were strongly impressed with the far-reaching effects of this collaborative project. We could see the positive effects of cooperative learning when combined with CMC and other related

technologies. The children appeared to gain a positive sense of empowerment, and obtained considerable learning experience with democratic
processes. They also gained greater technological sophistication.

In 1995 I presented a paper which described similar uses of CMC through
the medium of a "netnews group" (Sherman, 1995). The conference at which
this paper was delivered was entitled "CSCL'95: The First International
Conference on Computer Support for Collaborative Learning." It was at
this conference that I began to see the introduction of constructivist
theory based upon Piaget and Vygotsky. Koschmann (1996) has described
this as a major "paradigm shift." It certainly was a major paradigm shift for
me as I came in contact with a variety of computer support for collaborative
learning (CSCL) approaches called computer-supported intentional learning
experiences, or CSILEs.

Scardamalia and Bereiter (1993) and Scardamalia et al. (1992) have
described CSILE as "a networked database system which encourages
students intentional learning through progressive discourse." Oshima,
Bereiter, & Scardamalia, (1995) elaborate on this definition of CSILE as
follows:

> Students are allowed to externalize their thoughts in the database in the form of
> texts or graphics, then manipulate their represented knowledge in building further
> knowledge. The database is accessible to anyone who is registered as a member.
> Students can asynchronously collaborate through mutual commentaries. They can
> create comment notes to add to their reflective thoughts on their peers' thoughts.
> Thus, students with CSILE work as members of the classroom community in pursu-
> ing their inquiries on study topics (p. 259).

CSILE is not just software, but rather a process that is many times
implemented on the World Wide Web (WWW or Web) as a "chat room"
dialogue space where strands and threads of dialogue as well as graphic
images can be stored, accessed, viewed, and contributed. Business and
industry are using a variety of software to accomplish similar objectives; for
example, Lotus Notes. My own institution, Miami University, supports a
software product called "Blackboard.com" (Blackboard, Inc., 1999), where
CSILE activities might take place for the purposes of course instruction.
Basic Support for Cooperative Work (BSCW, 1999) is another product that
provides software for cooperative and interactive learning in a CSILE-like
structure.

All of my courses make use of an adaptation of a program called
WWWBOARD (WWWboard, 1995) available from Matt's Script Archive
at http://www.worldwidemart.com/scripts/wwwboard.shtml. This program
allows "strands" and "threads" of dialogue to emerge publicly in an organized fashion in an "on-line dialogue space" on the Web. I have begun to use
this dialogue space as a medium through which my own cooperative structure, dyadic essay confrontations, or DEC, is accomplished. DEC as a cooperative learning strategy is discussed elsewhere (Millis et al., 1993; R. C.

Sherman, 1998, 1999; Nolinske & Millis, 1999). However, it must be noted here that DEC is predicated on a postmodern and Lewinian based theory of cooperatively determined transactional communications.

A special issue of the APA *Monitor on Psychology* (APA, 2000) explores how the Internet is changing psychology as we know it, that is, Koschmann's (1996) paradigm shift. In this special issue Murray (2000) describes several applications of on-line discussion chat room resources. She includes several very helpful suggestions on how to avoid pitfalls of Web discussion. Problems relating to cooperative learning in Web-based discussions include students making assertions without providing evidence; difficulties connecting on-line comments to specific course concepts; students being hesitant to be critical on-line; a lack of peer camaraderie; instructors jeopardizing student interaction by falling into the lecture mode on-line; and difficulties forming a "community of learners" on-line. Solutions to these common problems are suggested in Murray's (2000) article.

Increasingly, evidence of the importance of peer learning and CMC may be seen in a variety of places. A major APA journal, *Teaching of Psychology*, has a separate section devoted entirely to "Computers in Teaching" where the majority of articles for the past five years have focused on web-based applications. Many of these articles are using CSILE-like cooperative activities, for example, Richard Sherman's report on social psychology class instruction on the Web (Sherman, 1998). Other journals also put a considerable emphasis on Web-based peer learning experiences, for example, *Instructional Science* (Hara, Bank, and Angeli's (2000) article on content analysis of on-line discussions) and *CyberPsychology and Behavior* (volume 3, issue 1, is devoted entirely to articles on Web-based applications (Hall, 2000)). An examination of the *Educational Media and Technology Yearbooks* (Ely & Minor, 1994 to the present) provides additional evidence of this increasing reliance upon Web-based technologies, many of which make use of cooperative learning structures.

Hara et al.'s (2000) article on content analysis of on-line discussions has provided a particularly interesting example of CMC research: specifically, it attempted both quantitative and qualitative analyses of text-based dialogues in a virtual environment. Unlike face-to-face discussions where the dialogue is "fleeting" (unless recorded on either audio or video tape), on-line discussions allow one to analyze the texts which students contribute. Hara et al. (2000) examined participation rates, interaction patterns, social cues within student messages, cognitive and metacognitive components, and depth of processing. They concluded that messages became more lengthy and cognitively deeper over time. The messages were also embedded with peer references, became more interactive over time, and were thus indicative of a student-oriented environment. It is interesting to note that one of their qualitative tools of analysis was a mapping of the dialogues, as in who responded to whom, which looked similar to traditional sociometric mapping of friendship patterns, an approach pioneered by earlier group dynamics research.

Researchers from the cooperative learning community have had an interest in examining the ongoing group experience of students engaged in the cooperative learning process (e.g., Webb & Kenderski, 1984; Webb, 1992; Weinstein, 1991). Different cooperative structures (behavior settings) may yield different interaction patterns. This was certainly suggested by Slavin (1983) and the Johnsons (Johnson, Maruyama, Johnson, Nelson, & Skon, 1981; Johnson & Johnson, 1987) in their meta-analysis of achievement and cooperative learning. Researchers taking a Lewinian psychological ecology perspective have also had a continuing interest in the analysis of group processes (Kounin & Sherman, 1979; Kounin & Gump, 1974; Weinstein, 1991). Hara et al.'s (2000) study has a similar focus, albeit in a virtual environment, rather than a video-taped one like Kounin and Gump (1974) described. Nevertheless, this return to examining the interactions of participants in a collaborative virtual environment is an important research focus and opportunity to study group dynamics at a distance.

Although some might be critical of examining text-based dialogue of collaborating groups because of the "unnatural" nature of these communications (being virtual, text-based, asynchronous, and on the web), it may be closer to the actual way people transact business in a postmodern world. Perhaps this mode of behavior is what Koschmann (1996) describes as the "paradigm shift." Perhaps this is why the U.S. Secretary of Labor's SCANS Report recognized and put so much emphasis on the development of skills that would lead to successful collaboration with others via the use of technology.

V. CONCLUSIONS

Earlier interest in computer support for collaborative learning has led to several technological innovations. Cooperative learning and computer-supported intentional learning environments have strong roots in the cognitive field psychology of Kurt Lewin. Learning settings that would be described as cooperative structures may be differentiated from those that are competitive or individualistic. While other cognitive psychology theories have been influential (Piaget and Vygotsky), the primary focus of this chapter has been to describe issues regarding group processes. These peer learning strategies are also linked to the world of work for which we are preparing our students. For these reasons, CSILEs are an integral part of a technologically enriched cooperative classroom.

Applied social psychological strategies for learning in highly diverse school environments were inspired by the earlier research of Morton Deutch (1949), who demonstrated the positive effects of promotive interdependence, that is, cooperative learning. Learning settings that could be described as cooperative structures can be defined and differentiated from those that are competitive or individualistic. The primary focus of this chapter has been to raise some issues regarding group processes, especially as they are being used in web-based collaborative learning experiences. Some promising new research goals have also been described.

References

APA (1999). Social psychology: Once overlooked, now a staple. APA *Monitor*, 30, 21.

APA (2000). APA *Monitor on Psychology* 31 (4), whole issue.

Aronson, E., Blaney, N., Sikes, J., Stephan, G., & Snapp, M. (1975, July). The jigsaw route to learning and liking. *Psychology Today*, 43–59.

Aronson, E., Blaney, N., Sikes, J., Stephan, G., & Snapp, M. (1978). *The Jigsaw Classroom*. Beverly Hills, CA: Sage.

Blackboard, Inc.(1999). http://company.blackboard.com/index.html

Blaney, N. J., Stephan, S., Rosenfield, D., Aronson, E., & Sikes, J. (1977). Interdependence in the classroom: A field study. *Journal of Educational Psychology*, 69, 121–128.

Bloom, B., Hastings, J., & Madaus, G. (Eds.), (1971). *Handbook on formative and summative evaluation of student learning*. New York: McGraw-Hill.

Brody, C. M. (1995). Collaborative or cooperative learning? Complementary practices for instructional reform. *Journal of Staff, Program & Organizational Development*, 12, 133–143.

Bruner, J. (1990). *Acts of meaning*. Cambridge, MA: Harvard University Press.

Bruner, J. (1996). *The culture of education*. Cambridge, MA: Harvard University Press.

BSCW (1999). *Basic support for cooperative work*. Bonn, Germany: GMD. Available: http://bscw.gmd.de/

Carroll, D. (1986). Use of the jigsaw technique in laboratory and discussion classes. *Teaching of Psychology*, 13 (4), 208–210.

Clement, J., & Abrahams, J. (1994). Networking in 1993. In D. P. Ely & B. B. Minor, (Eds.), *Educational media and technology yearbook*, (Vol. 20, pp. 106–119). Englewood, CO: Libraries Unlimited.

Coleman, J. S. (1966). *Equality of educational opportunity*. Washington, DC: U.S. Government Printing Office.

Dansereau, D. F. (1985). Learning strategy research. In J. W. Segal, S. F. Chipman, & R. Glaser (Eds.), *Thinking and learning skills: Vol. 1. Relating instruction to research*. Hillsdale, NJ: Erlbaum.

Dansereau, D. F. (1987, April). Transfer from cooperative to individual studying. *Journal of Reading*, 614–618.

Dansereau, D. F., Hythecker, V. I., O'Donnell, A., Young, M. D., Lambiotte, J. G., & Rocklin, T. R. (1986). Technical training: An application of a strategy for learning structural and functional information. *Contemporary Educational Psychology*, 11, 217–228.

Dembo, M. H. (1994). *Applying educational psychology in the classroom* (4th ed.). New York: Longman.

Deutsch, M. (1949). A theory of cooperation and competition. *Human Relations*, 2, 129–152.

Ely, D. P., & Minor, B. B. (Eds.), (1994). *Educational media and technology yearbook* (Vol. 20). Englewood, CO: Libraries Unlimited.

Fantuzzo, J. W., Riggio, R. E., Connelly, S., & Dimeff, L. A. (1989). Effects of reciprocal peer tutoring on academic achievement and psychological adjustment: A component analysis. *Journal of Educational Psychology*, 81, 173–177.

Friedman, B. M. (1999). The power of the electronic herd. *The New York Review of Books*, 46, 40–44.

Friedman, T. L. (1999). *The Lexus and the olive tree*. New York: Farrar, Straus and Geroux.

Gnagey, W. (1988, October). STAD *in educational psychology*. A paper presentation to the Midwestern Educational Research Association meetings, Chicago, IL.

Goldman, S. (1996). Mediating microworlds: Collboration on high school science activities. In T. Koschmann (Ed.), CSCL: Theory and practice of an emerging paradigm. Mahwah, NJ: Erlbaum.

Good, T. L. & Brophy, J. E. (1990). Educational psychology (3rd ed.). New York: Longman.

Hains, D. B., & McKeachie, W. J. (1967). Cooperative versus competitive discussion methods in teaching introductory psychology. Journal of Educational Psychology, 58, 386–390.

Hall, R. (Ed.) (2000). The virtual university: Education, hypermedia, and the World Wide Web. [Special issue.] CyberPsychology and Behavior, 3.

Hara, N., Bonk, C. J., & Angeli, C. (2000). Content analysis of online discussion in an applied educational psychology course. Instructional Science, 28, 115–152.

Hertz-Lazarowitz, R., & Miller, N. (Eds.). (1992). Interaction in cooperative groups: The theoretical anatomy of group learning. Cambridge: Cambridge University Press.

Hewstone, M., & Brown, R. (Eds.). (1986). Contact and conflict in intergroup encounters. New York: Basil Blackwell.

Johnson, D. (1979). Educational psychology. Englewood Cliffs, NJ: Prentice-Hall.

Johnson, D. W., & Johnson, F. P. (1991). Joining together: Group theory and group skills (4th ed.). Englewood Cliffs, NJ: Prentice-Hall.

Johnson, D. W., & Johnson, F. P. (1994). Joining together: Group theory and group skills (5th ed.). Scarborough, Ont.: Prentice Hall.

Johnson, D. W., & Johnson, R. T. (1975). Learning together and alone. Englewood Cliffs, NJ: Prentice-Hall.

Johnson, D. W., & Johnson, R. T. (1987). Research shows the benefits of adult cooperation. Educational Leadership, 45, 27–30.

Johnson, D. W., & Johnson, R. T. (1991). Learning together and alone: Cooperative, competitive, and individualistic learning (3rd ed.). Needham Heights, MA: Allyn and Bacon.

Johnson, D. W., Maruyama, G., Johnson, R. T., Nelson, D., & Skon, L. (1981). Effect of cooperative, competitive and individualistic goal structures on achievement: A meta-analysis. Psychological Bulletin, 89, 47–62.

Kohn, A. (1992). No contest: The case against competition. New York: Houghton Mifflin.

Koschmann, T. (Ed.) (1996). CSCL: Theory and practice of an emerging paradigm. Mahwah, NJ: Erlbaum.

Kounin, J. S., & Gump, P. V. (1974). Signal systems of lesson settings and the task-related behavior of preschool children. Journal of Educational Psychology, 66, 550–552.

Kounin, J. S., & Sherman, L. W. (1979). School environments as behavior settings. Theory into Practice, 18, 145–151

Lamberights, R. (1988). Effects of task interdependence and peer tutoring in original and alternative jigsaw sessions. Paper presentation to the Fourth Convention of the International Association for the Study of Cooperation in Education, Kibbutz Shefayim, Israel, July 5–8.

Lankard, B. A. (1995). SCANS and the new vocationalism [on-line]. ERIC Digest No. ED389879. Available (February 25, 2000): http://www.ed.gov/databases/ERIC_Digests/ed389879.html

Lewin, K. (1948). Resolving social conflicts: Selected papers on group dynamics. New York: Harper & Row.

Lucker, G. W., Rosenfield, D., Sikes, J., & Aronson, E. (1976). Performance in the interdependent classroom: A field study. American Educational Research Journal, 13, 115–123.

Messick, D. M., & Mackie, D. M. (1989). Intergroup relations. Annual Review of Psychology, 40, 45–81.

Millis, B. J. (1990). Helping faculty build learning communities through cooperative groups. In L. Hilsen (Ed.), To improve the academy: Resources for student faculty, and institutional development (Vol. 10, pp. 43–58). Stillwater, OK: New Forums Press.

Millis, B. J., Sherman, L. W., & Cottell, P. G. (1993). Stacking the DEC to promote critical thinking: Applications in three disciplines. Cooperative Learning and College Teaching, 3, 12–14.

Murray, B. (2000). Reinventing class discussion online. APA Monitor on Psychology, 31 (4), 54–56.

Newmann, F. M., & Wehlage, G. G. (1993). Five standards of authentic instruction. Educational Leadership, 50, 8–12.

Nolinske, T., & Millis, B. (1999). Cooperative learning as an approach to pedagogy. *American Journal of Occupational Therapy*, 53, 31–40.

O'Donnell, A., & King, A. (Eds.). (1999). *Cognitive perspectives on peer learning*. Mahwah, NJ: Erlbaum.

Oshima, J., Bereiter, C., & Scardamalia, M. (1995). Information-access characteristics for high conceptual progress in a computer-networked learning environment. In J. L. Schnase & E. L. Cunnius (Eds.), *Proceedings of CSCL '95: The first international conference on computer support for collaborative learning*. Mahwah, NJ: Erlbaum.

Riel, M. (1996). Cross-classroom collaboration: Communication and education. In T. Koschmann (Ed.), *CSCL: Theory and practice of an emerging paradigm*. Mahwah, NJ: Erlbaum.

Scardamalia, M., & Bereiter, C. (1993). Technologies for knowledge building discourse. *Communications for the ACM*, 36, 37–41.

Scardamalia, M., Bereiter, C., Brett, C., Burtis, P. J., Calhoun, C., & Smith-Lea, N. (1992). Educational applications of a networked communal database. *Interactive Learning Environments*, 2, 45–71.

Schmuck, R. A. (1995). Timely adolescent reminiscences: The IASCE and why I became an educator. *Cooperative Learning: The Magazine for Cooperation in Education*, 15, 10–14.

Schmuck, R. A., & Schmuck, P. A. (1997). *Group processes in the classroom* (7th ed.). Dubuque, IA: Wm. C. Brown.

The Secretary's Commission on Achieving Necessary Skills (1991). *What work requires of schools*: A SCANS *report for America* 2000. Washington, DC: U.S. Department of Labor.

Sharan, R., Sharan, S., Kagan, S., Hertz-Lazarowitz, R., Webb, N., & Schmuck, R. (Eds.). (1985). *Learning to cooperate, cooperating to learn*. New York: Plenum Press.

Sharan, S. (1980). Cooperative learning in small groups: Recent methods and effects on achievement, attitudes, and ethnic relations. *Review of Educational Research*, 50, 241–258.

Sharan, S. (1994). *Handbook of cooperative learning methods*. Westport, CN: Grenwood Press.

Sharan, S. (2000). 2002 by 2000: Recent research on cooperative learning. *International Association for the Study of Cooperation In Education Newsletter*, 19 (1), 2–15. Available: http://www.muohio.edu/~iascecwis//iasce_nl19–1/nl19–1–2000.html

Sharan, Y., & Sharan, S. (1992). *Expanding cooperative learning through group investigation*. New York: Teachers College Press.

Sherman, L. W. (1976). Formative evaluation, mastery grading, and peer directed small group discussions in an introductory educational psychology class. In J. B. Maas & D. A. Kleiber (Eds.), *Directory of teaching innovations in psychology* (pp. 445–446). Washington, DC: American Psychological Association.

Sherman, L. W. (1979). *Computer-managed correspondence in large lecture courses*. Paper presentation to Division 15 (Educational Psychology), 87th Annual Convention of the American Psychology Association. ERIC Document ED 247698.

Sherman, L. W. (1986). Cooperative vs. competitive educational psychology classrooms: A comparative study. *Teaching and Teacher Education: An International Journal of Research Studies*, 2, 283–295.

Sherman, L. W. (1989). A comparative study of cooperative and competitive achievement in two secondary biology classrooms: The group investigation model versus an individually competitive goal structure. *Journal of Research in Science Teaching*, 26, 55–64.

Sherman, L. W. (1990). *A pedagogical strategy for teaching developmental theories through writing: Dyadic essay confrontations*. Paper presentation to the 5th International Convention on Cooperative Learning, Baltimore MD July 6–10. ERIC Document 321–721.

Sherman, L. W. (1991). *Cooperative learning in post secondary education: Implications from social psychology for active learning experiences*. A presentation to the annual meeting of the American Educational Research Association, Chicago, IL. Available: http://miavx1.muohio.edu/~lwsh-erman/aera906.html

Sherman, L. W. (1995). A postmodern, constructivist and cooperative pedagogy for teaching educational psychology, assisted by computer mediated communications. In J. L. Schnase &

E. L. Cunnius (Eds.), *Proceedings of CSCL '95: The first international conference on computer support for collaborative learning*. Mahwah, NJ: Erlbaum.

Sherman, L. W. (1998). *CSILE as applied to teaching cooperatively*. A presentation to the 18th Annual Lilly Conference on College Teaching. Oxford, OH, November 18. Available: http://miavx1.muohio.edu/~shermalw/lilly98_wholepaper2.htmlx

Sherman, L. W. (1999). *Computer support for collaborative learning (cscl) in higher education: A postmodern, constructivist pedagogy for teaching educational psychology cooperatively*. Paper presentation to the 1999 Annual Meetings of the American Educational Research Associatio, Montreal, Canada, April 20. Available: http://miavx1.muohio.edu/~shermalw/aera99_wholepaper.htmlx

Sherman, L. W. (2000). Postmodern constructivist pedagogy for teaching and learning cooperatively on the web. *CyberPsychology and Behavior*, 3, 51–57.

Sherman, L., McMahon-Klosterman, K., Meyer, S., & Stephens, P. (1994). *"Kids can make a difference, too!": A demonstration of an interagency collaborative project using cooperative learning and telematiques*. A presentation to the 8th International Conference of the International Association for the Study of Cooperation in Education (IASCE), Lewis & Clark College, Portland, OR, 9–11 July.

Sherman, L. W., & Woy-Hazelton, S. (1988). *The student team project: A long-term cooperative strategy in graduate environmental studies*. Paper presentation to the Fourth Convention of the International Association for the Study of Cooperation in Education. Kibbutz Shefayim, Israel, July 5–8. ERIC Document ED 299–872.

Sherman, R. C. (1998). Using the World Wide Web to teach everyday applications of social psychology. *Teaching of Psychology*, 25, 212–216.

Slavin, R. E. (1978a). Student teams and achievement divisions. *Journal of Research and development in education*, 12, 39–49.

Slavin, R. E. (1978b). Student teams and comparison among equals: Effects on academic performance and student attitudes. *Journal of Educational Psychology*, 70, 532–538.

Slavin, R. E. (1983). When does cooperative learning increase student achievement? *Psychological Bulletin*, 93, 429–445.

Slavin, R. E. (1995). *Cooperative learning: Theory, research, and practice* (2nd ed.). Boston: Allyn and Bacon.

Slavin, R. E. (2000). *Educational psychology: Theory into practice* (5th ed.). Boston: Allyn & Bacon.

Webb. N. M. (1992). Testing a theoretical model of student interaction and learning in small groups. In R. Hertz-Lazarowitz & N. Miller (Eds.), *Interaction in cooperative groups: The theoretical anatomy of group learning* (pp. 153–170). Cambridge: Cambridge University Press.

Webb, N. M., & Kenderski, C. M. (1984). Student interaction and learning in small-group and whole-class settings. In P. L. Peterson, L. C. Wilkinson, & M. Hallinan (Eds.), *The social context of instruction* (pp. 153–170). New York: Academic Press.

Weinstein, C. S. (1991). The classroom as a social context for learning. *Annual Review of Psychology*, 42, 493–525.

Whetzel, D. (1992). *The secretary of labor's commission on achieving necessary skills*. ERIC Digest No. ED339749. Available: (February 25, 2000) http://www.ed.gov/databases/ERIC_Digests/ed339749.html

Wilber, K. (1998). *The marriage of sense and soul: Integrating science and religion*. New York: Random House.

Wolfe, C. R. (1995). Homespun hypertext: Student constructed hypertext as a tool for teaching critical thinking. *Teaching of Psychology*, 22, 29–33.

Wolff, R. P. (1969). *The ideal of the university*. Boston: Beacon.

Woolfolk, A. E. (1999). *Educational psychology* (7th ed.). Boston: Allyn & Bacon.

WWWboard (1995). *Matt's script archive*. Available: http://www.worldwidemart.com/scripts/wwwboard.shtml

CHAPTER

7

From Real to Virtual Communities

Cognition, Knowledge, and Intention in the World Wide Web

GIUSEPPE RIVA

Department of Psychology, Catholic University, Milan

I. INTRODUCTION

Distance learning, where student and teacher are connected by technology instead of a classroom, is becoming a viable option to traditional teaching methods, and is poised for major growth over the next several years. According to a recent market analysis (IDC, 1998), technology-based training (including Internet-based approaches) represented only 2% of the overall information technology (IT) training market in 1998. By 2003, however, the report predicts it will compose 14% of that market. According to the same research, the number of college students enrolled in distance-learning courses will reach 2.2 million in 2002, up from 710,000 in 1998. As noted by Federico (1999), "we are in the midst of a paradigm shift in education and training from classroom centric to network centric" (p. 653). However, understanding how to use the World Wide Web (Web) to support training and learning activities presents a substantial challenge for the designers and evaluators of this emerging technology. On one side, they have to explore the possibilities of successfully instructing via networks while proving the learning and cost effectiveness of these innovative systems. On the other side, they have to understand how communication and interaction, two key features of the learning process, are changed by computers.

The development of information technology has slowly changed the way people interact with computers. Technological advances have gradually shifted the focus away from computers as such, and toward what people actually do with them. In response to the environment in which people find themselves working and living, people appropriate the technology for their own needs. The most evident sign of this change has been the creation of totally new interactive communication environments like computer-mediated communication (CMC), computer-supported intentional learning experiences (CSILEs), and computer-supported collaborative work (CSCW) made possible by the increasing power and flexibility of today's information technology. In fact, the diffusion of these environments is creating a new social space, usually called cyberspace (Rheingold, 1991, 1993), that is the fertile ground for knowledge, new social relationships, roles, and a sense of self. Although CMC is not a novelty, its current spread is casting a blaze of light on the new environments created by electronic communications. The social and behavioral sciences are increasingly interested in understanding the characteristics of CMC and its effects on people, groups, and organizations (Riva & Galimberti, 1997).

Perhaps the most important change in psychosocial terms is in the concept of communication: the model of communication as the passage of information from one person to another is becoming obsolete. This model, usually called the "parcel-post model" (Shannon & Weaver, 1949; Tatar, Foster, & Bobrow, 1991), is now being radically challenged, partly because of some of the peculiar features of electronic environments, such as the asymmetry between message sender and message receiver. The information-transfer model of communication does not consider the cooperative component, very important in each learning or training activity, which stimulates reciprocal responsibility for successful interaction and a series of subtle adaptations among interlocutors. As Dohény-Farina (1991) notes, "the theory of communication as information transfer separates knowledge from communication; it treats knowledge as an object that exists independently of the participants in the innovation venture. With this independent existence, information becomes an object that can be carried through channels" (p. 8). However, it is possible to communicate only to the extent that participants have some common ground for shared beliefs, recognize reciprocal expectations, and accept rules for interaction which serve as necessary anchors in the development of conversation (Clark & Schaefer, 1989). Thus, CMC is generating a new, alternative concept of communication as the shared construction of meanings (Ghiglione, 1986; Kraut & Streeter, 1995).

Another important psychosocial change brought about by CMC lies in the concept of interaction (Riva & Galimberti, 1998a). Formerly, the physical copresence of both interacting subjects has been used to distinguish "interaction" from "relationship," with the latter implying intersubjective communication that can be maintained even at a physical distance. However, even in telephone communication, which predates digital computer technology, there can be no doubt that interlocutors do interact, even though they cannot see each other.

This chapter presents a framework for the development of web-based learning environments defining different psychosocial roots by which the knowledge and subjectivity of user are built. This has resulted in new ways of describing cyberspace; the virtual space inhabited by electronic network users. Community, for persons interacting in a technological environment, is shifting from culture-defining mass media to a proliferation of media as alternative sources of mediated experience. In fact, the key feature of cyberspace is interaction, from which a new sense of self and community can be built. A conceptual model of context is also presented here to account for interaction, identity, and knowledge construction processes. Context, according to the proposed model, is not restricted to the physical copresence of other people but consists of the interlocutory space which provides the subject with socially recognizable meanings. The author also considers some implications of this approach for current research in communication studies, with particular reference to the role of context and the link between cognition and interaction. The possible consequences of this model on web-based teaching and learning activities are outlined.

II. COGNITIONS IN THE NET: A NETWORKED APPROACH TO KNOWLEDGE

According to cognitive psychology, as opposed to traditional behaviorist theories, the acquisition and retention of knowledge are the product of different cognitive operations. Within this framework students are perceived (Federico, 1999) as "processors of information input, manipulators of intellectual throughput and producers of performance output" (p. 658). In fact, the activities that learners usually perform include selecting, encoding, organizing, retrieving, decoding, and generating information. But, how are these cognitive processes generated?

> The higher mental functions are dialogic processes derived from interpersonal activity. [They] develop through the progressive internalization of semiotically manifested perspectives on reality.... The emergence of these functions in the context of social activity constitutes the cultural line of development. (Fernyhough, 1996, pp. 47–48)

> Cognitions emerge ... from the conversational interactions in which children participate from a very early age ... Far from being circumscribed by experimental laboratory settings, cognitive activities are routine daily activities. In other words, it is in everyday life, and in conversational interaction especially, that we put our cognitive skills to practical use. (Trognon, 1992, p. 113)

These two quotations illustrate very well the so-called "dialogic approach" (Fernyhough, 1996; Saito, 1996) which seeks to assess how cognition relates to interaction, and to conversational interaction especially. Although methodological problems still have to be solved, cognitive studies are increasingly concerned with defining and exploring the relationship between cognition and interaction.

The essential groundwork for this new approach, in psychological terms at least, is provided by Bakhtin (1981, 1986), Bartlett (1932), Gergen (1982), Piaget (1995), and, of course, Vygotsky (1978). Though they differ in detail on many points, all of them agree that the social system should be seen as a network of relationships providing the *space* in which cognitions are elaborated. As hinted in the introduction, this space cannot be understood in physical terms only. That interaction no longer has to depend on the physical copresence of interlocutors is now taken for granted in the construction of nonphysical interactive settings (most typically, virtual reality) characterized by increasingly higher levels of simulation. Moreover, this shift in emphasis has revealed key structural features of interaction which have hitherto been concealed by dogmatic insistence on the physical copresence of subjects. The copresence of utterances, rather than the physical copresence of interlocutors, is now seen as the key to the construction and performance of cognitive functions (Galimberti, 1994). In this context, "copresence of utterances" is typical of the communicative exchange described by Goffman (1967) in which two interlocutors are able to influence each other's actions, and regulate the nature of their communication, through some form of feedback. Thus, cognition has a clear social connotation (Conein, De Fornel, & Quere, 1990). It is

> action, to the extent that those who take part in it have to organize a flow of shared activities by coordinating and concatenating their actions ... |and| communication, to the extent that the interlocutors make themselves mutually accessible, or render explicit the elements that enable them to understand each other and act together. (p. 19)

Most researchers, or at least, those who adopt a psychosocial approach to cognition, would find little to disagree with here. What is new, however, is that cognitive activities are increasingly being performed in networked contexts which, to varying degrees, are undeniably virtual. The network model is therefore essential to the functioning of the matrices of cognitive functions, or what De Kerckhove's calls brainframes (De Kerckhove, 1997; De Kerckhove & Lumsden, 1988). The construction of brainframes, and the overall configuration of the knowledge system, has been described by Pierre Lévy's (1994) recent concept of collective intelligence particularly well.

The concepts of "interbrainframe" and "collective intelligence" are especially useful because they enable us to describe this type of cognition in terms of two levels, micro and macro, depending on "closeness" to subject.

These levels are interconnected by a self- and other-oriented process of self-definition. Their common root is the social approach to cognition: cognition has lost its traditional connotation as a private event, and is now regarded as both a coordinated activity (in terms of process) and a networked reality (in terms of how the products of the process are distributed).

A. Interbrainframe: The Cognitive Skills Needed to Handle Hypermedia

According to De Kerckhove (1997; De Kerckhove & Lumsden, 1988) the fundamental stages in human historical "cognitive" development parallel the ways in which communication techniques and technologies have shaped not only interpretations of the human mind and brain function, but also views of society and the world over the ages. Marshall McLuhan, De Kerckhove's teacher, claimed that societies are always informed more by the means used to convey information than by the content of the information itself. Developing this insight further, De Kerckhove has identified three types of brainframe — alphabetic, video, and cybernetic — which determine how we perceive the world. The personal computer allows us to respond in a personal way to what we see on the screen (alphabetic brainframe), but the nature of our response is dictated by the rigid, inexorable logic of the program (videoframe). According to De Kerckhove, the unique feature of the cybernetic brainframe is that it enables us to externalize mental awareness; in other words, television has transformed us into image consumers, whereas the computer, by projecting us outside our own nervous systems and giving us access to, and power over, all aspects of the environment (cyberspace) we find ourselves in at any time we choose, has transformed us into information producers.

The next step from television-induced mass culture is the culture of speed and "personalized access." Networking now enables us to access any sort of information without having to move. By becoming nodes in a network, individuals can analyze the information they have access to with ever greater thoroughness and freedom of manipulation, and since networking can take you anywhere you want, it opens the way to global interaction. Developing on De Kerckhove's idea, recent advances in communications suggest that we may now be seeing the emergence of an interbrainframe, that is, the brainframe that results from the networking of minds (Riva & Galimberti, 1998b). The interbrainframe places the accent on networking, the interconnecting of a multiplicity of cognitive frames which are all simultaneously present and active in communicative interaction. This implies (Riva & Galimberti, 1998b) that "technology and human minds are linked by feedback (circular causality and reciprocity), and that this feedback generates the interaction which both structures, and is structured by action" (p. 299).

How is the concept of an interbrainframe related to web-based learning tools? Usually these tools can be considered a particular form of hypermedia. Hypermedia refers to any sort of computer-stored information which is related and retrieved via links (Federico, 1999). Although connectivity among nodes is linked to the characteristics of the specific networked environments, navigational paths through the nodes are ultimately determined by the users, who freely control the movement among nodes, according to their intrinsic interests and present goals. However, for students to thrive in these new instructional environment they must possess an adequate brainframe providing sufficient domain knowledge, experience, and ability (Shyu & Brown, 1995). As noted by Trumbull and Gay (1992), "many potential users of hypermedia systems lack the cognitive skills; the motivation or the attitude toward learning required to take full advantage of these systems" (p. 315). Consequently, students who do not possess an appropriate brainframe will likely need guidance or coaching in order to exercise effective and efficient learner control for navigating multimedia subject matter (Federico, 1999; Snow, 1980).

B. Collective Intelligence: The Instructional Ecosystem Created by the Net

The concept of collective intelligence recently proposed by Pierre Lévy (1994) is, in some ways, the anthropological equivalent of the interbrainframe. Since it is both a form of "networked reality" and a "coordinated activity," collective intelligence is the social complement of the cognitive interbrainframe concept (in terms of product and process). Lévy (1994) says that "collective intelligence is not a purely cognitive object," where intelligence has the explicit or implied meaning of phrases like "using one's intelligence," "by common accord," or "mutual understanding with the enemy" (p. 31). The emphasis is on a plurality of subjects, and the coordination and convergence of the actions they undertake. In this sense, collective intelligence should be seen as a ubiquitous intelligence which is continually being enhanced and coordinated in real time — an intelligence which mobilizes cognitive competencies. If this is true, we must also look carefully at how the products of this intelligence are handled in the space "between" minds where knowledge is generated and competencies develop. Thus, cognition can be seen as something that happens between, instead of inside, subjects. It is a media-structured loop that begins and ends with the subjects themselves — a continuous communicative exchange which generates a shared construction of reality at the interface between individual and collective (Fernyhough, 1996; Riva & Galimberti, 1997; Saito, 1996).

Naturally, the configuration of such a reality calls for a suitable type of communication technology. As Lévy himself says, "beyond a given quantitative threshold, the coordination of intelligence in real time perforce requires the use of digital information technology" (p. 56). Thus, collective intelligence relies on technological systems which enable members of a community to coordinate their interactions within the same virtual universe of knowledge, as usually happens in hypermedia. In fact, in these educational environments, "the learner is viewed as part of an instructional ecosystem, simultaneously shaping and being shaped by the instruction encountered" (Barab, Bowdish, & Lawless, 1997, p. 24).

Clearly, the web is the medium which best meets these requirements because it transforms collective intelligence into "a ubiquitous coordinated intelligence which is constantly being enhanced, coordinated and mobilized in real time" (Lévy, 1994, pp. 34–35). Hypermedia allows learner control: the creation of links and connection of different pieces of information. Obviously, the network must be intelligent, and it must also facilitate human contact by enabling subjects to recognize each other in and through the network. Facilitating human contact implies exploiting the "diversified range of knowledge and awareness" other people possess, and encouraging new, positive definitions of self by motivating other users, and eliciting in them the sense of gratitude that in turn facilitates the development of socially rather than individually oriented projects (Lévy, 1994). In the end, learning can be considered as acquisition and reorganization of knowledge structures: semantic or neural networks, or associative architectures or schemata. When students, using a specific brainframe — the interbrainframe — are engaged in hypermedia contexts, controlling acquisition by the creation of links and connections, they are also intrinsically modeling the learning process by making their own knowledge assemblies or associations in a coordinated environment (Barab et al., 1997; Federico, 1999).

III. COMMUNICATION IN THE NET: A PSYCHO-SOCIAL APPROACH TO CMC

The Introduction noted that the redefinition of communication itself is the most important psychosocial change resulting from CMC: the "parcel-post model" of communication as the passage of information from one person to another through channels is becoming obsolete. However, communication is possible only if participants have some common ground for shared beliefs, acknowledge each other's expectations, and accept interactive rules which serve to keep the developing conversation on track (Clark & Schaefer, 1989). In this sense CMC is giving rise to a new, alternative concept of communication as the shared construction of meanings (Ghiglione, 1986; Kraut & Streeter, 1995).

The starting point of this new approach is the awareness of the contractual nature of communication — the notion that something is at stake when people communicate with each other. According to this view is possible to describe communication as a coordinated attempt to construct possible worlds (Ghiglione & Trognon, 1993; Potter & Wetherell, 1987; Riva & Galimberti, 1997, 1998a; Trognon, 1992). As Ghiglione (1986) says, "communication is the co-construction of a reality using a system of signs and a mutually acceptable set of principles which make exchange possible and provide the rules needed to govern it" (p.102). Since this approach — usually referred as the "interlocutory model" — defines communication as a contractual process jointly negotiated by interlocutors, the concept of the interlocutor also has to be redefined. Each communicative event is seen as a dialectical encounter between two processes — one expressive, in which a communicating "I" addresses a receiving/uttering "you," and the other interpretative, in which an interpreting "you" in turn construes the image of an uttering "I." The two processes intertwine in a subtle interplay of mutual recognition and acknowledgment between the interlocutors involved.

A. Virtual Conversation: The Characteristics of Conversation in CMC

The first step in our analysis of CMC is the identification of two distinct types of CMC (Dix, Finlay, Abowd, & Beale, 1993): synchronous and asynchronous. Synchronous CMC is produced when communication happens simultaneously between two or more users, as in any normal telephone or face-to-face conversation. Asynchronous CMC is produced when communication is not simultaneous. The basic difference between the two is temporal (Riva & Galimberti, 1998a): for CMC to be synchronous, computers must be linked in real time.

The commonest form of asynchronous CMC is e-mail, in which a sender leaves a message in a receiver's electronic letterbox, which the receiver must open before he or she can read the message. Another more sophisticated type of asynchronous CMC is a newsgroup, an electronic notice board on which users can post messages referring to a specific topic or area of interest. Users can read the messages by opening the notice board and send their own messages in turn. As with e-mail, there is no real-time link between the computers of the interacting subjects.

Despite the predominance of the textual mode, it has been shown that asynchronous CMC differs in psychosocial terms from nonelectronic written communication, as well as from other existing means of communication. Experimental studies designed to compare CMC and nonelectronic written communication (Lea, 1991; Rice, 1993) have revealed significant differences in their respective degrees of social presence and media richness. Social presence is the user's perception of the ability of the means of communication to marshal and focus the presence of communicating subjects (Short, Williams, & Christie, 1976), while media richness is the ability of the means of communication to interlink a variety of topics, render them less ambiguous, and enable users to learn about them within a given time span (Daft & Lengel, 1986). Studies by Rice (1992, 1993) have shown that there is significant variation in user perceptions of the degree of social presence and media richness in e-mail and videoconferencing compared with other means of communication like the telephone and written text.

Unlike asynchronous CMC, the essential feature of synchronous CMC is that it does provide a real-time link between users' computers (Riva & Galimberti, 1998a). Although the most often cited example is videoconferencing, the most widespread system is Internet Relay Chat, or IRC. IRC is a form of synchronous CMC which enables a group of users (a chat) to exchange written messages and interact with each other in two different ways — by sending a message either to a specified user or to all members of the chat (Riva & Galimberti, 1998b). One IRC variant of particular interest to communication researchers is MUDs (originally "MULTI-USER DUNGEONS" or Dimensions, also a MOO, MUSH, or VEE),

> a software which accepts the multi-user link through a certain type of network ... and gives each user access to a shared databank of rooms, exits and other objects. Each user consults and manipulates the databank from inside one of the rooms, see[s] only the objects in that room, and moves to other rooms mostly by using the exits that link them. (Curtis, 1996, p. 229)

In practical terms, MUDs may be regarded as a form of network-accessible, multi-participant, user-extensible virtual reality whose interface is entirely textual. This approach enables users not only to speak to each other (as in IRC) but also to explore the space they find themselves in, and to interact with the objects in it (Parks & Floyd, 1996). Another feature of MUDs is that they enable users to interact in more complex ways than are possible with IRC. As well as sending written messages, MUD participants can use metacommands to describe their emotions and perform complex actions like striking another user or giving him objects (Curtis, 1997; Parks & Floyd, 1996).

Educational MUDs are an important presence on the Internet (Cherny, 1999). They range from MUDs designed as educational play spaces for children to MUDs for college students in which structured classroom activities happen (Bruckman, 1997). For instance, MicroMUSE, also known as "Cyberion City" is an educational play space founded by Stan Lim in 1990 and whose membership has reached 800, of whom half are children. Other educational MUD efforts have involved older students using MUDs as extensions of classroom activities, for instance, in conjunction with composition classes (Cherny, 1999).

One fairly recent form of synchronous CMC is the Internet Phone, an IRC mode that replaces written text with voice messages. But the latest and

TABLE 7.1
Shared Hypermedia Tools

Tool	Developer	Website
Firetalk	Multitude	http://www.firetalk.com
Gooey4	Hypernix	http://www.gooey.com
ICQSurf	ICQ	http://www.icq.com/icqsurf
Instant Rendezvous	Multimate	http://www.multimate.net
Odigo	NovaWiz	http://www.odigo.com

most interesting forms of synchronous CMC, especially for their possible use in learning activities, are shared hypermedia (SHY). SHY comprise new Internet tools attaching IRC to web browsing (see Table 7.1 for a set of SHY tools). In fact, these tools enable people who are simultaneously browsing the same web site to communicate with each other. The twist is that the chatters automatically have something in common: the web page they are reading. On any web site SHY users can see a list of other users and talk with them on group and private levels. By assembling people with similar interests and surfing habits, this new Internet platform transforms Web browsing into a social activity. SHY further enhances the user experience by consolidating different forms of CMC (e-mail and IRC) into one fully integrated interface. The most advanced SHY tools (i.e. Firetalk) have an option called the *web tour* that is very interesting for its potential use in teaching. During a web tour a leader can guide the browsing of a small group of users, who are forced to follow him, interacting with them in real time. Synchronous CMC also has special features which distinguish it from other forms of communication. According to Newhagen (1996) these include (especially in synchronous CMC via the Internet) multimediality, hypertextuality, packet switching, synchronicity, and interactivity.

There is a technical reason for these differences between synchronous and asynchronous CMC. Communication with a keyboard and computer screen takes longer than normal face-to-face communication, and the absence of metacommunicative features like facial expression, posture, and tone of voice encourages users to find other ways of making communication as complete as possible. These limitations make CMC interaction more rarefied than the kind of interaction that happens in normal conversation (Riva & Galimberti, 1997). It is rarefied in the sense that CMC uses mainly textual devices, that is, abbreviations and smiles (Dix et al., 1993) as well as MUD metacommands (Curtis, 1997), to reproduce the metacommunicative features (emotions, illocutionary force) of face-to-face conversation. Some common abbreviations (in English) are CUL8R ("See you later"), HowRU ("How are you?"), 2B ("to be"), IMHO ("In my humble opinion"), and

WRT ("with respect to"), and many of them are used to add an emotional dimension on the literal meaning of messages. For example, IMHO adds funny overtones to a sentence. Smiles — graphic symbols depicting a stylized smiling face — are also much used. The most popular are : –) to convey positive emotion,: - (to convey negative emotion, and : – o to convey surprise.

However, the differences between CMC and face-to-face conversation are important. While face-to-face conversation happens in a cooperative environment constantly regulated by mutual adjustment and correction (Galimberti, 1994; Goodwin & Heritage, 1990), CMC occurs in a much less cooperative environment because of the special conditions imposed by the medium itself (Brennan, 1991). In most CMC environments, and in asynchronous CMC environments especially, two typical features of face-to-face conversation are missing (Mantovani, 1996b): The collaborative commitment of participants to the coformulation of the message and the feedback which allows the social meaning of the message to be processed immediately.

CMC in no way guarantees that a user's declared identity is the real one. The use of false identities, often of a different sex, is widespread in electronic communities and in MUDs especially (Curtis, 1997; Mantovani, 1995, 1996a; Parks & Floyd, 1996; Riva & Galimberti, 1998b; see Jazwinski, chapter 9 of this volume, for a discussion of gender identities on the Internet). In this sense, CMC may be regarded as an example of virtual conversation (Riva & Galimberti, 1997), that is, a necessarily "pared-down" or, more precisely, rarefied form of conversation which lacks the rules on which effective interaction depends. Computer mediation creates an asymmetrical imbalance in the sender–receiver relationship: the sender can transmit information and get cooperation under way, but has no guarantee that the receiver receives the transmission, while the receiver has no guarantee that the sender's declared identity is the real one (Riva & Galimberti, 1998a).

Ghiglione's (1986) definition of communication as the co-construction of a reality using systems of signs and rules applies equally well to CMC as an instance of virtual conversation, with the important difference that in CMC a reality is asymmetrically co-constructed because the receiver can decide at will to terminate interaction or to continue it by turning himself into a sender. This decision is far from casual: it depends on how the receiver interprets the situation, what his aims are, and the social rules that govern his behavior. Some researchers have even used the term "electronic opportunism" to describe this feature of CMC (Rocco & Warglien, 1995). In this sense, CMC may be defined as a process by which a group of social actors in a given situation negotiate the meaning of the various situations which arise between them (Stasser, 1992).

IV. COMMUNITY IN THE NET: CREATING SHARED CONTEXTUAL MEANING

A. Understanding Situations: The First Step toward Shared Contextual Meaning

Stasser's definition of CMC may seem straightforward enough, but it has two important implications which have had a decisive effect on CMC studies. If CMC is a process of negotiation then the only way to understand it is by analyzing the subjects involved in it, and in the environment in which they operate. This means that the social context in which CMC occurs plays a crucial role. This also suggests that new processes and activities will develop which challenge and change the initial relationship between subject and context. Most researchers would broadly agree that these two statements are true. According to Mantovani (1996a) the early 1990s saw changes in the study paradigms of person–computer and person–computer–person inter-action. The main result of this has been the realization that interaction can only be fully understood through detailed analysis of the social context in which it happens (Mantovani, 1996a):

> At this point we should no longer see people simply as "users" of given systems, but as social "actors." In other words, whether expert computer users or not, people act independently and have their own reasons for what they do, and it is computers and systems that have to adapt to people, not vice versa. (p. 63).

This idea is also shared by many educational psychologists. Many of them have asserted that no single teaching method is best for all students (Cronbach & Snow, 1977; Glaser, 1976). As noted by Schroeder and Grabowsky (1995), "in a highly learner controlled hypermedia environment, learners navigate through the information creating a personal interpretative representation of that information. Each individual can take a different path, encountering different amounts and types of information" (p. 313). If this is true then students, when using web-based learning tools, will be able to reach educational goals more efficiently when instructional procedures are adapted to individual differences. And this calls for both the knowledge of the different aptitudes of the users and the knowledge of the social context where the learning activity will happen. But, how can we analyze the social context of web-based learning tools?

Our starting point is the situated action theory (SAT) developed within the field of sociocognitive research known as "cognition in practice." Though based on traditional cognitivist analyses of information processing and symbolization, SAT introduces a change of perspective in that it sees action not as the execution of a ready-conceived plan, but as adaptation to context (Suchman, 1987). As noted by Federico (1999),

> if hypermedia can be considered a knowledge base, then students' navigational paths through this semantic network-like structure can show what nodes they linked,

> thereby uncovering what concepts are associated. This, in turn, can reveal semantic structures constructed by individuals as they attempt to learn the entire knowledge base, or acquire the course content. (p. 669)

This means, as Suchman notes, that "instead of separating action from the circumstances in which it occurs as the execution of a carefully thought out plan ... [SAT] tries to study how people use circumstances to develop an intelligent course of action" (1987, p.167). This necessitates profound changes in how "social context" has previously been defined. In SAT, social context is not something physical and highly stable like an organization or the power structure within it. As Mantovani (1996a) stresses, contexts are not given, but made. Context is conceptual as well as physical: actors perceive situations using cultural models, and act accordingly in cultural ways. However, context is unstable: cultural models are constantly changed by subjects' actions and choices.

Applying SAT to CMC, Mantovani (1996a,b) concludes that CMC participants cannot be regarded simply as technology users. Rather, they are social actors with their own aims and autonomy in situations, and it is technology which must adapt to them. This idea poses serious problems. If social actors actively respond to their environment and end up changing it, how can context ever be analyzed properly? Mantovani meets the difficulty with a three-level model of social context which links situation and social norms to the use of computer technology. The first level is social context in general, the second, ordinary situations of everyday life, and the third, local interaction with the environment via computers.

The links between the three levels can be studied in either direction, starting from use of computers or from social context. Thus, the use of computers may be regarded as part of everyday life, which is in turn part of the broader social context. By interacting with each other, the physical environment, and the social context, subjects activate a spiral of actor–environment exchanges. First-level person–computer interaction leads to interaction in everyday situations, and thence to cultural changes. Working in the opposite direction, social context supplies the elements needed to interpret situations correctly, and situations generate the aims which determine local interaction with the environment via computer. So, as we have seen, social context may be defined as the symbolic system of a given culture which is continually being altered by practical human intervention; it cannot be explained exclusively in terms of the interpersonal relationships, or physical environment, in which information exchanges take place. Social context is a prerequisite of communication — "a shared symbolic order in which action becomes meaningful, and so generates meaning" (Mantovani, 1996b, p. 106).

Thus, SAT implies a radical redefinition of the meaning of communication. Context may be co-constructed by social actors, but they use communication to exchange meanings, not pieces of information. More precisely, the content of communication is the interpretation of the situations which actors are involved in. In this sense, the most effective way of clarifying the meaning of messages is to relate them to a shared context of meaning. However, a number of students do not have sufficient metacognitive experience (brainframe) in monitoring and controlling their learning in these network-based instructional settings. As underlined by Federico (1999), "these individuals have limited situation assessment skills and decision making schemata that allow them to exercise efficiently and effectively learner control in these hypermedia settings. Consequently, what is needed is a practical means of tracking students' navigation paths through this content" (p. 669).

B. Creating Community: The Second Step toward Shared Contextual Meaning

Shared hypermedia (SHY) may be an answer to the problem of students' lack of adequate metacognitive abilities. A teacher using SHY can employ a number of techniques, including monitoring the learners' routes through the hypermedia content; providing feedback to individuals about their navigational paths and consequences for acquisition; and guiding students' interactions with the subject matter. However, to be effective, SHY-based learning systems calls for conceptual mechanisms with which groups can be built and vehicles through which groups can express themselves (Oravec, 1996). Usually learners view themselves in the shared web experience in terms of how they manage the other users with which they are associated, particularly by relating to such cultural objects as "consistency," "integration," or "balance."

Studies of positioning theory (PT) have served to reinforce this view. As recently formulated by Rom Harré (1989; Harré & Van Langenhove, 1991), PT replaces the traditional concept of "role" with the concept of "positioning." The main difference between the two is that a role is a stable and clearly defined category, while positioning is a dynamic process generated by communication. Positioning theory adds new ideas about the relationship between mental and communicative processes to its analysis of context. As we have seen, there is indeed a link between mental and communicative processes which leads to the formation of specific mental structures called brainframes. However, PT is mainly concerned with the relationship between communication, social context, self, and identity.

The notion that discourse and conversation are closely linked to both mental processes (including attitudes and emotions) and social context is typical of Russian thought. One example is Vygotsky's analysis of the link between mental processes and social context in adult–child conversation. As is well known, Vygotsky (1978) believed that this culture-specific form of conversation is internalized by the child to become a part of her mental processes: "Each function in the child's cultural development appears twice: first between people (interpsychology) and then within the child (intrapsychology)" (p. 57). In reality, external language and interior dialogue are intimately related, and the link plays, as we have already seen, a crucial role in the formation of the subject's identity and higher mental processes (Fernyhough, 1996; Saito, 1996). The way interaction with other subjects mediates meaning is fundamental to this shift from external language to interior dialogue. In conversation, the subject not only acts as a goal-directed individual/self, but also actively collaborates in the positioning process. As Davies and Harré (1990) point out, subjects' selves during interaction "participate in an observable and subjectively coherent way in the joint production of story lines" (p. 48). In this phase subjects see themselves as "contradictors" (Davies & Harré, 1990) and use the positioning process to construct "a variety of selves" (p. 47) closely linked to the outcome of interaction. This is very similar to the "transactional contextualism" developed by anthropologists and sociologists. For example, Rosaldo (1984) says that the notion of self develops not from some internal essence relatively unaffected by the social world, but from experience accumulated in the world of meanings, images, and social relationships in which each person is unavoidably involved.

In psychology, these ideas have carried over into the work of Gergen (1982) and Bruner (1993). Gergen specifically has looked in detail at the construction of self in studies of how an individual's self-esteem and concept of self vary in different situations. These studies show that the concept of self varies both in relation to the kind of people the subject associates with and in response to the positive and negative comments they make. Altogether, then, the self may be seen as a product of the situation in which the subject acts. For his part, Bruner, though accepting the subject's autonomy, speaks of "creatures of history" whose selves are both "a guarantee of stability and a barometer reflecting changes in the cultural climate" (1993, p. 108).

So, the critical question is: in which way is a SHY-based learning experience related to the co-construction processes typical of positioning? Our starting point will be CMC. As previously discussed, Riva and Galimberti (1997) regard CMC as a form of virtual conversation, that is, rarefied, pared-down conversation lacking the rules which alone can ensure that effective interaction happens. Computer mediation creates an asymmetrical relationship between sender and receiver which enables the sender to send information and initiate cooperation, but does not guarantee that others receives the message. It also offers the receiver no guarantee that the sender's declared identity is the real one.

That this dual effect is a powerful influence on positioning and construction of self is more than evident in Internet communication (Riva & Galimberti, 1997). Hypermedia itself can be considered a kind of interlocutor because it adds to the positioning process objects and meanings which are alien to the interacting subjects. The concepts of cyberspace and collective intelligence clearly show that hypermedia is a "parallel universe" created and maintained by the networks in which subjects interact. Moreover, in shared hypermedia there is no guarantee that the declared identities of the interactors are real (Mantovani, 1995, 1996b). It is surely no accident that members of electronic communities very often adopt false "nickname" identities and openly accept them in others. Within the same community, a person may "construct and project mask-like identities which function as delegated puppets [or] agents" (Stone, 1991, p. 105). Gender switches are also commonly made, often for rather specific reasons — to get to know people of the opposite sex with a view to meeting them, or exploring the emotions of people of the opposite sex — although the fun of simply "dressing up" and pretending to be someone else is also a factor (see Jazwinski, chapter 9, this volume).

However, there is a problem here: how can you communicate and activate the positioning process in a shared hypermedia without staking your own identity on the outcome? As we have seen, communication always needs a framework of rules and meanings, and this is especially true of CMC in which many features of face-to-face conversation are "rarefied." According to Stone (1991), one solution is to represent yourself by "coding cultural expectations at a symbolic level" (p. 102). In constructing a false identity, the subject has to make wider use of social stereotypes than would be the case in normal conversation if he wishes his identity to be recognized and accepted. This means that CMC may force subjects to resort to massive use of stereotypical attitudes and behaviors — otherwise they are unlikely to achieve any shared understanding of actions and situations (Mantovani, 1996a).

As Meyrowitz (1985) points out, our social context has changed because of the technology of communication. The influence of social context on the construction of identity is beginning to wane, especially in younger people, as reference communities like the family, school, or church, which in the past anchored social contexts in shared sets of rules, gradually loosen their grip. The present situation would seem to be that the new media are accelerating the dissolution of traditional rule-based social contexts whose gradual disappearance is progressively emptying the media themselves of meaning. Many of the developers of shared hypermedia are aware of this trend and are conscious of the need to "create community" in the context of their efforts (Oravec, 1996). Even if many of the traditional means for creating community are not available, a great effort is given to the creation of virtual auditoriums or meeting rooms. According to Coate (1992) the work of maintaining virtual communities is similar to the one of an innkeeper: facilitating interaction and keeping order among patrons. In fact, if shared hypermedia has to serve as community for its users, it has to embody, or replace with adequate substitutes, some functions of community life that parallel those currently provided by "traditional" communities.

According to Cutler (1995), in the socially constructed space of cyber-space, where interaction produces culture, information is the only real medium of exchange an individual has with which to build a presence. Information exchange becomes the carrier for expressing self-concept and eliciting emotional support. Affiliations which form around general and special interests are limited only by the ability of individuals to process all the interactions that flow through the network to the desktop. The range and relative newness of affiliations mean that they have little or no time-bound histories. As noted by Cutler (1995), "commitment to relationships and community does not come out of previous relationships but out of the temporal mutuality of interests" (p. 21). At the same time, however, there may be changes in how personal identity develops. Identity building through communication works because people can interact. Thus, the opportunity for interaction becomes the key to understanding places where identity may be formed and affiliations made. Through discourse made possible by a shared hypermedia, individuals find or form groups that share interests.

V. CONCLUSIONS

Internet-based information and communication are changing how instruc-tion and assessment are being conducted in innovative schools, colleges, and universities throughout the world (Federico, 1999). In fact, many acade-mic institutions and private corporations are now recognizing the need for learning at a distance. However, understanding how to use the web to support training and learning activities presents a substantial challenge for the designers and evaluators of this emerging technology. In particular, they have to understand how communication and interaction, two key features of the learning process, are modified by the use of computers. This chapter explored these changes and defined some guidelines for the development of web-based learning tools.

Web-based learning tools can be considered a particular form of hypermedia: computer-stored information which is related and retrieved via links. In hypermedia, navigational paths through the nodes are ultimately determined by the users, who freely control the movement among nodes, according to intrinsic interests and present goals. In fact, in these educa-tional environments "the learner is viewed as part of an instructional ecosys-tem, simultaneously shaping and being shaped by the instruction encountered" (Barab et al., 1997 p. 24). However, for students to thrive in hypermedia they must possess an adequate brainframe providing sufficient domain knowledge, experience, and ability. When this happens, students can intrinsically model the learning process by making their own knowledge assemblies or associations in a coordinated environment (Barab et al., 1997; Federico, 1999).

The evolution of hypermedia has led to shared hypermedia — new Internet tools attaching IRC to web browsing. In SHY, different users who are simultaneously browsing the same web site can communicate with each other. On any web site with SHY, users can see a list of other users and communicate with them on both group and individual levels. By assembling people with similar interests and surfing habits, this new Internet platform transforms web browsing into a social activity. The most advanced SHY tools also have a web tour option allowing a leader to both guide the browsing of a small group of users and interact with them in real time. However, to be effective, the use of SHY-based learning systems calls for conceptual mechanisms with which groups can be constructed and vehicles through which groups can express themselves.

This analysis has enabled us to identify three nearly parallel theoretical tracks of great use to creators and users of web-based learning tools. The first leads from intersubjective interpretation of cognitive processes to the notion that cognition is a coordinated activity whose products are situated not in the mind, but in the space between minds. The second leads from communication as a linear process to the use of interlocutory models as paradigms of communicative interaction. The third leads from the essential passivity of communication technology users to active participation in the functioning of a tool (the hypermedia), which also influences user individuation and identity.

As we have seen, each has important methodological and technical implications for the study and development of web-based learning tools. On the one hand, "teacher" and "student," both of which are abstract, monofunctional entities, have been replaced by interlocutors endowed with thoughts, emotions, affects, and a psychosocial identity which expresses their positioning within groups, organizations, and institutions. On the other hand, we must now look carefully not only at the social impact but also (and more importantly) at the implications for users' identities and understanding of what actually happens in networked interaction in shared communicative environments. I believe that this integrated model can prove a useful framework and might stimulate the development of future studies taking into account the important link between cognition, knowledge, and interaction. An understanding of the inherent integration of cognition, knowledge, and social interaction is also necessary if web-based learning tools are to live up to their potential.

References

Bakhtin, M. M. (1981). Discover in the novel. In M. Holquist (Ed.), *Dialogic imagination: Four essays by M. M. Bakhtin* (pp. 259–422). Austin, TX: University of Texas Press.

Bakhtin, M. M. (1986). *Speech genres and other late essays*. Austin, TX: University of Texas Press.

Barab, S., Bowdish, B., & Lawless, K. (1997). Hypermedia navigation: Profiles of hypermedia users. *Educational Technology Research and Development, 45*, 23–41.

Bartlett, F. C. (1932). *Remembering: A study in experimental and social psychology.* Cambridge, MA: Cambridge University Press.

Brennan, S. E. (1991). Conversation with and through computers. *User modeling and user-adapted interaction,* 1 (1), 67–86.

Bruckman, A. (1997). *MOOSE crossing: Construction, community and learning in a networked virtual world for kids.* Unpublished Ph.D. dissertation, Massachusetts Institute of Technology, Cambridge, MA.

Bruner, J. (1993). *Acts of meaning.* Jerusalem: Harvard University Press.

Cherny, L. (1999). *Conversation and community: Chat in a virtual world.* Stanford, CA: CSLI Publications.

Clark, H. H., & Schaefer, E. F. (1989). Contributing to discourse. *Cognitive Science,* 13, 259–294.

Coate, J. (1992). Innkeeping in cyberspace. *Proceedings of directions and implications of advanced computing.* Palo Alto, CA: Computer Professionals for Social Responsibility.

Conein, B., De Fornel, M., & Quere, L. (1990). *Les formes de la conversation* (Vol. 1). Paris: CNET.

Cronbach, L., & Snow, R. (1977). *Aptitudes and instructional methods: A handbook for research on interaction.* New York: Irvington.

Curtis, P. (1996). Comunicazione via MUD: I fenomeni sociali delle realta virtuali basate su testo [Communication via MUD: Social phenomena of virtual reality based on text.]. *Sistemi Intelligenti,* 8 (2), 229–253.

Curtis, P. (1997). Mudding: Social phenomena in text-based virtual realities. In K. Sara (Ed.), *Culture of the Internet* (pp. 121–142). Mahwah, NJ: Erlbaum.

Cutler, R. H. (1995). Distributed presence and community in cyberspace. *Interpersonal Computer and Technology,* 3 (2), 12–32.

Daft, R. L., & Lengel, R. H. (1986). Organizational information requirements, media richness and structural design. *Management Science,* 32, 554–571.

Davies, B., & Harré, R. (1990). Positioning: The discursive production of selves. *Journal for the Theory of Social Behaviour,* 20, 43–63.

De Kerckhove, D. (1997). *Planetary mind: Collective intelligence in the digital age.* New York: HardWired.

De Kerckhove, D., & Lumsden, C. J. (Eds.). (1988). *The alphabet and the brain.* New York: Springer Verlag.

Dix, A., Finlay, J., Abowd, G., & Beale, R. (1993). *Human-computer interaction.* New York: Prentice Hall.

Dohény-Farina, S. (1991). *Rhetoric, innovation, technology: Case studies of technical communication in technology transfers.* Cambridge, MA: MIT Press.

Federico, P. A. (1999). Hypermedia environments and adaptive instructions. *Computers in Human Behavior,* 15 (6), 653–692.

Fernyhough, C. (1996). The dialogic mind: A dialogic approach to the higher mental functions. *New Ideas in Psychology,* 14 (1), 47–62.

Galimberti, C. (1994). Dalla comunicazione alla conversazione [From communication to conversation]. *Ricerche di Psicologia,* 18 (1), 113–152.

Gergen, K. J. (1982). *Toward transformation in social knowledge.* New York: Springer.

Ghiglione, R. (1986). *L'homme communiquant.* Paris: A. Colin.

Ghiglione, R., & Trognon, A. (1993). *Où va la pragmatique.* Grenoble: PUG.

Glaser, R. (1976). Components of a psychology of instruction: Toward a science of design. *Review of Educational Research,* 46, 1–24.

Goffman, E. (1967). *Interaction ritual: Essays on face-to-face behavior.* New York: Doubleday.

Goodwin, C., & Heritage, J. (1990). Conversation analysis. *Annual Review of Anthropology,* 19, 283–307.

Harré, R. (1989). Language and science of psychology. *Journal for the Theory of Social Behaviour and Personality,* 4, 165–188.

Harré, R., & Van Langenhove, L. (1991). Varieties of positioning. *Journal for the Theory of Social Behaviour,* 21, 393–408.

150   Giuseppe Riva

IDC (1998). *Worldwide and U.S. IT education and training markets, 1998–2003.* Framingham, MA: International Data Corporation.

Kraut, R. E., & Streeter, L. A. (1995). Coordination in software development. *Communication of the ACM*, 38 (3), 69–81.

Lea, M. (1991). Rationalist assumptions in cross media comparisons of computer mediated communication. *Behavior and Information Technology*, 10 (2), 153–172.

Lévy, P. (1994). *L'intelligence collectif* [Collective intelligence]. Paris: La Découverte.

Mantovani, G. (1995). Virtual reality as a communication environment: Consensual hallucination, fiction, and possible selves. *Human Relations*, 48 (6), 669–683.

Mantovani, G. (1996a). *New communication environments: From everyday to virtual.* London: Taylor & Francis.

Mantovani, G. (1996b). Social context in HCI: A new framework for mental models, cooperation and communication. *Cognitive Science*, 20, 237–296.

Meyrowitz, J. (1985). *No sense of place: The impact of electronic media on social behavior.* New York: Oxford University Press.

Mitchell, W. J. (1995). *City of bits.* Cambridge, MA: MIT Press.

Newhagen, J. E. (1996). Why communication researchers should study the Internet: A dialogue. *Journal of Communication*, 46 (1), 4–13.

Oravec, J. A. (1996). *Virtual individuals, virtual groups: Human dimension of groupware and computer networking.* Cambridge: Cambridge University Press.

Parks, M. R., & Floyd, K. (1996). Making friends in cyberspace. *Journal of Communication*, 46 (1), 80–97.

Piaget, J. (1995). *Sociological studies.* London: Routledge.

Potter, J., & Wetherell, M. (1987). *Discourse and social psychology.* London: Sage.

Rheingold, H. (1991). *Virtual reality.* New York: Summit Books.

Rheingold, H. (1993). *The virtual community: Homesteading on the electronic frontier.* Reading, MA: Addison-Wesley.

Rice, R. R. (1992). Contexts of research on organizational computer-mediated communication: A recursive review. In M. Lea (Ed.), *Context of computer-mediated communication* (pp. 113–143). Hemel Hempstead: Harvester-Wheatsheaf.

Rice, R. R. (1993). Media appropriateness — Using social presence theory to compare traditional and new organizational media. *Human Communication Research*, 19 (4), 451–458.

Riva, G., & Galimberti, C. (1997). The psychology of cyberspace: A socio-cognitive framework to computer mediated communication. *New Ideas in Psychology*, 15 (2), 141–158.

Riva, G., & Galimberti, C. (1998a). Computer-mediated communication: Identity and social interaction in an electronic environment. *Genetic, Social and General Psychology Monographs*, 124 (4), 434–464.

Riva, G., & Galimberti, C. (1998b). Interbrain frame: Interaction and cognition in computer-mediated communication. *CyberPsychology & Behavior*, 1 (3), 295–310.

Rocco, E., & Warglien, M. (1995). La comunicazione mediata da computer e l'emergere dell'opportunismo elettronico [The growth of electronic opportunism in computer-mediated communication]. *Sistemi Intelligenti*, 7 (3), 393–420.

Rosaldo, M. (1984). Toward an anthropology of self and feeling. In R. A. Shweder & R. A. LeVine (Eds.), *Culture theory: Essays on the mind, self and emotion* (pp. 124–136). Cambridge: Cambridge University Press.

Saito, A. (1996). Social origins of cognition: Bartlett, evolutionary perspective and embodied mind approach. *Journal of the Theory of Social Behaviour*, 26 (4), 399–422.

Schroeder, H., & Grabowsky, B. (1995). Patterns of exploration and learning with hypermedia. *Journal of Educational Computing Research*, 13, 313–335.

Shannon, C. E., & Weaver, W. (1949). *The mathematical theory of communication.* Urbana, IL: University of Illinois Press.

Short, J., Williams, E., & Christie, B. (1976). *The social psychology of telecommunications.* London: Wiley.

Shyu, H., & Brown, S. (1995). Learner-control: The effects of learning a procedural task during computer based videodisk instruction. *International Journal of Instructional Media*, 22, 217–231.

Snow, R. (1980). Aptitude, learner control, and adaptive instruction. *Educational Psychologist*, 15, 151–158.

Stasser, G. (1992). Pooling of unshared information during group discussion. In S. Worchell, W. Wood, & J. A. Simpson (Eds.), *Group processes and productivity* (pp. 48–67). Newbury Park, CA: Sage.

Stone, A. R. (1991). Will the real body please stand up? Boundary stories about virtual cultures. In M. Benedikt (Ed.), *Cyberspace: First steps*. Cambridge, MA: MIT Press.

Suchman, L. (1987). *Plans and situated action*. Cambridge: Cambridge University Press.

Tatar, D. G., Foster, G., & Bobrow, D. G. (1991). Design for conversation: Lessons from Cognoter. *International Journal of Man-Machine Studies*, 34, 185–209.

Trognon, A. (1992). Psicologia cognitiva e analisi delle conversazioni [Cognitive psychology and conversation analysis]. In C. Galimberti (Ed.), *La conversazione. Prospettive sull'interazione psicosociale* [Conversation: Perspectives in psychosocial interaction] (pp. 110–122). Milan: Guerini e Associati.

Trumbull, D., & Gay, G. (1992). Students' actual and perceived use of navigational and guidance tools in a hypermedia program. *Journal of Research on Computing in Education*, 24, 315–318.

Vygotsky, L. S. (1978). *Mind in society: The development of higher psychological processes*. Cambridge, MA: Harvard University Press.

CHAPTER

8

How Can the Web Support the Learning of Psychology?

NICK HAMMOND AND ANNIE TRAPP

Department of Psychology, University of York, United Kingdom

I. INTRODUCTION

Forms of learning are diverse. We learn on our own, and we learn from others; we learn from abstractions, and we learn by doing; we learn through exploration and discovery, and we learn through repetition and focus; learning may be a by-product of mere exposure, or it may only be achieved through hard work. Examples of all of these can be seen in learning with the Web. As psychologists, we claim to have some understanding of how different learning tasks and contexts map onto underlying constructs, and thus which situations may result in more or less effective learning outcomes (e.g., Laurillard, 1993). But our understanding is patchy and limited. Specifying a precise model of the cognitive changes which occur during a close encounter with an artifact as mundane as a textbook, let alone the Web, is not yet a feasible exercise — we do not know enough about the detailed mechanisms of learning. However, in designing effective environments for learning, this lack of precision may not be so important. What matters is that we have some understanding of the situations and conditions that promote effective learning, even if we do not entirely understand what is going on in the learner's head. For instructional design, it is the "engineering" rather than the science of learning that is important.

Vincent and Whalley (1998) have recently characterized the Web as an enormous CD-ROM. Indeed they point out that this analogy has been exploited by developers who produce Web and CD-ROM applications which share the same browser for each medium. While this aptly captures the aspects of the Web as an extensive and rich resource of information, we consider it to be only a partial analogue because the analogy is too static. The Web is not just a technology to learn *from*, it is a technology to learn *with*. The Web has creative, dynamic, and communicative aspects that go beyond a CD-ROM. The Web is creative in that learners can construct and share their own representations. It is dynamic in helping learners make sense of diverse materials, and in supporting facilities for reflection and integration. The Web is also communicative in broadening opportunities for communication with peers, teachers, and communities of practice.

We start this chapter with a brief consideration of the main theoretical positions that have influenced thinking about uses of the Web to support learning. This chapter is not primarily about theoretical issues, and we will not pin our flag to the mast of a single theoretical position. Rather, we will attempt to draw out some of the common themes and principles that are relevant to learning with the Web, and suggest a framework to help categorize different uses of the Web to support the learning of psychology. In particular, we will focus on the Web as a tool that both enables learners to broaden their experience and supports them in making sense of their experiences. We see this "sense-making" as a theme common to diverse theoretical views about learning, and one that is especially relevant to effective use of the Web. The next, and main, section of the chapter explores uses of the Web reported in a number of case studies from departments of psychology in the United Kingdom (UK). Finally, we provide a summary of points arising from this brief review.

II. EDUCATIONAL THEORY AND WEB-BASED LEARNING

Educational and instructional design is informed by a range of theoretical positions — unfortunately, at times, with insufficient consideration of their applicability to the particular learning situation and its context. Different theoretical camps adopt distinct but overlapping explanatory frameworks, and tend to apply them to distinct but overlapping learning situations. Before considering mainstream approaches, we will dismiss a surprisingly common view which has been termed the "homeopathic fallacy" (McKendree, Reader, & Hammond, 1995): this is that the analogous network-like structure of both the Web and the central nervous system (or, perhaps more plausibly, between the Web and the associative structure of memory) somehow enhances a more direct transfer of information from computer screen to the mind. One comment will suffice to illustrate this point of view: "The book is a wonderful invention, but it has one major flaw — the linear artifact. Computers allow information to be stored and accessed relationally, thereby mimicking the central nervous system" (Noblitt, cited in McKendree et al., 1995). To draw the inference that this similarity is a contributor to effective learning is a little like claiming that porridge is good for learning because it looks like the gray matter of the brain. What matters is the mechanisms and processes that are brought to bear in different learning situations, not whether there is some general structural similarity, and it is to these we turn

A cognitivist may focus largely on how individuals recruit their cognitive capabilities (memory, attention, knowledge representation, motivation, and so forth) to support learning tasks (e.g., Anderson, 2000). This view largely adopts an acquisitional or a tutoring approach to instructional design, where an analysis of both the information to be learned and the cognitive requirements lead to appropriate sequences or procedures to optimize learning. This may, for example, be in the form of mastery learning (e.g., Guskey & Gates, 1986) or of intelligent tutoring (e.g., Koedinger, Anderson, Hadley, & Mark, 1997). Constructivists, on the other hand, emphasize the importance of supporting learners in constructing personal meanings for events and activities (e.g., Jonassen, Peck, & Wilson, 1999; Papert, 1990). Learning, according to this view, is primarily developed through activity rather than through direct knowledge-acquisition strategies such as rehearsal. It is not hard to see that cognitivists and constructivists share some common theoretical ground (for instance, both stress the importance of meaning and understanding); the difference is more in terms of their recipes for educational practice. For constructivists, computers are best seen as "mindtools" to help learners make activities more meaningful (e.g., Mayes, 1992).

Educationalists in the situated learning camp place the main emphasis on the influences of the social contexts in which the acquired skills or knowledge are typically embedded (Glaser, 1990; Wenger, 1998). There are actually two aspects to the notion of social context, as pointed out by Barab and Duffy (2000). The first is the claim that learning activity must be "authentic," and therefore situated as closely as possible in the context of real use. There are clear links here with cognitivist notions of context-dependent learning, though the situated learning view raises questions about how learners can successfully abstract out general principles and avoid becoming context-bound. The second claim is that the wider context is important, and this has led to the concept of a community of practice being influential in shaping the individual's relationship with what is to be learned (e.g., Wenger, 1998).

The cognitivist and constructivist positions are not mutually incompatible, although of course they have areas of dispute and conflict. Each may be appropriate in particular domains of study, or at different stages of learning. Quite different learning tasks may be recruited within different areas of study. For example, Trapp, Condron, and Hammond (1999) compared the use of information and communications technology (ICT) to support small groups in psychology departments, physics departments, and various areas of the humanities. It was evident that the use of discussion as a learning method in the humanities was both far more common and largely served a different purpose (for critical analysis) than was the case in physics (where discussion sessions were rare and usually for remediation). Usage in psychology departments fell between that in the humanities and that in physics. Thus, in modeling the use of the Web to support discussion in these different discipline areas, different theoretical positions will be applicable depending on the learning objectives and the material under study.

Mayes (1995) has proposed a simple framework for considering the stages or processes that a learner typically passes through in a learning cycle of gaining understanding of a topic. Mayes' framework is based, in part, on Rumelhart and Norman's (1978) description of three modes of learning — structuring (involving the formation of new schemata), accretion (adding new knowledge to existing schemata), and tuning (the fine adjustment of knowledge to the demands which are made of it). The framework (with some adaptations) allows us to consider different uses of the Web in terms of four key aspects of learning. Figure 8.1 shows our adapted version of Mayes' learning cycle.

In the "reception" stage, the learner acquires some of the basic facts or substantive content that an understanding of the topic is based upon. This may be achieved through reading, listening, or exploring factual information in some other fashion. We can consider this as an acquisition phase where

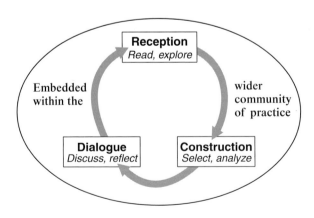

FIGURE 8.1.
The learning cycle.

traditional cognitive models of learning and memory apply most directly. This is not to imply that acquisition of new information does not occur during other phases, nor indeed that cognitive principles do not inform understanding of the other stages. And of course adult learners will, from the outset, interpret new information in the context of what they already know. However, the emphasis in the reception stage is on factual retention within the context of existing schemata. For example, with the fact-based methods of assessment (such as multiple choice tests) common in many introductory courses, it may be that the student will see no need to progress any further in the learning cycle. Newstead and Findlay (1997) have neatly demonstrated that as students approach their assessment, they adopt an increasingly surface approach to learning as measured by Entwistle and Ramsden's (1983) *Approaches to Studying Inventory.* As exams approach, initial good intentions to develop deep conceptual understanding are displaced by rote learning of material. It is perhaps not surprising that retention of material in the period subsequent to factually based assessment can be so poor (Schank, 1999).

Once learners have acquired some basic knowledge of the topic, they move into the "construction" stage, and more actively interpret their newly acquired knowledge in terms of their personal goals, motivations and prior understanding in order to construct new perspectives. Construction involves linking and classifying information in new ways — in short, building up personal meanings. This may be achieved through self-directed activity or through externally defined assignments, such as writing an essay or answering a question requiring the learner, for instance, to take a new angle or interpret an example within a broader context. This construction process may be helped through tools of selection, analysis and exploration. It is in understanding this stage that the principles of constructivism may be most applicable.

In the third "dialogue" stage, the learner benefits from reflecting upon, sharing, and discussing his or her understanding. The understanding has reached a point where key concepts can be articulated, evaluated, and refined through both self-reflection and discussion with others. The processes of articulation, understanding another's point of view, and judging a different perspective against one's own are often hard for learners to achieve, and may involve yet more construction and, to use Rumelhart and Norman's (1978) terminology, the tuning of knowledge and schemata to accommodate new information. Within traditional teaching, such activities as one-to-one tutorials, seminars, problem sessions, and other small–group methods call upon dialogue as a means for enhancing learning and understanding in different ways. These processes involved in dialogue (and indeed the construction process) will lead to the formulation of new questions or the identification of further issues for study, thus closing the loop.

This framework focuses largely on the individual learner, but the cycle as a whole can be considered to be embedded within a wider context (or "community of practice" as indicated in Figure 8.1). This leads to a fourth aspect of the use of the Web in terms of learning: providing the organizational or community context (in this volume, see Sherman, chapter 6, for more on cooperative learning, and Riva, chapter 7, on virtual communities).

III. WAYS OF USING THE WEB IN LEARNING PSYCHOLOGY

Web-based courses are developing rapidly: according to one estimate (Philips & Yager, 1998) there were over 195 accredited U.S. universities offering a thousand or more distance learning courses. However, it is claimed that the ease of implementation of Web-based approaches results in a low level of innovation, with Web courses based closely on traditional materials and methods, with a consequent widespread failure to make the best use of the potential of the Web (e.g., Fowler & Mayes, 2000). In this section we will look at some examples of using the Web to support the learning of psychology; while there may be some truth in Fowler & Mayes' claim, there are also plenty of examples of innovative usage.

The learning cycle framework of Figure 8.1, together with our brief review of educational approaches, provides us with a simple taxonomy of uses of the Web to support learning. We will explore the use of this taxonomy and evaluate whether it is useful in categorizing examples of using the Web to support the learning of psychology.

A simple division of Web resources is as follows:

- Reception. For acquisition of primary content materials.
- Construction and integration. Relevant materials to support or enable learning activities; tools to facilitate exploration and integration.
- Dialogue. Tools to support communication and sharing with tutors and other learners; tools for self-reflection.
- Communities of practice. Facilities to support the management of learning and to define and support communities of learners.

However, we should bear in mind that a single resource can serve several purposes, and so it will not be possible to apply definitively a categorization scheme based on supposed purpose of use. It is certainly the case that many of the publicly available materials on the Web relevant to the teaching of psychology were originally intended primarily as materials for acquisition. An example of a collection of such material is shown in Figure 8.2, the start of the psychology page on the World Lecture Hall, which provides links to pages created by faculty worldwide who are using the Web to deliver university-level academic courses. The great majority of the materials in these sites are support materials for specific courses, including assignments, readings, tutor notes, and class details. Without the benefit of the wider context of the particular courses, it is not clear how useful much of these materials are as primary sources for study. However, for students or lecturers who wish to browse or search the materials, they do contain much of interest on specific topics which would be of use as secondary support materials. The provision of such collections enhances the sharing and quality of resources used by the global community of teachers of psychology. Thus this kind of collection serves a range of purposes; indeed it is likely that it is only within their original context that they actually provide direct course support.

It is perhaps not surprising that much of the published Psychology instructional material on the Web is text-based course support information. This is so because it is relatively easy to convert text to a Web-based form, and to some degree materials of this sort are separable from their immediate context of use, in much the same way as is a textbook. It is harder

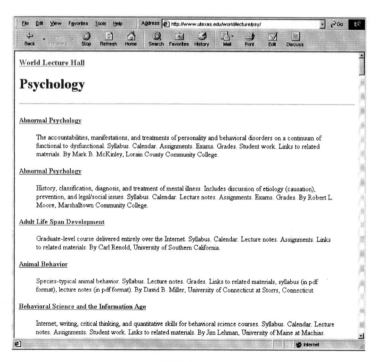

FIGURE 8.2.
Part of the World Lecture Hall Web page.

to publish Web-based facilities that support processes of construction or communication in a useful and shareable form.

However, when we look at use of the Web by individual departments of psychology, a rather different picture emerges. We are in a fortunate position at the University of York of having access to developments in psychology departments within the UK as we run a center which provides advice on the use of learning technology in psychology. LTSN Psychology (or the Learning and Teaching Support Network Subject Centre in Psychology, to give it its full name) promotes good practice in all forms of teaching and learning within psychology. (LTSN Psychology replaced the earlier CTI Psychology — the Computers in Teaching Initiative Centre for Psychology — at the start of 2000.) One activity of the center has been to collect case studies from psychology departments on aspects of their use of learning technology. These case studies were not commissioned but submitted by departments themselves as a shared resource and published both in a newsletter and on the Web. Some of the case studies can be seen at www.psychology.ltsn.ac.uk/case_studies.html. In many cases, pointers to the materials discussed are included. The case studies were mostly written in 1998 and 1999.

Table 8.1 summarizes instances of the use of the Web to promote learning drawn from case studies from 11 departments of psychology in universities in the UK (in the table, each institution is identified by the identification or "Id" column; some institutions contributed more than one case study). The instances are categorized first in terms of the taxonomic scheme described above, and second in terms of the general class of use. A further general category, "facilities for teachers," was also identified. We will discuss each category in turn.

A. Reception

Only 3 (out of 29) instances described using the Web to deliver primary materials in place of lectures (and in 1 case, the delivery was via e-mail). One case study described the use of a complete web-based Introduction to Psychology course that was run in parallel to a conventionally delivered course. Although all materials were web-based, tutorials were face-to-face. The outcomes for the two versions (in terms of marks for examinations) were the same. In a second case, materials (distributed by e-mail) were developed to replace individual lectures, and comparisons between the two formats (in terms of multiple choice question examination performance) showed no significant differences. Evaluation showed that the format was popular with students, who identified the key strengths as having complete sets of lecture notes; working with lecture material at own pace; and a facilitation of student–tutor communication.

TABLE 8.1
Summary of Uses of Web from Case Studies

Category	Use	Id	Brief description
Reception	Course delivery	1	Complete Introduction to Psychology course on Web
		2	E-mail delivery of material replaces lectures
		2	Convert eight lectures to multimedia for Web delivery
Construction and integration	Explore examples	3	Web multimedia clips of developmental and social behavior
	Support for lectures	4	Overheads and exercises on Web
		5	Provision of internal (e.g., course notes) and external (e.g., support materials for course texts) material
		6	Demonstrations and simulations adapted for Web
		2	E-mail used to deliver support materials
		7	Lecture handouts and old exam papers on Web
		8	Web resources to support research methods course
	Student projects	6	Software used for demo purposes earlier in course is subsequently used for project work
	Use in lab	3	Web clips on observational methods used in lab
	practicals	6	Remote access to analysis packages
	Assessment	5	Web-based multiple choice test with feedback
Dialogue	Communication	1	Group tutorials on Web, with e-mail questions and answer sessions
		2	One-to-one student-tutor discussion
		7	Students ask questions over e-mail
	Communicate with resources	9	Use of simulated environment (MOO) for seminar, with resources, assignments, and discussion facilities
		8	E-mail dialogue with tutor and FAQ list integrated with support resources for research methods course
	Preparing for face-to-face	2	E-mail used to circulate information and instructions about tutorial sessions
Community of practice	Reuse of prior work	10	Use of Web to share experiment-generator scripts (developed by staff and students)
		11	Students prepare "briefing notes" on topics for use by students in the following year
		3	Sharing of examples of children's writings collected by students
	Course administration	5	Web pages contain information and resources for course as a whole and specific modules
		6	Web-based communications software used by faculty and administration staff for management of teaching
		2	Use e-mail to distribute general course information
		7	Handbooks, timetables, etc., on Web for students
	Student community	7	Course run jointly with U.S. institution, with students communicating and sharing materials
Facilities for teachers		3	The accumulation of a large corpus of departmental web resources enables tutors to assemble components into support materials for their courses

B. Construction and Integration

Eleven of the 29 instances could be classified as use of the Web to assist in constructing, refining or integrating information that was primarily conveyed by other means. The majority (6 instances) involved the provision of supplementary information to support lectures, usually course notes or handouts and copies of overheads, but also supplementary simulation and demonstration materials. Supplementary information in a text-based form may well have been circulated in a paper form prior to the use of the Web. In this case, the advantage of its provision on the Web may be in terms of convenience of access (a single point of access for students, and an archive during the period of the course) rather than in terms of any changed impact on learning. Nevertheless such access advantages may have substantial benefits. Where more innovative support resources were provided which were not previously available in paper form, good take-up by students was reported.

Other case studies described the use of support materials to explore the categorization of behavior using video clips, to teach observational methods (also using video clips), and to support student experimental projects. The use of video clips of behaviors which it is otherwise impossible or hard for students to experience can be a compelling use of the Web. One department has a large collection of clips including infants reacting in a variety of ways to people and objects around them, school-age children responding to standard Piagetian tasks, and examples of free play in early childhood, as well as shots of various kinds of social interaction. The Web "library" includes audio clips of interviews and conversations involving children or young people, such as addressing the standard Kohlberg moral dilemmas or revealing metacognitive knowledge. This kind of resource is not only popular as a supplement to lecture courses, but is also stimulating a basis for critical discussion and analysis of many basic psychological phenomena not readily encountered through everyday experience.

It is noteworthy that our case studies did not use any examples of students creating Web materials as a learning task, an approach advocated by constructivists at least at the secondary educational level (Jonassen, 2000). However, there are examples of materials created by psychology students available on the Web, such as at Miami University's Psybersite (http://miavx1.muohio.edu/~psybersite/index.htx), which provides a gateway to web tutorials on a variety of topics in the field of psychology. All of the educational modules at this site have been created by advanced undergraduate and graduate students at Miami University (Sherman, 1998). We also note that there were no examples in our case studies of the use of specific facilities to aid the construction of "personal representations," such as concept mapping tools. This is not to say that such learning activities do not take place, but if they do they are probably relatively rare.

The Web-supported learning activities from our case studies were all based on psychology-specific content materials.

C. Dialogue

The six examples of use of the Web to support dialogue processes in learning fell into three types of usage: preparing students for later face-to-face communication, using the Internet for either one-to-one or group discussion, and an elaboration of this where the contributors also shared electronic resources upon which the discussion was focused. At the simplest level, the use of e-mail provides a highly convenient method of communication with which the student has time to compose a question or comment without having to wait for the tutor to be available, and the tutor can answer at a convenient time and with a due level of reflection. In one case study, student questions that might be of interest to others were compiled together with answers into a "frequently asked questions" resource made available to all students. The disadvantage, of course, is that queries that require much iteration (for example, to clarify the question) may be much better dealt with face to face.

There is a considerable body of literature on the use of computer-mediated communication that we will not discuss here (see Riva, chapter 7, this volume). However, a number of the case studies noted that group communication using the Web was not without problems, and that suitable moderation may be required. There was only one case study which reported the use of a "virtual environment," and in this case the technological difficulties may have been something of a barrier. The department's report of the case study notes that "it has proved to be an enlightening and enjoyable experience for most students; however, some students have failed to reach a level of efficiency with typing and with the language of the MOO to allow them to pass the frustration barrier." The student evaluations indicated that there were some disadvantages compared to face-to-face seminars.

More recently we have identified a number of departments using virtual learning environments (such as WebCT) which enable the integration of support materials, assessment and other learning activities, and various communication facilities. These systems have somewhat simpler interfaces for the student as well as allowing the tutor to create or edit materials using standard tools. An example from one of our own courses is shown in Figure 8.3. Use of these environments serves various purposes. They can be used as stand-alone teaching materials or as support tools to free up time for more interactive work during face-to-face periods with students and lecturers.

This idea of shifting the balance in activity is also exemplified in the final case study within this category. Here the Web is used not to support dialogue directly but to provide materials and instructions to ensure that all students are "up to speed" prior to a face-to-face meeting. With increasing

FIGURE 8.3.

Example of a virtual learning environment.

student numbers, small-group teaching sessions are an expensive form of learning and so it makes sense for staff and departments to ensure that when small-group teaching does happen, it is as effective as possible. The Web can be used not only to precirculate materials, but also for supporting preliminary exercises or quizzes. In our own teaching, we have used the Web to make available summaries of papers by students which all members of the group are required to read before the face-to-face session.

D. Community of Practice

Four departments described use of the Web for making available general information about courses and departmental procedures available to students. In one case, the focus was on staff (both teaching and administrative) using facilities to share information. This use of the Web for archiving and making available administrative information is of course widespread, and when well designed it is integrated into the provision of specific course information. This means that students have a single point of access for all the information required about their courses. It is notable that departments did recognize this as a benefit to learning (and not just for administrative convenience) — as evidenced by the fact that several put it forward as an example of innovation in teaching or learning.

Three departments described the use of the Web for what has been termed "tertiary courseware" (Mayes, 1995) — the use of materials which had been created as part of a prior learning episode. In one case, the task for students was explicitly to create briefing notes on topics for students in the following year. The lecturer made the best of these available along with his own comments. In the other two cases, the materials were produced as part of project work (scripts and materials for running experiments, and samples of children's writing from studies conducted in schools). Selected material was then made available for subsequent reuse by students. It is likely that students may benefit not only from the reuse of such resources directly, but also by learning from the processes and outcomes of their peers. This idea of "vicarious learning" has been explored by McKendree and Mayes (1997) in terms of the benefits which may accrue when students observe their peers participating in discussions as learners.

A final example given in one of the case studies serves as a good example of extending the "community of learners." This was a third-year undergraduate course in Human Communication and Technology, where the department linked up with a similar course at a university in the United States. Students communicated over the Internet with their American peers via e-mail and computer conferences to exchange views and completed group-based collaborative course assignments. Students enjoyed the highly interactive nature of this course and appreciated the added intercultural dimension to their studies, to the extent of working hard to overcome inevitable problems caused by transmission delays and time differences.

A final category was evident from the case studies — the use of the Web to facilitate the preparation of teaching materials. Although only one example was given (the use of Web resource materials for tutors to assemble specific teaching or support materials), other such instances no doubt occur.

IV. SUMMARY AND CONCLUSIONS

A. Variety and Context of Use of the Web

All in all, we have been able to use our simple taxonomy to categorize quite effectively a diverse snapshot of case studies from departments of psychology in the UK. The range of uses of the Web for teaching and learning within departments is wide, with all the main "cells" of our taxonomy exemplified. In the case studies we have reported, with the benefit of a description of the purpose and nature of the intervention from a member of the faculty, categorization was a relatively straightforward matter. As we noted earlier, resources made publicly available over the Web and shorn of their original context will be harder to categorize, though may, if transferable, have the potential of serving a variety of purposes.

The examples we have discussed illustrate another point about the learning context. We see that many of the developments have grown from the motivation to develop and enrich existing methods and activities by adding to the resources available for students, making resources more accessible, and enabling better communication. Innovation can thrive within the warp and weft of locally delivered courses as well as from the spur of novel educational approaches or markets. Nevertheless, we also see the introduction of new methods and directions for learning: sharing materials of past students with future students, and sharing among students with differing perspectives from elsewhere; relying more on the generation and exploration of concepts; and shifting the emphasis toward supporting understanding and communication on the part of the students rather than relying on authoritative dissemination from the teacher.

B. Emerging Issues

Use of the Web for learning is part of a broader shift toward an emphasis on self-directed and student-centered learning. This change in emphasis is driven in part by the economics of education, in part by the changing market (mature and part-time students, and distance and flexible courses) and student expectations, and in part by educational theory. Change is enabled by developments in technology and the Internet. However, for this shift to become a larger reality in terms of educational practice, both students and their teachers need to take on new responsibilities. Making resources available is of little use if students do not use them effectively; some uses of the Web may be intrinsically motivating, appealing or convenient, but certainly not all. Studying even highly appealing materials may still require expert support and guidance, and opportunities for reflection — easy access to relevant materials on its own is not enough. Students will therefore need to take new responsibilities for aspects of their own learning, but new ways also have to be found for linking individual and group activities to the wider context of communication and "social embedding," and of assessment and progression. Faculty who have previously taken for granted the balance of teacher and student roles within the familiar context of lectures, tutorials and practicals may have difficulty in developing appropriate models for how to act as a tutor, for example, for an asynchronous electronic discussion, how to integrate a Web-based simulation within a laboratory class, or just what support to provide for students who are studying from Web-based resources.

Some changes will come through explicit staff development or training programs, but more important is to ensure a culture for change at individual, departmental, and institutional levels. Opportunities to become informed about innovation, support to explore new methods, and time to evaluate the outcomes of new approaches are all vital ingredients. Evolution requires a culture for reflecting about developments and making further changes in the light of evidence and feedback; excessive bureaucracy in course administration and in the application of quality management procedures can all too easily stifle innovation. In a period of change it is doubly important to question both the purpose of a new development and whether the approach is fit for that purpose: does it do the job to the satisfaction of all parties? If psychologists cannot apply some of their methodological and conceptual tools to enrich the quality of education, what hope is there for the rest of higher education?

A further issue evident in a number of the case studies is how the Web can provide integration for the management of learning. This can be from the student's perspective (a "one-stop shop" for course information and materials, or a means for communicating with peer students, faculty, and administrators) or from the department's (a medium for sharing and communicating about the administration of courses, or a means for controlling the quality of course documentation). The ubiquity of the use of the Web and the growing use of local area networks (LANs) mean that these changes will accelerate as both faculty and administrators see the benefits to student learning and to the organization and management of educational provision. Much of the change will be in the form of a silent revolution. Many departments have made the shift to carrying out their administrative and day-to-day business by e-mail and other Internet facilities (if you are in such a department, think back to how things have changed over the past decade); these changes often happen "by the back door" rather than through management dictate.

So how will the Web be supporting the learning of psychology in five year's time? Undoubtedly there will be a growth in the provision of distance on-line courses and other flexible forms of delivery. Such courses will mainly be delivered electronically, but with provision for a range of support from on-line tutors and from other students, as well as, perhaps, from electronic guides and help systems. Locally delivered courses will be enhanced by a great range of Web-based resources, and the role of faculty may have shifted further toward "learning facilitator" rather than "key purveyor of knowledge." Teachers will have to learn new skills in supporting the learning of students, perhaps using Web-based communication tools, and students will have to take more responsibility for their own learning activities. Nevertheless, traditional forms of delivery, such as lectures, will still have their place, but their importance may be reduced and their purpose shifted away from the primary means of conveying the curriculum. Greater sharing of resources between institutions will be possible, though this may be limited by the acceptable balance of competition and cooperation (we may see divergences between Europe and the United States here in view of different funding models for universities). Greater explicitness and accountability in course management through the use of local area networks is likely to be a

two-edged sword: it can work to the great benefit of students and departments through enabling more effective information flow and evaluation, but
the temptation for institutions to impose unwieldy centrally managed
systems may restrict flexibility and innovation.

References

Anderson, J. R. (2000). *Learning and memory.* New York: Wiley.
Barab, S., & Duffy, T. (2000). From practice fields to communities of practice. In D. H. Jonassen &
    S. Land (Eds.), *Theoretical foundations of learning environments* (pp. 25–55). Mahwah, NJ: Erlbaum.
Entwistle, N., & Ramsden, P. (1983). *Understanding student learning.* London: Croom Helm.
Fowler, C. J. H., & Mayes, J. T. (2000). Learning relationships from theory to design. *Association for
    Learning Technology Journal, 7,* 6–16.
Glaser, R. (1990). The re-emergence of learning theory within instructional research. *American
    Psychologist, 45,* 188–195.
Guskey, T. R., & Gates, S. (1986). Synthesis of research on the effects of mastery learning in
    elementary and secondary classrooms. *Educational Leadership, 43,* 73–80.
Jonassen, D. H. (2000). *Computers as mindtools for schools: Engaging critical thinking.* Columbus, OH:
    Prentice-Hall.
Jonassen, D. H., Peck, K. L., & Wilson, B. G. (1999). *Learning with technology: A constructivist approach.*
    Upper Saddle River, NJ: Prentice-Hall.
Koedinger, K. R., Anderson, J. R., Hadley, W. H. & Mark, M. (1997). Intelligent tutoring goes to
    school in the big city. *International Journal of Artificial Intelligence in Education, 8,* 30–43.
Laurillard, D. (1993). *Rethinking university teaching.* London: Routledge.
Mayes, J. T. (1992). *Cognitive tools: A suitable case for learning.* In P. A. M. Kommers, D. H. Jonassen, &
    J. T. Mayes (Eds.), Cognitive tools for learning (pp. 7–18). Berlin: Springer-Verlag.
Mayes, J. T. (1995). Learning technology and Groundhog Day. In W. Strang, V. Simpson, & D.
    Slater (Eds.), *Hypermedia at work: Practice and theory in higher education* (pp.21–37). Canterbury,
    UK: University of Kent Press.
McKendree, J., & Mayes, J. T. (1997). *"The vicarious learner": Investigating the benefits of observing peer
    dialogues.* Paper presented at CAL97, University of Exeter, March 23–26.
McKendree, J., Reader, W., & Hammond, N. (1995). The "homeopathic fallacy" in learning from
    hypertext. *Interactions, 2,* 74–82.
Newstead, S., & Findlay, K. (1997). Some problems with using examination performance as a
    measure of teaching ability. *Psychology Teaching Review, 9,* 23–30.
Papert, S. (1990). An introduction to the fifth anniversary collection. In I. Harel (Ed.),
    Constructionist learning (pp.7–15). Cambridge, MA: MIT Media Laboratory.
Philips, V., & Yager, C. (1998). *Best distance learning graduate schools: Earning your degree without leaving
    home.* Princeton, NJ: Random House.
Rumelhart, D. E., & Norman, D. A. (1978). Accretion, tuning and restructuring: Three modes of
    learning. In J. W. Cotton & R. L. Klatzky (Eds.), *Semantic factors in cognition* (pp.37–53). Hillsdale
    NJ: Erlbaum.
Schank, R. (1999). *Teaching the questions instead of the answers: How creativity can be fostered.* Presentation
    at the 197th Annual Convention of the American Psychological Association, Boston, 20–24
    August.
Sherman, R. C. (1998). Using the World Wide Web to teach everyday applications of social
    psychology. *Teaching of Psychology, 25,* 212–216.
Trapp, A., Condron, F., & Hammond, N. (1999). Using C&IT to support small-group learning
    activities in psychology. In *Proceedings of Association for Learning Technology Conference* (ALT-C 99).
    Oxford: Association for Learning Technology.

Vincent, T., & Whalley, P. (1998). The Web: Enabler or disabler In M. Eisenstadt & T. Vincent (Eds.), *The knowledge web: Learning and collaborating on the net*. London: Kogan Page.

Wenger, E. (1998). *Communities of practice: Learning, meaning and identity*. Cambridge: Cambridge University Press.

Gender Identities on the World Wide Web

CHRISTINE H. JAZWINSKI

Department of Psychology, St. Cloud State University

I. INTRODUCTION

The Internet has transformed the way we work, learn, play, socialize, and shop. To buy books, I usually go to the World Wide Web (WWW or Web) address of my favorite on-line bookstore. I am personally greeted by "Hello, Chris Jazwinski! We have recommendations for you." I can click on several links for books on the topic of cyberspace. They know what I like! I can view information about any book that I choose, including a picture of the book cover, a table of contents, and reviews of the book. I can also see what other books have been purchased by people with interests similar to mine. The computer interface is much more user-friendly than many live clerks at real life bookstores.

Geographical space need not be traversed in order to accomplish many goals. It is possible to purchase just about anything from the comfort of one's networked home computer. Virtual libraries of on-line documents are replacing the need for paper copies (and decreasing the use of physical facilities). The new millennium will introduce ever-growing numbers of people to e-commerce and Internet communities. Virtual marriage ceremonies (Danet, 1998; Reid, 1994), as well as virtual birthday parties, funerals, and other social events, will become more commonplace. On-line relationships will probably grow in importance, and people may become isolated from one another in real life as they spend more time interacting with on-line friends

(Kraut et al., 1998). The Internet will probably create fundamental changes in the way that we think about ourselves as people and members of the world community.

As oft-mentioned science fiction writer William Gibson so aptly described, personal identity in cyberspace is no longer situated in the physical body (Gibson, 1984). New virtual identities can be forged easily through the physical contact of fingertips with computer keyboards. Electronic circuitry, cables, computer networks, and software applications deliver the virtual person. Any one of a variety of identities can be selected, some of which may not even be singular or human (e.g., a swarm of insects). "Gender swapping" (Bruckman, 1993), that is the choice of female identities by men as well as male identities by women, is commonplace on the Internet (Reid, 1994). Virtual identities may coincide with real life or be elaborate constructs. Appearance and context are no longer available and new means of presenting an identity have been developed (see Riva, chapter 7, this volume, for a discussion of the relationship between identity, on-line interaction, and learning).

Experimenting with personal identities is easy on-line. "The Internet is another element of the computer culture that has contributed to thinking about identity as multiplicity. On it, people are able to build a self by cycling through many selves" (Turkle, 1995, p. 178). The playfulness that can be observed in chat rooms and MUDs (Multiple User Domains that are text-based virtual interactive forums; Reid, 1994; Shefski, 1995) has been compared to festival and theater performances (Danet, 1998, Danet, Ruedenberg, & Rosenbaum-Tamari, 1998). New identities can be easily attempted and discarded. Kolko & Reid (1998) maintain that the ease of relinquishing identities leads to shallow and rigid on-line personas and structurally weak virtual communities with ineffective conflict resolution strategies. Many newsgroups have no moderator and users can post any message. Instead of resolving conflicts, interactants can simply exit by signing off.

In some text-based forums, gender identity can be explored by logging in as male, female, or a person of neuter gender (Bruckman, 1993). Multiple gender options (11 in all) have been added to LambdaMOO and MediaMOO (Danet, 1998). Gender identity determines the pronouns that are used by the computer program in reference to a particular game participant (Reid, 1994). One of the new gender options, "spivak" (named after mathematics professor Michael Spivak who used gender-neutral language in his textbooks), was found to be fourth most popular in 1996 after male, female, and neuter choices (Danet, 1998). Gender swapping can be thought of as a growth experience, a form of therapy, or just a game of "dressing up" (Danet, 1998; Danet et al., 1998). However, cycling through selves begs the question of psychological aftereffects.

Cyberspace allows people from all over the world to come into contact with one another. Close physical proximity is not required when forming groups and communities. Two people can be continents apart physically and yet present together in the same virtual space. Social psychologists have found that physical proximity (or propinquity) determines the likelihood that people will become friends (Brehm, 1992). It is possible that proximity effects will be less important in the future. Functional distance (ease of contact) will be based on access to the same virtual space.

Modern means of transportation (e.g., the automobile and the commercial airplane) have made us increasingly mobile. In past centuries, the connections of people to geographical areas were much more tenacious. People were born and usually lived out their entire lives in just one location. If we assume that speech and thought are based on the social and physical world one lives in (Voiskounsky, 1998), then it is not surprising that people's self-concepts used to be relatively simple and constant (Baumeister, 1987). Several social categories were sufficient for self-description, for instance, family membership, residence in a particular locale, and station in life.

As social and geographic mobility increased, the self became more complex, variable, and prone to problems of identity. Today people change geographical location, socioeconomic status, and relational ties more easily and frequently. As a result, these categories no longer automatically define them (Baumeister, 1987). Identity is more fluid and the self-concept must be periodically redefined. If physical mobility and changes in life circumstances have made self-identity a problem, then how will virtual traversing of cyberspace impact self-identity? Acquiring and discarding multiple identities in cyberspace can be expected to have psychological effects. Will identity become more fragmented and the self even more of a problem (Baumeister, 1987), or will the possibility of rehearsing possible selves (Markus & Nurius, 1986) increase cohesiveness and integration of the self in real life?

This chapter is about the mutual relationship of gender and virtual social interaction, particularly on the Web. Psychologists use the phrase "doing gender" to mean that gender is constructed through social interactions (Burn, 1996; Deaux & LaFrance, 1998). In other words, gender is not a quality that resides within a person, but rather it is a set of behaviors and role relationships that are setting-dependent. If gender is "constructed" as people interact, then it can surely become something new and different in cyberspace.

We know that gender, as a variable, is associated with social status, and that being male can confer an advantage (Burn, 1996). Higher-status individuals wield greater social influence and power (Deaux & LaFrance, 1998). A great deal of optimism has been voiced regarding the potentially democratizing effects of electronic communication (Sproull & Kiesler, 1991). When physical appearance and social context cues are missing, gender, age, disability, and formal social status are harder to determine. Therefore, these variables should have less influence. In cyberspace, people can experiment with new, creative, and more egalitarian ways of relating to one another (Turkle, 1995). It has been found that group participation of previously marginalized (lower status) individuals does increase and that social influence becomes more balanced in electronic groups communicating via e-mail (Sproull & Kiesler, 1991).

The opposing, more pessimistic view is that traditional gender roles and hierarchical status relations may not just be duplicated but even magnified in virtual encounters (e.g., Hall, 1996; Lea & Spears, 1995; Postmes, Spears, & Lea, 1998). The anonymity of virtual interactions can lead to depersonalized perceptions of the self and others (Postmes et al., 1998; Shamp, 1991). Because little individuating information is available in many on-line interactions, people may respond to others as representatives of salient social categories. A person's sex is a particularly salient category in many virtual spaces. In chat rooms a common question posed to newcomers is "M/F?" which means "are you male or female?" followed often by a question about age (cf. Clark, 1998). Category salience and lack of individuating information create conditions that are ripe for the activation of sex-role stereotypes and resulting social status dynamics (Bodenhausen & Macrae, 1998). The following sections will explore the social psychological characteristics of virtual social interaction and gender as they relate to computer technology.

II. VIRTUAL SOCIAL INTERACTION

A. Definitions

Virtual social interaction means social interaction that is mediated over a computer network. When computer technology began to permeate work, school, and home environments, psychologists began to investigate its use and impact (e.g., McGrath & Hollingshead, 1994; Sproull & Kiesler, 1991). However, the rapid development of new interactive computer technologies, especially the more recent Web, has created a paucity of tested research methodologies and techniques for collecting reliable and internally valid data.

Social interaction mediated by technology is not new. For example, the telegraph and telephone made such mediated social interaction widely available to many people. Today, the convenience and widespread use of the Internet, cell phones, and fax machines have further increased the number of mediated interactions. New technology elicits a range of reactions from fear and avoidance to enthusiastic appreciation and adoption. Although there are vast regional and socioeconomic differences in access to Internet services, the number of people who are on-line and interacting is growing rapidly (Gray, 1996). New generations growing up with computer technology will consider it ubiquitous.

B. Dimensions of Virtual Interaction

Virtual social interaction is multifaceted. People log on to computer networks for many reasons, and use a variety of software applications. People go on-line to work, socialize with family or friends, gather information about the community, retrieve health-related information, shop, or simply have fun. Some people are primarily searching for information and are not interested in meeting people. Others may consider making friends their primary goal. Internet support groups can bring similar people together in a safe, anonymous setting. For instance, McKenna and Bargh (1998) found benefits of newsgroup participation among people with stigmatized, concealable identities.

Differences in goals and objectives of Internet use are reflected in choice of software applications and Internet services. Multitasking, where several activities occur simultaneously, is fairly common, especially among more expert computer users (Turkle, 1995). Web browsers were originally developed for viewing Web (HTML, or hypertext markup language) documents. However, Web browsers can now be used as front-end applications for many services (e.g., FTP, newsgroups, e-mail, and SHY; see Riva, chapter 7, this volume, for a description of SHY).

Virtual social interactions are initiated with people known to us or with strangers. Anonymous interactions of strangers using false identities have received popular attention. The 1980s case of a male psychiatrist posing as a disabled woman on CompuServe is frequently cited in the literature on computer culture (Lea & Spears, 1995; Stone, 1998). The psychiatrist discovered that posing as a female enabled him to interact with women at a higher and more satisfactory level of intimacy. When his true identity was discovered, the many women who had become his friends felt angry and betrayed. Today, subterfuge in electronic forums is well known. It is taken as a given that aliases are sometimes adopted to playfully deceive. For instance, the use of graphical aliases or "avatars" in the Web-based chat environment of the Palace (an on-line community) is intended to allow for the expression of fantasies (Suler, 1999a,b).

The playful nature of anonymous virtual interactions is reminiscent of the games of "dress up" many of us played as children. Fascination with costumes, disguises, carnivals, and theater contains two elements: mystery and experimentation with new identities or possible selves (Danet, 1998, Danet et al., 1998; Markus & Nurius, 1986; Suler, 1999b). The concept of possible selves (introduced by Markus and Nurius in 1986) consists of imagined, future visions of what one may become. A balance between hoped for and feared versions of possible selves is necessary for psychological adjustment (Oyserman & Markus, 1990). Possible selves may receive role-playing rehearsal through participation in interactive electronic forums. Perhaps this is what makes anonymous virtual interactions so enticing.

Virtual interactions can occur among people who are well known to each other. For example, e-mail may be used to supplement daily face-to-face interactions in a work organization (McGrath & Hollingshead, 1994). The early research of psychologists studying electronic communication was intended to relate such functions to organizational productivity. When people are interacting with known others who are encountered face-to-face as well as virtually, entirely different social psychological dynamics would be expected than when interactants remain anonymous (Postmes & Spears, 1998). It is important to distinguish various electronic interaction media from one another if they are different along psychologically meaningful dimensions. The following dimensions will be considered: bandwidth, interactivity, and relative anonymity.

C. Comparison of Virtual Interaction Media

It is misleading to consider all virtual interaction media as resulting in psychologically identical effects. Newer media, such as the Web, support wider bandwidth, that is, presentation modalities that require faster Internet connections and larger disk storage space (especially video). The degree of anonymity is also variable, with Web pages being among the least anonymous and chat or MUD environments among the most anonymous. Some media are highly interactive, allowing multiple cycles of social interaction approximating real time if the hardware and network connections are fast enough (MUD, chat), while others are equivalent to a one-way radio or television broadcast with limited feedback opportunities (e.g., noninteractive Web pages). Even when using the same medium, users can customize their client software, thus changing important characteristics of the computer–user interface. For instance, one can choose to check e-mail relatively frequently (and receive faster updates) or infrequently.

Computer-mediated communication can be traced to simple protocols used on large computer systems such as TALK (UNIX systems) and PHONE (VMS systems). These protocols were used primarily for private, work-related conversations. A comparison of virtual communication media by Chen and Gaines (1998) is based on the following criteria: timing (synchronous or "real time" versus asynchronous) and group size supported (individual dyads vs. a large community). Using this classification scheme, UNIX-based TALK would fall into the category of synchronous and dyadic communication, while a registered newsgroup would fall into the classification of asynchronous communication supporting a large community.

A decrease in bandwidth is characteristic of all virtual interactions relative to those that occur face-to-face (Hall, 1966). On the Internet fewer channels of communication are available. Visual, auditory, tactile, and olfactory social cues, as well as the environmental setting that contains them, are unavailable or greatly attenuated. Narrow bandwidth has been thought to result in a reduction of social cues that normatively guide social behavior (Kiesler, Siegel, & McGuire, 1984). The result may be disinhibition and violation of social norms. When typing text at a computer keyboard it can be difficult to realize that the recipient of the message is another human being (cf. Shamp, 1991).

The most widely studied virtual social interactions have been those that are entirely text-based, such as MUDs (Reid, 1994; Turkle, 1995). "MUDs are networked, multi-participant, user-extensible systems" (Reid, 1994). Text-based media should be considered narrowest in bandwidth (one channel, low information load). However, MUD software allows tremendous customizability by experienced users. One can build virtual, text-based worlds, as well as interact with objects, environments, and people in a synchronous manner (Shefski, 1995). Although e-mail and newsgroups (USENET) are also text-based, both are asynchronous and offer far less complexity than MUDs. Unlike MUDs, newsgroups and e-mail offer low anonymity. Bandwidth should probably not be considered in isolation from the variables of anonymity, interactivity, and customizability.

The Web can be used as merely a broadcast medium (for on-line publishing), or can be used interactively with multiple cycles of data input and feedback (using CGI or common gateway interface programming). Chen and Gaines (1998) consider the Web to be a publication service (one-way communication) utilizing rich media (pictures, movies, color). They see it as an unusual instance of cooperation where service providers contribute a resource to unknown and relatively anonymous users.

The masking of personal identity is probably the most commented-on feature of social interactions in cyberspace. The use of aliases or handles can mask the personal identity and sex of interactants. However, the anonymity of virtual interactions is almost never complete, even with software that masks or encrypts user information. The computer system administrator, or "superuser," can access information to partially or fully determine user identity. Spears and Lea (1994) utilize the metaphor of the panopticon (a surveillance device proposed for use in correctional institutions by philosopher Jeremy Bentham) to illustrate the relationship of users to each other and to the superuser. The panopticon does not allow the inmates to see one another though they are clearly visible to the prison administrator.

System administrators can set anonymous access to services such as Web pages. This means that anyone who can get on the computer network can also access these resources without having an account on the server providing the Web or newsgroup services. Even so, the superuser can find the IP (Internet Protocol) address of the computer from which the request for services was made by scanning the computer access logs. Although the identity of the user may be unknown, it is often still possible to obtain information on the computer that was used.

D. Theoretical Accounts

Several theoretical frameworks have been advanced to account for the presumed behavioral characteristics of computer-mediated social interaction. One account is based on the idea that during virtual interactions people become deindividuated (Zimbardo, 1969) and normative control of behavior is disrupted. Deindividuation in cyberspace is thought to be the result of anonymity, large groups with unclear boundaries, and intense task absorption that may reduce self-focus (Joinson, 1998). The lack of empirical support for the deindividuation model (Postmes & Spears, 1998), and the question of when conditions for deindividuation are met in the various virtual media, makes the deindividuation framework difficult to apply at this time. Although an early hypothesis, evidence for behavioral disinhibition during virtual interaction (e.g., increases in self-disclosure, harassment, or flaming) is still lacking.

Other accounts focus on the decrease in information available during virtual social interactions (narrow bandwidth). Nonverbal and contextual cues that guide behavior along the path of existing social norms are missing (Sproull & Kiesler, 1991). Status differences that are usually evident in real life groups would be expected to decline. Therefore, balanced group participation and decentralized social influence would be expected in virtual groups. Support for this framework is mixed. Although the early work of Kiesler and her colleagues (Sproull & Kiesler, 1991) showed democratizing effects of e-mail group discussion, later studies were not always supportive. For example, Weisband, Schneider, and Connolly (1995) found that status differences did not decrease in electronic groups compared to face-to-face groups. Thus, the "cues filtered out" approach is not fully supported by the data.

A social identity model is proposed by Postmes and his colleagues (Postmes & Spears, 1998; Postmes et al., 1998). According to the model, when individuating information about the self and others is missing (due to anonymity or lower bandwidth), people will rely more strongly on any social categories that are salient and will interact with others as if they were representatives of these categories. In the world of virtual social interaction, one such category is gender, particularly when gender information is available while other, individuating information is not. Women in virtual forums are often numerically scarce compared to men. Under these conditions it is expected that female gender will become particularly salient and that female sex-role stereotypes will be activated and used as interaction guides (Bodenhausen & Macrae, 1998; Fiske & Taylor, 1991).

Finally, a personal growth approach can also be proposed. The Internet can be considered to be a form of theater (Danet, 1998, Danet et al., 1998) or a place where people can rehearse possible selves (Markus & Nurius, 1986). The growth potential of rehearsing various options can be particularly valuable to those who are renegotiating their identity due to a developmental crisis (Oyserman & Markus, 1990) or who need to cope with a concealable stigma (McKenna & Bargh, 1998).

II. VIRTUAL GENDER

A. Gender

Psychological gender is a system of beliefs, expectations, social relations, and social roles. Gender is dependent on the socialization practices within a culture and should be distinguished from biological sex (Burn, 1996). The term "sex" will be used to mean biological maleness or femaleness (cf. Burn, 1996; Eagly & Wood, 1999). Earlier in history it was thought that biological sex determined psychological characteristics (Millett, 1970). However, most psychologists today agree that gender is learned and that it is situation specific (Deaux & LaFrance, 1998). The impact of social psychological variables on gender is readily obvious in reviews of gender research (Burn, 1996; Deaux & LaFrance, 1998).

Gender is not only an aspect of self-presentation and social identity, it is also part of the self-concept, and a lens through which the world is viewed (Fiske & Taylor, 1991). Developing an identity as a male or a female is an important part of the human experience (Burn, 1996). Children learn about their biological sex and fully grasp the concept only very gradually. Sex typing of children's clothing, toys, and activities teaches children that social role expectations go along with a particular biological sex. Restrictions are placed on activities that are considered sex-inappropriate, especially with boys (Burn, 1996). The presence of growing numbers of people in anonymous virtual interactive forums offers unprecedented opportunities for the exploration of gender identities.

B. Virtual Gender

Virtual gender is the result of a complex interaction between culture and computer technology. Computer hardware, network connections, and software place constraints on how people can relate to each other. Virtual gender is therefore a technology-dependent phenomenon. The social construction of gender is very obvious in the virtual computer interaction medium. Physical appearance, tone of voice, and other social and environmental cues are not available. Biological sex can easily be concealed and a variety of new gender identities explored.

Virtual gender is the social construction of gender in cyberspace. Psychologists talk about "doing gender," which means that gender can be observed in people's social interactions (Deaux & LaFrance, 1998). If gender is so constructed then it may become something quite different virtually than it is when people interact face-to-face (Danet, 1998). Virtual interaction is narrow in bandwidth compared to face-to-face interaction. New ways of communicating have developed to replace unavailable communication channels (e.g., nonverbal cues, appearance, and context).

As in real life, "doing" gender virtually occurs on several levels. On the one hand, it can be a deliberate act of selecting a male, female, or other identity when prompted (e.g., logging into a MUD; Bruckman, 1993; Reid, 1994). Gender can also be constructed less self-consciously when habits that are characteristic of face-to-face interaction carry over into virtual space (e.g., male and female language differences; Lakoff, 1975). Gender can be masked in cyberspace and individuals may even engage in gender bending. Finally, new means of communicating in the reduced bandwidth of the Internet have appeared. Some of these, such as emoticons [e.g., "smileys," :–)], may be used differently by women and men.

C. Virtual Gender Differences

To what extent do people play out the same gender roles (including existing power and status relations) in cyberspace? The virtual medium has been thought of as a liberating place where people may be able to discard outdated habits and relate in new ways. The cultural ballast of traditional gender roles and sex role stereotypes is still with us today even though the conditions that fostered their development (sex-based division of labor) existed a long time ago (Eagly & Wood, 1999). The research on virtual gender differences is very limited at this time, and is based largely on older text-based newsgroup and e-mail technology.

1. Participation and Power

Sex is associated with social status and power differentials in our society. Men's earnings consistently exceed women's (Lexus-Nexus Universe, 2000) and men hold a greater number of leadership positions. Even when status differences are unknown, sex may be used as a basis for inferring men's higher status (Wood & Karten, 1986). Higher-status individuals talk more and are more influential in small groups (Deaux & LaFrance, 1998).

Women and men do not participate equally on the Internet. The 1998 WWW survey of Internet usage conducted by the Graphics, Visualization, and Usability Center (GVU) of Georgia Tech found that among 5022 respondents, women composed only 35.8% of the U. S. part of the sample compared to 64.2% men. Participation by European women was even lower at 18.4%.

Alarmingly, the biggest sex difference in the United States occurred among the young age group of 11 to 20 year olds. Concerning experience, the greatest gender gaps occurred in the categories of the most experienced (women were at 26.2% of total) and most expert users (women at 21.8% of total).

Because there are differences among women and men in access and expertise with the Internet, most virtual spaces are more populated by men than women. The computer industry, including mainframes, servers, computer games, and personal computers, has largely been a male province from its inception (Morahan-Martin, 1998; Stone, 1998). Men have designed the virtual spaces that we populate. The ultimate power over the virtual person is in the hands of the system administrator, and these positions are more likely to be filled by men. The 1998 GVU survey found that of 423 individuals overseeing Web server activities, only 13.2% were women.

2. Preference for the Virtual Salon

The Internet is a place where people can meet, socialize, and have fun. Do men and women differ in their level of participation in highly interactive virtual meeting places? In the GVU 1998 survey of Web browser use, of 3291 respondents, 9.4% of all female respondents reported daily use of chat groups compared to 7.1% of males. On the other hand, only 15.8% of the women reported daily use of newsgroups while 22.9% of men did. These differences may reflect the fact that chat provides a synchronous, and therefore more interactive, computer interface compared to newsgroups.

Females may prefer the interactive quality of the chat given that in real life they are also more adept at forming intimate relationships (Burn, 1996). Clark (1998) investigated the phenomenon of teenage "cyberdating" in chat rooms (i.e., meeting someone and going into a private chat room with them). She found that the girls in her study were more enthusiastic about the possibilities of cyberdating than were the boys. The female participants enjoyed decreased fears of social rejection, the fact that their physical appearance did not matter, and the way that their excellent verbal skills translated into superb cyberdating skills.

3. Emotional Expressiveness: Emoticons and Flames

In face-to-face interaction, a wide array of nonverbal signals such as facial expressions, tone of voice, body position, and gestures convey emotion. How can one express emotion when interacting in the relatively low bandwidth of the Internet? Several means have been developed. Smileys (plain text drawings), as well as the use of stage direction commentary (e.g., <sigh>, <laugh>), can enrich the otherwise impoverished bandwidth.

In real life, women have been found to be somewhat more emotionally expressive than men are, but the differences are small (Burn, 1996; Deaux &

LaFrance, 1998). The caretaking social roles traditionally performed by women, such as tending infants and children, require women to convey warmth and caring. On the other hand, the overt expression of anger and aggression is more in keeping with the protective roles traditionally performed by men, as well as with their higher social status (Burn, 1996; Eagly & Wood, 1999).

Are gender differences in emotional expressiveness also observed in virtual settings? Two behaviors displayed in virtual settings relate to this issue: the use of emoticons and flaming. Emoticons or smileys are graphical symbols of feeling states created using plain text characters [e.g. smiles :–) or someone sticking out their tongue :–P] or stage direction indicators (e.g., <sigh>). Witmer and Katzman (1998) performed a content analysis of the use of graphic accents in a newsgroup. In this study, emoticons were grouped with "emodevices" (use of all capital letters, repeating punctuation marks, etc.) and "articons" (use of plain text to make a drawing). Posts with graphic accents included 29.7% by women, while only 16.4% of all posts with discernable gender were written by women, thus indicating a greater preference for use of emoticons by women than by men.

Flaming in virtual interactions involves expression of anger, including name-calling and provocative, insulting statements. While the virtual medium has been described as one which promotes antisocial behavior (Kiesler et al., 1984), there is disagreement as to the prevalence of flaming and other aggressive behaviors (Rafaeli & Sudweeks, 1998). In their study of a newsgroup, Witmer and Katzman (1998) also coded the newsgroup posts for flaming. They found that women flamed more frequently than men. However, when Savicki, Lingenfelter and Kelley (1996) coded 100 sequential messages posted in each of 30 on-line discussion groups, they found no differences in flaming among groups based on the sex composition of the group (ranging from 50 to 100% male). At this time, there is little support for sex differences in flaming, and the evidence for use of emoticons is too meager to draw firm conclusions.

4. Virtual Agency and Communion

Agency and communion are believed to fundamentally describe the content of male and female sex roles, respectively (Deaux & LaFrance, 1998). Men are believed to be independent and to show initiative (agency), while women are believed to be caring and responsive to others' needs (communion). Herring (1996) analyzed the message content and structure from two e-mail discussion lists to test the hypothesis that women use the Internet to relate to others interpersonally while men use it to exchange information. One list was populated predominantly by men and the other predominantly by women. On both lists women's messages tended to be more supportive of others then men's messages. Men's messages were more likely to oppose and criticize.

Ferris (1996) reported findings of sex differences in message content similar to Herring's, using a different coding and analysis system, and a different e-mail discussion list. She also found that men were more likely to initiate topics that were responded to by the list members (women's topics were more often ignored), and that men's messages were between two and eight times as long as women's messages. In the Savicki et al. (1996) study, men were the larger group, composing 73% of the participants. Men's posts made up 75% of all messages, which is only slightly larger than their proportion in the sample. In this study men were not dominating the conversation. Groups with higher proportions of females used more self-disclosive and tension-reducing statements. On the other hand, groups with higher proportions of males used more fact-oriented language and calls to action. All in all, there appears to be some support for sex differences in agency and communion.

D. Masking Gender: Gender Bending and Gender Concealment

Gender bending involves the presentation of either ambiguous or contradictory cues indicative of biological sex. Gender concealment is the avoidance of cues indicating one's sex. In cyberspace concealing or changing one's sex is easy. "Without makeup, special clothing, or risk of social stigma, gender becomes malleable in MUDs" (Bruckman, 1993). Social interaction in virtual reality offers unprecedented possibilities for exploratory role playing, with few costs. While there has been much debate about whether Internet groups can possibly develop a sense of community (e.g., Kraut et al., 1998; Lockard, 1996), it is precisely the absence of a link to real life consequences that allows creative experimentation. One can log on to a server as a man, a woman, a person of neuter gender, or another available variant (Bruckman, 1993). Because one can choose to remain anonymous to most other users, it is possible to practice new behaviors without fear of ridicule. The present section will discuss what is known about gender-bending and gender concealment in cyberspace.

The incidence of gender masking in various media is unknown and estimates are imprecise. Danet (1998) indicates that a only a minority of nicknames used in IRC (Internet Relay Chat) channels have a clear gender linkage, thus pointing toward commonly occurring gender concealment in IRC. In MUDs the situation is completely different with an explicit choice of gender required to log on. It is estimated that a considerable number of men in MUDs log on as women (Reid, 1994; Suler, 1999b), and that more men gender bend than do women (Bruckman, 1992, 1993). The motivations for gender bending are not well known. Men who gender bend may desire to experience what it feels like to be a woman. Another reason for gender bending may be the increased attention from men that women in a male-dominated medium can receive (Bruckman, 1993; Suler, 1999b). Bruckman (1992), the founder of two virtual communities on the Internet, states that "the impact of gender on social interactions is sometimes subtle in real life, but is obvious in MUDs. New female players are often swarmed with male players vying for their attention" (p. 26).

Jaffe, Lee, Huang, and Osshagan (1995) randomly assigned male and female participants (75 in all) to two electronic conferences. One conference required that they use their real life identity, while the other conference required a pseudonym. Unfortunately, Jaffe et al. (1995) combined the categories of gender bending with concealment of gender in their analysis. It was found that women used pseudonyms that either involved gender concealment or gender bending more often than men did. Additionally, females were more supportive and made more self references (used first-person pronouns) than males overall. However, the condition of pseudonym use increased men's use of supportive statements and self-references. It appears that anonymity allowed the men in this study to engage in out-of-sex-role-behavior.

Historically, the presentation of male sex by women was the more common phenomenon. Gender bending by women has been linked to limitations of the female gender role (Bullough, Bullough, & Elias, 1997). Famous cases of cross-dressing or use of male noms de plume abound, such as that of the 19th century writer George Sand (in reality Aurore Dupin) or Joan of Arc. These women were able to successfully fulfill their life's ambition by posing as men (Sand was an accomplished writer, while Joan of Arc was a great military leader). However, the situation began to change in the 19th century and reversed entirely in the 20th century with much larger numbers of men wishing to change their sex to female. This shift can be seen as the result of increasing restrictions placed on the male sex role (Bullough et al., 1997).

The evidence for sex differences in concealment of gender and gender bending on the Internet is not strong, due to the scarcity of data. However, given what we know about virtual interaction, sex roles, and gender bending (Bullough et al., 1997), it would seem likely that men engage in gender bending more than women, but that women engage in more gender concealment. Women may conceal their gender in order to escape the stereotyping and possible harassment that they could encounter. Men may gender bend in order to explore aspects of their selves that have been restricted by limitations of a strictly enforced male gender role (Burn, 1996).

III. CONCLUSIONS AND FUTURE DIRECTIONS

The social psychological study of the Internet is still in its infancy. Most of the research reported in this chapter was drawn from the field of communications, where the predominant methodology is ethnography. Established methods for collecting internally valid data on the Internet do not yet exist — however, see Joinson and Buchanan, chapter 11 of this volume for a detailed account of doing psychological research on the Web. The openness and lack of regulation of the Internet are its defining features. Yet, these characteristics also impede the scientific study of social behavior on the Internet.

The psychological implications of many Internet phenomena are far reaching. We cannot afford to ignore the tremendous increase in the use of the Internet (cf. Kraut et al., 1998). New technologies are likely to change important characteristics of virtual social interactions. The use of the World Wide Web as a platform for social interaction is likely to replace older text-based media. As bandwidth and speed of information transfer increase in computer networks, richer media (e.g., video) will be increasingly available and are likely to be incorporated into virtual social interactions.

What can the electronic medium teach us about gender? Anonymous virtual interactions allow for either gender concealment or gender bending. For instance, a person may decide to not reveal her sex. She could use a pseudonym and leave out any personal information linked to biological femaleness. Avoiding all gender-stereotyped language and self-descriptions could be more difficult. Misinformation via the presentation of contradictory information would help mask gender (e.g., stating preferences for both "masculine" and "feminine" activities). Gender concealment and gender bending can teach us about skill in deception, the process of stereotyping, and gender roles. Explorations of gender identity can result in valuable self-knowledge and personal growth.

What are the implications of research on virtual gender for Web-based instruction? The gender bias that exists in a real life classroom can easily extend to a Web-based learning environment. In the absence of personally individuating information, gender categories can activate the use of sex-role stereotypes. However, a virtual learning environment offers the possibility of gender masking. Students could be assigned gender-ambiguous aliases for their virtual social interactions. The long-term feasibility of gender masking is probably limited. If aliases remain constant over the academic term, then it is likely that gendered virtual identities will eventually emerge. Whether these identities will consist of a simple two-category system of male and female or contain a larger number of gender variations will depend on prior gender schemata. It is much more feasible to mask gender for a shorter period in a classroom exercise.

In social psychology, gender roles are often explored in Psychology of Women courses. Students could be assigned aliases that either conceal or bend their gender. Gender bending can be thought of as an exercise in role reversal. An increase in perspective-taking and sensitivity to problems, privileges, and challenges experienced by members of the other sex would be a desirable outcome. On the other hand, gender concealment (ambiguous gender) can help illustrate the construction of gender-specific questions. Who can and who cannot conceal gender? How can one conceal one's gender successfully? What is it about gender concealment that might cause discomfort? The influence of gender categories on thought, feeling, and behavior can be fruitfully explored in this manner.

The lower access and participation of women and girls in the world of computers creates a challenge when utilizing the Web for instruction. In order for Web-based instruction to provide a nonoppressive growth experience for girls and women, several means can be utilized. First, it should be made known that virtual interactions are being monitored and that the course instructor may sometimes participate. Second, an explicit code of conduct prescribing respect and prohibiting gender harassment should be provided to students. These devices should work to deter the development of virtual group norms fostering harassment (i.e., Postmes et al., 1998). A further increase of Web course friendliness to women and girls can be achieved by increasing their access and expertise. Aspects of group dynamics related to sex composition should be considered; in particular, imbalanced groups containing few women and a larger number of men may decrease the value of the Web-based instruction for women. Instructors may wish to consider including one or more same-sex group experiences for on-line discussions in Web-based courses.

Whether fundamental changes in our concept of gender will result from virtual experimentation is a question that cannot be easily answered at this time. Access and control in electronic forums is still the province of men and boys. Men are much more likely to administer server computers and to write the computer code which shapes virtual interactional spaces. The potential for change will not be possible to assess until women increase their impact in the computer field. The creation of Web sites specifically targeted towards girls and women is a positive trend (Morahan-Martin, 1998), and female-friendly sites may draw increasingly larger numbers of girls and women into the computer arena.

References

Baumeister, R. F. (1987). How the self became a problem: A psychological review of historical research. *Journal of Personality and Social Psychology*, 52, 163–176.
Bodenhausen, G. V., & Macrae, C. N. (1998). Stereotype activation and inhibition. In R. S. Wyer, Jr. (Ed.), *Advances in social cognition: Vol. 11. Stereotype activation and inhibition* (pp. 1–52). Mahwah, NJ: Erlbaum.
Brehm, S. S. (1992). *Intimate relationships*. New York: McGraw-Hill.
Bruckman, A. (1992). *Identity workshop: Emergent social and psychological phenomena in text-based virtual reality*. Unpublished manuscript.
Bruckman, A. S. (1993). *Gender swapping on the Internet*. Paper presented at the Internet Society, San Francisco, CA [On-line]. Available: ftp://ftp.cc.gatech.edu/pub/people/asb/papers/gender-swapping.txt

Bullough, B., Bullough, V. L., & Elias, J. (Eds.). (1997). *Gender blending*. Amherst: Prometheus Books.

Burn, S. M. (1996). *The social psychology of gender*. New York: McGraw-Hill.

Chen, L. C., & Gaines, B. R. (1998). Modeling and supporting virtual cooperative interaction through the World Wide Web. In F. Sudweeks, M. McLaughlin, & S. Rafaeli (Eds.), *Network & netplay: Virtual groups on the Internet* (pp. 221–242). Menlo Park, CA: AAAI Press/The MIT Press.

Clark, L. S. (1998). Dating on the Net: Teens and the rise of "pure" relationships. In S. Jones (Ed.), *Cybersociety 2.0: Revisiting computer-mediated communication and community* (pp. 159–183). Thousand Oaks, CA: Sage.

Danet, B. (1998). Text as mask: Gender, play, and performance on the Internet. In S. Jones (Ed.), *Cybersociety 2.0: Revisiting computer-mediated communication and community* (pp. 129–158). Thousand Oaks, CA: Sage.

Danet, B., Ruedenberg, L., & Rosenbaum-Tamari, Y. (1998) In F. Sudweeks, M. McLaughlin, & S. Rafaeli (Eds.), *Network and netplay: Virtual groups on the Internet* (pp. 41–76). Menlo Park, CA: AAAI Press/The MIT Press.

Deaux, K., & LaFrance, M. (1998). Gender. In D. T. Gilbert, S. T. Fiske, & G. Lindzey (Eds.), *The handbook of social psychology* (Vol. 1, pp. 788–827). Boston: McGraw-Hill.

Eagly, A. H., & Kite, M. E. (1987). Are stereotypes of nationalities applied to both women and men? *Journal of Personality and Social Psychology*, 53, 457–462.

Eagly, A. H., & Wood, W. (1999). The origins of sex differences in human behavior: Evolved dispositions versus social roles. *American Psychologist*, 54, 408–423.

Ferris, S. P. (1996, October). Women on-line: Cultural and relational aspects of women's communication in on-line discussion groups. *Interpersonal Computing and Technology: An Electronic Journal for the 21st Century*, 4, 29–40. Available: http://www.helsinki.fi/science/optek/1996/n3/ferris txt

Fiske, S. T., & Taylor, S. E. (1991). *Social cognition*. New York: McGraw-Hill.

Gibson, W. (1984). *Neuromancer*. New York: Ace Books.

Graphics, Visualization, and Usability Center (GVU) (1998). *GVU's 8th WWW user survey*. Atlanta: *Georgia Tech Research Corporation*. Available: http://www.cc.gatech.edu/gvu/user_surveys/

Gray, M. (1996). *Internet growth: Raw data* |On-line|>. Available: http://www.mit.edu/people/mkgray/net/printable/internet-growth-raw-data.html

Hall, E. T. (1966). *The hidden dimension*. New York: Doubleday.

Hall, K. (1996). Cyberfeminism. In S. C. Herring (Ed.), *Computer-mediated communication: Linguistic, social and cross-cultural perspectives* (pp. 147–170). Amsterdam: John Benjamins.

Herring, S. C. (1996). Two variants of electronic message schema. In S. C. Herring (Ed.), *Computer-mediated communication: Linguistic, social and cross-cultural perspectives* (pp. 81–106). Amsterdam: John Benjamins.

Jaffe, J. M., Lee, Y., Huang, L., & Osshagan, H. (1995). *Gender, pseudonyms, and CMC: Masking identities and baring souls* |On-line|. Available: http://research.haifa.ac.il/~jmjaffe/gender-pseudocmc/

Joinson, A. (1998). Causes and implications of disinhibited behavior on the Internet. In J. Gackenbach (Ed.), *Psychology and the Internet: Intrapersonal, interpersonal, and transpersonal implications* (pp. 43–60). San Diego: Academic Press.

Kiesler, S., Siegel, J., & McGuire, T. W. (1984). Social psychological aspects of computer-mediated communication. *American Psychologist*, 39, 1123–1134.

Kolko, B. and Reid. E. (1998). Dissolution and fragmentation: Problems in on-line communities. In S. Jones (Ed.), *Cybersociety 2.0: Revisiting computer-mediated communication and community* (pp. 212–229). Thousand Oaks, CA: Sage.

Kraut, R., Patterson, M., Lundmark, V., Kiesler, S., Mukopadhyay, T., & Scherlis, W. (1998). Internet paradox: A social technology that reduces social involvement and psychological well-being? *American Psychologist*, 53, 1017–1031.

Lakoff, R. T. (1975). *Language and women's place*. New York: Harper Colophon Books.

Lea, M., & Spears, R. (1995). Love at first byte? Building personal relationships over computer networks. In J. T. Wood & S. Duck (Eds.), *Under-studied relationships*. Off the beaten trac (pp. 197–233). Thousand Oaks, CA: Sage.

Lexus-Nexus Universe (2000). Available: http://Web.lexis-nexis.com/universe

Lockard, J. (1996). Progressive politics, electronic individualism and the myth of virtual community. In D. Porter (Ed.), *Internet culture* (pp. 219–231). New York: Routledge.

Markus, H., & Nurius, P. (1986). Possible selves. *American Psychologist*, 41, 954–969.

McGrath, J. E., & Hollingshead, A. B. (1994). *Groups interacting with technology*. Newbury Park, CA: Sage.

McKenna, K. Y. A., & Bargh, J. A. (1998). Coming out in the age of the Internet: "Demarginalization" through virtual group participation. *Journal of Personality and Social Psychology*, 75, 681–694.

Millett, K. (1970). *Sexual politics*. Garden City, NY: Doubleday.

Morahan-Martin, J. (1998). Males, females and the Internet. In J. Gackenbach (Ed.), *Psychology and the Internet: Intrapersonal, interpersonal, and transpersonal implications* (pp. 169–198). San Diego: Academic Press.

Oyserman, D., & Markus, H. R. (1990). Possible selves and delinquency. *Journal of Personality and Social Psychology*, 59, 112–125.

Postmes, T., & Spears, R. (1998). Deindividuation and antinormative behavior: A meta-analysis. *Psychological Bulletin*, 123, 238–259.

Postmes, T., Spears, R., & Lea, M. (1998). Breaching or building social boundaries? SIDE-effects of computer-mediated communication. *Communication Research*, 25, 689–715.

Rafaeli, S., & Sudweeks, F. (1998). Interactivity on the nets. In F. Sudweeks, M. McLaughlin, & S. Rafaeli (Eds.), *Network and netplay: Virtual groups on the Internet* (pp. 173–190). Menlo Park, CA: AAAI Press/The MIT Press.

Reid, E. (1994). Cultural formations in text-based virtual realities [On-line]. Available: http://www.eden.rutgers.edu/~mlwld/cult-form.html

Savicki, V., Lingenfelter, D., & Kelley, M. (1996). Gender language style and group composition in Internet discussion groups. *Journal of Computer Mediated Communication*, 2 (3). Available: http://www.ascusc.org/jcmc/vol2/issue3/savicki.html

Shamp, S. A. (1991). Mechanomorphism in perception of computer interaction partners. *Computers in Human Behavior*, 7, 147–161.

Shefski, W. J. (1995). *Interactive Internet: The insider's guide to MUDs, MOOs, and IRC*. Rocklin, CA: Prima Publishing.

Spears, R., & Lea, M. (1994). Panacea or panopticon? The hidden power in computer-mediated communication. *Communication Research*, 21, 427–459.

Sproull, L., & Kiesler, S. (1991). Computers, networks and work. *Scientific American*, 65, 116–123.

Stone, A. R. (1998). *The war of desire and technology at the close of the mechanical age*. Cambridge, MA: The MIT Press.

Suler, J. (1999a). *Avatar psychotherapy* [On-line]. Available: http://www.rider.edu/users/suler/psycyber/avatarther.html

Suler, J. (1999b). *Do boys just wanna have fun? Gender-switching in cyberspace* [On-line]. Available: http://www.rider.edu/users/suler/psycyber/genderswap.html

Turkle, S. (1995). *Life on the screen: Identity in the age of the Internet*. New York: Simon & Schuster.

Voiskounsky, A. E. (1998). Telelogue speech. In F. Sudweeks, M. McLaughlin, & S. Rafaeli (Eds.), *Network and netplay: Virtual groups on the Internet* (pp. 27–40). Menlo Park, CA: AAAI Press/The MIT Press.

Weisbad, S. P., Schneider, S. K., & Connolly, T. (1995). Computer-mediated communication and social information: status salience and status differences. *Academy of Management Journal*, 38, 1124–1152.

Witmer, D. F., & Katzman, S. L. (1998). Smile when you say that: Graphic accents as gender markers in computer-mediated communication. In F. Sudweeks, M. McLaughlin, & S. Rafaeli

(Eds.), *Network and netplay: Virtual groups on the Internet* (pp. 3–12). Menlo Park, CA: AAAI Press/The MIT Press.

Wood, W., & Karten, J. (1986). Sex differences in interaction style as a product of inferred sex differences in competence. *Journal of Personality and Social Psychology, 50*, 341–347.

Zimbardo, P. G. (1969). The human choice: Individuation, reason and order, vs. deindividuation, impulse and chaos. In W. J. Arnold & D. Levine (Eds.), *Nebraska symposium on motivation* (pp. 237–307). Lincoln: University of Nebraska Press.

Caught in the Web: Research and Criticism of Internet Abuse with Application to College Students

JANET MORAHAN-MARTIN

Bryant College

I. INTRODUCTION

Since the early 1990s, Internet use has proliferated from a small group of scientists, engineers, and mathematicians to over 304 million users world-wide. In the United States and Canada, there are 136 million Internet users (NUA, 2000). The rapid growth of this medium, as well as its potential to change the way we communicate and gather information, has brought much positive and negative publicity as we try to sort out the meaning of the myriad changes promised by this new technology. On the positive side, the Internet has been heralded as the Information Superhighway, a medium that will facilitate the flow of information worldwide, and as the Electronic Agora which will allow communication between individuals worldwide without distinctions of nationality, race, gender, or class. On the negative side, concerns about what kind of information can be accessed, and with whom one socializes on-line, have alarmed some. Parents, teachers, and others have been frightened by reports of pornography and pedophiles on-line and distressed by a loss of the ability to monitor children's Internet use. These concerns can be worsened by parents' relative lack of Internet sophistication compared to their children's. The combination of the rapid growth of the Internet, not knowing the effects of Internet use, and concerns about the negative consequences of Internet use has created a climate where bad news can become magnified. This is the context for alarm about yet another negative consequence of Internet use: Internet addiction.

Some have argued that Internet addiction is a creation of the media. Clearly, this has been a story that the media finds fascinating. Stories of Internet addiction have received wide coverage, as has some of the research on the topic. It is easy to dismiss existing research on Internet addiction because of its media attention and the tentative nature of the research thus far. There have not been any randomized epistemological studies of pathological Internet use to date, and the results so far are based on limited samples. However, research on Internet abuse has begun to document that some people do indeed develop serious problems from their Internet use. This research is beginning to delineate characteristics of both the Internet and users that are associated with Internet abuse.

Even more importantly, the cries of affected individuals demand that psychologists and others understand their needs. Many feel helpless and out of control, and report job and school impairments, interpersonal problems, divorces, and impaired health resulting from their Internet use. Many are clamoring for help, some on-line and some clinically. The on-line support group Internet Addiction Support Group (*iasg@netcom.com*), though founded by Ivan Goldberg as a joke because he did not (and still does not) believe in Internet addiction, is widely used by individuals desperate for help with their out-of-control use of the Internet. Other individuals are coming to the attention of clinicians (Young, Pistner, O'Mara, & Buchanan, 1999) and centers such as the Computer Addiction Service at McLean Hospital, a psychiatric hospital affiliated with the Harvard Medical School.

Despite professionals' arguments about applying the addiction model to Internet-related behavior, "Internet addiction" is the term many individuals have applied to themselves and reflects the sense of powerless many of them feel about their Internet use. The extension of the model of addiction from substances to compulsive, repetitive behaviors which individuals feel they have no control is controversial. Although researchers who endorse the broadened concept of addictive behaviors differ in their specific definition, "(t)he common denominator is that the individual appears to others to have diminished control over the behaviors or report a sense of disequilibrium, loss, distress, or craving when the object or substance is unavailable or the behaviors are curtailed" (Jaffe, 1990, p. 1425). Since the 1970s, parallels have been drawn between behaviors associated with substance abuse and specific activities such as eating, exercise, television, shopping, computer games, gambling, and sex (e.g., Jacobs, 1986; Milkman & Sunderwirth, 1982). A diagnosis of substance abuse required physical tolerance and/or withdrawal until the 1987 introduction of the revised third edition of the *Diagnostic and Statistical Manual of Mental Disorders*, (DSM-III-R) by the American Psychiatric Association (APA). Unlike prior editions, the DSM-III-R required a specified number of symptoms that may or may not include dependence or tolerance. This change arguably accelerated the push in popular culture toward applying the term "addiction" to compulsive behaviors. This in turn is reflected in commonly used terms, used both jokingly and seriously, such as "chocoholics," "shopaholics," "relationship addicts," "sex addicts," "video game addicts," "computer addicts," and now "Internet addicts."

This chapter reviews research on Internet abuse, as well as other relevant research, to summarize and highlight trends and differences across studies. It first documents the incidence and demographic differences found in on-line and offline studies of Internet abuse, and then explores characteristics of the Internet, and of those who abuse the Internet, which may explain underlying factors. Next, alternative explanations for Internet abuse are discussed. Finally, it explores the impact of Internet abuse on the lives of college students.

II. RESEARCH ON INTERNET ABUSE

Researchers who have studied Internet abuse have differed in nomenclature, using terms such as "Internet addiction" (Chou, Chen, & Hsiao, 1999; Chou, Chou, & Tyan, 1999; Egger, 1996; Lin & Tsai, 1999; Suler, 1996; Young, 1998), "Internet dependency" (Anderson, 1999; Kubey, Lavin, & Burrows, 1999; Lavin, Marvin, McLarney, Nola, & Scott, 1999; Scherer, 1997), "pathological Internet use" (Morahan-Martin & Schumacher, 2000), and "compulsive Internet use" (Greenfield, 1999). In this chapter, the term "Internet abuse" (IA) is used to describe the phenomenon although the other terms are used in keeping with their use by the varied authors.

Internet abuse studies have been conducted in both offline and on-line settings. Offline studies have consisted of surveys of college students in the United States (Anderson, 1999; Kubey et al., 1999; Morahan-Martin & Schumacher, 2000; Scherer, 1997; Welsh, 1999), Europe (Anderson, 1999), and Taiwan (Chou, Chen, et al., 1999), and high school students in Taiwan (Lin & Tsai, 1999). On-line surveys consist of self-selected participants who have responded to announcements posted on-line. The 17,251 participants in Greenfield's study (1999), the largest to date, responded to a posting at the ABC News website (abcnews.com) following a cover story on Internet use and addiction. Participants in other, smaller, on-line studies have been recruited by announcements posted on sites for Internet and other addicts (Brenner, 1997; Egger, 1996; Petrie & Gunn, 1998; Thompson, 1996; Young, 1997a,b, 1998; Young & Rodgers, 1998) or in response to an electronic mailing to all undergraduates at a small university (Lavin et al., 1999).

A. Assessment of Internet Abuse

No studies have defined Internet abuse by the amount of time spent on-line. In two studies, participants self-identified themselves as "Internet addicts" (Petrie & Gunn, 1998) or "psychologically dependent on the Internet" (Kubey et al., 1999). In the rest of the studies, Internet abuse was defined by the impact of Internet use on users' lives. The specific questions and cutoffs used to assess Internet abuse have varied, although for all, the criteria have included tolerance, withdrawal, and continued use despite recurrent Internet-related problems. Using the Internet to escape negative feelings also was a criterion for all of the preceding studies except the Taiwanese ones (Chou, Chen, et al., 1999; Lin & Tsai, 1999). Duration of disturbed use has not been considered. That is, no studies have explored how long the symptoms existed. This may inflate the incidence rate in these studies because they include those who are experiencing transient problems with their Internet use. In other domains, criteria for abuse often delineate a minimum duration of abuse for inclusion.

B. Incidence

Despite differences in specific criteria for inclusion and definition of Internet abuse, the incidence of IA among college and high school students in the United States, Europe, and Taiwan consistently has been in the 5.9–13% range. In Taiwan, the incidence of Internet abuse was 10.9% in a stratified sample of 616 high school students across the country (Lin & Tsai, 1999) and 5.9% in a study of 12 universities (Chou, Chen, et al., 1999). Studies in the United States have had similar results. Of the undergraduates who responded to a college-wide electronic posting in Lavin et al.'s study (1999), 12.5% were Internet dependent. Scherer (1997) found that 13% of undergraduates who used the Internet once a week or more were Internet dependent. In studies of undergraduates who have used the Internet at least once, Morahan-Martin and Schumacher (2000) and Welsh (1999) found 8%, and Anderson (1999) 10%, to be Internet abusers. In contrast, in Anderson's 1998 survey of 1078 undergraduates from the United States and Europe, only 3% of students self-reported that they had serious problems resulting from Internet use; 15% reported that they knew someone who was an Internet addict. Kubey et al. (1999) found 9% of students labeled themselves as psychologically dependent on the Internet.

Several studies of the general population have been conducted on-line (see Joinson & Buchanan, chapter 11 of this volume, for guidelines on conducting psychological research on-line). In the largest study to date of Internet addiction, Greenfield (1999) found that 6% of the 17, 251 participants were addicted to the Internet. He cautions that because the survey was added to a story on Internet use and addiction, there may be a "bias in the responses, as we assumed that anyone who may be having difficulty with their on-line use is likely to read a story about Internet addiction" (p. 404). As discussed in the next section, the self-selection bias of on-line studies is evident in other on-line studies of the general population. For example, in two on-line studies 74 to 80 % of participants qualified as Internet addicted (Thompson, 1996; Young, 1998).

C. On-line versus Offline Studies

Characteristics of Internet abusers vary between on-line and offline studies. With the exception of Lavin et al.'s (1999) study with college students, the on-line populations are older (average age in the thirties vs. the early twenties), use the Internet more, and appear to be more pathological than those in the offline studies. Average time spent online has been significantly higher in all on-line studies than in offline studies. For example, in Greenfield's study (1999), non IA participants reported that they used the Internet an average of 6.33 hours daily, while according to Internet industry studies (CyberAtlas, 2000), the average amount of time U.S. Internet users spent on-line for a month was 8.28 hours in December 1999, and 9.43 hours in January 2000. All of the on-line studies recruited participants on-line. That alone biases the sample to those who use the Internet more. In addition, all except one (Kubey et al., 1999) recruited participants on sites which would attract those who have Internet-related problems such as sites for Internet addicts.

The level of pathology reported in online studies reported on here was substantially higher than that of offline studies, reflecting a self-selection bias. For example, 74 to 80% of those who participated in two on-line studies met the criteria for IA (Thompson, 1996; Young, 1998) while in non-self-selected off-line studies the incidence of IA has varied from 8 to 13% (see above). The number of participants who identified themselves as having Internet-related problems was also higher in on-line versus off-line studies. In one on-line study, 46% of the respondents reported that they were addicted to the Internet (Petrie & Gunn, 1998), while in an off-line study the number of self-reports of problems related to Internet use was 3% of the total (Anderson, 1999), and in another the number of those psychologically dependent on the Internet was 9% of the total (Kubey et al., 1999).

D. Time On-line

Not surprisingly, all studies have found that IA participants spend significantly more time on-line than others, although there is considerable variation. In all of the considered studies except one (Morahan-Martin & Schumacher, 2000), the amount of time spent online by all participants, Internet abusers and not, was significantly higher than that found in large, representative studies. In the United States in January 2000, one estimate of the average amount of time spent on-line was 9.43 hours for a month (CyberAtlas, 2000). In another study, 15% spent less than 1 hour per week on-line, 49% spent 1 to 5 hours, and 14% spent more than 10 hours (O'Toole, 2000). In the off-line studies of college students, the average weekly use (in hours) for those with IA versus others was 8.48 versus 3.18 in Morahan-Martin & Schumacher's study (2000), 13 versus 6.7 in Lavin et al. (1999), 16.45 versus 9.31 in Welsh (1999), 20.52 versus 8.47 in Lin and Tsai (1999), 23.68 versus 13.89 in Chou, Chou, et al. (1999), and 23 versus 5–10 hours in Chou, Chen, et al. (1999). Time spent on the Internet was higher for studies done on-line. Young (1998) found Internet abusers reported spending 38.5 hours per week online, while nonabusers used the Internet 4.9 hours per week. Participants in Greenfield's study (1999) reported the most use of the Internet; Internet abusers reported being on-line 9.01 hours *daily*, while nonabusers reported being on-line 6.33 hours *daily*.

E. Demographics

I. Gender

Among studies that included gender as a variable, there are differences between on-line and offline measurements in the reported gender ratio of those with IA. Offline studies consistently have found males two to five times more likely to have IA than females. The percentage of males versus females who were Internet abusers was 17% versus 8% in Scherer's (1997) study, 12.2% versus 3.2% in Morahan-Martin and Schumacher's (2000) study, 15.8% versus 2.7% in Anderson's (1999) study, and 12% versus 5.3% in Welsh's (1999) study. This is consistent with other studies which have found males spend more time on-line than females both in the general population (Graphics, Visualization, and Usability Center [GVU], 1999; O'Toole, 2000) and among college and teenage users (Kraut, Scherlis, Mukhopadhyay, Manning, & Kiesler, 1996; Morahan-Martin & Schumacher, 1997). Teenage and young adult males are more likely than their female counterparts to use technologies such as video games and television to relax and escape pressure (Sax, Astin, Korn, & Mahoney, 1999). They also are more likely to use the Internet for activities with a high risk of abuse such as gambling, MUDs (Multiple User Dungeons or Domains), and Net sex (Cooper, Delmonico, & Burg, in press; Cooper, Scherer, Boies, & Gordon, 1999; Greenfield, 1999; Morahan-Martin & Schumacher, 1997, 2000; Scherer, 1997; Welsh, 1999).

On-line studies present a different pattern of Internet use with respect to gender. Those on-line studies that that reported gender differences have found either no differences (Brenner, 1997; Egger, 1996; Greenfield, 1999; Petrie & Gunn, 1998; Thompson, 1996) or that females are more likely to be Internet abusers (Young, 1998). It is probable that this is caused by the methods used to recruit participants in these studies. Females are more likely to seek help for problems (Weissman & Payle, 1974) and to participate in psychological studies (Rosnow & Rosenthal, 1996), and thus may be more likely to respond to posts for Internet addicts, which was the method used to recruit participants in these on-line studies.

2. Age

All off-line studies have been with high school and traditional college-aged students. In studies of traditional college-aged students, one study found first-year students more likely to report being psychologically dependent on the Internet than other students (Kubey et al., 1999), while a second study found no difference by age (Morahan-Martin & Schumacher, 2000). On-line studies universally have reported that the average person with disturbed Internet use was in his or her late 20s to early 30s, which is the median age range of Internet users. Again, on-line studies have a self-selection bias so it is impossible to know if this age group is more prone to Internet abuse in the general population. It is probable that the incidence of IA is higher among teens and young adults because they have been found to be the heaviest users of the Internet and particularly sites used by those who develop IA (GVU, 1999; Kraut, 1997; Morahan-Martin & Schumacher, 1997). The HomeNet study of residential use of the Internet found "teenagers most vulnerable to the poten-tial negative effects" of the Internet (Carnegie Mellon, 1998, p. 2). Brenner (1997) reported that younger participants in his on-line study experienced more problems from Internet use than older individuals, and Greenfield (1999) found that younger people at increased risk of being Internet addicts.

F. Ways of Using the Internet

Despite these differences in how IA studies have been conducted, and who is included in these studies, there is consistency among all studies in both which sites Internet abusers use and the reasons they use the Internet. Internet abusers are more likely than others to use socially interactive aspects of the Internet, including chat rooms (IRCs, or Internet Relay Chat), discussion groups (newsgroups), bulletin boards systems (BBSs), and MUDs. Chat rooms, discussion groups, and bulletin boards provide arenas to meet people, exchange ideas, find support, and become part of an on-line community. MUDs provide a recreational outlet, a place to meet new people, and an escape from everyday realities. E-mail is the most widely used on-line activity; it is the first thing most people do when they go on-line (GVU, 1999; Kraut et al., 1996; O'Toole, 2000). Primarily used to interact with those one knows, e-mail both supplements and replaces traditional mail and telephone communication. Some studies have found e-mail both helps maintain existing relationships and serves as a social activity (Activmedia, 1998; Kraut, 1997; O'Toole, 2000). Most studies of Internet abuse have found that Internet abusers use e-mail more than others (Chou, Chen, et al., 1999; Lin & Tsai, 1999; Lavin et al., 1999; Welsh, 1999; Young, 1998), but some have found no significance between the two groups (Chou, Chou, et al., 1999; Morahan-Martin & Schumacher, 2000). In Morahan-Martin and Schumacher's study, differences were in this direction, but fell short of significance (p =. 07).

Internet abusers also are more likely than others to gamble on-line and engage in cybersex. Some studies also have found Net abusers more likely to surf the World Wide Web (Chou et al., 1999; Greenfield, 1999; Lavin et al., 1999; Lin & Tsai, 1999; Morahan-Martin & Schumacher, 2000) and visit technologically sophisticated sites (Morahan-Martin & Schumacher, 2000). No differences between those with IA and nonabusers were found in information gathering or using the Internet for work or school.

III. EXPLANATIONS FOR INTERNET ABUSE: CHARACTERISTICS OF INTERNET ABUSERS

Explanations for causative factors for IA have focused on characteristics of the user and of the Internet. Several studies have found that those with IA are more likely than others to be disturbed in other areas of their lives. In comparison to nonabusers, Internet abusers have been found to be more lonely on the UCLA loneliness scale (Morahan-Martin & Schumacher, 2000), to be more depressed on the Beck Depression Inventory (Young & Rodgers, 1998) and the Zung Depression Inventory (Young, 1997a), and to have a high incidence of relatives with addictions (Thompson, 1996; Young, cited in King, 1996). Some studies have found an overlap between IA and sexually compulsive behavior (Cooper et al., in press) and self-reports of sex addiction (Greenfield, 1999).

Personality correlates of IA have been examined as well. Welsh (1999) found differences in coping styles between those with IA and nonabusers, with abusers less likely to use task-oriented styles and more likely to use emotional coping styles and to have a more external locus of control (p =. 057). That is, dependents were more likely to use coping strategies based on emotional reactions rather than directly changing the situation causing the problem, and to perceive that they had little control over their lives. Lavin et al. (1999) tested the hypothesis that Internet abusers may be similar to video game users and seek stimulation on-line. They found, contrary to predictions, that Internet dependents were less likely to be sensation seeking on the Zuckerman Sensation Seeking scale. These studies raise questions about the relationship between IA and other disorders. A major unanswered question is whether IA is symptomatic of other disorders or whether IA causes or exasperates other problems. This is discussed later.

Another debate is whether Internet abuse is more prevalent among "geeks" and others who are more technologically savvy. In studies of college students, Anderson (1999) and Welsh (1999) found a higher incidence of IA among college students in technological, science, and object-oriented fields than those in other majors, and Morahan-Martin and Schumacher (2000) report that those with IA were more likely than others to be technologically sophisticated. However, Young (1997b, 1998), in an on-line study, did not find a higher incidence with "techies." Some of the interest in the link between technological sophistication came from early reports of compulsive Internet use among computer hackers (e.g., Curtis, 1992; Rheingold, 1993; Turkle, 1995). As Internet use becomes more widespread among the general population, and as the Internet becomes easier to use, technological sophistication should diminish as a factor in IA. However, characteristics of computer hackers may make them more susceptible to IA. Hackers, mostly male, use the computer and the Internet for work and play. They often are lonely, socially isolated, and lack social skills (Shotten, 1991; Turkle, 1995). For them, the Internet may provide a source for social interaction, excitement, and escape from negative feelings.

IV. EXPLANATIONS FOR INTERNET ABUSE: CHARACTERISTICS OF THE INTERNET

A. Changes in Social Interaction

The changes in social interactions made possible by the Internet are a key component underlying Internet abuse. Interviews as well as survey data support that social communication on some Internet sites is a major factor in the development of IA. Communication in chat rooms, newsgroups, MUDs, and the like is radically different than preexisting communication in "real life" (RL in cybertalk), whether face to face (ftf), on the telephone, through written communication, or even via e-mail. The Internet allows individuals to meet and interact in text-based anonymous environments with a wide range of people, many with similar interests, and with whom one might never communicate in real life. This change of social interaction alters communication patterns from person to person to "many to many" (Rheingold, 1993, p. 12). It can provide new social networks and communities (cybercommunities) which not only broaden horizons for new social contacts and friends (cyberfriends), but also provide mutual support and are available 24 hours a day. On-line, individuals can self-present from the relative safety of a computer screen. Even when communicating in real time (RT in cyberspace; synchronous time in social psychology), the delay in communication while typing can allow one to compose one's thoughts and present a more enhanced image. Individuals may feel less hampered by perceived or real defects.

The lack of ftf communication and anonymity on-line can lessen social risk and lower inhibition (Walther, 1996), which can allow users to try out new ways of relating and new roles and identities — even sexual identity (Curtis, 1992; Turkle, 1995). Additionally, communities and social relations on-line can provide a safe haven for users who can also control social distance from others, thus providing controlled intimacy (Dinty Moore, 1995) and companionship without the demands of friendship (Turkle, 1995). On-line, people can express controversial or hidden thoughts and feelings without the fear of RL judgment, rejection, and confrontation. Additionally, the climate of shared intimacies of many on-line communities fosters a strong sense of acceptance. When asked what he liked about playing MUSHs (Multiple User Shared Habitats), a form of on-line game that is generally less aggressive and more cooperative than MUDs, one male said,

> You can do anything you want. It is not like society. There is no bias to anything. You can have the name you want. There are no arguments, no fighting. There is … no race. You can be yourself…. I spend more time on the computer than with people (because) it is more comfortable. (Cited in Dinty Moore, 1995, p. 59)

Differences in Internet use between Internet abusers and others supports the idea that the changed social interaction made possible on-line may be particularly appealing to those who develop IA. Young (1997b) notes that people who do not have Internet-related problems use the Internet to maintain existing friendships and gather information while those with IA use the Internet primarily to meet and socialize with new people. Kubey et al. (1999) found those who self reported as psychologically dependent on the Internet to be more likely than others to say they felt alone and would use the Internet less if they had more friends at school. In Greenfield's study (1999), those with IA were twice as likely as nonabusers to report that they experienced more intense feelings of intimacy on-line than in ftf relationships (75% vs. 38%).

Scherer (1997) found that those who were dependent on the Internet were much more likely than others to use the Internet to meet new people and to socially experiment. Although there was no difference between Internet-dependent and nondependent undergraduates in self-description of sociability, there were strong differences between the groups in comparing face-to-face versus Internet socialization (all p <. 01). Ninety-one percent of nondependents versus 71.4% of dependents reported that they socialize more ftf than on the Internet; 5.7% of nondependents versus 18.4% of dependents reported that they socialized equally ftf and on the Internet; and 1.5% of nondependents versus 6.1% of dependents reported that they socialize more on the Internet than ftf. Four percent of dependent and 1.8% of nondependents reported that they socialize "seldom|ly|; I do not socialize much face to face."

Morahan-Martin and Schumacher's research (2000) provides further insight into the differences between how those with and without IA interact socially on-line. This study differentiated 3 groups, those who had no symptoms of IA (27.2 %), those with limited (1–3) symptoms (64.7 %), and those with patho-logical Internet use (PIU, 8.1 %). Pathological users differed markedly from the other two groups in how being on-line changed social behavior, friendship patterns, and use of role playing (all differences, p <. 01). As can be seen in Figure 10.1, those with PIU were much more likely than others to report that the Internet made it easier for them to communicate (91% vs. 56%). They were more likely to report that they found on-line anonymity liberating, felt more themselves on-line than off, opened up more on-line, were friendlier, shared intimate secrets, and preferred on-line to ftf communication.

Friendship patterns also differed between those with PIU and others. Compared to those with no or limited symptoms, those who abuse the Internet were more likely to report a network of on-line friends, that they have more fun with on-line friends than other friends, and that their on-line friends understand them better than others. They also were more likely to say that it is easier to make friends on-line, with 18% saying *most* of their friends were on-line friends. Finally, they were more likely to go on-line when they were lonely. There were differences between the three groups in role playing on the Internet as well. Internet abusers were more than twice as likely than others to pretend that they were someone they are not, and to gender swap on-line. Thus, for Internet abusers, Internet communication

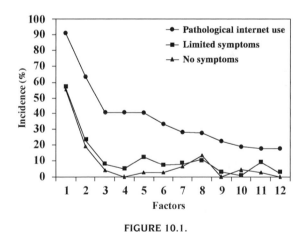

FIGURE 10.1.

The Internet changes social behavior and friendship patterns. Factor: 1, easier to communicate; 2, anonymity liberating; 3, shared intimate secrets; 4, more myself online; 5, network of online friends; 6, friendlier; 7, prefer to face to face; 8, open up more; 9, more fun with online friends; 10, online friends understand me better; 11, easier to make friends online; 12, most friends made online. Source: Morahan–Martin & Schumacher (2000).

appears to be liberating — the Prozac of social communication. On-line, their social behavior is enhanced, which facilitates their ability to make friends.

As the Internet evolves, there will be changes in social interaction patterns on-line. The introduction of instant messaging has extended the capacity to communicate in real time. Currently, the Internet is primarily a text-based medium, but increasingly, sound and visual communication are becoming available on-line. These additional channels will drastically alter the nature of on-line communication. For example, anonymity will be compromised, as will the ability to alter self-presentation. Instantaneous verbal agility will be favored, unlike current text-based responses that allow time for composing thoughts. This will advantage some users at the expense of others, and the attractiveness of the Internet will diminish for some and increase for others.

B. Escape, Relaxation, and Excitement

The Internet can also provide a place to relax, escape pressures, and seek excitement. In Morahan-Martin and Schumacher's study (2000), half of Internet abusers went on-line to escape pressures, while only one-quarter of those with limited symptoms, and one-eighth of those with no symptoms, went on-line to escape pressures. Internet abusers also were more likely than others to use the Internet for recreation, relaxation, and wasting time. Two Taiwanese studies also have found Internet abusers more likely to go on-line for escape, fun, and excitement (Chou, Chen et al., 1999). Some outlets such as gambling, Net sex, and MUDs provide stimulation and excitement. All studies that have included these on-line activities have found that those who abuse the Internet are more likely to go on-line for gambling and for sexual purposes (Chou, Chen, et al., 1999; Greenfield, 1999; Morahan-Martin & Schumacher, 2000; Scherer, 1997). The use of sexual outlets and gambling on-line are associated with a higher incidence of IA.

Using the Internet for sexual purposes — Net sex or cybersex — is widespread. In fact, in on-line search engines, the word "sex" has generally been the most widely searched term (Cooper, 1998). Those with IA are more likely than others to engage in cybersex (Brenner, 1997; Greenfield, 1999; Morahan-Martin & Schumacher, 2000; Scherer, 1997; Young, 1997b). For example, in Scherer's study of undergraduates, when asked reasons that they use the Internet, dependents were more likely than others to report using it to seek sexual material (41.7% vs. 11.6%, $p < .01$) and to seek illegal or immoral material (37.5% vs. 9.2%, $p < .01$), while 50% of those with IA versus 15% of others reported engaging in Net sex in Morahan-Martin and Schumacher's study (2000). Brenner (1997) also found a higher incidence of Net sex among those with IA. Perhaps because the nature of solicitation of their on-line study, Greenfield (1999) found a higher percentage of individuals who said that they have accessed pornography on-line: 46% of nonaddicts versus 62% of addicts. In Greenfield's (1999) on-line study, 20% of Internet addicts described themselves as sex addicts.

More psychological disturbances are associated with the use of sexually explicit chat rooms than seeking sexual explicit Web sites. In Cooper, Scherer, et al.'s study (1999), those who used sexually explicit chat rooms were more likely to spend more time on-line for sexual pursuits and to report that their Internet use interfered or jeopardized important aspects of their lives. According to the authors, this suggests "that for both men and women the most powerful and potentially problematic types of [sexual] interactions [on-line] take place in chat rooms with other Internet users" (p. 160). They suggest that preexisting social isolation, often associated with sexual compulsivity, may underlie why some individuals compulsively use sexually explicit chat rooms. On-line, they find both social support and sexual gratification. Unfortunately, this study did not distinguish *type* of chat room used for cybersex. The range of sexuality in chat rooms ranges from flirting to one-night cyber-stands, romantic relationships, and acting out of sexual paraphilias. It is probable that disturbed behavior is more likely to be associated with paraphilias being acted out on-line and, perhaps for some at-risk people, romantic involvement on-line.

C. Mood Alteration

Those with IA are more likely than others to go on-line to escape negative emotions. Morahan-Martin and Schumacher (2000) found that, compared to others, those with IA were more likely than others to use the Internet to escape pressure when down, anxious, or isolated. Those with IA become totally absorbed when on-line. Anderson (1999) and Welsh (1999) also found Internet abusers likely to use the Internet to control moods. Bromberg (1996) has suggested that when on-line,

> some people do, in fact, experience altered states of consciousness while connected to virtual worlds. The promise of eroticism, mastery, connectivity, and identity exploration are significant as they all have the potential to contribute to producing these altered states, with the computer as the interface. (p. 149)

Users' perception of reality as well as their sense of time, space, and self can become altered on-line. On-line environments provide alternate realities. They can be intensely absorbing and many users become intensely involved, sometimes resulting in altered perceptions in time and loss of boundaries (Greenfield, 1999). Mood alterations may be facilitated by these distortions. Altered perceptions on-line may mimic dissociative states. Eastman (1998) hypothesizes that for some people the activity of watching a computer screen may be hypnotic and thus contribute to the addictive process.

D. Power and Mastery

Achieving a sense of power and mastery on-line has been suggested as an aspect that can be appealing to some users, especially if they cannot achieve mastery and power in the real world (Curtis, 1992; Turkle, 1995; Young, 1997b). In chat rooms as well as on-line sexual outlets, power and mastery are achieved through social and/or sexual interactions. In MUDs, players can achieve status and prestige by perseverance and computer prowess. Proficient MUD players can gain rank and control over other players because of their ability. A sense of power can also be derived from users' ability to master the virtual environment. A critical component of the fascination with virtual reality, according to Novak, "is the promise of control over the world by the power of the will. ... [I]t is the ancient dream of magic that finally nears awakening into some kind of reality" (p. 228). The ability to control their environment may be particularly attractive to people who do not have control in the their everyday life.

V. INTERNET ABUSE: SYMPTOM, CAUSE, OR EFFECT?

There is a heated debate about whether Internet abuse should be considered a separate disorder or a symptom of another pathology. There also is no consensus about whether there is a cause and effect relationship between Internet abuse and other disorders. With some types of applications, the Internet is redefining how pathology is expressed. For example, for those who are sexually compulsive and/or have sexual paraphilias, the Internet is providing a new channel to act out their pathologies. The Internet provides relatively easy access to sexually explicit material, anonymity, 24-hour availability, on-line disinhibition, a wide choice of sexual partners, and new ways of interacting sexually. These characteristics are opening new avenues for sexual expression, which are poorly understood. Researchers such as Cooper and his colleagues have begun to delineate how the Internet affects the development and acting out of normal and abnormal sexuality, including paraphilias and other sexual pathologies. It is probable that Internet-related sexual disturbances arise from preexisting underlying pathology. However, some individuals may not have acted out this pathology without exposure to cybersex (Cooper, Putnam, Planchon, & Boies, 1999). Further, because of the ready availability of cybersex and anonymity, the patterns of expression of these pathologies may be altered, especially for children who may be exposed to cybersex at increasingly younger ages.

There is some evidence that people with preexisting conditions may be turning to the Internet. A small scale study of 14 self-selected Internet addicts who were recruited by advertising found that most had preexisting pathology (Shapira, 1998). Young asserts that 50% of the self-selected individuals with IA had a prior history of another addiction (reported in King, 1996). Rheingold (1993) observed that users of on-line support and recovery groups were vulnerable to Internet abuse. Egger (1996) found confirmation of this observation. It is possible that on-line recovery groups fill a gap in individuals' lives as they pull away from the social support that may have been given before recovery (Orzak, 1997, personal communication). On-line support groups have a confessional quality which offers both instant intimacy and acceptance as a member of a deviant group. As is common with other Internet social outlets, on-line support groups may provide companionship with the safety of anonymity and geographical distance. On-line disinhibition and a climate of shared intimacies may allow individuals to open up more in these on-line support groups and provide the illusion or reality of social support that they are missing.

A. Cause and Effect

The cause and effect relationship of findings such as the higher incidence of loneliness and depression among Internet abusers is uncertain. For example, are lonely people drawn to the social aspects of the Internet or are people lonely because their Internet usage isolates them from real life social support? Do depressed individuals turn to the Internet, or are people depressed because of their Internet usage? The relationship may be bidirectional. People who are lonely and/or depressed may turn to the Internet to alleviate painful feelings and because they can find companionship and support on-line which is lacking in real life. Once on-line, they may find the companionship, social support, and sense of community so compelling that they increasingly rely on on-line support at the expense of fostering RL contacts and support, which may exacerbate negative affect (Morahan-Martin, 1999; Morahan-Martin & Schumacher, 1999). There is a paucity of longitudinal studies that could help clarify the cause and effect relationship.

The results of one longitudinal study support the contention that Internet use causes pathology. This research, part of the HomeNet study, found increases in loneliness and depression resulting from Internet use (Kraut et al., 1998). Participants in this study consisted of 93 families (169 individuals) in Pittsburgh, Pennsylvania, who were provided free or reduced cost computers, training, and Internet access for two years. In exchange, participants allowed their Internet use to be documented and provided self-reports on their psychological and social characteristics before beginning Internet use as well as at 1-year intervals after they began using the Internet. Neither participants' reported loneliness nor depression at the beginning of the study predicted the amount of subsequent Internet use, but both loneliness and depression increased with greater Internet use once on-line. The authors attributed the increases in loneliness and depression to decreases in family communication, social activities, happiness, and the number of individuals in one's social network, which also were associated with increased Internet use.

Additional confirmation of the adverse effect of Internet use on social relationships was found by the Stanford Institute for the Quantitative Study of Society (SIQSS) whose study of a representative sample of 4113 American adults found that social isolation increased with Internet use. O'Toole (2000) found that the quarter of respondents who used the Internet more than five hours a week believed that their time on-line reduced their time with friends and family either in person or on the phone, and 10% said they spent less time attending social events outside the home. This conforms to a popular image of Internet use as isolating users from the real world and depriving them from a sense of belonging. It bolsters those who argue that Internet use abets technological alienation. For example, Carducci and Zimbardo (1995) argue that "voice mail, faxes and e-mail give us the illusion of being 'in touch' but what's to touch but the keyboard? This is not a Luddite view of technology but a sane look at its deepest causes.... The danger, however, is that technology will become a hiding place" (p. 82).

It is worth noting that other studies have found social connections are augmented on-line (Activmedia, 1998; Katz & Aspden, 1997). Even the HomeNet study confirmed positive social effects of Internet use; a separate analysis from the same study indicates participants use of e-mail actually supported existing relationships (Kraut, 1997). It is probable that the overall social impact is mixed: it increases social connections in some contexts but decreases social connections in other.

Morahan-Martin (1999) argues that lonely people may use and abuse the Internet more than others do because the Internet offers possibilities that are especially well suited to their needs. That is, the Internet is a place lonely people can go to escape painful feelings and to combat isolation, and where they may be able to interact more easily than in the real world. Support for this was found in Morahan-Martin and Schumacher's (1999) study that compared how lonely and nonlonely people used the Internet. Lonely people used the Internet more than others, and used it in ways consistent with escaping negative feelings. They were more likely to go on-line when down, anxious, or lonely; to be totally absorbed when on-line; and to use the Internet to relax and waste time. They preferred on-line to ftf communication, and enjoyed the anonymity of being on-line. On-line, they found companionship. Compared with others, the lonely were more likely to meet new people, make on-line friends, interact with others, and find emotional support. They also were more likely to have more fun with their on-line versus ftf friends, and to believe their on-line friends understood them better. The social behavior of lonely people was enhanced on-line. They opened up more, shared intimate secrets, felt more themselves, and were friendlier. However, despite enhanced social interactions and behavior on-line, the lonely also reported that their Internet use interfered with real life social activities and with school and work performance, and was causing guilt. Thus, using the Internet facilitated more prosocial behavior that resulted in more rewarding friendships on-line while also causing problems in non-Internet social interactions. "This suggests a vicious circle whereby lonely individuals go on-line to fill social voids and emptiness in their lives, but their on-line time creates voids in their RL social life" (1999, p. 13) and supports the idea that the relationship between loneliness and Internet use and abuse may be bidirectional.

Other studies have found a similar pattern with Internet abusers. For example, in Anderson's study (1999), Internet abusers were more likely than others to say they would spend less time on-line if they had more friends on campus while also acknowledging that their Internet use had interfered with their making new friends. Similarly, Internet abusers in Morahan-Martin and Schumacher's (2000) study were more likely to go on-line when feeling isolated, feel socially confident on-line, and make friends on-line. However, they also reported that being on-line interfered with their RL social activities.

As discussed earlier, many use the Internet to modulate moods. This is especially true of those who are Internet abusers. Some argue that this proves that the real problem with those who abuse the Internet is the underlying disorder that causes the negative affect, and that Internet abuse is irrelevant or at best symptomatic. People have long self-medicated by using substances and becoming involved in activities such as gambling and compulsive eating. Depression frequently coexists with a number of other disorders such as substance abuse, pathological gambling, eating disorders, anxiety disorders, and borderline personality disorders (APA, 1994; Becona, Lorenzo, & Fuentes, 1996). Loneliness, too, is associated with a number of other psychological problems such as depression, interpersonal hostility, anxiety and personality disorders (Forsyth & Elliot, 1999), and sexual compulsivity (Cooper, Putnam et al., 1999). Because two disorders coexist does not mean that one caused the other nor that directionality or causality can be determined. Given the limited state of research on Internet abuse, it may be more productive at this point to acknowledge the coexistence of both disorders.

B. Alternative Explanations

A common concern is that IA research is inappropriately pathologizing Internet use and negating positive aspects of the Internet. Many argue that models of pathology that focus on Internet use are inappropriate. Alarm about the Internet being addictive may reflect fears about a new form of technology from those who are themselves intimidated by that technology (Turkle, 1995). The rapid expansion of the Internet combined with the perceived and real sense of lack of control of access to information and social contact frightens many. Historically, fear of the effect of new technology has accompanied the introduction of other communication technologies as well. The introduction of the telephone and television, two other technologies which altered access to information and people, also were accompanied by widespread concern.

1. Quality of On-line versus Real Life Interactions

The Internet is altering how and with whom people socialize. A related objection to the concept of Internet abuse concerns the quality of on-line versus real life relationships. Some argue that many Internet researchers make the implicit assumption that the quality of on-line interactions and friendships are inferior to those in RL. Grohol (1999), arguing that, "maybe they're just healthy social relationships," states,

> Researchers seem to have not considered that perhaps people who spend a lot of time on-line are simply engaging in normal, healthy social relationships with other human beings around the world…. (T)here is very little to suggest that individuals who prefer virtual friends over real-world friends are less well-adapted or have a lower overall quality of life. It is a *different* way of interacting, but is not necessarily a *lesser-quality* interaction. In fact, because of the unique psychological components of on-line social interactions, on-line friendships and relationships may be of higher quality or value to some. (p. 399, author's italics)

Variants of this argument are found in many discussions of Internet use and abuse. Rather than view on-line social relationships as weak, artificial, "superficial personal relationships of pseudocommunity" (Beniger, 1987, p. 369), some argue that on-line relationships are just as valid, if not more so, than real life relationships. On-line contacts can provide support otherwise missing precisely because they are not part of people's real world, and this might make it easier to discuss problems. For example, Stewart, who used MUDs to talk about his real life problems, said,

> I find it a lot easier to talk to people on[line] about … [problems] because they're not there. I mean, they are there but they're not there. I mean, you could sit there and you could tell them about your problems and you don't have to worry about running into them on the street the next day. (Turkle, 1995, p. 198)

In a similar vein, Curtis argues that virtual friendships and communities provide social connectedness.

> If someone is spending a large portion of their time being social with people who live thousands of miles away, you can't say they've turned inward. They aren't shunning society. They're actively seeking it. They're probably doing it more actively than anyone around them. (Quoted in Rheingold, 1993, pp. 151–152).

In fact, on-line communities can provide a strong sense of community, companionship, acceptance, and social support (see Riva, chapter 7 of this volume, for a thorough discussion of virtual communities). Many on-line friendships are transferred into real life as well (Parks & Floyd, 1996). However, the question remains as to when and for whom on-line support is beneficial. Stewart, quoted above, did *not* benefit from his on-line relationships, and felt he was addicted to the Internet. He later said, "When you feel you're stagnating and you feel there's nothing going on in your life, and you're stuck in a rut, it's very easy to be on there [the Internet] for a very large amount of time" (Turkle, 1995, pp. 198–199).

2. Drug Addiction Model

The appropriateness of the drug addiction model to explain *any* habitual or compulsive behavior, even those that are self-destructive behaviors, is questioned by many. This argument extends to all behaviors which have an addictive quality, including disorders such as pathological gambling and binge eating which are recognized inthe fourth edition of the DSM (DSM-IV; APA, 1994), as well as those not formally recognized, such as compulsive sexuality and shopping. Jaffe (1990) maintains that the broadened use of the term "addiction" not only trivializes the concept of substance-related addiction, but is detrimental to understanding specific etiology and treatment approaches for both substance-related and compulsive, repetitive behaviors. Further, Peele argues that the concept of addiction itself causes "addictive behaviors to grow because it excuses uncontrolled behaviors and predisposes people to interpret their lack of control as the expression of a disease that they can do nothing about" (cited in Jaffe, 1990, p. 1426).

3. A Temporary Phenomenon?

Some have questioned whether Internet abuse is a temporary phenomenon among new users (newbies) who become enthralled when first exposed to on-line friendships and the vast possibilities of on-line activities — the "newbie effect" (King, 1996). Young (1998) reports that most of those who have developed IA had done so within one year of going on-line. However, given that Internet use was doubling every six months at the time of her study, the large numbers of new users may reflect their actual ratio in the on-line population at the time. Clark (1998), in a study of teens and chat rooms, reports that many had "periods of intense experimentation in the chat rooms, sometimes devoting more than four hours a day to on-line chats for a period of several weeks or even months" (pp. 161–162). However, this was usually curtailed, often following parental intervention. The HomeNet study, which monitored actual Internet use, found that the heaviest Internet use with new users, especially teens, peaks within the first few weeks of being on-line (Mukhopadhyay et al., 1996). However, studies of on-line use, including the HomeNet study, find that Internet use is higher among experienced users than inexperienced ones (GVU, 1998; O'Toole, 2000). Questions about the "newbie effect" raise two issues about Internet abuse. The first is whether new users are more prone to Internet abuse than others. Studies of Internet abuse report contradictory results. Kubey et al. (1999) found that the incidence of IA increases the longer individuals have been on-line, while Morahan-Martin and Schumacher (2000) found no difference in Internet abuse by years on-line. The second issue is whether Internet abuse is a temporary phenomenon. Unfortunately, none of the IA studies reviewed in this chapter considered duration of the symptoms. Thus, it is not known whether they documented temporary, perhaps even momentary, phenomena. Certainly, future researchers must specify how long symptoms must be present before the individual has a problem. Additionally, future study needs to explore the development and the duration of symptoms.

VI. COLLEGE STUDENTS AND INTERNET USE AND ABUSE

The Internet has become an integral part of college life. Eighty five percent of college students in U.S. campuses are on-line, with 50% having access from their dorms (Greenfield On-line, 1999). Students use the Internet for both work and play. Courses increasingly have at least an on-line component (see Hammond and Trapp, chapter 8 of this volume, for a discussion of the Web in higher education). Research capacities are enhanced on-line. Students and faculty can interact with each other through e-mail. Some courses use chat rooms and bulletin boards. Distance education is a rapidly growing educational option.

Students also use the Internet nonacademically. Increasingly, the Internet is becoming a way to socialize, waste time, and have fun. E-mail, instant messaging, and e-cards allow them to stay in touch with friends and family. They go on-line for news, weather, and other information. Chat rooms and newsgroups can be places to socialize, hang out, or just have fun. Some also find stimulation in cybersex and on-line gambling, both new variants of behaviors that have long been popular with college-aged students, especially males. For many, the Internet and computers simply provide new ways to procrastinate. One college student recently described his fellow classmates as "playing Tomb Raider instead of going to class, tweaking the configurations of their machines instead of writing the paper due tomorrow, collecting mostly useless information from the World Wide Web instead of doing a math problem" (Stulman, 1999, p. A19). None of these behaviors are problematic, and the vast majority of social and recreation use of the Internet among college students is beneficial or neutral. However, some students' on-line behavior is out of control and is causing serious problems in their lives. In fact, some of the earliest studies of Internet abuse were initiated by college counselors in response to students coming to counseling centers with Internet-related problems (Anderson, 1999; Kandell, 1998; Scherer, 1997).

College students have been the most systematically studied population of Internet abusers. For these students, their Internet use is negatively affecting academics, sleep patterns, and real life social interactions. Students who are Internet abusers are more likely than others to be missing classes and to report academic performance slipping because of their Internet use. They also are more likely to stay up late to be on-line and be tired as a result. Their time on-line is interfering with meeting new people and/or causing disturbances in relationships with people in their real world.

Although Internet abuse is a new phenomenon among college students, it may better be thought of as a new manifestation of the tendency of some students to abuse substances and engage in compulsive behaviors such as eating disorders and pathological gambling. However, the Internet may become the chosen object of abuse because some on-line activities uniquely meet the needs of college students. The following sections will discuss common issues underlying disturbed behaviors among college students, and then look at developmental issues specific to the Internet which may explain why some become Internet abusers.

A. Developmental Issues of College Students

The college years are very stressful. Traditional-aged students are dealing with developmental issues of identity, separation, and autonomy, and the establishment of intimate relationships (Kandell, 1998), while balancing the social, academic, and often work-related demands of college. Freshman year for many is the first time many leave home. At the same time students are dealing with separating from their families and high school friends, they are trying to fit into their new environment: meeting new people, finding friends and confidants, and adjusting to roommates and dorm life. Academics are usually much more demanding than they were in high school, and frequently there is less help available to them; many find grades slipping. Sometimes, it seems as if everyone else is adjusting except them.

College students have much freedom: freedom from parental restrictions and from the rigid structure of high school. Freedom is both exhilarating and terrifying. Many suddenly have much unstructured time, with increased opportunities for boredom and/or loneliness. Others are overburdened with demands of school and outside work. Distractions are numerous. They must learn new ways of coping at many levels: study and time management skills, dealing with peer pressure, and social and negotiation skills. Simultaneously, students are dealing with existential issues surrounding identity and life's meaning while making practical choices such as choosing majors and careers. Romantic involvement can alleviate or accentuate insecurities. Some students also bring unresolved personal or family issues that can undermine their adjustment. For students, this is a period when they must gain autonomy. Not all students or families are ready for this transition. "The role of the family and the student's ability to gain sufficient independence from the family system are crucial at this point.... If parents ... do not allow the child to form an independent identity (or if the child is not ready), many problems can and do occur" (Kandell, 1998, p. 14).

Given the upheaval of the college years, it is not surprising that many escape into binge drinking, drugs, and other addictive behaviors. These behaviors allow them to escape pressures, and numb them to the pain associated with their life situation. They also may allow some individuals, consciously or unconsciously, to resolve issues related to separating from their families. If they "become addicted to drugs, gambling, the Internet, whatever, [they] become unable to care for [themselves] in an independent way. Thus, the family is forced to accept [their] return ... back ... to the [family] system," which can resolve the crisis at an individual and family level (Kandell, 1998, p. 15). Arguably, the Internet is just the newest outlet for some students to act out their problems.

B. Why the Internet?

Although the underlying reasons some students may become dependent on the Internet are similar to those associated with drug abuse or other addictive or compulsive behaviors, the Internet may be the object of choice for reasons related to both properties of the Internet and of college students. First of all, the Internet is available 24 hours a day, 7 days a week, and many students can go on-line whenever they wish. Many use the Internet as a distraction while working, going back and forth between working and recreational or social Internet applications. For example, students working on a paper may activate instant messaging and interrupt their paper to respond to messages. MUD users may multitask between a school-related task and their MUD games. There always is another world just a click away. For some, this is a short distraction, but for others the temptation to abandon the task at hand may be too great.

The Internet provides a virtual playground for many college students. The current generation of college students has been called the Net generation (Tapscott, 1998). They are more comfortable with technology than most of the older generations. Most have grown up using computers, often for entertainment. Most, especially boys, have used computer and video games extensively in their childhood (Sax et al., 1999; National Public Radio, 2000). In the late 1990s, going on-line became prestigious. Polls in the United States and Britain report that it is "in" to be on-line (Burke, 1999; Tapscott, 1998). Internet users "are held in high esteem by teenagers .... [They] are described as 'clever', 'friendly', 'cool', 'trendy', and 'rich'" (NOP Research reported in Burke, 1999). Once on-line, students find themselves in a virtual playground with endless possibilities to play, connect with others, and just have fun. More than any generation, teens and young adults use the Internet to socialize and enjoy themselves (GVU, 1999). They dominate chat rooms and MUDs (Adamse & Motta, 1996; Clark, 1998; GVU, 1999). Not surprisingly, they are the heaviest users of the Internet (GVU, 1999; Kraut et al., 1996).

College students may be the most prone to use and abuse the Internet because the virtual playground provides not only fun, but also unique ways to deal with developmental and social issues common in the college years: isolation, intimacy, identity, sexuality, and dating relationships. People who are feeling isolated can readily find companionship on-line "24/7" in socially interactive activities such as chat rooms, newsgroups, BBSs and MUDs. Becoming part of a cybercommunity can enhance feelings of acceptance and may validate the individual in ways not possible in their real life. Additionally, the Internet can fulfill unmet intimacy needs. The intense intimacy of some of these groups can counteract the lack of perceived intimacy in their real life. Some people who have problems in intimacy report that it is easier to be intimate on-line. This may be related to the hyperpersonal nature of some on-line groups, as well as the socially liberating effects of disinhibition and anonymity (Morahan-Martin, 1999). Many learn social skills that generalize to their real life through their on-line interactions (Adamse & Motta, 1996; Clark, 1998; Morahan-Martin, 1999). On-line activities such as chat rooms and MUDs also provide social arenas to act out and perhaps resolve many issues. These activities can serve as identity workshops. One can consciously or unconsciously work through issues relating to identity in group interactions and role playing on-line (Turkle, 1995). Also, these activities provide places to experiment with issues related to dating and sexual identity. Many consider cybersex the ultimate safe sex, allowing users to explore erotic fantasies in an anonymous environment without real world consequences (Young, 1997a). For the vast majority of college students, flirting, sexual experimentation, and on-line sexual behaviors are not problematic. However, college students who use cybersex are the most likely groups of cybersex users to develop cybersex compulsivity. That is, they are both sexually compulsive and use the Internet for sexual purposes more than 10 hours per week. This is much higher than the incidence of cybersex compulsivity among those who are employed or "at home" (Cooper et al., in press).

The popularity of the Internet among college students may, in part, be related to the unique way that Internet activities can enable them to explore and work through these issues. For most students, using the Internet to meet these needs is not problematic, and may even be beneficial. However, some individuals, in seeking resolution of needs on-line, become trapped there and develop disturbed patterns of Internet abuse. Thus, for some individuals, the appeal of the Internet is that it allows them to meet and express unresolved needs, but, unfortunately, their Internet use causes further problems rather than resolving them. Whether this is a temporary phenomenon is not known. However, to the extent that individuals become dependent on the Internet to meet their needs, they are not resolving them in real life.

VII. CONCLUSIONS

For the vast majority of Internet users, going on-line has been beneficial and expanded their world in positive ways. However, for some, their use of the Internet has led to serious problems in their lives. As with many behaviors, it is difficult to determine when use becomes problematic. For example, communication on the Internet can foster friendships and communities. However, when Internet communication impedes building skills and connections in the real world, it can be detrimental. At what point does this occur? Research to date has documented that a small percentage of Internet users develop problematic behaviors. The changed social interaction patterns made possible by on-line communication, especially with those one would not know in real life, appear to be critical underlying factors in the development of Internet abuse. Additionally, Internet abusers are more prone than others to go on-line seeking excitement and escape from negative emotions. Some may achieve a sense of power and mastery on-line that is unavailable to them in the real world. Internet abusers are more likely to develop problems when using some Internet activities: chat rooms, newsgroups, MUDs, Palaces, on-line gambling, and cybersex. Each of these activities has unique features that appeal to different users, but more research needs to delineate these differences. Some notable areas of Internet activity where some users may develop disturbed patterns of use have not been studied, including on-line stock trading, auctions, and shopping.

Internet abuse among college students may be similar to other addictions common to their peers. Like substance abuse, and behaviors such as eating disorders, students may be abusing the Internet in attempts to escape from the pressures of their lives. However, the Internet offers unique properties that may underlie disturbances among college students being expressed through it rather than in other ways. It can provide an arena where students can work through developmental issues of isolation, identity, sexuality, and dating relationships. This is positive for most, but for a small minority may result in their developing disturbed patterns of Internet use and creating further problems. Like substance abuse among college students, Internet abuse could be a temporary phenomenon.

However, in the meantime, affected individuals are not able to resolve key issues.

Research on Internet abuse is limited. There are no standardized criteria for Internet abuse, and no studies to date have considered the duration of symptoms. There is much need for a study of a random sample of Internet users — preferably one that follows users over time, with a special focus on differences between specific Internet applications — to clarify the development and course of Internet abuse. Serious questions remain about Internet abuse. Is IA a separate disorder or symptomatic of other disorders? Are researchers inappropriately pathologizing Internet behavior, perhaps expressing Luddite fears of the effects of new technology? Is the addiction model appropriate? Internet abuse research to date arguably ignores the positive potential of some forms of Internet use to facilitate growth.

Daily life is being transformed for Internet users. People are going on-line for shopping, news, and entertainment, resulting in a redistribution of time (O'Toole, 2000). Increasingly, entertainment will be sought on-line as individuals use the Internet to access more traditional entertainment media such as music, radio, and television. The introduction of the MP3 music format already is altering the music industry and changing how people listen to music. In fact, by one account, "MP3" replaced "sex" as the most frequently searched term on-line in January 2000 (Ni hEilidhe, 2000). High-speed access promises to change the delivery of entertainment as well, and to make text-based communication obsolete. These changes will alter patterns of Internet use in ways that are difficult to predict. In discussions of Internet use and abuse, it is important to recognize how the Internet is changing and reorganizing peoples' working and nonworking time. For many, especially teens and males, being on-line is becoming a preferred way of wasting time, replacing other leisure, recreational, and social activities. The Internet provides a virtual playground, with activities such as games, chat rooms, instant messaging, and e-mail just a click away. Some of these are variants of other activities that when done off-line do not cause concern. Excessive MUD playing raises alarm, but not playing pinball machines or bridge, or going bowling. Chat rooms and newsgroups often are akin to social clubs that allow people to communicate with others with similar interests, but use of chat rooms alarms many. Finally, the Internet is a constantly evolving medium. Changes such as voice and camera capacity will change the nature of communication on-line as well as the appeal of the Internet to users. Existing research on Internet abuse is largely based on interaction that is primarily text-based. Social presence will increase and anonymity will decrease with the addition of voice and visual cues. How this will effect on-line communication and Internet abuse is not known.

References

Activmedia. (1998, September 4). *Web improves relationships.* Available (September 21, 1998): http://www.nua.ie/surveys/index/cgi?service=view_survey&survey_number=959&rel.htm

Adamse, M., & Motta, S. (1996). *On-line friendship, chat-room romance and cybersex.* Deerfield Beach, FL: Health Communications.

American Psychiatriac Association. (1987). *Diagnostic and statistical manual of mental disorders* (3rd ed., rev.). Washington, DC: Author.

American Psychiatriac Association. (1994). *Diagnostic and statistical manual of mental disorders* (4th ed., rev.). Washington, DC: Author.

Anderson, K. (1999, August). *Internet dependency among college students: Should we be concerned?* Paper presented at the 107th Annual Convention of the American Psychological Association, Boston, MA.. Available (February 21, 2000): http://www.rpi.edu/~anderk4/research.html

Becona, E., Lorenzo, M., & Fuentes, M. (1996). Pathological gambling and depression. *Psychological Reports, 78,* 635–640.

Beniger, J. R. (1987). Personalization of mass media and the growth of pseudo-community. *Communication Research, 14,* 352–371.

Brenner, V. (1997). Psychology of computer use: XLVII. Parameters of Internet use, abuse and addiction: The first 90 days of the Internet Usage Survey. *Psychological Reports, 80,* 879–882.

Bromberg, H. (1996). Are MUDs communities? Identity, belonging and consciousness in virtual worlds. In R. Shields (Ed.), *Cultures of the Internet: Virtual spaces, real histories, living bodies* (pp. 143–154). London: Sage.

Burke, B. (1999, July 19). Meeting generation Y: NUA analysis. Dublin: NUA. Available (January 31, 2000): http://nua.ie/surveys/?f=vs&art_id=905355157&rel=true

Carducci, B., & Zimbardo, P. (1995, November/December). Are you shy? *Psychology Today,* 34–40, 64, 66, 68, 70, 78, 82.

Carnegie Mellon. (1998, September). *Carnegie Mellon study reveals negative potential of heavy Internet use on emotional well being* (Press release). Available (February 21, 2000): http://homenet andrew.cmu.edu/progress/research.html

Chou, C., Chen, S., & Hsiao, M. (1999). *Internet addiction, usage and gratification—The Taiwanese college students' case.* Paper presented at the 107th Annual Convention of the American Psychological Association, Boston, MA.

Chou, C., Chou, J., & Tyan, N. (1999). An exploratory study of Internet addiction, usage and communication pleasure — The Taiwanese case. *International Journal of Educational Telecommunications, 5,* 47–63.

Clark, L. (1998). Dating on the Net: Teens and the rise of "pure" relationships. In S. Jones (Ed.), *Cybersociety 2.0: Revisiting computer-mediated comunication and community* (pp. 159–183). Thousand Oaks, CA: Sage.

Cooper, A. (1998). Sexuality and the Internet: Surfing into the new millennium. *CyberPsychology & Behavior, 2,* 187–193. Available (May 22, 2000): http://www.sex-center.com/Internetsex_folder/Sexual&Internet%205

Cooper, A., Delmonico, D., & Burg, R. (In press). Cybersex users, abusers, and compulsives. *Sexual Addiction and Compulsivity: Journal of Treatment and Prevention.*

Cooper, A., Putnam, D., Planchon, L., & Boies, S. (1999). On-line sexual compulsivity: Getting tangled in the Net. *Sexual Addiction and Compulsivity, 6,* 79–104. Available (May 22, 2000): http://www.sex-centre.com/sex1comp_Folder/On-line%sexual%20Compulsivity

Cooper, A., Scherer, C., Boies, S., & Gordon, B. (1999). Sexuality on the Internet: From sexual exploration to pathological expression. *Professional Psychology: Research and Practice, 30,* 154–164. Available (October 20, 1999): http://www.sex-centre.com/Internetsex_Folder/MSNBC_Study_pp.htm

Curtis, P. (1992). MUDDING: Social phenomena in text-based virtual realities. In *Proceedings of Directions in Advanced Computing Conference* (DIAC '92). Available (February 21, 2000): http://moo.di.uminho.pt/~pmoo/papers/pap_virt.en.html

CyberAtlas. (2000, February 22). January 2000 Internet usage stats. [on-line] Available (February 22, 2000): http://cyberatlas.internet.com/big_picture/demographics/article/0,1323, 5931_308301.html

Eastman, G. (1998, February). *The effect of electronic imaging on our experience of reality.* Paper presented at the Eastern Psychology Association, Boston, MA.

Egger, O. (1996). *Internet and addiction.* Semester thesis, Swiss Federal Institute of Technology, Zurich [on-line]. Available (September 14, 1999): http://www.ifap.bepr.ethz ch/~egger/ibq/iddres.htm

Forsyth, D. & Elliott, T. (1999). Group dynamics and psychological well being: The impact of groups on adjustment and dysfunction. In R. Kowalski and M. Leary (Eds.), *The social psychology of emotional and behavioral problems: Interfaces of social and clinical psychology* (pp. 339–361). Washington, DC: American Psychological Association.

Graphics, Visualization, and Usability Center (GVU). (1999). GVU's WWW *user surveys.* Atlanta, GA: Georgia Tech Research Corporation. Available (February 21, 2000): http://www.gatech.edu/user_surveys

Greenfield, D. (1999). Psychological characteristics of compulsive Internet use: A preliminary analysis. *CyberPsychology & Behavior,* 2, 403–412.

Greenfield On-line. (1999, July 9). *College students provide a vibrant Net market.* Dublin: NUA. Available (February 21, 2000): http://www.nua.ie/?f=VS&art_id=905355016&rel=true

Grohol, J. (1999). Too much time on-line: Internet addiction or healthy social interactions. *CyberPsychology & Behavior,* 2, 395–402.

Jacobs, D. (1986). A general theory of addictions. *Journal of Gambling Behavior,* 2, 15–31.

Jaffe, J. (1990). Trivializing dependence. *British Journal of Addiction,* 85, 1425–1427.

Kandell, J. (1998). Internet addiction on campus: The vulnerability of college students. *CyberPsychology & Behavior,* 1, 11–17.

Katz, J., & Aspden, P. (1997). A nation of strangers? *Communications of the Association for Computing Machinery,* 40, 81–86.

King, S. (1996). *Is the Internet addictive or are addicts using the Internet?* [on-line]. Available (February 21, 2000): http://concentric.net/~Astorm/iad.html

Kowalski, R., & Leary, M. (Eds.). (1999). *The social psychology of emotional and behavioral problems: Interfaces of social and clinical psychology.* Washington, DC: American Psychological Association.

Kraut, R. (1997, August). HomeNet: A *study of residential Internet use* [On-line HomeNet slide presentation]. Available (February 21, 2000): http://homenet.andrew.cmu.edu/progress/homenettalk/sld001.htm

Kraut, R., Patterson, M., Landmark, V., Kiesler, S., Mukophadhyay, T., & Scherlis, W. (1998). Internet paradox: A social technology that reduces social involvement and psychological well being? *American Psychologist,* 53, 1017–1031.

Kraut, R., Scherlis, W., Mukhopadhyay, T., Manning, J., & Kiesler, S. (1996). The HomeNet field trial of residential Internet services. *Communications of the* ACM, 39, 55–63.

Kubey, R., Lavin, M., & Barrows, J. (1999, May 27). *Heavy Internet use and collegiate academic performance.* Paper presented at the meeting of the International Communication Association, San Diego, CA.

Lavin, M., Marvin, K., McLarney, A., Nola, V., & Scott, L. (1999). Sensation seeking and collegiate vulnerability to Internet dependence. *CyberPsychology & Behavior,* 2, 425–430.

Lin, S., & Tsai, C. (1999). *Internet addiction among high schoolers in Taiwan.* Paper presented at the 107th Annual Convention of the American Psychological Association, Boston, MA.

Milkman, H., & Sunderwirth, S. (1982). Addictive processes. *Journal of Psychoactive Drugs,* 14, 177–192.

Moore, David. (2000, February 23). *Americans say Internet makes their lives better* (Poll release). Princeton: Gallup Organization. Available (February 25, 2000): http://www.gallop.com/poll/releases/pr000223.asp

Moore, Dinty. (1995). *The emperor's virtual clothes: The naked truth about Internet culture.* Chapel Hill, NC: Alogonquin.

Morahan-Martin, J. (1999). The relationship between loneliness and Internet use and abuse. *CyberPsychology & Behavior*, 2, 431–440.

Morahan-Martin, J., & Schumacher, P. (1997, August). Gender differences in Internet usage, behaviors and attitudes. In G. Salvendy, M. Smith, and R. Koubek (Eds.), *Proceedings of the Seventh International Conference on Human-Computer Interaction* (p. 122). Amsterdam: Elsevier.

Morahan-Martin, J., & Schumacher, P. (1998). *Pathological Internet use* (Study). Unpublished data.

Morahan-Martin, J., & Schumacher, P. (1999, August). *Loneliness and social uses of the Internet*. Paper presented at the 107th Annual Convention of the American Psychological Association, Boston, MA.

Morahan-Martin, J., & Schumacher, P. (2000). Incidence and correlates of pathological Internet use among college students. *Computers in Human Behavior*, 16, 13–29.

Mukhopadhyay, T., Kraut, R., Szczypula, J., Kiesler, S., Scherelis, & Buskirk, S. (1996, October). HomeNet: *Residential Internet use over time* [on-line]. Available (February 21, 2000): http://www.homenet.andrew.cmu.edu/progress/tspaper.html

National Public Radio (NPR). (2000). *Survey shows widespread enthusiasm for high technology.* Washington DC: NPR On-line. Available (March 1, 2000): http://www.npr.org/programs/specials/poll/technology/index.html

Ni hEilidhe, S. (2000, February 7). A musical shakeout. NUA *analysis: Weekly editorial* [on-line]. Available (March 1, 2000): http://www.nua.ie/surveys/analysis/editorial/archives/issue1no112.html

Novak, M. (1993). Liquid architectures in cyberspace. In M. Benedikt (Ed.), *Cyberspace: First steps*. Cambridge, MA: MIT Press.

NUA. (2000, March). *How many on-line?* [on-line]. Dublin: NUA Internet Surveys. Available (May 21, 2000): http://www.nua.ie/surveys/how_many_on-line_/index.html

O'Toole, K. (2000, February 16). Study offers early look at how Internet is changing daily life [on-line]. *Stanford News*. Available (February 21, 2000): http://www.stanford.edu/dept/news/pr/00/000216internet.html

Parks, M., & Floyd, J. (1996). Making friends in cyberspace. *Journal of Computer-Mediated Communication*, 1 (4). Available (February 21, 2000): http://jmc.huji.ac.il/vol1/issue 4/parks.html

Petrie, H., & Gunn, D. (1998, December 15). Internet "addiction": *The effects of sex, age, depression*. Paper presented at the British Psychological Society, London. Available (February 21, 2000): http://www.phoenix.psy.herts.ac.uk/sdru/Helen/inter.html

Rheingold, H. (1993). *The virtual community: Homesteading on the electronic frontier*. Reading: MA: Addison-Wesley.

Rosnow, R., & Rosenthal, R. (1996). *Beginning behavioral research: A conceptual primer*. Englewood Cliffs, NJ: Prentice-Hall.

Sax, L. J., Astin, A. W., Korn, W. S., & Mahoney, K. (1999). *The American freshman: National norms for fall 1999*. Los Angeles: Higher Education Research Institute, UCLA.

Scherer, K. (1997). College life on-line: Healthy and unhealthy Internet use. *The Journal of College Student Development*, 38, 655–664.

Shapira, N. (1998, May). *Problematic Internet use*. Paper presented at the annual meeting of the American Psychiatric Association, Toronto, Ontario.

Shotten, M. (1991). The costs and benefits of computer addiction. *Behavior and Information Technology*, 10, 219–230.

Stulman, N. (1999, March 15). The great campus goof-off machine. *The New York Times*, A19.

Suler, J. (1996). *Why is this thing eating my life? Computer and cyberspace addiction at the "Palace"* [on-line]. Available (February 21, 2000): http://www.rider.edu/users/suler/psycyber/eatlife.html

Tapscott, D. (1998). *Growing up digital: The rise of the Net generation*. New York: McGraw-Hill.

Thompson, S. (1996). *Internet connectivity: Addiction and dependency study* [on-line]. Unpublished honors thesis, Pennsylvania State University. State College, PA. Available (October 17, 1997): http//www.personal.psy.edu/sjt/112/iads/thesis/html

Turkle, S. (1995). *Life on the screen: Identity in the age of the Internet.* New York: Simon & Schuster.

Walther, J. (1994). Anticipated ongoing interaction versus channel effect on recreational communication in computer-mediated communication. *Human Communications Research, 20,* 473–501.

Walther, J. (1996). Computer-mediated communication: Impersonal, interpersonal, and hyperpersonal interaction. *Communication Research, 23,* 3–43.

Weissman, M., & Payle, E. (1974). *The depressed woman: A study of social relationships.* Evanston, IL: University of Chicago Press.

Welsh, L. M. (1999). *Internet use: An exploration of coping style, locus of control and expectancies.* Unpublished doctoral dissertation, Northeastern University, Boston.

Young, K. (1997a, April). The relationship between depression and pathological Internet use. In *Proceedings and abstracts of the Annual Meeting of the Eastern Psychological Association* (Vol. 68). Washington, DC: EPA.

Young, K. (1997b, August). *What makes on-line usage stimulating: Potential explanations for pathological Internet use.* Paper presented at the 105th Annual Convention of the American Psychological Association, Chicago, IL.

Young, K. (1998). Internet addiction: The emergence of a new clinical disorder. *CyberPsychology and Behavior, 1,* 237–244.

Young, K., Pistner, M., O'Mara, J., & Buchanan, J. (1999). CyberDisorders: The mental health concern for the new millennium. *CyberPsychology and Behavior, 2,* 475–479.

Young, K., & Rodgers, R. (1998). The relationship between depression and Internet addiction. *CyberPsychology, 1,* 25–28.

CHAPTER

11

Doing Educational Research on the Internet

ADAM N. JOINSON

The Open University

TOM BUCHANAN

University of Westminster

I. DOING RESEARCH ON THE WEB

A. What Is On-line Research?

What is on-line research? It may just be the most exciting and useful extension to the toolbox of psychology researchers since the invention of the personal computer. The World Wide Web, for many psychologists, is fast becoming a World Wide Laboratory, allowing us to explore questions of psychological importance with thousands of participants from around the globe. At the time of writing, there is still a degree of novelty associated with on-line research. However, it is unlikely to be many years before asking questions such as, "Can one do meaningful psychological research over the Internet?" (c.f. Buchanan & Joinson, 2000) will seem as odd as asking, "Can one do meaningful psychological research using pencil and paper?"— or stand-alone computers, or tachistoscopes, or any other "traditional" technology one might care to name.

As demonstrated by other chapters in this volume, the Internet has great potential as a medium for teaching and learning, as well as presenting a fascinating new sphere of human expression and interaction in its own right. The extension of psychological research into this sphere allows for the

identification and investigation of factors which may affect the design —
and success — of on-line learning paradigms, and the exploration of the
context in which these paradigms are implemented. In fact, given the attractiveness of the new technologies available to us, it is essential that the
psychological factors underpinning "what works" in on-line teaching be
understood. As is the case with off-line computerized teaching packages, the
best are likely to be those which are driven by sound pedagogical principles,
rather than those being showcases for the latest technology.

On-line psychological research, then, is not just an exciting and innovative extension to our existing methods for exploration of many aspects of
human behavior, it is also crucial to the success of learning and teaching on
the World Wide Web (WWW or Web).

B. Issues in On-line Research

There are many ways in which the Internet can be used in teaching
and learning, and many opportunities for both theoretical and applied
research on the psychology of on-line education. Such research may be
considered a subarea (though an important one) of on-line psychology
research in general, and will be informed by the lessons learned — and
potential problems identified — in the broader field to date.

It may be useful to clarify exactly what we mean by "on-line psychological
research." There are in fact two main (overlapping) spheres of activity that
could be described in this way. One is an extension of the longstanding
social-psychological tradition of research into computer-mediated communication (CMC), which is now informing our understanding of how people
interact and behave "on the Internet" (in this volume see Sherman, chapter
6, and Riva, chapter 7, for more on CMC). The implications of what we
already know about the psychology of on-line behavior will be addressed
later in this chapter.

The second variety of on-line research really began in the mid–1990s
(Krantz & Dalal, 2000) — though there were antecedents in the shape of on-
line studies performed using other media, such as e-mail) — when people
began to wonder about the possibility of extending the traditional psychological laboratory into cyberspace. Given that many laboratory research
paradigms (especially within cognitive psychology) involve participants
sitting at computers, responding to on-screen stimuli, why not ask people
to do this outside the laboratory, using their own computers and in their
own time?

The reasons for using the WWW as a research lab are numerous. Musch
and Reips (2000) surveyed a number of active WWW experimenters, asking
about their motivation for doing this kind of work. The main reasons
provided by respondents were (1) the large sample sizes and resultant high
levels of statistical power made possible by the WWW; (2) the speed of WWW

experimentation compared to traditional laboratory studies in that large numbers of participants can be acquired in a very short stretch of time (not least because participation can be round-the-clock, and is not contingent on the timetable of the experimenter or hours when the laboratory is open); and (3) the ease of access to participants from other countries around the world (facilitating what Pagani & Lombardi, 2000, have described as "intercultural" research).

To these, one might add more mundane factors such as cost. Compared to traditional laboratories that must be equipped, staffed, and maintained, the cost to the on-line experimenter is minimal: participants are essentially providing their own equipment and materials. Data can be written automatically to file, saving the time (and transcription errors) associated with data entry. Yet another advantage is the potential to recruit from special populations which might be difficult to access through traditional means (e.g., Smith & Leigh, 1997).

In addition to these practical considerations, there are also more psychologically grounded motives for doing research on-line (e.g., Buchanan & Joinson, 2000; Buchanan & Smith, 1999a; Hewson, Laurent, & Vogel, 1996; Joinson, 1999; Reips, 2000). For example, Hewson et al. (1996) suggest that the greater (potential) anonymity of both respondent and experimenter may serve to reduce experimental demand characteristics and experimenter bias (alternatively, one might propose that automation will control for these factors by keeping them constant for all participants). The increased candor and self-disclosure traditionally associated with on-line communication (e.g., Joinson, 1998a) might well serve to increase the validity of on-line techniques (although, as a caveat, it might also lead to different patterns of responding — in which case, which technique is the "right" one?). Reips (2000) has suggested that on-line research is likely to have greater ecological validity than traditional laboratory studies using student samples (on which psychology still relies to a disturbing extent — e.g., Banyard & Hunt, 2000; Buchanan & Smith, 1999a). Reips argues that the WWW gives us access to much more heterogeneous samples, and that when people participate in environments of their own choosing their behavior is likely to be more "natural" than it is under "artificial" laboratory conditions.

However, early attempts to do research on the WWW were cautious in nature, and mainly aimed at establishing the viability of such an endeavor (e.g., Krantz, Ballard, & Scher, 1997; Buchanan & Smith, 1999a). There were sound motives for this caution. There are many possible reasons why the validity of WWW-mediated research might be suspect. Reips (2000) discusses many of these, including self-selection of participants, the representativeness of samples given known (but changing) sampling biases, and ethical issues.

Among these, the biggest question is probably whether or not WWW and traditional studies will reflect the same psychological phenomena.

Accordingly, this point has been addressed by a number of researchers, who have — across different research areas and methodological approaches — performed studies which permit comparison of data sets acquired via both the WWW and traditional means. In some cases, the parallel comes from inclusion of lab-based comparison conditions, and in others, from comparison with existing data. What follows will not be a comprehensive review, but rather an account of several studies which allow inferences about the validity of on-line research to be drawn.

Stanton (1998) used what is probably the simplest of psychological research tools, the questionnaire-based survey, to measure perceived fairness in employee–supervisor relations. Participants under one condition were solicited by e-mailing people in 20 different organizations and asking them and their colleagues to participate in the WWW condition by going to the appropriate page. In the comparison condition, packets of pencil-and-paper questionnaires were mailed out to a comparable sample. The findings suggested that the two datasets were fundamentally equivalent: an analysis of latent structure suggested that the same factor structure and inter-subscale correlations were present in both.

Almost as easy to implement (if not to construct) are personality questionnaires. The first published account of a study comparing on- and off-line versions of a scale was probably that of Pasveer and Ellard (1998). The test in question was a new measure of "self-trust." In the course of developing this new measure, both WWW and traditional (in terms of recruitment and testing situation) samples were employed. This allowed various comparisons to be made between the two groups, and led to the observation that reliability (Cronbach's alpha) and latent structure were very similar for the two types of dataset. Again, this suggested equivalence of the scales in terms of their psychometric properties.

Work in this vein was also done by Buchanan and Smith (1999a) using a test designed to measure the construct of Self-Monitoring (Snyder, 1974). A WWW version of the scale was developed, and data acquired using it were compared with those acquired from a paper- and-pencil comparison sample and previously published analyses. Again, reliability and factor structure were very similar, suggesting psychometric equivalence. Indications of the validity of the on-line scale have also been found (Buchanan & Smith, 1999b): using a criterion-group approach to validation it was found that groups of respondents who theoretically should differ in self-monitoring scores, did differ in self-monitoring scores. Further work (Buchanan, 2000a) has replicated the findings of traditional laboratory studies on self-monitoring as a moderator of attraction, adding further weight to the claim that the WWW version of the test is a valid one.

Moving to a more experimental approach, Krantz et al. (1997) asked respondents — both on the WWW and in the laboratory — to rate the attractiveness of female silhouettes whose characteristics (e.g., weight, breast size) were systematically manipulated. They found a very close match between the two types of sample, leading them to conclude that the same psychological processes were driving responses in both samples: the things that made a figure attractive in a WWW study were the same as those which made it attractive in the laboratory.

This is echoed by the work of Pagani and Lombardi (2000), who asked WWW and laboratory respondents to rate schematic faces for degree of surprise. Again, various characteristics were manipulated, and again the same pattern of main effects and interactions was found. The same psychological processes seemed to be operating in both the WWW and the laboratory versions of the study.

In general, therefore, the results of these studies have been encouraging. The most common finding is that the same psychological processes underpin participant responses in both WWW and off-line explorations of the same topics. This implies that psychological research can be viably performed on the WWW, and that by extension the same is true of educational psychology research. This would seem to make sense. Just as one would go to the classroom to investigate the processes occurring in that mode of pedagogy, it is appropriate that one should use the medium of the WWW to investigate the psychology of teaching and learning which is taking place in that medium.

There many ways in which this could be done. For instance, there is evidence that personality variables may affect learning — as a specific example, extraverts and introverts may prefer different study environments and be affected to different degrees by distracting stimuli (Furnham & Heaven, 1999; see Anderson, chapter 3 of this volume, for more on the role of personality in learning from web-based courses). As indicated above, there are strong indications that personality traits can be validly assessed using on-line measures (e.g. Buchanan & Smith, 1999a,b; Buchanan, 1999, 2000b; Pasveer & Ellard, 1998). It is easy to envision, therefore, an experiment where respondents first complete a WWW-based personality inventory, and then use a set of on-line learning materials. The effect of extraversion on how they use the materials could be assessed by tracking their movements (e.g., using WWW server log files, or "hits" on Web sites as used by Joinson, 2000b) — one might, for example, expect that people high in extraversion would move through the pages faster, paying less attention to detail, or preferring more stimulating materials. If learning is also to be assessed on-line (a topic addressed later in this chapter), then the effect of personality on performance could be assessed. Participants might even be randomly assigned to different conditions testing the efficacy of different on-line teaching techniques (e.g., multimedia or text based).

That is an example of research that *could* be done. There are also examples from the existing literature of WWW research which *has* been done, and which has implications for education in general, not just on-line teaching. It has been hypothesized that discovery-based learning in elementary computer programming (specifically using the language LOGO during childhood) can reduce mathematics anxiety (e.g., Papert, 1980). Mueller, Jacobsen, and Schwarzer (2000) tested this prediction, surveying over 2000 adult participants with an on-line questionnaire. Among other things, they found that people with LOGO experience did report greater generalized self-efficacy. This seems to provide some support for Papert's claims — and more than any end-of-course evaluation would, given the long time interval between any LOGO experience and this study. However, further analyses suggested the benefit was not unique to LOGO experience: other kinds of computer experience also seemed to have a positive effect on self-efficacy. This is one concrete example of how WWW research methods can be used to evaluate the outcomes of educational interventions. There is clearly much else that must be done in this sphere of on-line research.

Some research findings — along with extrapolations from CMC research — suggest differences between on- and off-line behavior. For example, previous research supports reliable differences in levels of disinhibition and interactions of the medium with the construct being explored (Buchanan & Joinson, 2000) which have implications for the conduct of WWW research. These differences can only be identified, and their impact assessed, by research on the psychology of on-line behavior itself: researching the psychology of the WWW, as well as using the WWW to perform psychology research.

These differences have further implications for education on the Internet. To fully understand how people will learn on-line — the ways in which they will interact with on-line teaching materials, and what they will gain from them — we will need to know how they behave on-line and why. Such an understanding will inform the design of educational materials. For instance, if we knew that people tend to avoid graphics-heavy sites, or that multimedia instruction is not effective on-line, our teaching materials could be constructed in such a way as to maximize their efficacy and likelihood of use. In short, therefore, an understanding of how people use the Internet, and the psychological processes involved in or associated with various on-line activities, is key to the design and implementation of on-line learning paradigms.

II. BEHAVIOR ON THE INTERNET AND EDUCATION

A. Why Be Interested in Internet-Based Behavior?

The Internet is rapidly becoming a ubiquitous part of people's lives. According to current forecasts, over half of the U.S. population will be using the Internet in some form within the next few years. The development of a wireless Internet, interconnected using wireless application protocol (WAP) technology, promises to increase the penetration of the Internet into people's lives. While much of the planned use of the Internet will almost certainly be hidden (e.g., kitchen appliances communicating with each other), it is likely that the increased linking of households to the Internet will create a corresponding increase in social and educational uses of the Internet. Similarly, the increase in access will make an understanding of behavior on the Internet all the more important — especially to educators.

B. How Can Internet Behavior Be Characterized?

Internet behavior is normally considered in comparison to similar behaviors in "real life" or "face to face." Thus, people respond to Internet-based surveys in a less socially desirable manner than pen-and-paper tests (Kiesler & Sproull, 1986; Joinson, 1999). For instance, Robinson and West (1992) found that people reported more previous visits to the Sexually Transmitted Diseases clinic and more unsafe sexual practices to a computer than to a person. People are more likely to "flame" others (e.g., express open hostility) using CMC than face-to-face (FtF) communication (Dyer, Green, Pitts, & Millward, 1995).

On the other hand, Walther (1996) has argued that *sometimes* Internet users act in a more "socially desirable" manner than would be expected face to face. Walther (1996) termed this the "hyperpersonal" nature of computer-mediated communication, that is, people behaving in an overly positive or socially desirable manner toward others. Walther (1996, 1999) reports anecdotal and experimental evidence for higher intimacy in on-line communication, and greater attraction and affiliation within CMC workgroups.

1. Communication on the Internet

There is an accumulating body of research to suggest that CMC is character-ized by less inhibited communication compared to FtF communication (Joinson, 1998a). This disinhibited communication is usually taken to mean "flaming," that is, overly hostile or negative behavior on-line (e.g., Siegal, Dubrovsky, Kiesler, & McGuire, 1986). For instance, when Siegal et al. compared face-to-face communication and CMC they found higher levels of hostile comments such as swearing, name calling, and insults under the CMC condition. The finding that CMC is characterized by uninhibited communication (usually defined as "flaming") has been replicated a number of times (see Joinson, 1998a). This led Selfe and Meyer (1991) to conclude that "heated, emotional, sometimes anonymous, venting ... is a common, if not universal, feature of computer-based conferences" (p. 170).

However, as the literature on flaming came under closer scrutiny, some dissenters emerged. For instance, Lea, O'Shea, Fung and Spears (1992)

argue that "flaming is in fact radically context dependent; that it is a compar-
atively rare occurrence in CMC, but that for various reasons specific
instances are observed or remembered by large numbers of people, thereby
contributing to the illusion of universality" (p. 108).

Walther, Anderson, and Park (1994) similarly argue that much of the
acceptance of flaming as a widespread phenomenon during CMC is based
on "erroneous analysis and reporting practices" (p. 463). Joinson (1998a)
argues that the present emphasis on flaming by researchers masks other,
more prevalent forms of disinhibition. He argues that "on-line communication, whilst disinhibited, may not be characterized by flaming. That is, flaming may be a sub-set of disinhibited behavior on the Internet, but it is not
the only disinhibited behavior on the Internet" (p. 47).

One such disinhibited behavior is heightened levels of intimacy in at
least *some* computer-mediated communication (Walther, 1996). Although
early empirical research found CMC to be desocialized and task focused,
outside the laboratory CMC is replete with occurrences of intimate, social
communication (Joinson, in press; Walther, 1996). Perhaps highly intimate
communication is as characteristic, if not more so, of CMC than flaming. For
instance, Wallace (1999) argues that "the tendency to disclose more to a
computer ... is an important ingredient of what seems to be happening on
the Internet" (p. 151). Parks and Floyd (1996) found that over 60% of Usenet
participants report forming personal relationships with fellow newsgroup
users. Significantly, Parks and Floyd also found high levels of self-disclosure
in on-line relationships. Similarly, McKenna and Bargh (1998) argue that
participation in on-line newsgroups gives people the benefit of "disclosing a
long secret part of one's self" (p. 682). Medical patients report more symptoms and undesirable behaviors when interviewed by computer rather than
face-to-face (Greist, Klein, and VanCura, 1973; Robinson and West, 1992).
The UK branch of the Samaritans, an advice service, reports that around 50%
of e-mail contacts report suicidal feelings, compared to 20% of telephone
callers (The Scotsman, Feb. 24, 1999).

This self-disclosure is not just confined to traditional CMC: Rosson (1999)
analyzed 133 stories posted by Internet users on a resource called "Web
Storybase" and found that 81 of the stories contained personal information
of some sort. Rosson concludes that "users seem to be quite comfortable
revealing personal — even quite intimate — details about their lives in this
very public forum" (p. 8). This tendency to disclose more about the self
during on-line interaction also extends to the completion of psychological
measures. Kiesler and Sproull (1986) report that, compared to a pencil-and-
paper survey, answers to an electronic survey are less socially desirable and
lead to the disclosure of more information about the self. Joinson (1999)
found that participants completing questionnaires on the WWW respond in
a less socially desirable manner than participants completing the same
measures on paper, regardless of their level of anonymity.

2. Web Behavior

Research into WWW behavior has been relatively slow to develop compared to CMC research. This is partly due to the relative newness of the WWW compared to CMC, and to the earlier difficulties in tracking precisely how people navigate WWW sites. There are still difficulties in following users' WWW browsing outside sites under direct experimenter control — recording key strokes or screen movies, to be effective, requires special equipment. The analysis of log files goes some way toward enabling the study of WWW behavior (e.g., Joinson, 2000b). However, a universal problem is the use of caches by both local and regional servers and individual web browsers. For instance, if someone hits the "back" button on his or her browser, it is unlikely that this action will register as a hit. Indeed, if the site is popular, it is likely that the pages will be cached both locally and on servers between the browser and the server being studied (Goldberg, 1995), so even if a user is visiting a site for the first time, they might not register as a "hit." The development of Java applets to record page hits circumvents this particular problem somewhat (as do counters that subvert caching by changing at every visit). Similar techniques developed by psychological researchers, for instance, to randomly allocate participants to a condition using Java could also be applied to be study of WWW behavior per se. To be sure, studying WWW behavior, unless you stood behind the user (however metaphorically) as they browse, is full of problems.

Those precautions in mind, there is some evidence that browsing behavior differs from normal information seeking. For instance, Joinson (2000b) found that, contrary to behavior in "real life," soccer fans did not stop seeking information about their team on the WWW following a defeat. Provisional data from Teddle, Banyard, and Joinson (2000) suggest that the seeking of cancer-related information on the WWW closely matches actual prevalence, while information seeking on telephone help lines tends to avoid socially embarrassing cancers (e.g., prostate or testicular cancer). Joinson and Banyard (1998) compared information seeking about alcohol across traditional sources and on the WWW. They found that people not planning to reduce their drinking were more likely to seek antidrinking messages on the WWW than on paper. Conversely, those contemplating or planning to reduce their drinking were more likely to seek prodrinking information than those seeking paper sources of information were. To circumvent any caching problems, Joinson and Banyard (1998) created a Common Gateway Interface (CGI) form where participants' choice of information, instead of being recorded as hits, was submitted as a CGI form on the WWW server. As outlined above, the work of Rosson (1999) suggests that people may also be more willing to disclose personal information about themselves by posting it on the WWW. This may also extend to people's homepages (see Joinson, 1998a).

The research cited above suggests that people's browsing behavior on the WWW may be significantly different than comparable behaviors in "real life." We strongly encourage more observational research, not using "hits," into naturalistic WWW browsing behavior. Later in this chapter we will consider how browsing behavior might impact the design of educational material.

C. Models of Internet Behavior

Because the literature on Internet behavior has tended to concentrate on the differences between on-line and real life behavior, models that explain, for instance, both task focus and intimacy have been relatively rare. In the main, theories have focused on the medium itself and its impact on behavior via psychological variables rather than characteristics of the environment and the individual that interact to produce the behaviors outlined above. For instance, early researchers argued that the reduced social cues inherent in CMC effectively desocialized communication, leading to both task-oriented communications and flaming (because the users became "deindividuated"). Similarly, the application of social identity theory to CMC, despite its original specific situational constraints (e.g., anonymity, salience of group identity), has been applied to a number of Internet behaviors (e.g., flaming; Lea et al., 1992).

Walther (1996, 1999) has presented a social information processing model that goes some way to explaining both hyperpersonal and "desocialized" Internet behavior. He argues that the limited time span used in most experimental studies of CMC encourages task-focused communication, while longer-term CMC groups have emergent social properties (Walther et al., 1994). According to Walther (1992) users of CMC have the same interpersonal needs as FtF communicators. Due to the reduced channels of communication and time limitations often imposed during CMC experiments, "users will adapt their linguistic and textual behaviors to the solicitation and presentation of socially revealing, relational behavior" (p. 463).

Walther also argues that some of the defining characteristics of CMC — visual anonymity and asynchronous communication — encourage intimacy and "hyperpersonal" communication, that is, interaction which is "more stereotypically socially desirable or intimate than normal" (Walther, 1996, p. 34). One of the main factors hypothesized to cause "hyperpersonal" interaction is visual anonymity. Being visually anonymous allows communicants to focus on their private self rather than their public persona, and to carefully construct a self-presentation without the cognitively taxing need to control nonverbal cues. Indeed, there is considerable evidence to suggest that visual anonymity encourages within-group affiliation (Spears & Lea, 1992). Conversely, still pictures of the discussants reduces attraction within long-term CMC groups (Walther, Slovacek, & Tidwell, 1999).

A similar model of Internet behavior argues that in some circumstances (e.g. when anonymous) users' self-foci change. Matheson and Zanna (1988) and Joinson (1998a, 1999, 2000b) have argued that during CMC, users experience heightened private self-focus and reduced public self-focus. Combined, these self-foci lead to a reduction in concerns about evaluation by others and an increased focus on one's own attitudes, beliefs, and morals.

Despite the increasing proliferation of models of Internet behavior, thus far no one model goes any distance toward explaining the array of behaviors seen on the Internet. The considerable overlap between social information processing and the self-focus models suggests that a model will emerge that takes into account users' focal state, the content and aims of that focus, the environment, constraints and norms within which they behave, and the medium itself. Indeed, the number of confounding variables between the models (e.g., visual anonymity confounds with public and private self-awareness, group salience, deindividuation, and reduced social cues) suggests that a model incorporating parts of existing models occurring within certain situational confines is likely sooner rather than later. More importantly, a series of reasonably well-accepted empirical findings of Internet-based behavior are beginning to emerge from the array of sometimes contradictory results, suggesting a number of factors to be taken into account when designing and evaluating educational material on the Internet.

III. INTERNET BEHAVIOR AND EDUCATIONAL MATERIAL DESIGN

It would be unheard of to design and write a student textbook without some consideration of pedagogy. Similarly, the mantra that people can only concentrate for 45 minutes is writ large in the planning of face-to-face lecturing. However, when educational materials are designed for Internet delivery, little recognition is made of the different behavioral patterns on the Internet compared to real life, and the potential implications for students' interaction with educational material. In this section we consider the main uses of the Internet in education, and consider how they might interact with models of Internet-based behavior per se.

A. Web-Based Material Delivery

The WWW should be an excellent device for the delivery of traditionally print-based materials. It can be easily and quickly updated, it provides interaction between students and their peers and between the teacher and his or her students, and it is relatively cheap. However, many teachers' experience of WWW provision is that students usually "print and run," so any potential benefits derived are removed by rendering a hypertext delivery back to a paper-based one (Joinson, 1998b). In part this is certainly due to the generally lower flexibility of timing and location of any Information and Communication Technology (ICT) teaching. It may also be due to an enduring dislike among people of screen-based reading.

A first sight, people seeking information on the Internet might not seem to have many implications for the provision of educational material digitally. However, a number of areas of Internet research map directly onto the design of educational material on the WWW. First, an increasing number of researchers are using psychological methods for analyzing Web traffic to study students' interaction with educational material. This provides an unparalleled opportunity to understand how students work through educational material — unsurprisingly often not in the order intended by the author. Work within the human–computer interaction (HCI) usability paradigm would also suggest that lessons leared from other spheres about, for instance, the optimum number of levels on a Web site or the user interface should be translated to educational material. Perhaps most important is the potential role of the Internet to open education to a global market of often nontraditional students.

The apparent willingness of people to post personal information on the WWW should also enable a degree of "experience sharing" between students using the WWW to study. As much of the current emphasis within education is on reflective activities to enhance learning, the WWW and its associated behaviors should prove to be excellent at encouraging the sharing of such experiences. Moreover, if indeed self-focus is increased during Internet use, this suggests that such reflective exercises may be more successful on the WWW than in traditional settings. A further potential boon of the WWW in teaching is the potential for increased student–student and student–faculty interaction. This is discussed in more detail in the following section.

B. Computer Conferencing

Computer-based tutorials have seen rapid uptake and adoption among teachers. This is because they promise a number of potential benefits. First, the anonymity of much computer conferencing may encourage students to engage in a tutorial process more freely and to contribute more willingly (Reader & Joinson, 1999). Second, many potential students find it impossible to attend seminars at a particular time and place, and would welcome the opportunity to participate in an asynchronous discussion where they can select the time and place of their contributions themselves. Third, writing something down is more effortful than, say, stating it, and as such may encourage "deeper" learning (see Walther, 1999). Fourth, CMC allows text to be stored, archived for future generations of students, and moved easily from one group to another. Finally, reading others' discussions may encourage learning vicariously (McKendree, Stenning, Mayes, Lee, & Cox, 1998).

However, a number of problems have emerged from academics' experiences of CMC in education. The main problem is that students do not tend to post much — it is not unusual for teachers' postings to make up 50% of all postings (Light & Light, 1999), and for these postings to be considerably longer than the students'. The usual answer is to make CMC an assessed component of a course, but of course, this removes the potential role of anonymity in encouraging freedom of expression and opens questions about what exactly to assess (e.g. the quantity or quality of students' postings).

Reassuringly, models of CMC behavior suggest that visual anonymity is more important than "pure" anonymity in encouraging affiliation within groups and hyperpersonal interaction. So, just because we know someone's name, does not mean that the potentially disinhibiting role of CMC is removed (although this may depend on the context — other issues relating to anonymity are discussed later in this chapter). Perhaps more importantly, the use of CMC in education can encourage the development of highly affiliated groups when students are visually anonymous and share a social identity (Spears & Lea, 1992). This potential for CMC to create on-line communities rather than on-line tutorials has been overlooked by most educators. Indeed, the tendency among many academics is to discourage social communication with the intention of encouraging course-based discussions. We would argue that the two go hand in hand, and that CMC facilitators risk reducing CMC use to a mere trickle if genuine social interaction, and the resulting on-line communities, are not allowed to develop naturally.

However, these same conditions, while encouraging in-group affiliation and the development of on-line communities, are also likely to increase conformity to a group norm (Spears & Lea, 1992). While this is positive as far as encouraging group cohesion is concerned (especially important for distance education students), it is not likely to encourage opinionated discussions. Thus, if the aim of CMC is to effectively create a support group on-line, visual anonymity combined with in-group membership (and the salience of that membership) will increase group cohesion, affiliation, and conformity. If the aim is for free and open discussions, the educator will need to combine visual anonymity with salience of personal identity and opinions, and underplay any potential shared-group memberships.

The vicarious learning position is also complex — while it is relatively well documented that potentially students can learn vicariously (McKendree et al., 1998), there is some evidence that those students who do not post much to CMC tutorials are also less likely to read the messages posted by others (Joinson, 2000a). Still, such close attention is not paid to lack of listening in FtF tutorials, and at least electronically teachers can identify which people are posting and reading (and thus focus their efforts in the required direction). To a certain extent, CMC tutorials are still aiming for a

Socratic ideal — one that has long since been effectively abandoned in most face-to-face teaching environments.

To use what is known about behavior on the Internet to successfully enable CMC tutorials, educators need to recognize that the environment they create for the students must match the aims of the teaching. An option which has been successfully applied at the Open University in the United Kingdom is to create a number of environments for different aims — a cafe for group cohesion, a working conference for structured activities, and a notice board for general information. Similarly, a clear and well-defined structure within a teaching conference, perhaps based a round an activity such as peer review and reply or text-based simulation, is more likely to enhance learning compared to an unstructured discussion forum (Reader & Joinson, 1999). However, educators must be careful not to distribute postings across too many different "rooms," nor to be too strict about restricting use of a teaching area for social communication — this may risk impoverishing the CMC experience for all students by sterilizing their on-line communication.

C. Assessment and the Web

A natural accompaniment to on-line teaching is on-line assessment. Courses taught via the web need not necessarily be assessed via the web. However, there are reasons (e.g., logistical considerations in the case of distance learners) why it is often appropriate that this should be the case. Accordingly, and given the fact that certain forms of assessment (notably multiple choice tests) are easy to adapt for on-line administration, WWW-based assessment procedures are seeing increasing use.

It is common to distinguish between two major functions of assessment: summative and formative. Note that these two types differ in function, not form — the same assessment procedure could be used for both functions. The important distinction is between the uses to which the information derived from the assessment is put. In the case of summative assessment, this information is used to rank or grade students in terms of performance or achievement of learning outcomes — for instance, in the award of academic qualifications. In the case of formative assessment, the information is fed back to students in an appropriate form to guide their future learning.

It has been argued that on-line assessments are best used in a formative manner (e.g., Buchanan, 1998a). Features making them especially appropriate for this function are the facts that feedback — perhaps tailored to the individual student — can be instantly provided, and that individuals with different learning styles or levels of ability can use formative assessment tools at their own pace and convenience. There are also problems (security being an important one) with on-line summative assessment. To misquote a famous cartoon, on the Internet nobody knows if your dog is doing your homework for you. Thus, this discussion will focus on assessments serving a formative function.

Given their increasing use (e.g., Burgess, Lund, Keeney, & Audet, 1998; Stockburger, 1998; Charman & Elmes, 1998), it is important that the efficacy of on-line assessment procedures be evaluated. In the case of formative procedures, obvious questions are whether students will actually use them, and whether they will actually add to the learning experience. Earlier in this chapter, we asserted that design of on-line learning paradigms must be guided by an understanding of how people think and behave on-line. This has been clearly demonstrated in the case of research about on-line assessment.

Taraban, Maki, and Rynearson (1999) reported on the use of on-line quizzes as part of an introductory psychology course delivered via the WWW. Taking these tests was required for course credit, and there were regular deadlines for completion of certain tests as students moved through the syllabus. It was found that students made most use of the on-line quizzes in the two days prior to the deadline, rather than pacing their work (this was true for other study materials made available on-line as well as the quizzes). Buchanan (1998a,b) reported the use of similar on-line multiple choice tests in a comparable course, which was otherwise conventionally delivered. Again, students were most likely to use the tests immediately before an important deadline (in this case, the end-of-semester examination).

This phenomenon of massed practice is not unique to computerized assessments and study aids: typically, students report spending more time on all kinds of study as examinations draw nearer (e.g., Rosen, Petty, Nolan, & Harcum,1999; Taraban et al., 1999). However, observations such as those by Taraban et al. demonstrate that students do not always interact with on-line materials in the way that instructors intend. Knowing how they do actually interact with the materials we create will inform the design of on-line curricula.

While massed practice may not be unique to WWW learning, there are other aspects of the ways in which students interact with on-line materials that are. For example, the Internet often gives us the opportunity to manage our self-presentation and to conceal our real identity. In some virtual spaces, anonymity is highly prized. One reason why this might be the case is that anonymity gives people the freedom to "test out bizarre ideas ... [and] ask questions that might reveal their stupidity" (Wallace, 1999, p. 240) without the same perceived threat to peer or self-esteem that might be present had they asked the same thing in a nonanonymous setting (e.g., a traditional FtF seminar class).

There are indications that at least some users of on-line assessment materials are keen to take advantage of such an opportunity. Buchanan (1998b, in press) asked students to enter identification numbers when completing on-line formative assessments (however, the system would still work if they did not), and found that on many occasions they chose not to (e.g., 1243 anonymous hits, compared to 1056 hits from identifiable students). In a second study, where entering an ID number was mandatory, some students entered false numbers in order to be able to use the system anonymously. Aside from simple rebellion or a desire to preserve privacy, the reasons for this are not clear. However, a clue comes from examination of log files generated during the study: cases were identified where students seemed to use the system repeatedly (multiple hits from the same IP address in a short space of time), trying to identify the correct answers on the basis of the feedback they received. Once they were sure of the answers, they would then emerge from anonymity, enter their ID numbers, and submit a "perfect" attempt at the test. This desire for anonymity — which is entirely consistent with Wallace's suggestion — is not only interesting but important. The message for designers of this type of on-line material is clear: if you wish students to make full use of the system, allow them to do so anonymously.

IV. CONCLUSIONS AND NEW HORIZONS

A. Future Challenges for Web Research

Is everything rosy in the garden of WWW research? It is perhaps too early to tell. The bulk of the evidence to date suggests that research using the Internet as a laboratory can be successful, but there are unanswered questions and unresolved issues. For example, we have suggested above that there may be cases where individual differences (for example, in computer anxiety or aversion) may interact with the medium to affect the outcomes of a study. There are indications that this may be the case from research using stand-alone computers (see, for example, Tseng, Tiplady, Macleod, & Wright, 1998). It is easy to imagine how a study such as that of Mueller et al. (2000) could be affected by such a phenomenon, and there may be other, as yet unidentified, potential confounds with serious implications. This points once again to the fact that research on on-line behavior is required to inform on-line research on behavior.

Practical and ethical issues also arise. Recall the imaginary experiment outlined earlier in the chapter, where participants' personalities were assessed and then their progress through on-line materials tracked. In one of the studies cited above (Buchanan, in press) it was found that students preferred to use on-line assessment materials anonymously — so much so that when they were required to enter identification numbers there were cases of fraudulent information being entered. Unless participants are to be coerced — which would probably affect their behavior in other ways — getting them to enter identifying information for the purpose of tracking their progress through on-line materials may be problematic. Of course, we have the ability to do this covertly. We can snoop on participants by tracking IP addresses in the WWW server's log files, or use cookies to track what the users of individual machines are doing. Is this ethical? One might construe it as akin to following a student around their classes, monitoring what they are doing, without their knowledge.

Codes of ethical practice for psychologists (for example, the British Psychological Society's statement of ethical principles, by which the authors of this chapter are bound) would suggest that observational research should only take place in settings where the people being observed might expect to be the object of public scrutiny. As an example, analysis of people's postings to Usenet newsgroups — which people expect to be read around the world — would be just as acceptable in ethical terms as scanning the personal ads sections of a newspaper to compare the notices placed by men and women, or examining official statistics to see if murder rates really do increase in hot weather. However, it is not clear that tracking people's on-line movements without their knowledge falls into the same category. While it is technically feasible to do this, and the more technically savvy user might be aware of the fact, it is likely that most people sitting alone at their computers think themselves to be in a much more private and anonymous situation than is actually the case.

At this point, we do not wish to prescribe what should or should not be done. However, those of us working in on-line research —whether educational or otherwise — must be aware of these issues and the possibility that new guidelines for ethical research on the WWW may be required.

B. General Web Teaching Issues

The era of ubiquitous information and communication technology in education has encouraged academics and teachers to reflect on their own teaching and to experiment with their students' learning experience. While this reflection must be welcomed, the degree of effective failure in applying ICT to education must be questioned. In some cases, the use of ICT and the Internet might be best seen as the "tail wagging the dog" — a round learning experience being squeezed into a square technology. There is also a degree of techno-utopianism associated with what are inevitably enthusiasts using technology to teach. With their associated high ambitions, a high failure rate would be expected. The tendency for WWW-based teaching materials to focus on the understanding of material, rather than the evaluation or synthesis of such material, is also a major concern — if WWW-based teaching is failing at the first pedagogical hurdle, we have to ask whether it is capable of delivering more ambitious learning goals.

Quite aside from this slightly pessimistic vision of the Internet in teaching, few educators have tackled the question of equal access to technology and its implications for education. We are in danger of creating more advantages for the privileged Western middle classes, and further widening the gap between the relatively well off, educated "wired" classes and the relatively poor, "unwired" groups. As well as being a within-nation and international issue, the equal access contraindication also applies across age groups — while the young and aged have tended to take up the Internet with relish, a group of people aged 35–55 with little technological savvy does not bode well for visions of lifelong learning aided by the WWW. A further issue is whether the increasing use of the Internet in teaching actually improves learning. For instance, Oppenheimer (1997) argues that "there is no good evidence that most uses of computers significantly improve teaching and learning" (p. 45). Similarly, Turkle (1997) asks whether "we are using computer technology not because it teaches best, but because we have lost the political will to fund education adequately," (p. 80).

It is clear that a concerted effort is required to investigate the impact of the Internet on students' learning and to address pedagogical concerns about Web-based teaching. Perhaps more importantly, educators need to move beyond the evaluation of the technology itself, and begin concerted evaluations of its impact on the students. An understanding of how students learn, alongside some thought of how people behave on the Internet, should help this cause. It is our belief that when carefully planned, with clear aims and pedagogy, using the Internet to teach can be of clear benefit to students' learning experiences. However, only full evaluative efforts can confirm this.

C. New Medium, New Learning?

Associated with the need to evaluate (and understand) how students learn on the Internet, there is also the possibility that the Internet does not simply enhance students' learning, but that it might introduce new ways of learning. Laurillard (1993) suggests that the use of information technology in learning will change the traditional balance of students' educational experience, with less emphasis (and time) on reading, and more on practicing and "doing." Similarly, the role of the educator will change, although recent work on CMC tutorials suggests that while fellow students are seen as a potential source of expertise, existing notions of the professor or tutor as having the "final say" still exist (Joinson, 2000a). As mentioned above, there is also the possibility that students' learning experiences could be tailored to their own learning styles (see Anderson, chapter 3 this volume). Perhaps more importantly, the digitization of education may also encourage the development of "pick and mix" education, where a traditional course can be served up in smaller blocks, or even combined with other courses to produce new educational experiences. As teaching becomes increasingly WWW-based, we may also see that educational material becomes less associated with a specific tutor, and more of a public (or university) resource to be used in a number of settings and manners. This does not bode well for teachers who see their teaching materials as effectively their "babies" to be guarded and controlled. Traditional teaching is still based on notions of learning developed, in some cases, three millennia ago. The development of WWW-based teaching at least allows the development of new ways of teaching that more closely match students' learning.

D. A Look to the Future

What might we achieve in the future? One possibility — firmly grounded in current research — is tailoring on-line educational materials to fit the needs of the individuals using them. We have indicated above that on-line personality assessment is feasible and suggested ways in which the efficacy of different types of material for different individuals might be assessed. As well as personality (and let us not forget intelligence!), it has been shown that individuals differ in learning style (Furnham & Heaven, 1999). Given that learning styles are typically assessed through questionnaires (much like personality tests), there is no reason why it should not be possible to do this remotely via the WWW. Indeed, a quick search using the Lycos and AltaVista search engines revealed a number of sites, both amateur and professional, purporting to do exactly that.

It is also common nowadays to come across Web sites which exist in parallel versions (e.g., versions with or without frames, or high or low in graphical content) to cater for people using different browsers or different speeds of Internet connection. It has been demonstrated that individuals differ in the speed at which they learn from computerized materials (Clariana, 1997). Might the same not be true of the *type* of materials which different people find most effective? If that is the case, users might first complete an on-line assessment of personality or learning style, and then automatically be directed to a version of the on-line materials likely to be most suitable for them (see Anderson, chapter 3, for more on individual differences and Web-based courses).

This may seem like pie-in-the-sky, but it is in fact a realistic and achievable scenario in terms of current technical capability and psychological knowledge. The only real question is whether it would actually be worth doing — would significant benefits actually arise from tailoring materials to individuals? The only way in which the question can be answered is through research: a case, once again, of the need for on-line research into on-line learning to underpin the design of on-line teaching materials.

A second possibility is the tailoring of education to meet students' immediate needs. So, you need a quick refresher course on Java programming? Have it sent to your mobile phone to study this week! Not only is there little need for a university to exist in a physical sense, but there will be little requirement for students to take a relatively lengthy course of, say, one semester. If visions of lifelong learning emerge, the role of ICT and the WWW in changing people's conception of what it means to be student will need to be radically altered. With the help of the Internet, and inevitably a wireless version, a university degree may just be seen as the starting block preparing us for a life of learning.

References

Banyard, P., & Hunt, N. (2000). Reporting research: Something missing? *The Psychologist*, 13, 68–71.

Buchanan, T. (1998a). Using the World Wide Web for formative assessment. *Journal of Educational Technology Systems*, 27, 71–79.

Buchanan, T. (1998b, November). *The efficacy of a World-Wide Web mediated formative assessment.* Paper presented at the Meeting of the Society for Computers in Psychology, Dallas, TX.

Buchanan, T. (1999, October). *On-line personality assessment: Equivalence of traditional and WWW personality measures.* Paper presented at German On-line Research '99, Nuremberg, Germany.

Buchanan, T. (2000a). *Internet research: Self-monitoring and judgments of attractiveness.* Manuscript submitted for publication.

Buchanan, T. (2000b). Potential of the Internet for personality research. In M. H. Birnbaum (Ed.), *Psychological experiments on the Internet* (pp. 121–140). San Diego: Academic Press.

Buchanan, T. (2000). The efficacy of a World-Wide Web mediated formative assessment. *Journal of Computer Assisted Learning*, 16, 193–200.

Buchanan, T., & Joinson, A. J. (2000). *Doing psychology research on the Web.* Manuscript submitted for publication.

Buchanan, T., & Smith, J. L. (1999a). Using the Internet for psychological research: Personality testing on the World-Wide Web. *British Journal of Psychology*, 90, 125–144.

Buchanan, T., & Smith, J. L. (1999b). Research on the Internet: Validation of a World-Wide Web mediated personality scale. *Behavior Research Methods, Instruments, & Computers*, 31, 565–571.

Burgess, C., Lund, K., Keeney, M., & Audet, C. (1998, November). *A generic multiple choice test program for Web-based applications.* Paper presented at the Meeting of the Society for Computers in Psychology, Dallas, TX.

Charman, D., & Elmes, A. (1998). *Computer based assessment: (Volume 1): A guide to good practice.* SEED Publications, University of Plymouth.

Clariana, R. (1997). Pace in mastery-based computer-assisted learning. *British Journal of Educational Technology*, 28, 135–137.

Dyer, R., Green, R., Pitts, M., & Millward, G. (1995). What's the flaming problem? CMC — Deindividuating or disinhibiting? In J. R. Kirby, A. Dix, & J. Finlay (Eds.), *People and computers* X. Cambridge: Cambridge University Press.

Furnham, A., & Heaven, P. (1999). *Personality and social behavior.* London: Arnold.

Goldberg, J. (1995). *Why web usage statistics are (worse than) meaningless* [on-line]. Available (February 16, 2000): www.cranfield.ac.uk/docs/stats/

Greist, J. H., Klein, M. H., & VanCura, L. J. (1973). A computer interview by psychiatric patient target symptoms. *Archives of General Psychiatry*, 29, 247–253.

Hewson, C. M., Laurent, D., & Vogel, C. M. (1996). Proper methodologies for psychological and sociological studies conducted via the Internet. *Behavior Research Methods, Instruments, & Computers*, 28, 186–191.

Joinson, A. N. (1998a). Causes and implications of disinhibited behavior on the Net. In J. Gackenbach (Ed.)., *Psychology of the Internet* (pp. 43–60). New York: Academic Press.

Joinson, A. N. (1998b). Supporting psychology teaching using the Internet. In J. Radford, D. Van Laar, & D. Rose (Eds.), *Innovations in psychology teaching* (pp. 103–111). Birmingham: Seda Publications.

Joinson, A. N. (1999). Anonymity, disinhibition and social desirability on the Internet. *Behavior Research Methods, Instruments, and Computers*, 31, 433–438.

Joinson, A. N. (2000a). *Computer-conferencing to the converted*. Student Research Center Paper, Institute of Educational Technology, The Open University, UK.

Joinson, A. N. (2000b). Self-disclosure in computer-mediated communication. *European Journal of Social Psychology*. (In press)

Joinson, A. N. (2000c). Information seeking on the Internet: A study of soccer fans. *CyberPsychology and Behavior*, 3 (2), 185–191.

Joinson, A. N., & Banyard P. (1998). *Disinhibition and health information seeking on the Internet. Presentation to the World Congress of the Society for the Internet in Medicine*, St. Thomas' Hospital, London.

Kiesler, S., Siegal, J., & McGuire, T. W. (1984). Social psychological aspects of computer mediated communication. *American Psychologist*, 39, 1123–1134.

Kiesler, S., & Sproull, L. S. (1986). Response effects in the electronic survey. *Public Opinion Quarterly*, 50, 402–413.

Krantz, J. H., Ballard, J., & Scher, J. (1997). Comparing the results of laboratory and World-Wide Web samples of the determinants of female attractiveness. *Behavior Research Methods, Instrument, & Computers*, 29, 264–269.

Krantz, J. H., & Dalal, R. (2000). Validity of Web-based psychological research. In M. H. Birnbaum (Ed.), *Psychological experiments on the Internet* (pp. 35–60). San Diego: Academic Press.

Laurillard, D. (1993). *Re-thinking university teaching: A framework for the effective use of educational technology*. London: Routledge.

Lea, M., O'Shea, T., Fung, P., & Spears, R. (1992). "Flaming" in computer-mediated communication. In M. Lea (Ed.), *Contexts in computer-mediated communication*. London: Harvester Wheatsheaf.

Light, P., & Light, V. (1999). Analyzing asynchronous learning interactions: Computer-mediated communication in a conventional undergraduate setting. In K. Littleton & P. Light (Eds.), *Learning with computers: analysing productive interactions* (pp. 162–178). London: Routledge.

Matheson, K., & Zanna, M. P. (1988). The impact of computer-mediated communication on self-awareness. *Computers in Human Behavior*, 4, 221–233.

McKendree, J., Stenning, K., Mayes, T., Lee, J., & Cox, R. (1998). Why observing a dialogue may benefit learning. *Journal of Computer Assisted Learning*, 14, 110–119.

McKenna, K. Y., & Bargh, J. (1998). Coming out in the age of the Internet: Identity "demarginalization" through virtual group participation. *Journal of Personality and Social Psychology*, 75, 681–694.

Mueller, J., Jacobsen, D. M., & Schwarzer, R. (2000). What are computing experiences good for: A case study in on-line research. In M. H. Birnbaum (Ed.), *Psychological experiments on the Internet* (pp. 195–216). San Diego: Academic Press.

Musch, J., & Reips, U.-D. (2000). A brief history of web experimenting. In M. H. Birnbaum (Ed.), *Psychological experiments on the Internet* (pp. 61–87). San Diego: Academic Press.

Oppenheimer, T. (1997). The computer delusion. *The Atlantic Monthly*, 280, 45–62.

Pagani, D., & Lombardi, L. (2000). An intercultural examination of facial features communicating surprise. In M. H. Birnbaum (Ed.), *Psychological experiments on the Internet* (pp. 169–194). San Diego: Academic Press.

Papert, S. (1980). *Mindstorms: Children, computers and powerful ideas*. New York: Basic Books.

Parks, M. R., & Floyd, K. (1996). Making friends in cyberspace. *Journal of Computer-Mediated Communication*, 1 (4). Available (December 10 1999): http://jmc.huji.ac.il/vol1/issue4/parks.html

Pasveer, K. A., & Ellard, J. H. (1998). The making of a personality inventory: Help from the WWW. *Behavior Research Methods, Instruments, & Computers*, 30, 309–313.

Reader, W., & Joinson, A. N. (1999). Promoting student discussion using simulated seminars on the Internet. In D. Saunders & J. Severn (Eds.), *The simulation and gaming yearbook: Games and simulations to enhance quality learning* (Vol. 7, pp. 139–149). London: Kogan Page.

Reips, U.-D. (2000). The Web experiment method: Advantages, disadvantages, and solutions. In M. H. Birnbaum (Ed.), *Psychological experiments on the Internet* (pp. 89–117). San Diego: Academic Press.

Robinson, R., & West, R. (1992). A comparison of computer and questionnaire methods of history-taking in a genito-urinary clinic. *Psychology and Health*, 6, 77–84.

Rosen, E. F., Petty, L. C., Nolan, E., & Harcum, E. R. (1999, November) *Study time distribution in a computer-assisted statistics course*. Paper presented at the meeting of the Society for Computers in Psychology, Los Angeles, CA.

Rosson, M. B. (1999). I get by with a little help from my cyber-friends: Sharing stories of good and bad times on the Web. *Journal of Computer-Mediated Communication*, 4 (4). Available (November 10, 1999): http://jcmc.huji.ac.il/vol4/issue4/rosson.html

Selfe, C. L., & Meyer, P. R. (1991). Testing claims for on-line conferences. *Written Communication*, 8, 163–192.

Siegal, J., Dubrovsky, V., Kiesler, S., & McGuire, T. (1986). Group processes in computer-mediated communication. *Organizational Behavior and Human Decision Processes*, 37, 157–187.

Smith, M. A., & Leigh, B. (1997). Virtual subjects: Using the Internet as an alternative source of subjects and research environment. *Behavior Research Methods, Instruments, & Computers*, 29, 496–505.

Snyder, M. (1974). Self-monitoring of expressive behavior. *Journal of Personality and Social Psychology*, 30, 526–537.

Spears, R., & Lea, M. (1992). Social influence and the influence of the "social" in computer-mediated communication. In M. Lea (Ed.), *Contexts in computer-mediated communication*. London: Harvester Wheatsheaf.

Sproull, L., & Kiesler, S. (1986). Reducing social context cues: Electronic mail in organizational communication. *Management Science*, 32, 1492–1512.

Sproull, L., & Kiesler, S. (1991, November). Computers, networks and work. *Scientific American*.

Stanton, J. M. (1998). An empirical assessment of data collection using the Internet. *Personnel Psychology*, 51, 709–725.

Stockburger, D. W. (1998, November). *Automated grading of homework assignments and tests in introductory and intermediate statistics courses using active server pages*. Paper presented at the Meeting of the Society for Computers in Psychology, Dallas, TX.

Taraban, R., Maki, W. S., & Rynearson, K. (1999). Measuring study time distributions: Implications for designing computer-based courses. *Behavior Research Methods, Instruments, & Computers*, 31, 263–269.

Teddle, S., Banyard, P., & Joinson, A. (2000). *Seeking information about cancer: A comparison of Internet searching and telephone helpline requests*. Unpublished manuscript.

Tseng, H. M., Tiplady, B., Macleod, H. A., & Wright, P. W. (1998). Computer anxiety: A comparison of pen-based personal digital assistants, conventional computer and paper assessment of mood and performance. *British Journal of Psychology*, 89, 599–610.

Turkle, S. (1997). Seeing through computers: Education in a culture of simulation. *The American Prospect*, 31, 76–82. Available (Feb. 29, 2000): http://www.prospect.org/archives/31/31turkfs.html

Wallace, P. (1999). *The psychology of the Internet*. Cambridge: Cambridge University Press.

Walther, J. B. (1992). Interpersonal effects in computer-mediated interaction: a relational perspective. *Communication Research*, 19, 52–90.

Walther, J. B. (1996). Computer-mediated communication: Impersonal, interpersonal and hyperpersonal interaction. *Communication Research*, 23 (1), 3–43.

Walther, J. B. (1999, May). *Visual cues and computer-mediated communication: Don't look before you leap*. Paper presented at the Annual Meeting of the International Communication Association.

Walther, J. B., Anderson, J. K., & Park, D. W. (1994). Interpersonal effects in computer-mediated interaction: A meta-analysis of social and antisocial communication. *Communication Research*, 21, 460–487.

Walther, J. B., Slovacek, C. L., & Tidwell, L. C. (1999). *Is a picture worth a thousand words? Photographic images in long-term and short-term computer-mediated communication*. Paper presented at the Annual Meeting of the International Communication Association.

chapter 12

The Mental Web
Pedagogical and Cognitive Implications of the Net

JENNIFER WILEY
University of Illinois at Chicago

JONATHAN W. SCHOOLER
University of Pittsburgh

I. INTRODUCTION

Every new information technology from the first cave drawing to the invention of the alphabet and the advent of the television and the modern computer has sent ripples through society, forever altering ways that we communicate, interact, and perhaps even think. The emergence of the Internet (net) and the World Wide Web (web) is likely to be no exception, although the precise manner in which their impact is to be felt is still an area of marked speculation. In the domain of education, whether the emergence of the web and its uses in teaching and learning cause a true paradigm shift in educational practice, or a more modest reconceptualization, there are clearly major differences between teaching and learning from the web versus more traditional educational media. That, at least in principle, could have broad significance. In the following chapter, we briefly consider some of the potential pedagogical implications of differences between the web and both traditional classroom and text learning contexts. We then consider some areas that this review suggests are in particular need of further research. We close with a discussion of the pedagogical and cognitive implications of a

243

potentially fundamental aspect of the web, namely, its capacity to emulate and instantiate many of the processes of the mind.

II. DIFFERENCES BETWEEN THE WEB AND CLASSROOM LEARNING CONTEXTS

The present volume has enumerated many points of interest where traditional classroom practices diverge from the affordances of the web. The following is a summary of some of these central differences.

A. Physicality

The most obvious contrast between virtual media and traditional forms of education is the basic difference in physicality. In traditional classroom settings, the teacher and students are physically co-present, and texts are written in permanent form on pieces of paper. Some paper is compiled in books that are made available to students as assigned texts. Printed texts and conversation partners are physically present, and provide rich stimulation to the senses. However, the supply of books, partners, and perspectives is limited by physical space. In contrast, in virtual educational settings, discussion and information emerge from pixels on a computer screen. The physical context stays constant, a student interacts with a single computer and screen and keyboard, but the information that can be accessed is practically infinite. As a number of chapters have discussed, from these simple physical differences emerge many far-reaching implications.

B. Social Interactions

Perhaps the topic that has received the most attention has been the differences in social contexts between real and computerized settings. In the case of virtual learning environments, the lack of physical co-presence in itself alters the social context of the exchange of information. There has been great concern over the limited social interaction that may be available in virtual education. The HomeNet studies at Carnegie Mellon (Kraut et al. 1998) suggesting that people who spend too much time on-line tend to have disturbed interaction patterns, and are more likely to experience depression and loneliness, are often cited as evidence that computer use leads to negative consequences. But more recent studies, such as one reported by the Pew Internet and American Life Project (2000), have found different results. Women, in particular, who spend more time on-line tend to be better socially adjusted, as they often spend their time on-line connecting with distant relations and friends, and renewing old acquaintances. Even the original HomeNet studies found that in some ways, and for some people, computer use supported social interaction in positive dimensions. Indeed as Reyna, Brainerd, Effken, Bootzin, and Lloyd (chapter 2) observe, there are good reasons to expect that as with many other aspects of the web, individual differences may play a critical role in determining the costs and benefits of the web relative to more traditional educational media. In particular, introverts, who can be intimidated by the social context of the classroom, may be able to contribute and even start friendships over the web in a manner that they might otherwise never have been able to achieve.

Other chapters also speak to the opportunities for on-line social interaction that may actually surpass live or "real" classroom interaction. For example, Sherman (chapter 6) traces the importance of social interaction in educational contexts in a review of literature on cooperative learning. He identifies several on-line tools that can be recruited to support cooperation and collaboration in computerized learning environments. He points out that these on-line tools can substitute for "real" interaction in a number of ways, and offers evidence that they are being used with increasing frequency, especially for distance learning courses.

Riva (chapter 7) takes the notion of on-line communication one step further by examining the differences between on-line communication and virtual discussions, and exploring notions of how the unique capabilities of on-line interactions may be best understood. Instead of merely viewing communication, and a sense of community, as something that occurs only when students are physically co-present, new technologies have forced a reexamination of conventional definitions. It has been argued that the definition of communication may be better viewed as elocutionary co-presence, and the definition of community may be better viewed as people with common interests, and not simply physical common ground (see also Jazwinski, chapter 9, and Morahan-Martin, chapter 10). Requiring physical co-presence or proximity for meaningful interaction has become obsolete.

C. Conversational Pragmatics

Other concerns about the quality of computer-mediated versus classroom interactions stem from the fact that most on-line communication uses written language, while in "real" classroom discourse the predominant mode of communication is oral. On-line written communication suffers from a lack of social presence, and many metalinguistic and pragmatic cues, like gesture, expression, tone of voice, speaker volume, and distance, are unavailable. Further, the relationship between speaker and listener is altered, as consent or commitment on the part of the listener cannot be assumed, as it may be in face-to-face interaction. But some advantages of on-line, written dialogue also can be noted. The discussion is often preserved in its entirety, whereas oral conversations are not usually preserved. The transmission of normal conversation is fleeting and therefore not entirely available for reflection either by the participants or by others who may be observing the discussion. While writing comments takes more time than speaking, this too may have its advantages as writing may require more effort, more planning, and more reflection than speaking (Joinson & Buchanan, chapter 11). Further, although on-line written discussions are frequently asynchronous, taking away the immediacy of the experience of participating in a group activity or community, many students may find the flexibility and lack of time pressure more convenient and conducive to deep thought.

On-line communication resources not only allow the learner to be more flexible in terms of where and when they participate in a dialogue, they may also allow a wider audience to read and participate in a discussion. This potentially means that more perspectives can be entertained and a more heterogeneous sample may be encountered (see chapters 9, 10, and 11).

D. Depersonalization

A related concern to the loss of social interaction in virtual space is the loss of identity. By talking through a machine, many have feared that computers are a dehumanizing and depersonalizing influence, resulting in socially undesirable behaviors like "flaming." However, depersonalization or anonymity can also have its advantages. Anonymity, along with the flexibility of communicating when and where you have time to think about the issues in an asynchronous on-line community, also allows more voices to be heard — particularly, students who may feel marginalized in a live classroom setting, women, minorities, and others who fear voicing an unpopular opinion or perspective may be more likely to communicate in an on-line arena. Students may also be more inclined to respond truthfully about their behaviors or their confusions in an anonymous interaction. And, anonymity can allow students to try out new roles or ways of relating to others (Jazwinski, chapter 9).

III. DIFFERENCES BETWEEN WEB LEARNING AND TEXTBOOK LEARNING

Along with differences between face-to-face and on-line conversation, there are also a number of important contrasts between textbook learning and web-based learning, mostly centered around the greater interactivity of electronic text or hypertext.

A. Diversity of Resources

The most striking difference between print and electronic media is the number and diversity of resources immediately available to students, and the student's ability to choose what to read. Students using the web have easy access to a seemingly infinite number of resources, many of them including multimedia presentations. Sources can be obtained representing many heterogeneous perspectives on any one issue or topic. Further, less structure is imposed on the order in which information can be read, so students have choices about how to navigate through information.

B. Permanence

Britt and Gabrys (chapter 4) discuss a number of differences in the "permanence" of written and electronic texts. Electronic sources can be altered and updated easily. This leads to some problems, as the content of pages can change, making the location of referred to information unreliable, and links frequently die. Even the layout of content on pages is not static. This is particularly so on sites with scrolling text. Students may not be able to have a reliable memory for "where" they read something, and even if they do, the site may not be there tomorrow.

C. Authenticity

In chapter 4, Britt and Gabrys also note that printed and electronic text differ in the sense of their writer's presence or identity. Anonymity is a two-edged sword in electronic text, much as it is in electronic discourse. Anyone can publish an opinion on the web. This makes authenticating information more difficult than from physically published material. On the other hand, since adding to the web is so easy, students have the ability to add, edit, and alter sources that they find, thereby having creative opportunities to contribute to the web in a way not possible with hard copies of texts (Hammond & Trapp, chapter 8).

D. Motivation

At least for the present, the novelty of web-based materials may be quite motivating for some students. In addition, considerable evidence suggests that web usage can be addictive (see Morahan-Martin, chapter 10). Although problematic in some contexts, the addictive nature of the Internet may also be quite useful for education, as textbook reading is almost never characterized as addicting. One intriguing, though rarely mentioned, possible source of the motivating quality of the Internet is its uneven quality. When surfing the web, good "hits" are typically interspersed with more mediocre ones.

Thus, individuals may experience random intermittent reinforcement, which is well known to encourage prolonged engagement in the reinforced activity. One curious implication of this view is that at least in some educational venues, some variety in the quality of materials might actually enhance participants' motivation to explore more thoroughly.

E. Familiarity

Although the unique novelty of web-based materials is likely to enhance students' motivational qualities (at least for some of them) the lack of experience and familiarity associated with such materials may also have significant costs. Due in part to our experience with published media, paper has a number of advantages, especially in the way we are used to reading text. Given a choice, most people will print out an electronic document in order to really read it. On-line reading is usually more like skimming or browsing than studying. There is a sense of immersion that people get from reading a book that people rarely get in reading an on-line article. Thus, Wolfe suggests in chapter 5 that brief presentations of text are best in an electronic or hypertext environment, and this seems suited to a browsing style of reading.

F. Multimodality

In the design of the Dragonfly Web Pages (Wolfe, chapter 5), the texts are actually both short and illustrated. The capability for including images seems one of the most obvious advantages of on-line text. Images can make text more interesting, or more meaningful. Multimedia capabilities can allow for more authentic learning environments and simulations. They can convey abstract principles to students. Similarly, tools that allow students to create or manipulate their own images can allow readers to solidify their understanding and make their abstract notions more concrete and available to others. At the same time, however, such images can result in overload, and can distract readers from important points in text (Reyna et al., chapter 2). Previous research advises that images and visualization tools like animation must be included judiciously when relevant for conceptual learning, or else the reader suffers too many demands on their attention (Harp & Mayer, 1998; Hegarty, Quilici, Narayanan, Holmquist, & Moreno, 1999; Wright, Milroy, & Lickorish, 1999).

G. Flexibility versus Linearity

Perhaps the feature of the web that has prompted the most techno-optimism, in terms of its educational promise, is its capacity for flexible, dynamic, and adaptive presentation of information. There are a number of theorists who have suggested that the web represents a tremendous educational resource for students, especially because of its potential for self-directed and active learning. A reader may choose his or her own path through web documents, reaching beyond the confines of the narrow narrative path that traditional text must follow. With such flexibility the reader experiences the joys of discovery-based learning. Self-directed control of what is read next leads to more intrinsic interest in content, more motivation to learn, and more excitement in the learning process. Further, the reading of texts in an unstructured way requires students to generate their own sense of connection and coherence between the documents. Encountering isolated texts, instead of a single text, can in itself prompt more active processing of information, more reflection, and the recognition of novel connections between ideas. Thus, there are a number of romantic notions that hypertext may engender deeper thought and richer learning as learners navigate on paths of their own choosing through a network of ideas, and must actively construct meaning for themselves.

However, as many studies of text comprehension have demonstrated, the linear structure of a text serves an important function, as it gives the reader a way to navigate through information and a starting point for developing a representation of the text. While students may enjoy the empowerment and freedom of having their own navigational control, navigational choices may also overload the capabilities of the reader in some cases. While the linear structure inherent in most lectures and texts limits readers, it also supports their understanding. Access to an infinite number of choices gives readers the agency to follow their own interests and may allow for more intrinsic motivation to enter the learning context, but unless the reader has a great deal of knowledge about the content, or a good understanding of the web space, a lack of organizational structure can often leave students "lost in hyperspace." A major question for web-based education is how to support both navigation and representation while allowing for flexibility.

In chapter 7, Riva suggests an intriguing and important new tool, shared hypermedia (SHY), that may provide a good balance of student-initiated navigation and guidance. Shared hypermedia applications may be used to allow learners to choose their own destination, preserving their sense of agency and allowing them to follow their own interests. But, once at a site, students may be guided through the hypertext links and web pages in an instructor-led tour. This may provide enough support for learners to get their bearings within a site and get a sense of the important features and concepts, so that they can get the most out of their web experience.

A second way in which the dynamic, flexible, and adaptive nature of on-line text can benefit learning is through the inclusion of interactive features that force students to refine their understanding of the subject matter. There has been a great deal of converging evidence demonstrating that activities that require learners to engage in active, constructive, and integrative tasks lead to the best understanding of the subject matter (e.g., Bereiter & Scardamalia, 1996; Brown & Campione, 1996; Kintsch, 1994; Mayer, 1989). Web environments in particular can be designed and used to capitalize on these modes of learning. Giving students an environment where they actively manipulate information and construct their own conceptual representation of the subject matter seems to be the best way to capture the benefits of new technologies. Wolfe's Dragonfly Web Pages provide an excellent example of this kind of learning opportunity.

H. Customization

A final advantage of the dynamic, adaptive, and flexible nature of on-line presentation is the capacity for all kinds of text, from short warnings to whole sites, to be customized to the specific needs of readers. By using short on-line assessments, as suggested by Joinson and Buchanan (chapter 11), readers can be directed to sites that are tailored for their needs. Anderson (chapter 3) has suggested a number of personality and cognitive styles that may benefit from sites with particular features. Alternatively, all students may be provided with a single version of a site, but prompts may provide individual-specific feedback or scaffolding in response to certain behaviors. Students can receive feedback, prompts, or background information when an intelligent program recognizes certain patterns of use, or when wrong or right answers are recognized in on-line exercises. They can thus be tutored on necessary skills, like how to perform effective searches. Dynamic processes can also be used to model expert behavior, and as mentioned in the SHY example, students can be guided through sites by a teacher, or directed to important concepts by links or hints.

It has long been held that there is an optimal match between reader and text that may result in the best learning outcomes. The adaptive nature of web presentation holds the promise to fit readers to ideal conditions by screening readers and altering the information that is presented to them in a manner suited to their abilities. Or alternatively, web environments could support readers into using behaviors and styles that are more appropriate for on-line learning.

IV. FUTURE RESEARCH

The chapters here have done a good job of laying out many possibilities for virtual education. What remains, as many have noted, is the empirical investigation of exactly which features of face-to-face and virtual learning environments lead to the best educational outcomes in which circumstances. Few of the chapters here included a formal assessment of learning outcomes or other evidence that the ideas they have suggested will actually translate into better student learning. Unfortunately, this is also the case in the broader literature, as few studies on educational use of electronic text or multimedia resources have actually shown significant learning gains (Chen & Rada, 1996; Clark, 1983; Dillon & Gabbard, 1998; Landauer, 1995). In fact, few have measured learning outcomes in controlled experiments. While multimedia resources hold great promise as an educational tool, it is clear that putting a student in front of a computer screen, a web browser, or any other multimedia format does not necessarily lead to better learning. There are a wide range of outcomes that can be evaluated.

The most frequently reported outcome measure in the educational computing literature is preference or liking for a learning experience. While there need be no direct relation between enjoyment and actual learning, to the extent that preference measures predict whether students will return to the web in the future, and therefore have the opportunity to learn new content or skills, then liking seems to be an important variable to consider. Similarly attitudes toward technology may be an important mediating or outcome variable. More to the point, however, it is important to test actual effects of web-based education on students' learning of skills or content. This can be achieved by observing the use of skills. For example, have students learned to seek out the source of information, or do they formulate good Boolean searches? Learning can also be assessed through the observation of behaviors. For example, do students spontaneously engage in higher-order mental processes, and do they look for contradictions? Learning can also be tested through the assessment of students' memory for facts or their understanding of concepts from web-based materials.

The previous chapters have suggested how the World Wide Web can support many student behaviors (i.e., interacting, active processing, sourcing) that may be important for better learning. Observation of which behaviors may be promoted by technology is an important first step. And all of the ideas mentioned here seem theoretically promising. We hope that the interactive game-like activities found on the Dragonfly Web Pages will lead to more active processing of information and therefore better understanding of the scientific concepts. We would hope that students who learn to consider the source of documents in their use of the web will develop a better understanding of the subject matter than students who accept information unquestioningly. We hope that readers who use "deeper learning strategies" will have better retention of what they read. We would also hope that students who receive feedback as they are learning will do better in a course. However, all of these practices need to be tested empirically, as sometimes the best practices are not intuitively obvious.

Under many conditions, learning from multimedia or electronic text can certainly lead to poorer learning than occurs from traditional formats (Mayer, 1997; Rouet, Levonen, Dillon, & Spiro, 1996; Wiley & Voss, 1999). There may be nothing in a given medium per se that ensures better learning.

However, there may be certain learning behaviors that one medium engenders better than another. The key for educational research is to figure out how to allow students to gain the most from each medium. Technology offers us a number of reasons to be excited about its potential, and there are a number of theoretical approaches that lend themselves to implementation in electronic environments, which in turn may lead to better learning. Interactive tutors can supply important pieces of domain knowledge and guidance through complex reasoning and problem-solving exercises. This may allow novice learners to complete tasks that they would otherwise be incapable of performing. Computer environments can simulate real-world situations and help students ground their learning in concrete problem-solving contexts. Further, multimedia environments can provide students with good models of difficult or abstract concepts — through illustrations, diagrams, or animations — that they would have trouble visualizing through text alone. An important goal of the educational computing literature needs to be to determine which specific instructional contexts allow for effective educational uses of web resources.

In a good example of the kind of study that is needed, Reyna et al. (chapter 2) describe how the effects of on-line presentation can be assessed. Among three types of graphic presentations that accompanied a unit on heart medication, Reyna et al. found that students who saw a balloon-like diagram were more likely to use the important concepts of "flow" and "pressure" (and use them correctly) in their discussion of their problem solving. This protocol analysis suggests that students in this condition were acquiring the key concepts of the unit more so than students in the two other conditions.

In a similar kind of analysis, Wiley and Voss (1996) investigated the advantages of learning from a multiple-source environment over a textbook-like environment. Using Sourcer's Apprentice, the environment designed and described by Britt and Gabrys in chapter 4, students were presented source texts about the Irish Potato Famine either as eight separate documents in a web site or as a textbook chapter that contained the same exact text in a single document. Thus, the presentation format, but not the content of the information, was varied. Further, the task that students were assigned to do as they read varied. Some students were asked to write an argument about what produced the changes in Ireland's population, while others were asked to write a narrative. The essays that the students wrote were analyzed, and when students wrote arguments from multiple sources their essays contained more causal terms than those in the other three conditions. Students in the multiple-source argument condition were also more likely to integrate information from different sources. These findings suggest that students were developing a better understanding when they had multiple sources and a task that required them to integrate the sources. Like the findings in the protocols from the Reyna et al. study, this analysis suggested which specific design features and uses of computerized learning environments lead to the best learning outcomes.

Although both of these studies used discourse analysis to probe the kinds of learning that occur in different learning contexts, there are also simpler ways of assessing whether deeper understanding is occurring. Verification tasks, although usually used for more superficial measures of memory, like retention of facts, can also be designed to test deeper levels of learning. Royer, Carlo, Dufresne, and Mestre (1996) have described how learning measures that tap multiple levels of representation can be developed. In a follow-up study, Wiley and Voss (1999), using the procedure of Royer et al., created three kinds of verification tasks to assess the kinds of learning that were occurring from the Potato Famine web site. In one task, students were simply assessed on sentence verification. In a second task, students were tested for inference verification and were asked to indicate whether a point seemed to follow from what they read. In a third test, a principle identification task, students were asked to rate the similarity of potential conceptual analogies to the cause of the Potato Famine. In this task, students were given four examples, one which was similar neither on the surface nor at a conceptual level, one which was similar at both the surface and the conceptual levels, one similar only on the surface level, and one similar only on an underlying conceptual level. The tests of most interest were those thought to reflect better understanding of the content: (1) good performance on the inference task, and (2) the recognition of the deep analogy. Consistent with the essay analyses, students who read from multiple sources and wrote an argument had the best performance on the inference and analogy tasks, indicating that they had indeed gained a better understanding of the subject matter.

Interestingly, students in the textbook and narrative condition of the Wiley and Voss (1999) experiment actually had the best performance on the verbatim memory task (the sentence verification task). This result is similar to that of others (e.g., Reyna et al., chapter 2). This discrepancy between verbatim memory and comprehension measures emphasizes the importance of including both retention and transfer outcome measures as learning assessments when measuring learning from the web. While multimedia and other computerized learning environments can be used to support more active learning, and potentially better understanding of the subject matter, students may actually have poorer surface or verbatim memory for information when compared to textbook or lecture-based learning.

Other examples of measures that test for understanding come from the studies of Mayer and his colleagues, who have investigated how images should be incorporated in text for effective learning (e.g., Harp & Mayer, 1998; Mayer, 1989). In these studies, he tests for "transfer" by giving a few short problem-solving tasks after students see units on scientific topics such as how brakes work and why lightning occurs. These problems involve troubleshooting questions, questions about how machines could be made more reliable and effective, and questions about how effects could be counteracted or changed by hypothetical factors. In a similar series of studies, Hegarty has developed multiple choice questions that relate to the creation of an accurate causal model about the mechanisms that are studied (Hegarty et al., 1999). Similarly Kintsch and his colleagues have employed sorting tasks, where an understanding of the subject matter leads students to sort ideas into piles based on underlying concepts instead of more superficial associations (i.e., Mannes & Kintsch, 1987). These examples of verification, problem solving, and sorting tasks are included to show that detailed protocol analysis, or time-consuming analysis of navigation logs, while an important source of information on how students use and learn from the web, are not the only means available for empirical evaluation. These shorter tasks may be easier to administer and will also yield important and much needed evidence about effective uses of the web in teaching and learning.

V. THE WEB AS AN EXTENSION OF THE MIND

Although much research is clearly needed before we will be able to flesh out the full pedagogical implications of the web, it seems safe to predict at least one dimension that is certain to play an important role is in shaping the way we think about thought itself. The web has more general implications for cognition, particularly as a metaphor for the mind. As Riva notes in this volume, various researchers have suggested that the web represents something akin to an "interbrain" in which "cognitive activities are increasingly being performed in networked contexts which, to varying degrees, are undeniably virtual" (Riva, chapter 7). Such parallels between the net and the mind raise intriguing possibilities about the potentially unique learning value that a medium with such a close affinity to the mind might have. Importantly, however, Hammond and Trapp (chapter 8) point out that we must be very cautious in assuming that the net, by virtue of the fact that it shares some similarities with brains, should be assumed to lead to enhanced learning. Hammond and Trapp refer to this false conclusion as the "homeopathic fallacy," that is, that "the analogous network-like structures of both the web and the central nervous system (or, perhaps more plausibly, between the web and the associative structure of memory) somehow enhances a more direct transfer of information from computer screen to the mind." As they aptly put it, "to draw the inference that this similarity is a contributor to effective learning is a little like claiming that porridge is good for learning because it looks like the gray matter of the brain" (chapter 8). Indeed, the fact that to date there have been few studies that unequivocally demonstrate that the web enhances learning over traditional methods illustrates that the web's parallels to the mind do not make it an unequivocally superior learning medium.

Although the parallels between the web and the mind have been thoughtfully considered in discussions of the web's potential pedagogical value, the mind–web metaphor has been largely ignored in traditional cognitive psychology theories, which still typically rely on the digital computer metaphor (Roediger, 1980). As Ulric Neisser observed, "models of the mind always follow the latest advances in gadgetry" (1982, p. 7). In the third century B.C., Plato likened the mind to a wax tablet. In the 17th century, Descartes fashioned many mental processes after the complex clock robots that were popular at the time. In the early 20th century, the mind was likened to a telephone switchboard, and of course, in the later part of the 20th century the mind was thought to resemble a digital computer. Given the relentless mapping between recent technology and the mind, it simply stands to reason that cognitive models will come to explore the parallels between the mind and the net.

In fact, when we consider the viability of the web as a metaphor for the mind, it is certainly far more apt than a wax tablet, and potentially provides a useful alternative or supplement to the still reigning (albeit with less strength than it once had) digital computer metaphor. There are certainly some significant parallels between navigation through the cyberspace of the World Wide Web and navigation through the mental space of the mind. In both cases, sophisticated search engines sort through a huge network of information to provide associations that are most relevant to the target information. Admittedly web search engines are not as effective as human search engines (yet), but perhaps as the parallels between the two become fleshed out, development of web search engines may become increasingly informed by our understanding of cognitive search mechanisms. Once one has landed on a particular location in search space (be it mental space or cyberspace), other associations present themselves. In both cases these associations are not random but rather are conceptually related in important respects to the target location. Just as we can choose which subsequent web sites to click on, so too do we move through mental space. Like lists from a search engine, multiple ideas often come to mind and we can "decide" which idea to pursue.

The web metaphor also nicely illustrates the relationship between conscious and unconscious processes. When we search our minds, we can control the basic topics that we choose to consider, and when alternatives come to mind we can choose between them. However, we have relatively little insight into the specific search processes that bring particular thoughts to mind, nor do we have much control over the nature of the specific thoughts that arise. Similarly, with the web, we can choose our search terms, but we cannot control what specific hits will come up. We can then choose what locations to visit, but we cannot control what those pages will look like.

Another useful attribute of the web analogy, in contrast to many of the other metaphors of the mind that have been introduced over the years, is that it includes a first-person perspective. We cannot imagine what it "feels" like to be a computer, and so the computer metaphor for the mind has always been hard to relate to. In contrast, it is easy to think about surfing one's internal mental space in a manner that resembles the way in which we search cyberspace because in both cases there is "someone" participating in the search. There are a number of exciting potential implications of the parallels in the subjective experience of searching mental space and cyberspace. First, it suggests that expertise in understanding how to navigate through the web may provide individuals with a natural and potentially rich knowledge domain for conceptualizing human information processing more generally. In short, the web metaphor of the mind may provide a particularly intuitive model of the mind that readily relates to a domain of universally increasing expertise.

In addition to providing a rich and accessible metaphor for conceptualizing human thought, the parallels between the web and the mind may actually influence the manner in which individuals ultimately learn to search through mental space. Surfing the web introduces a variety of formal demands for optimum searching. One needs to know how to define searches appropriately, how to assess the promise of the alternatives that arise, and to how maintain a general representation of what has been learned. All of these skills may similarly apply to searching mental space, suggesting that some of the information searching skills acquired through surfing the net might ultimately come to be internalized and used in searching one's own mind. Although provocative, the notion that individuals may come to internalize the information search skills that they use in exploring the web is consistent with a general view, originally articulated by Vygotsky (1978) and subsequently fleshed out by others (see Riva, chapter 7), that internal thought is a reflection of the social situations that individuals encounter. If, as a consequence of human interactions, individuals come to develop an internalized mode of thought that initially resembles something akin to social conversations, then it is not all that far-fetched to suggest that experiences on the Internet might result in a greater specialization of the modes of operation (such as defining problem searches and conceptualizing hyperlinked representations) that are particularly emphasized on the web. Indeed such claims are testable as they suggest that a relationship may be found (both correlationally and through extensive training) between individuals' experience with and proficiency in searching the web and their ability to search thoughts in their own minds. It may well turn out that although the web is not uniquely effective in getting information into our minds, it is uniquely suitable for encouraging the deft navigation of ideas within the complex representational network that constitute our personal "mental webs."

References

Bereiter, C., & Scardamalia, M. (1996). Rethinking learning. In D. R. Olson & N. Torrance (Eds.), *The handbook of education and human development: New models of learning, teaching and schooling* (pp. 485–513). Oxford: Blackwell Publishers.

Brown, A. L., & Campione, J. C. (1996). Psychological theory and the design of innovative learning environments: On procedures, principles, and systems. In L. Schauble & R. Glaser (Eds.), *Innovations in learning: New environments for education* (pp. 289–325). Mahwah, NJ: Erlbaum.

Chen, C., & Rada, R. (1996). Interacting with hypertext: A meta-analysis of experimental studies. *Human Computer Interaction*, 11, 125–156.

Clark, R. E. (1983). Reconsidering research on learning from media. *Review of Educational Research*, 53, 445–459.

Dillon, A., & Gabbard, R. (1998). Hypermedia as educational technology: A review of the quantitative research literature on learner comprehension, control and style. *Review of Educational Research*, 68, 322–349.

Harp, S., & Mayer, R. (1998). How seductive details do their damage: A theory of cognitive interest in science learning. *Journal of Educational Psychology*, 90, 414–434.

Hegarty, M., Quilici, J., Narayanan, N. H., Holmquist, S., & Moreno, R. (1999). Multimedia instruction: Lessons from evaluation of a theory-based design. *Journal of Educational Multimedia and Hypermedia*, 8, 119–150.

Kintsch, W. (1994). Text comprehension, memory, and learning. *American Psychologist*, 49, 294–303.

Kraut, R., Patterson, M., Landmark, V., Kiesler, S., Mukophadhyay, T., & Scherlis, W. (1998). Internet paradox: A social technology that reduces social involvement and psychological well being? *American Psychologist*, 53, 1017–1031.

Landauer, T. (1995). *The trouble with computers*. Cambridge, MA: MIT Press.

Mannes, S., & Kintsch, W. (1987). Knowledge organization and text organization. *Cognition & Instruction*, 4, 91–115.

Mayer, R. (1989). Models for understanding. *Review of Educational Research*, 59, 43–64.

Mayer, R. (1997). Multimedia learning: Are we asking the right questions? *Educational Psychologist*, 32, 1–19.

Neisser, U. (1982, January). *On the trail of the tape-recorder fallacy*. Paper presented at the symposium, "Influence Of Hypnosis And Related States On Memory: Forensic Implications," American Association for the Advancement of Science, Washington, DC.

Pew Internet and American Life Project (2000, May). *Tracking on-line life: How women use the internet to cultivate relationships with family and friends* [on-line]. Available (May 11, 2000): http://www.pewinternet.org/

Roediger, H. L. (1980). Memory metaphors in cognitive psychology. *Memory & Cognition*, 8, 231–246.

Rouet, J. F., Levonen, J., Dillon, A., & Spiro, R. (Eds.) (1996). *Hypertext and cognition*. Mahwah, NJ: Erlbaum.

Royer, M., Carlo, M., Dufresne, R., & Mestre, J. (1996). The assessment of levels of domain expertise while reading. *Cognition & Instruction*, 14, 373–408.

Vygotsky, L. (1978). *Mind in society: The development of higher psychological processes*. Cambridge, MA: Harvard University Press.

Wiley, J., & Voss, J. F. (1996). The effects of "playing" historian on learning in history. *Applied Cognitive Psychology*, 10, 63–72.

Wiley, J., & Voss, J. F. (1999). Constructing arguments from multiple sources: Tasks that promote understanding and not just memory for text. *Journal of Educational Psychology*, 91, 1–11.

Wright, P., Milroy, R., & Lickorish, A. (1999). Static and animated graphics in learning from interactive texts. *European Journal of Psychology of Education*, 14, 203–224.

Author Index

Subject Index